Twenty-Five Women Who Shaped . . . Series

The series *Twenty-Five Women Who Shaped . . .* shines a spotlight on the extraordinary women who helped to lay the cultural, political, or religious foundations of different historical eras. These meticulously researched books provide accessible and immersive introductions to influential female figures throughout the ages and across the globe, offering readers a deeper appreciation of women's enduring impact on history.

Twenty-Five Women Who Shaped the Italian Renaissance
Meredith K. Ray

For more information about this series, please visit:
www.routledge.com/Twenty-Five-Women-Who-Shaped/book-series/TFWWS

Twenty-Five Women Who Shaped the Italian Renaissance

Meredith K. Ray

Routledge
Taylor & Francis Group

LONDON AND NEW YORK

Designed cover image: Alamy

First published 2024
by Routledge
4 Park Square, Milton Park, Abingdon, Oxon OX14 4RN

and by Routledge
605 Third Avenue, New York, NY 10158

Routledge is an imprint of the Taylor & Francis Group, an informa business

British Library Cataloguing-in-Publication Data
A catalogue record for this book is available from the British Library

ISBN: 978-0-367-53398-4 (hbk)
ISBN: 978-0-367-53399-1 (pbk)
ISBN: 978-1-003-08180-7 (ebk)

DOI: 10.4324/9781003081807

Typeset in Times New Roman
by Apex CoVantage, LLC

Contents

List of Figures   *viii*

Introduction: Hidden Histories   1

PART ONE
Politics and Power Brokers   17

 1 Lucrezia Tornabuoni (1427–1482): Medici
    Matriarch   19

 2 Caterina Sforza (c. 1463–1509): Countess,
    Warrior, Alchemist   31

 3 Isabella d'Este (1474–1539): Diplomat and
    Tastemaker   42

 4 Lucrezia Borgia (1480–1519): Entrepreneur
    From Italy's Most Controversial Family   53

 5 Bona Sforza (1494–1557): The Italian Queen
    of Poland   65

PART TWO
Poets, Reformers, and Courtesans   77

 6 Vittoria Colonna (1490?–1547): Divine Poet,
    Michelangelo's Mentor   79

7   Lucrezia Gonzaga (1522–1576): Epistolary
    Icon and Religious Dissident   90

8   Olimpia Morata (1526–1555): Humanist and
    Heretic   100

9   Laura Terracina (1519–c.1577): Bestselling
    Author, Defender of Women   111

10 Veronica Franco (1546–1591): Celebrity
    Courtesan   122

PART THREE
Musicians, Composers, and Performers   133

11 Gaspara Stampa (1523–1554): Renaissance
    Sappho   135

12 Tarquinia Molza (1542–1617): *Virtuosa* and
    Philosopher   147

13 Isabella Andreini (1562–1604): Diva of Stage
    and Page   158

14 Francesca Caccini (1587–post-1641): Opera's
    Star at the Medici Court   168

15 Barbara Strozzi (1619–1677): Trailblazing
    Composer   180

PART FOUR
Artists and Scientists   191

16 Sofonisba Anguissola (c. 1532–1625):
    Portraitist to Kings   193

17 Lavinia Fontana (1552–1614): Pioneering
    Professional Artist   205

18 Artemisia Gentileschi (1593–1656?): Fearless
Painter, Feminist Icon 216

19 Camilla Erculiani (d. post-1584):
Pharmacist-Philosopher 229

20 Margherita Sarrocchi (c. 1560–1617): Reader
of the Stars, Galileo's Correspondent 240

PART FIVE
Renaissance Feminists 251

21 Laudomia Forteguerri (1515–1555?): Queer
Poet, Civic Hero 253

22 Moderata Fonte (1555–1592): Visionary of
Women's Equality 264

23 Lucrezia Marinella (1571?–1653): Champion
of Women's History 275

24 Sarra Copia Sulam (1592–1641): Poet and
Polemicist in Venice's Jewish Ghetto 285

25 Arcangela Tarabotti (1604–1652): Rebel Nun,
Feminist Force 296

Notes and Further Reading *307*
Dates of Reign *339*
Acknowledgments *342*
Index *343*

Figures

0.1   *The Chess Game*, by Sofonisba Anguissola   7
0.2   *Portrait of a Woman*, attributed to Annibale Carracci   8
1.1   *Lucrezia Tornabuoni*, attributed to Domenico
      Ghirlandaio   20
1.2   *Adoration of the Magi*, by Sandro Botticelli   21
1.3   Exterior view of the Medici Palace, Florence   22
1.4   *The Procession of the Magi*, by Benozzo Gozzoli   23
2.1   *Primavera (Spring)*, by Sandro Botticelli   32
2.2   Partially encrypted page from Caterina Sforza's
      medical-alchemical manuscript   36
2.3   *Portrait of a Young Woman with Jasmine*, by
      Lorenzo di Credi   37
3.1   *Portrait of Isabella d'Este*, by Titian   43
3.2   *Minerva Expelling the Vices From the Garden of
      Virtue*, by Andrea Mantegna   45
3.3   Sketch of Isabella d'Este by Leonardo da Vinci   47
4.1   *Idealized Portrait of a Young Woman as Flora*, by
      Bartolomeo Veneto   54
4.2   Autograph letter of Lucrezia Borgia to Pope
      Alexander VI   57
4.3   *Lucrezia Borgia, Duchess of Ferrara*, portrait
      attributed to Dosso Dossi   63
5.1   Detail, woodcut of Bona Sforza   66
5.2   View of Wawel Castle with Sigismund Chapel   70
5.3   *Poisoning of Queen Bona*, Jan Matejko   74
6.1   Presumed portrait of Vittoria Colonna by Sebas-
      tiano Luciani (Sebastiano del Piombo)   80
6.2   Title page of Vittoria Colonna, *Rime*   86

6.3	Michelangelo's *Crucifixion*	89
7.1	Villa Badoer in Fratta Polesine	92
7.2	Portrait of Lucrezia Gonzaga in *Rime di diversi nobilissimi, et eccellentissimi auttori*	94
7.3	Title page of Lucrezia's Gonzaga's *Letters*	96
8.1	Portrait of Martin Luther by Lucas Cranach the Elder	101
8.2	Portrait of Olimpia Morata in Virginia Mulzazzi, *Scene della riforma*	102
8.3	Olympia Fulvia Morata with the burning Schweinfurt in background	108
9.1	*Portrait of Laura Terracina*, by Enea Vico	114
9.2	Gustave Doré, scene from *Orlando furioso*	115
9.3	Title page of Laura Terracina's *Discorso*	117
10.1	A–B Woodblock print of a Venetian courtesan	124
10.2	*Portrait of Lady*, by Tintoretto	125
10.3	Poem from Veronica Franco's *Rime*	127
11.1	Portrait of Collaltino di Collalto in Luisa Bergalli's *Rime di Madonna Gaspara Stampa*	139
11.2	Title page and opening sonnet of *Rime di Madonna Gaspara Stampa*	142
11.3	Portrait of Gaspara Stampa in Luisa Bergalli's *Rime di Madonna Gaspara Stampa*	145
12.1	Portrait of Tarquinia Molza	149
12.2	Portrait of Francesco Patrizi in his *Discussiones peripateticae*	152
12.3	A concert of women	155
13.1	Commedia dell'arte troupe	160
13.2	Presumed portrait of Isabella Andreini, by Paolo Veronese	161
13.3	A–B Commemorative medal by Guillaume Dupré	166
14.1	*Portrait of a Woman*, by Palma Vecchio	171
14.2	Christine of Lorraine, by Agostino Carracci	172
14.3	Fresco scene from *Orlando furioso*, by Niccolò dell'Abate	175
14.4	Title page of Francesca Caccini, *Il primo libro delle musiche*	177
15.1	*The Viola da Gamba Player*, by Bernardo Strozzi	183
15.2	Title page of Barbara Strozzi's *Il primo libro de' madrigali*	185

15.3   *Portrait of Vittoria della Rovere*, by Justus Sustermans   186
16.1   *Bernardino Campi Painting Sofonisba Anguis-*
       sola, by Sofonisba Anguissola   196
16.2   *Boy Bitten by a Crawfish*, by Sofonisba Anguissola   197
16.3   *Self-Portrait*, by Sofonisba Anguissola   199
16.4   *Minerva, Amilcare, and Asdrubale Anguissola*, by
       Sofonisba Anguisola   201
17.1   *Self-Portrait at the Spinet*, by Lavinia Fontana   207
17.2   *The Gozzadini Family*, by Lavinia Fontana   209
17.3   *Portrait of Bianca degli Utili Maselli and Her*
       children, by Lavinia Fontana   210
17.4   *Portrait of Antonietta Gonzales*, by Lavinia Fontana   211
17.5   *Minerva Dressing*, by Lavinia Fontana   214
18.1   *Judith Slaying Holofernes*, by Artemisia Gentileschi   217
18.2   *Susanna and Her Elders*, by Artemisia Gentileschi   219
18.3   *Allegory of Inclination*, by Artemisia Gentileschi   223
18.4   *Judith and Her Maidservant*, by Artemisia Gentileschi   225
19.1   *Early Italian Pharmacy* (Left Side of Pair) with
       women assistants   230
19.2   Miniature of Anna Jagiellon of Poland, by Lucas
       Cranach the Younger   233
19.3   Title page of Camilla Erculiani's *Lettere di*
       philosophia naturale   235
20.1   Title page of Margherita Sarrocchi's *Scanderbeide*   244
20.2   Portrait of Galileo Galilei, attributed to Domenico
       Robusti   247
20.3   Letter of Margherita Sarrocchi to Galileo Galilei   249
21.1   Portrait of Duchess Margaret of Parma, by
       Anthonis Mor   257
21.2   Portrait of Alessandro de' Medici, Duke of Flor-
       ence, by the workshop of Agnolo Bronzino   258
21.3   The storming of the fortress near Porta Camollia
       in Siena, by Giorgio Vasari   263
22.1   Portrait of Moderata Fonte, in *Il merito delle donne*   266
22.2   Title page of Moderata Fonte's *Tredici canti del*
       Floridoro   268
22.3   Title page of Moderata Fonte's *Il merito delle donne*   271
23.1   Depiction of Lucrezia Marinella, by Giacomo Pecini   276

23.2	Title page of Lucrezia Marinella, *La nobiltà et l'eccellenza delle donne*	279
23.3	*The Crusaders Conquering the City of Zara in 1202*, by Andrea Vicentino (Michieli)	283
24.1	Campo del Ghetto Nuovo, Venice	286
24.2	Possible portrait of Sarra Copia Sulam, attributed to Antonio Logorio	289
24.3	Title page of Sarra Copia Sulam's *Manifesto*	291
25.1	Convent of Sant'Anna in Castello	297
25.2	*Il parlatorio (The Convent Parlor)*, by Francesco Guardi	298
25.3	Title page of Arcangela Tarabotti's *La semplicità ingannata*	305

Introduction

Hidden Histories

Why bother with all the history books, when their authors – being men who are envious of women's worthy deeds – do not talk about women's noble actions, but instead consign them to silence?

— Lucrezia Marinella, 1601

"Renaissance Italy": the words evoke figures like Botticelli, Raphael, and Leonardo; Michelangelo, Machiavelli, and Monteverdi. These are the one-named "giants" we have come to associate with the Renaissance, the era that produced some of history's best-known works of art, literature, and music. Maybe we think of Petrarch, the great scholar and poet who mined the human psyche in his love lyric, or Galileo, the astronomer who jolted the earth from its position at the center of the cosmos. The Renaissance was an epoch of seismic shifts in art and culture, science and religion, politics and philosophy – in how people thought about the world and their place in it.

But what about the women of the Renaissance? Lorenzo "the Magnificent," the de facto prince of Florence, is credited with presiding over one of the most significant cultural centers of the fifteenth century – but his mother, Lucrezia Tornabuoni, was a poet and political force in her own right. The inspired verse of the "divine" Vittoria Colonna of Naples – the first woman to have a book of poetry published in Italy – made her one of the most famous figures of the age, her name synonymous with literary excellence. Friend and spiritual mentor to Michelangelo, she was immersed in the new religious currents that reverberated throughout Italy as the Protestant Reformation unfolded to the north. Lavinia Fontana painted vivid, complex portraits and large-scale religious, historical, and mythological paintings; by the time

DOI: 10.4324/9781003081807-1

she died, she rivaled Caravaggio as the most famous artist in Rome. In seventeenth-century Venice, the Benedictine nun Arcangela Tarabotti penned fierce condemnations of the oppression of women – and published them – a shockingly subversive act given her cloistered religious status. These women's names – and so many more – often go unrecognized in narratives of the Renaissance that reflexively privilege male genius. How can we recover these hidden histories? And why does it matter?

Centuries after the Renaissance, gender equality remains elusive. In many parts of the world, girls and women have access to education and healthcare, legal protections, self-determination, and financial stability – but there are significant gaps in, as well as retreats from, that progress. Women exert greater control and choice over their lives and career paths than they did in the Renaissance – but autonomy over their bodies remains in question, or actively denied. The wage disparity persists. Many countries, including the United States, have yet to elect a female head of state, and ideas about politics and gender are deeply fraught. As we continue working toward gender parity in the present and the future, we must also re-center women in our narratives of the past. This means writing women into history – intentionally, deliberately, and thoughtfully. It means shifting the lens through which we view the past, asking different questions, and valorizing a wider range of political and creative activity. When we see women represented in history – and when women see themselves there – it alerts us to their collective impact in shaping our world in profound, important ways. Rich, exciting conversations were happening all over Renaissance Italy, and women were a part of them. Why aren't we more aware of their presence?

This is not a new question: Renaissance writers were already considering it. In the mid-fourteenth century, Giovanni Boccaccio intertwined biographies of noted women from history and legend in his widely circulated *De claris mulieribus* (*Concerning Famous Women*). Though he highlighted their stories, Boccaccio saw his protagonists as exceptions to the (male) rule, musing, rhetorically, "what can we think except that it was an error of nature to give female sex to a body . . . endowed by God with a magnificent virile spirit?"[1] A half-century later, Christine de Pizan, writing in France, composed *Le Livre de la Cité des Dames* (*The Book of the City of Ladies*) in response to a flood of misogynistic literature (so blatant that it prompted her to "examine myself and my condition as a woman"), sparking a *querelle des femmes*, or "debate over women," throughout Europe that compelled writers and philosophers to either defend or defame them.[2] The debate about women's capabilities and "proper" roles was ongoing in the sixteenth century when Lodovico Ariosto, the Italian author of a beloved chivalric tale of knights and adventures populated by strong female characters, paused mid-poem to comment on historiography. "Women have achieved in every art/and craft the highest distinction," he observed – so why are their achievements "concealed"?[3] Ariosto posited that envy or ignorance was to blame, going on to praise a host of female contemporaries by way of recompense. History's inclination to gloss over or elide entirely the contributions of women, while highlighting and preserving those of men, had clearly not been resolved.

Renaissance women wrote about the same problem. In her own chivalric poem, the sixteenth-century Venetian writer Moderata Fonte picked up where Ariosto left off, insisting that women are "endowed by Nature with excellent judgement and great courage, and they are born no less well fitted than men to display wisdom and valor, if properly trained and nurtured." If they are provided the same opportunities as men, she noted – making a comparison to the mining of gold from unrefined ore – their worth will be revealed, for gold has innate potential, even before it is extracted and polished. Her compatriot Lucrezia Marinella amplified the point and made an even clearer recommendation. Women are excluded from education, she argued, because "men, fearing to lose their authority and become women's servants, often forbid them even to learn to read or write." Therefore, she asserted, it is essential for women to keep their own record – in essence, to create the discipline of women's history – because "history books" have been authored by men to their own advantage. The Neapolitan poet Laura Terracina likewise exhorted women to "dedicate ourselves to learning,/and make space for our neglected voices,/so they are not so quiet/that they cannot be heard above the writings of men." As each of these authors recognized, gender equality first requires visibility.[4]

If the accomplishments of a handful of accomplished Renaissance women were recognized even in their own time, how can we recapture the many more who have been relegated to undeserved obscurity? Over the past decades, feminist historians have led the way in asking important questions about women's roles in family, religion, culture, and politics.[5] Retracing the steps of Renaissance women can require some detective work: combing libraries for rare books or manuscripts, following the trail of an obscure footnote to discover the woman at its center, or paying attention to silences in the archives – to what is absent from the historical record as well as what is preserved.

I began my own search as a graduate student: while I loved the classics of the Italian literary canon, female names were noticeably absent from many of my reading lists. I was lucky to be able to learn from my own professors and other scholars working in the developing field of women and gender studies, and to glimpse what might be missing. It was a revelation: Renaissance women *did things*. I kept reading. I went to Italy and continued the quest. In the libraries of Florence and Venice – with their gorgeous reading rooms, lined with centuries-old volumes – and in archives from Milan to Rome, the most rewarding research moments came hidden within centuries-old *buste* of fragile, fading documents. Seeing the handwriting of a Renaissance woman whose story you have been trying to uncover – on a letter, a contract, or a will – or her name on an elaborate sixteenth-century title page can spark a strong and unexpected sense of connection to the past, as well as awareness of the many differences owed to time, geography, and circumstance. (Sometimes, there are other surprises, too, like the remains of a sixteenth-century scorpion preserved among the papers of a Venetian convent.) To write women's history requires searching in unexpected places – and to read it helps us to create a more expansive view of the past.

Whose Renaissance?

If the question of who writes history – and why – is at the heart of this book, as it was on the minds of Renaissance men and women themselves, so is another important question: what – and for whom – was "the Renaissance"? Did women (as the historian Joan Kelly famously asked more than three decades ago) have a "Renaissance"?[6] The French term "Renaissance," or rebirth, derives from the Italian *rinascita*, used to describe new developments in art and culture and the efforts of humanist scholars to recover the knowledge of the classical world and reconcile it with Christianity. But the word itself is rife with connotations and friction.[7] First, it presumes a tidy periodization – though historians differ on the precise dates of its beginning and end. Periodization is a convenient way to think about and organize changes in structures, political conflict, and cultural currents, but it always involves categorization and choices that prioritize some things (or people, or places) over others or assume neat resolutions to tensions or developments that unfolded over long stretches of time. It is freighted, too, with a long history of cultural associations that privilege an elite, Western, male experience – as well as an idealized concept of individual genius that overshadows the collaborative nature of much Renaissance achievement.

This volume deliberately incorporates "the Renaissance" into its title and pages to evoke the complicated nature of the term – one that should prompt us to wonder not only about collectivity and the experiences of the non-élite but also about women. Far from being universally silenced or subjugated, Renaissance women were everywhere. They were poets and composers, artists, political leaders, and philosophers. On the cusp of the Scientific Revolution and in the thick of the Reformation, they were at the forefront of transformational change in science and religion. They were present in the workplace and the marketplace and worked as artisans, apothecaries, midwives, and wetnurses. Some of their stories have been preserved, and others erased. But they are a critical part of the trajectory of Renaissance history. By focusing on the impact of women across multiple aspects of Renaissance culture, we reveal a richer, more interconnected Renaissance – one that brings into relief, too, the fluid connections between literary, musical, artistic, scientific, and religious culture.

In presenting the stories of twenty-five women, however, I have had – inevitably – to undergo a process of categorization of my own. Which twenty-five women to include? On what criteria? How to organize them, when so many Renaissance women were active in myriad spheres, and the lines between Renaissance disciplines – literature, science, philosophy, art – were hazy and permeable? It is impossible to be exhaustive. The stories presented here are a selection – my selection – and the presentation in five parts merely a suggestion, meant to help orient the reader to the many arenas in which women left their mark. I have chosen as my own chronological parameters the period spanning roughly the years from 1450 to 1650 – allowing for the emergence of print on the one hand (with its significant impact on women, literacy, and publication activity), and running through the Counter-Reformation and the end of the wars of religion on the other. The women included here illustrate a diversity of paths and circumstances – across education, social class, religion, and region. Some were born into the major dynastic families that ruled Italy, such as the Sforza, Medici, Este, or Borgia; others came from the professional or artisan classes. They hail from Milan and Cremona to Mantua and the

Po valley, from Venice and Florence to Naples and Bari. Though it was difficult, I have not included certain better-known figures like the Latin Humanists Laura Cereta, Cassandra Fedele, and Isotta Nogarola (who warrant their own extensive discussion) or Alessandra Macinghi Strozzi (whose letters offer wonderful insights into the lives of Renaissance women), Margherita Costa (a multifaceted writer whose life story also makes for fascinating reading), the botanical artist Giovanna Garzone, the poets Veronica Gambara or Chiara Matraini, the courtesan and philosopher Tullia d'Aragona, or countless others – but I hope interested readers will seek out their stories and others.

I have also focused on women whose lives can be amply reconstructed from historical accounts, writings, and records, incorporating some who may be less familiar to readers, such as Lucrezia Gonzaga and Laudomia Forteguerri, or focusing on less well-studied aspects of better-known figures, like Caterina Sforza and Lucrezia Borgia. But there are many more stories yet to be told – especially those of the "invisible women" of the Renaissance who are so often absent from the historical record: working women, servants, and enslaved and manumitted women. We glimpse the presence of such figures, sometimes only fleetingly. In Sofonisba Anguissola's painting *The Chess Game*, for example, a white-capped female chaperone looks on as the artist's three sisters play a gleeful round of chess. She is watching, even enjoying, the game – but she isn't playing. Perhaps she is too busy: domestic servants were tasked with a wide range of duties, from household management to child-rearing (see Figure 0.1). The same figure appears again, older and gaunter, in the background of a 1651 self-portrait by Sofonisba. What was her name? What was her life like? We might ask similar questions about the woman who holds the music for Lavinia Fontana in the cover image for this volume, also shown in Chapter 17. Her simple garments contrast with the artist-performer's elaborate gown and lace collar; she is at once unobtrusive and energetic. Her eyes are fixed intently on the spinet, and on Lavinia's fingers as they hover over the keys.

To an even greater extent than servants like those depicted by Sofonisba Anguissola and Lavinia Fontana, Renaissance women of color have been virtually lost to history. Biographical details are fragmentary, and I did not have enough information about any one such figure for a chapter here, but this does not mean that women of color were not present in early modern Italy – only that retracing their lives remains as complicated as it is essential. Again, Renaissance art can provide

Figure 0.1 The Chess Game, by Sofonisba Anguissola, 1555
(National Museum, Poznán, Poland)
Photo: Alamy

clues – and prompt more questions. A striking image by Annibale Car-racci, for example, depicts a Black sitter holding an ornate gold clock in her hand – a symbol of virtue, modernity, or simply luxury (see Figure 0.2). Clad in plain but costly black fabric, wearing pearl earrings and a neat middle part, the woman staring steadily back at the viewer has long been identified, reflexively, as an enslaved woman or simply as an African woman. However, some art historians contend that Carracci's figure may have been a seamstress, as suggested by the pins and needle tucked into her bodice, perhaps a free woman living and working in the environs of Bologna. The painting is a fragment: we can just barely make out the arm of a more richly dressed second figure, stretching out and partially obscuring her. What was their relationship, and what might future research reveal about the seamstress's identity, and about race, gender, class, and work in the sixteenth century?

Tensions of race and class were also deeply embedded in Renais-sance politics and power. Simonetta da Collevecchio, the mother of the

Figure 0.2 Portrait of a Woman, attributed to Annibale Carracci, c. 1580s
(Tomasso, UK)

first duke of Florence, is thought to have been a free African woman
living near Rome. Though Simonetta was described as a peasant, her
son Alessandro de' Medici rose to the heights of command. Alessandro's reign was brief: installed as leader by the Medici pope Clement
VII, he was assassinated by a cousin in 1537. Was the attack motivated
by race, class, politics, personal rivalries, or all of these at once? His
story – and that of his mother – raises important questions not only
about Blackness and power at Renaissance courts but also about his-
toricizing race, class, gender, and difference.[8]

Renaissance cities were more diverse, multicultural, and complicated than we may sometimes imagine, and much work remains to
be done to see them – and the women who inhabited them – in their
full complexity. In Venice, for example, a center of Mediterranean

trade and commerce, contacts between Italy, Africa, and the Levant abounded: the sounds of Turkish, Greek, Hebrew, and countless other languages mingled with Italian in the streets; and the ranks of the republic's famed gondoliers included free and manumitted Black Africans.[9] Yet Venice was also the site of Europe's first Jewish Ghetto, established in 1516 to contain and surveil its Jewish population, soon followed by Rome. Venice and many other Italian cities were involved in the Mediterranean slave trade, which had begun to shift toward the Atlantic by the end of the fifteenth century. The majority of those sold as slaves came from Eastern Europe and Central Asia; when ports along the Black Sea were closed to merchants amid tensions with the Ottoman Empire, the number of sub-Saharan African slaves increased. As historians note, the presence of Black Africans in Italian cities was at once significant enough by the sixteenth century that they could be portrayed as servants in paintings but scarce enough to be perceived as particularly "exotic" by Renaissance Italians – as in the case of Isabella d'Este of Mantua, who avidly sought to purchase black children for her court.[10] Manumitted slaves of diverse ethnicities – those granted free status after some period of domestic servitude – appear frequently in historical records as well as in artistic depictions.

References to racial difference abound in Renaissance art and literature, with tropes of blackness linked to intertwined theological and aesthetic binaries: good and evil, dark and fair. Petrarch's blonde Laura represented the ideal spiritualized feminine beauty for scores of poets from Italy to England (in contrast to Shakespeare's sexualized "dark lady"), while racialized narratives of crusade and conversion shape epics like those of Ariosto, Torquato Tasso, or the poet Margherita Sarrocchi. Artists often drew on Blackness to heighten the whiteness of European subjects; some scholars interpret the foundational artistic technique of "chiaroscuro" – the dramatic use of shadow and light – as an extension of this binary.[11] The term "Moor," invoking tensions with the Ottoman East, was used indiscriminately throughout the Renaissance in reference to black- and brown-skinned people from Africa, Central Asia, the Ottoman Empire, and the Eastern Mediterranean, as well as Italy. As this suggests, early modern notions of race – and racism – were not limited to color. Religion was inextricably entangled for white Europeans in the discourse of human difference and its associated categorizations, exclusions, discrimination, and oppression, racializing not only Black Africans but also Jews, Muslims, and other non-Christians. Racism and discrimination have long kept people of color – and especially women – at the margins of history, but scholars are mining not only art and literature but correspondence, music, and other sources to create a more expansive picture of this era in Italy and across the globe.[12]

Different Paths

The circumstances of Renaissance women's lives varied greatly according to social class, geography, education, and many other factors. Women's lives were shaped by different choices (often not their own), responsibilities, and social expectations than men. Education was accessible to some women, especially among the elite patrician class, to varying degrees, but it was not formalized. Cultural and religious norms placed the notion of female honor (i.e., virginity, and a host of accompanying ideas about female virtue and chastity) at the heart of ideas about Renaissance womanhood. Women were expected to preserve their honor, and that of their families, by marrying or entering a convent – a practice that was common across Italy and became increasingly fraught once the Church instituted new reforms to enclose female convents after the Council of Trent (1545–1563). Marriage was typically a practical, rather than romantic, arrangement – intended to bring mutual benefit to both families, whether economic, social, or political. Marriage and motherhood entailed a host of expectations and duties, many of them time-consuming and some of them, like childbirth, physically taxing and often life-threatening. These factors, obligations, and emotional ties affected – but did not exclude – opportunities for women. Patronage or the support of the family was often critical to success, especially in areas like music, art, or literature, but some women, like courtesans, operated largely independently (though prostitutes and courtesans were subject to a host of other risks and uncertainties). Some women carved out lives of spiritual dedication within the secular world, remained single (or embraced widowhood after a first marriage), or – increasingly over the decades – pursued professional careers, supporting themselves and their families as the primary breadwinner or head of household.

Part One of this book focuses on women who were active in the political sphere. The sixteenth century was an age of queens throughout Europe, from Isabela I of Castile, whose marriage to Ferdinand of Aragon united two Spanish kingdoms (a reign marked by the terrible expulsion of Jews from Spain and the institution of the Spanish

Inquisition, and the colonization of the New World), to the Florentine Catherine de' Medici in France and Elizabeth I in England (who famously ruled alone). In the early decades, the Italian queen of Poland, Bona Sforza – of the formidable Milanese dynasty – sat on the throne of the largest kingdom in Europe, which eventually passed to her daughter, the last in the royal Jagiellon line. In Italy, where the political landscape was comprised of a host of city-states – *signorie*, princedoms, duchies, and republics, and, in the south, the Kingdoms of Naples and Sicily, all fending off internal and external bids for dominance – women were also at the heart of power. From behind the scenes, they impacted political policies and decision-making by exerting their influence as daughters, wives, and mothers – like Lucrezia Tornabuoni, an astute diplomat who worked in partnership with her Medici husband and son. Women also ruled openly, in the stead of absent consorts or independently. Caterina Sforza controlled her state in the Romagna for over a decade, surviving the assassinations of two husbands; Isabella d'Este governed Mantua for long stretches while her husband was at war. The women of Italy's powerful families were treated as political pawns, their marriages often arranged – often when they were still children – for maximum political or economic benefit (Isabella d'Este was betrothed at six; Caterina Sforza was fourteen when she left Milan as a bride). Rodrigo Borgia (Pope Alexander VI) negotiated three marriages for his daughter Lucrezia, intervening through force or guile each time a better opportunity for the family's advancement presented itself. Despite these machinations, Lucrezia Borgia found her own power and agency as the duchess of Ferrara, where she engaged her formidable business instincts in real estate ventures and land reclamation projects.

Widening the lens to include the cultural presence of women, Part Two of this volume focuses on women writers of the Renaissance, who took up their pens to express their views on love, desire, power, spirituality, and religious reform. There are many connections among the women included here, although each one made her own unique mark. Many engaged, adapted, and innovated the dominant literary models of the sixteenth century. Laura Terracina reworked Ariosto's chivalric poem in her own voice, using it as a platform to question the exclusion of women from education and history. The learned Venetian courtesan Veronica Franco used the three-line stanza made famous by Dante Alighieri – author of the medieval masterpiece, *The Divine Comedy* – to write subversive, sensual verse that openly embraced female desire while also questioning the inequity, instability, and danger inherent to sex work. But the foremost reference for lyric poetry in Renaissance Italy was Petrarch, whose fourteenth-century "canzoniere" – a collection of poems written in Tuscan Italian for an abstract beloved called "Laura" – was revered. Building upon the Petrarchan model, Vittoria Colonna became one of the most influential poets of the Italian Renaissance and the standard against which other women writers were judged for many decades.

Active in the mid-sixteenth century, Vittoria Colonna was also involved in the evangelist religious currents that swept through Italy. As Catholic reformers promoted an intensely personal relationship between the individual and God, they found an audience – and valuable allies – in educated and influential noblewomen like Vittoria; her contemporary, Lucrezia Gonzaga, explored similar religious themes in her writing through another popular literary genre: the letter. Though the Council of Trent, convened by the Roman Catholic Church between 1543 and 1563 in response to the Protestant Reformation, would soon clamp down on heterodoxy – religious beliefs that did not conform to official Church doctrine – in the 1530s such views were still circulating freely in Italy. Both Vittoria and Lucrezia passed through the court of Renée of France in Ferrara, known for its hospitality to religious dissidents. The humanist Olimpia Morata, who tutored Renée's daughters, was so deeply affected by the Lutheran-leaning atmosphere at the duchess's court that she became a religious exile, fleeing Italy for Germany. Unlike the other poets discussed in this section, Olimpia wrote primarily in Latin, the better to exchange ideas with and participate in the Republic of Letters that connected humanists and intellectuals across Europe.

If poetry was often intertwined with religious and social commentary, women's creative expression overlapped in many other areas as well. The women of Part Three were poets, musicians, composers, actors – sometimes many of these things at once. Singing or performing on stage – "public" activities that were sometimes seen as endangering the reputation and moral virtue of both the performer and her public – often made women the target of criticism. By the mid-seventeenth century, a particularly extremist commentator on social mores, the Jesuit Giovanni Domenico Ottonelli, commented that the sweetness of a woman's voice in song threatened less resolute souls with "catching a spiritual and deadly plague"; likewise actresses, "with their sweet, melodious voices, and with their costumes and their grace,

just like the Sirens . . . enchant men and transform them into beasts."[13]
But such views were prescriptive rather than reflective of reality, for
Renaissance women were celebrated in music and theater and foundational to major developments in both. In mid-sixteenth-century Venice,
the *virtuosa* Gaspara Stampa – celebrated for her angelic voice – wrote
passionate love poetry infused with musicality; she often set her verse
to music and performed for private gatherings of the city's elite. The
actress Isabella Andreini of Padua, who published poetry and letters to
augment her stage persona, gained international renown as a diva of
commedia dell'arte theater, infusing the form with her unique style.
Many Italian city-states boasted rich cultural environments, or courts,
centered around their rulers (like the one captured in Baldassare Castiglione's famous *Book of the Courtier* of 1528, an idealized snapshot
of the court of Urbino) that proved especially fruitful for women performers. The celebrated poet and philosopher Tarquinia Molza was
associated with Ferrara's famed "concerto delle donne," known for its
members' highly ornamented style of singing. Being born into a musical family that provided training and instruction was also an important
factor in helping to launch a career. By the end of the sixteenth century,
Francesca Caccini, daughter of the composer Giulio Caccini, was the
highest-paid musician on the rolls of the Medici grand dukes in Florence. She was the first woman to compose an opera – performed at the
Medici court in 1625 – and published a volume of sacred and secular
vocal works. In seventeenth-century Venice, Barbara Strozzi was also
born into music: her father, Giulio Strozzi, wrote librettos for some
of opera's best-known composers. Barbara forged an independent
career as a composer not of operas but secular chamber music. Unlike
some of her counterparts, she did not perform in public. Instead, she
cemented her fame through print, publishing a staggering eight volumes of her compositions.

As in music, Renaissance women were increasingly visible in the
world of art. Without the same access to apprenticeships and training
as men, family support was again often vital; the court environment,
too, offered opportunities for patronage and recognition. Part Four
examines three female artists with different paths to success. In Cremona, Sofonisba Anguissola made her name with vivid, sympathetic
portraits of family members, domestic scenes, and genre paintings
before forging a career as painter to princes and popes. In Bologna,
a progressive university city that was especially hospitable to women

artists, Lavinia Fontana was inspired by Sofonisba's success. She, too, painted portraits of noblewomen and their families, infusing them with psychological depth. Working outside a court environment, Lavinia may have been the first woman in Italy to take on large-scale religious commissions – as well as the first known to have painted nudes, an unprecedented subject for women. Among the best-known Renaissance artists, Artemisia Gentileschi was also the daughter of a painter, training with her father Orazio in his workshop. After surviving a horrific rape and subsequent trial, Artemisia left Rome for Florence, where she set about building her career and her clientele, painting muscular, dramatic paintings that featured strong heroines.

Renaissance women were also active in science (or natural philosophy, in Renaissance parlance, an umbrella term for many related areas of scientific inquiry). Though the Counter-Reformation eventually had a chilling effect on such debates (a conflict between religion and faith epitomized by the "Galileo affair" – the Church's prosecution of Galileo Galilei for heresy – that stretched from 1610 to 1633), vigorous debates were underway on the cusp of the seventeenth century. In 1584, the apothecary Camilla Erculiani became the first Italian woman to publish a work of natural philosophy, offering material explanations for biblical phenomena like the flood. Though she tried to evade scrutiny by publishing the volume in Poland, she caught the attention of the Paduan Inquisition and underwent a trial, in which she defended herself, in part, on the basis that she separated theology from scientific argument. In Rome, the poet Margherita Sarrocchi defended Galileo's discovery of the moons of Jupiter, a major development in the case for Copernican heliocentrism. She exchanged letters with Galileo that touched on astronomy, astrology, and poetry; Galileo sent her his works for comment, and she invited him to provide feedback on her epic poem, *Scanderbeide*. Cases like these illuminate the many ways in which women participated in scientific culture at the dawn of the Scientific Revolution – and reveal the long history of women in science.

Part Five, finally, brings us full circle to the Renaissance feminists who believed it was imperative for women to have access to education and to be written into history. The formidable Laudomia Forteguerra, a fifteenth-century noblewoman in the republic of Siena, marshaled a battalion of women to defend her city against imperial attack. Laudomia was a vocal critic of women's lack of access to education, as well as an admired poet who penned passionate sonnets to Margaret of Austria, daughter of the Habsburg emperor Charles V.

Though scholars disagree on the nature of Laudomia's feelings for the woman she professed to love from afar, her poems are an important source for the study of same-sex desire in the Renaissance. The stories of the other four women in this section are centered on women who lived in the republic of Venice: a powerful and distinct political entity in Renaissance Italy that took pride in its history of freedom from foreign invasion and professed the civic ideals of justice and equality. Did those ideals apply to everyone, including women? That tension fueled the emergence in Venice of some of the most important feminist voices in early modern Europe, who argued that given the same opportunities as men, women could succeed equally well at any profession or skill they chose. Moderata Fonte imagined a conversation among female friends – each one representing a different phase in a woman's life – who discuss and question the gender inequality women routinely faced. Her dialogue was published posthumously as part of the literary "battle of the sexes" of which Venice was an epicenter by the late 1600s. The prolific Lucrezia Marinella raised many of the same points in her forceful treatise on the "nobility and excellence of women," using examples taken from ancient and modern philosophy to turn misogynistic arguments about women on their head. Her treatise is an important forerunner to modern feminist methodology. The final two examples consider two women, both confined within walls of different kinds, who navigated not only the tensions of Renaissance gender politics but those of religion. Writing from within the Venetian Ghetto in the early seventeenth century, the Jewish intellectual Sarra Copia Sulam discussed literature and religion with Christian writers who sought repeatedly to convert her. Remaining steadfast in her faith when falsely accused of denying the immortality of the soul – a Catholic heresy – she responded with a manifesto in defense of Judaism. Meanwhile, from inside the cloister, Arcangela Tarabotti corresponded with many of the same literary figures and denounced the tyranny of church, state, and family over women's lives. As an unwilling nun, she joined the ranks of thousands of women in early modern Italy forced to take religious vows despite a lack of vocation – a common practice that was widely considered an "honorable" alternative to marriage. She called the convent a hell on earth – a prison with no escape. But she refused to swallow her marginalization quietly, instead devoting her life to forging connections outside the convent and protesting with her pen. Her legacy is a significant chapter in the history of feminist and political thought today.[14]

The twenty-five examples presented here provide only a glimpse into the many hidden histories of "the Renaissance" – an era at once vibrant and violent, innovative and repressive. In a recent essay, the contemporary Italian writer Elena Ferrante – who reflects at length on some of the figures who appear in these pages – asserts, "I believe that the pure and simple joining of the female "I" to History changes History."[15] It is a conviction recognized and voiced by women throughout the centuries, and, after some six hundred years, it remains an ongoing and essential endeavor. These pages aim to bring the inspiring, influential women who helped to shape the Renaissance out of the shadows and into the light they are due.

Part One

Politics and Power Brokers

1 Lucrezia Tornabuoni (1427–1482)

Medici Matriarch

Was there any part of the state that Lucrezia did not oversee, manage, or
approve?. . . She worked on behalf of all citizens, no matter their rank . . .
she knew how to handle matters of the greatest gravity and how to comfort
the people in times of crisis.

– Francesco da Castiglione

In Domenico Ghirlandaio's famous likeness, Lucrezia Tornabuoni appears in elegant three-quarter profile, her Florentine features stern but serene. In keeping with the pragmatic style of the Medici family – the Renaissance powerbrokers who rose to prominence from their roots in banking – she wears a simple black gown. Only a hint of red bodice evokes her noble status, and a translucent veil covers her hair and shoulders (see Figure 1.1). The image subtly evokes twin aspects of Lucrezia's persona, each equally potent: modest and dutiful wife and mother on the one hand, political and cultural force on the other. Wife of the infirm Piero di Cosimo de' Medici (1416–1469), known as "The Gouty" (for the painful joint condition that afflicted the family), and mother to Lorenzo "The Magnificent" (1469–1492) – a figure synonymous with the golden age of Florentine art and culture – Lucrezia wielded her own form of power to guide and shape Medici fortunes. In politics, business, and the arts, Lucrezia – like her son – played an important role in fostering the vitality of early modern Florence. Hundreds of letters exchanged between Lucrezia and her contemporaries, along with her own writings, offer a portrait of an influential and creative Renaissance woman, one that adds depth and complexity to Ghirlandaio's iconic depiction.

DOI: 10.4324/9781003081807-3

Figure 1.1 Lucrezia Tornabuoni, attributed to Domenico Ghirlandaio, c. 1475
(Samuel H. Kress Collection)
[open access]

Born into another Florentine banking family – a branch of the élite Tornaquinci with noble roots – Lucrezia Tornabuoni was seventeen when she married into the Medici. The quintessential Renaissance dynasty was just beginning its rapid ascent. Piero, eleven years her senior, was the eldest son of Cosimo de' Medici (1389–1464), who had used his vast fortune to assume de facto political control over the city, manipulating the votes of municipal office holders even as he claimed to lack all political ambition. As one contemporary, the future Pope Pius II, observed, "Political questions are settled in Cosimo's house. The man he chooses holds office. He is king in all but name."[1] Astutely, Cosimo consolidated political power by deploying his great wealth to support cultural initiatives, a tactic later epitomized by his grandson

Lorenzo, who poured the equivalent of hundreds of millions of dollars into strategically selected public projects. Though Piero lacked Cosimo's political charisma, he too supported Florence's burgeoning humanist culture. Soon, with the innovative vision of Lorenzo – and the help of Lucrezia, on whose judgment Lorenzo depended – Florence would turn into a magnet for the most imaginative and gifted artists, philosophers, writers, and architects of the era. From Sandro Botticelli – who depicted Lucrezia's sons in his *Adoration of the Magi*, commissioned for a chapel in the Dominican church of Santa Maria Novella – to the Neoplatonist Marsilio Ficino and the multi-talented Leonardo da Vinci, the Tuscan city became synonymous with the flowering of Renaissance culture (see Figure 1.2).

Lucrezia brought status and a substantial, though not extravagant, dowry of 1200 florins to her match with Piero. Both were equally important to the Medici, who did not come from nobility and relied

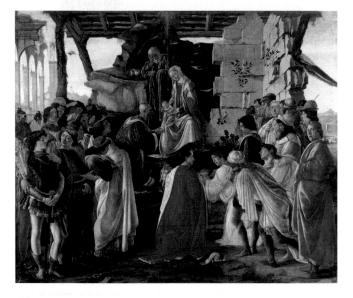

Figure 1.2 Adoration of the Magi, by Sandro Botticelli, c. 1475–1476
(Uffizi, Florence)
Photo: Alamy

Figure 1.3 Exterior view of the Medici Palace, Florence, 1930s
(Wellcome Collection)
[open access]

on the accumulation of new wealth. Piero and Lucrezia lived with Cosimo and his wife Contessina de' Bardi (1390–1473) in the then still-unfinished Palazzo Medici in Via Larga (today Via Cavour) (see Figure 1.3). Laid out by the architect Michelozzo, the imposing building – one of the finest of the Renaissance – reflected the essence of the Medici public image: the exterior somber and rather plain, designed to avoid stirring up envy among the people; the interior richly adorned with frescoes by Filippo Lippi and Paolo Uccello.

Figure 1.4 The Procession of the Magi, by Benozzo Gozzoli, c. 1459–1463
(Palazzo Medici-Riccardi, Florence)
Photo: Alamy

During the years of the palace's construction, the Medici supported numerous artistic commissions, from Benozzo Gozzoli's vivid frescoes for the Chapel of the Magi, portraying members of the family (see Figure 1.4), to Donatello's bronze *Judith and Holofernes* (which may have inspired Lucrezia's later poetic account of the Old Testament heroine). Lucrezia also spent much of her time at the Medici villas in the Tuscan countryside, particularly at Cafaggiolo, where she took refuge with her children for several months in 1458 to escape an outbreak of the plague.

Like many women of her social class, Lucrezia received an education intended to prepare her for marriage. If the Florentine architect and author Leon Battista Alberti, writing in 1434, stressed that the "ideal" young wife should be modest, chaste, and obedient, he also delegated to her the governance of the household, from raising children to overseeing domestic staff and supplies, making basic literacy, numeracy, and handwriting useful and practical skills.[2] While girls of Lucrezia's status did not attend formal school outside the house, unless in a convent setting, Lucrezia took advantage at home of the instruction provided to her brother and modeled on the ideals of humanism, the revived Renaissance interest in classical literature and philosophy. Her education stretched beyond the rudimentary parameters for women: she could read and write in Italian and likely Latin and composed her own poetry and religious narratives. After marrying, Lucrezia became close to some of Florence's leading literary voices. She commissioned Luigi Pulci to write an epic about Charlemagne, the great emperor said to have visited Florence during the Carolingian era (though Pulci's *Morgante* of 1483, a burlesque tale featuring a giant as its protagonist, was perhaps not quite what she had in mind). She also exchanged letters and literary opinions with the humanist Angelo Poliziano, who prized her company. Away from Florence in 1478, Poliziano complained: "Here I don't find my Mona Lucrezia in her room, to whom I can unburden myself, and I'm dying of boredom."[3]

Along with her literary interests, Lucrezia possessed a finely tuned political acumen which she turned to crafting Medici policy and promoting strategic alliances. As Piero's health declined, Lucrezia became an intermediary for her bedridden husband, hearing petitions and mediating requests from Florentine citizens. When the exiled Filippo Strozzi – a great rival of the Medici – sought a reconciliation, for example, he turned first to Lucrezia, offering her a gift of fine linen. Though Piero maintained that Florentine law forbade the dispensation Filippo requested, Lucrezia was persuasive, and the Strozzi's exile was lifted. Her political skill was no secret, and she deftly navigated between domestic and public worlds. Following Cosimo's death in 1464, her role in Medici affairs grew more active still: Piero, stepping into the role of Medici patriarch, kept his wife updated on political matters, and Lucrezia traveled on several diplomatic and cultural missions, often wielding her influence from behind the scenes. In many regards, this was the most effective – and often the only – way for Renaissance women to impact political decisions, by exercising their voices and guiding matters through unofficial channels of counsel and recommendation. Such intervention leaves little written record, but historians now widely acknowledge Lucrezia's role in helping to shape Medici affairs.

Lucrezia's letters and double-entry accounting book show that she also took an active and often imaginative hand in the family's private dealings and investments, primarily in the form of real estate and rentals. These were skills exercised by other Renaissance women, including Lucrezia's fellow Florentine, Alessandra Macinghi Strozzi – detailed in her own account book – and the entrepreneurial Lucrezia

Borgia. A principal initiative was the purchase and revitalization in 1477 of the old thermal baths at Bagno a Morba, near Volterra. Spas played an important role in early modern health practices, and proponents acclaimed the restorative powers of their waters as a cure-all for all kinds of ailments – including the joint pain that plagued the Medicis. A lively leisure culture sprang up around them, satirized by Niccolò Machiavelli in his comic play, *La Mandragola* (*The Mandrake*), which envisions an excursion to the baths as a pretext for an adulterous encounter. Lucrezia, said by her doctors to suffer from indigestion and depression, was a longtime devotee of taking the waters. In a 1446 letter to Piero she maintained "the baths have been very good for me," and she sometimes brought along Lorenzo, who was prone to eczema.[4] A savvy businesswoman, Lucrezia established a family residence at Bagno a Morbo, along with an inn that began receiving visitors in 1478, capitalizing on this lucrative early modern health craze.

Lucrezia's letters reveal an affectionate partner and a parent engaged in all aspects of her family's well-being, education, and future. When she was not in Florence, she sent Piero greetings, quotidian requests, and thanks for household items shipped from one residence to another – such as bedding and wine – as well as frequent updates on their children, to whom she referred warmly as their "brigata," or "little group." In 1458, she reassured him that "our little group is all in good health," adding that the children miss Piero and hope he will return soon, "for it seems like a thousand years since we've seen you." Taking a firm hand in her children's schooling, Lucrezia updated Piero on their activities regularly, noting that same year, for example, that "Lorenzo is learning the verses his teacher gave him, and he is teaching Giuliano, too." Lucrezia and Piero had five children: Lorenzo (b. 1449) and Giuliano (b. 1453); Bianca (b. 1445), who married into the rival de' Pazzi family in an unsuccessful effort to resolve bloody animosities; Lucrezia (b. 1447), nicknamed "Nannina," who married Bernardo Rucellai, host of the garden gatherings in the Orti Oricellari famously recollected by Machiavelli in his 1531 *Discorsi sopra la prima deca di Tito Livio* (*Discourses on Livy*); and Maria (date of birth unknown), rumored to be the illegitimate daughter of Piero but raised by Lucrezia as her own.

Lucrezia was strategic in arranging the marriage of her eldest son to an aristocratic Roman bride, Clarice Orsini (1453–1488). Matrimony, as Lucrezia was well aware from her own experience, was a complex matter that, for women of the élite, was dictated by social, economic, and political interest, not romantic love. The practical benefits to be reaped were great, and negotiations required care. Lucrezia thus insisted on traveling to Rome to meet Lorenzo's potential spouse herself, reporting back to Piero in a letter dated March 28, 1467, about the encounter with the fifteen-year-old Clarice. "She was dressed in the Roman style," Lucrezia wrote, "wearing a wrap, and dressed in that way she seemed very attractive, fair skinned and tall; but since the girl was all covered up, I couldn't see her as well as I hoped." In her letter from April 5, following a second meeting, Lucrezia provided more extensive detail:

> She is of appropriate height and fair skinned, as I have said, and has a sweet manner; she's not as refined as our [Florentine] girls, but she's very modest and could soon become accustomed to our ways. She's not blonde, because that isn't typical here; her hair is red and abundant, and she wears it loose. Her face is a bit roundish, which doesn't bother me.

Lucrezia went on to list Clarice's physical attributes further – all elements to be considered in a future wife and mother: she is a bit slim, her hands long and slender, her bust "of good quality." All in all, Lucrezia was satisfied, judging Clarice "well above average" (though again, "not to be compared" with her own daughters, "Maria, Lucrezia, and Bianca"). Just as important, however, were Clarice's connections: the niece of a Cardinal, she was related through both parents' sides to an array of well-placed nobility, her brothers and uncles had extensive land holdings, and "as far as I can learn they are well off, and every year doing even better." When Piero was not persuaded, Lucrezia was quick to reiterate that there was no "better girl here for [Lorenzo] to marry" and that they must "come to an agreement." Lorenzo and Clarice married in a four-day celebration in 1469.

Before his death the same year, Piero began taking steps to assure the transfer of power to his eldest son, securing approval for Lorenzo to take his seat on the Council of One Hundred, the governing body of Florence composed of select citizens. When Piero died on December 2, 1469, his passing was mourned by the city in a funeral procession that did not include Lucrezia, despite their closeness. Her position and authority, while well-known, were wielded privately and not officially. With Lorenzo and Giuliano now serving as co-rulers, Lucrezia – a widow at forty-two – had two options: with her dowry returned to her, she could return to her natal family, or she could remain – as her mother-in-law had done before her – with her sons. Lucrezia chose to stay in the Medici palace, where she could continue to exert influence, managing the household and hosting visitors (perhaps at the expense of Clarice, who retreated largely to the countryside).

With her sons rising to new prominence, however, tragedy struck. On 26 April 1478, Giuliano was assassinated. The doomed coup, known as the Pazzi Conspiracy and engineered by the Medici's long-standing rivals with help from Pope Sixtus IV, unfolded in full view of the crowd gathered in Florence's cathedral for Mass. Witnesses later described how the conspirators had escorted their unsuspecting targets to the Duomo under friendly guise, only to brutally attack them: a scenario so devious – and altogether emblematic of Renaissance dynastic politics – that it became the stuff of countless retellings (and, more recently, a central plot point in the bestselling historical videogame franchise *Assassin's Creed*). Giuliano was stabbed more than a dozen times, bleeding to death on the church's stone floor, while Lorenzo managed to shelter in a room to the side of the altar and from there escaped with his life. The event ended badly for the plotters, who were quickly apprehended and publicly executed: their bodies were hung from the windows of the Palazzo della Signoria, as depicted in a well-known drawing by Leonardo da Vinci (itself later reenacted in a macabre scene in the 2001 film *Hannibal*, directed by Ridley Scott). The Florentines deeply mourned Giuliano's death, and the episode left an indelible mark on Lucrezia. It also altered the trajectory of the Medici family, leading not to the disintegration hoped for by the Pazzi but to the further consolidation of Lorenzo's political power. As Lorenzo's authority and influence increased, so did that of his mother, his most trusted advisor. Lucrezia insisted on remaining by Lorenzo's side in Florence to face the aftermath of the episode and strengthen the show of Medici power and stability.

In her widowhood – and now in the wake of loss – Lucrezia, a gifted poet, turned in earnest to writing. Lorenzo's former tutor Gentile Baschi noted in a 1473 letter that Lucrezia's study was always "filled with books"; her friends ranged from the religious playwright Feo Belcari to the satirical poet Bernardo Bellincioni, with whom she exchanged playful sonnets, along with Pulci and Poliziano. A critical element of the Medici's "soft" cultural strategy was to encourage humanist scholarship and to meld it with Christian learning. For a time, these efforts had been primarily focused on Latin texts, since vernacular writing was reminiscent of the period before the Medici had taken over the Florentine republic. Under Lorenzo, however, the

Tuscan Italian promoted by Florence's "three crowns" – Dante Alighieri, Giovanni Boccaccio, and Francesco Petrarca (Petrarch) – came
into fashion, a shift evident in the poetry of both Lorenzo and Lucrezia.
For women writers, many of whom were not given a humanist education, Italian was also more accessible than Latin, and therefore not just
a matter of style. Many scholars suggest that Lucrezia influenced her
son's literary evolution toward vernacular poetry, and even that the two
were poetic collaborators.

Lucrezia was particularly interested in the stories of women (especially widows), and three of her *storie sacre*, longer religious poems,
center on biblical heroines who were well-known to Renaissance audiences: Judith, Susannah, Esther. Perhaps she admired her subjects for the
complex array of qualities they presented: from Susannah's chaste virtue and Judith's pious courage to the humility and discretion of Esther, a
popular subject in fifteenth-century Florence. Lucrezia hoped to engage
a female audience and in this she succeeded; a letter from Poliziano, to
whom she sent her poems, notes, "The women here enjoyed them very
much and [one in particular] learned them all by heart."[5]

Lucrezia's heroines each wield their own subtle but formidable
power, their honor and virtue always unshakeable. In her telling,
Esther is transformed from timid wife to authoritative queen, mediating among her people, her husband, and his court, much as Lucrezia herself did. Judith – like Lucrezia, a widow who chooses not to
remarry – is "gracious, noble and worthy, and goodness itself," while
at the same time possessed of a "valorous and manly spirit" that impels
her to take up the sword against the oppressor of the Jewish people.
Lucrezia describes the climactic scene in which the "valiant" Judith
slays Holofernes – one regularly depicted throughout the Renaissance,
from Donatello's sculpture for the Medici palace to the paintings of
Artemisia Gentileschi. "Once she had said her prayer," Lucrezia writes,

> Judith rose, her heart resolved,
> and in one hand she grasped a sword she had found
> leaning against a column or the wall,
> and so well did the young woman brandish it
> it would have been fitting for a strong and sturdy man;
> she struck him twice, with force,
> and his head rolled away from his shoulders.[6]

Lucrezia's strong heroines possess a mix of typically "masculine" and
"feminine" qualities, perhaps in a reflection of Lucrezia's own adept

navigation of public and private worlds. At the same time, her subject matter and tone were carefully chosen, for Lucrezia had to reckon with the treacherous cultural waters that sought to quell women's creative expression, often characterizing it as an expression of unchecked sexuality or unwelcome intellectual autonomy. By writing in Italian rather than Latin and by focusing on religious themes and virtuous women, Lucrezia avoided the criticism directed at many other women writers.

Lucrezia also composed *laudi* or lauds, shorter religious poems, four of which were set to the melody of a ballad by Poliziano, *Ben venga maggio (Welcome, May)*. Joyful in tone, if sometimes melancholic, her lauds focus on the praise of Christ, the saints, and the Virgin Mary. Lucrezia was well-known for her intense personal devotion to the Virgin and ordered special masses said in the Virgin's name (Pulci even imagines Mary reading Lucrezia's works in heaven). She was admired in Florence for her support of religious and charitable institutions – some Florentines referred to her warmly as a "font of charity" and "mother and helper of all the afflicted," terms conventionally used in descriptions of Mary.[7] Through these activities, Lucrezia helped reinforce the perception of Medici rule as supported by God and the people alike – a view the Medici family did not discourage.

Up to her death in 1482 (coincidentally, on the Feast of the Annunciation honoring Mary), Lucrezia – grandmother to two future popes, Leo X (Giovanni di Lorenzo de' Medici, 1475–1521), and Clement VII (Giulio de' Medici, 1478–1534) – remained at the center of Florence's political, cultural, and religious life. From her political activity to the strategic marriages she arranged for her children, from her poetry to her patronage and charitable works, her assiduous efforts all redounded to the benefit of the Medici. Indeed, it was thanks to Lucrezia's canny political instincts that the Medici not only preserved their wealth but also maintained and expanded their political base, particularly among the lower classes and within parts of the church bureaucracy. When she died, the canon of the church of San Lorenzo lamented that Florence had lost an important champion of their interests, and suggested that, in many ways, Lucrezia's contributions had been more consequential than those of her son, the "Magnificent" ruler of the city. Writing directly to Lorenzo, the canon noted:

> Was there any part of the state that Lucrezia did not oversee, manage, or approve? . . . Sometimes your mother's actions, from the political point of view, were more prudent than yours, for you attended only to great things and forgot the lesser. . . . She worked

on behalf of all citizens, no matter their rank, and she also admitted the humblest to her presence and all she sent away happy and contented. . . . She knew how to handle matters of the greatest gravity and how to comfort the people in times of crisis.[8]

Acknowledging Lucrezia's pivotal role as her son's most trusted advisor, he added: "but you know all this better than I do, for you never did anything without first consulting her." The grief-stricken Lorenzo echoed this sentiment himself, writing that when Lucrezia died, he lost not only his mother but also "an irreplaceable refuge from my many troubles and source of relief from numerous chores."[9]

The Medici dynasty transformed the political and cultural landscape of the Renaissance, and Lucrezia Tornabuoni was a driving force behind that legacy. Today, her role in molding Medici power is increasingly recognized: numerous editions and translations of her plays, poetry, and letters have been published, while, in popular culture, she has become known to a whole new generation, featured in novels and television series devoted to the Medici that spotlight her role at the head of her family. By restoring women like Lucrezia to the center of our narratives of Renaissance history and understanding the many facets of their lives, we begin to understand more clearly how women negotiated the gendered social norms of their age to actively shape their world.

2 Caterina Sforza (c. 1463–1509)

Countess, Warrior, Alchemist

Tall and beautiful, speaking little, she wore a satin dress with a long train, a black velvet hat in the French style, a man's belt and a purse filled with gold ducats, a curved sword at her side; and she was greatly feared among the footsoldiers and horsemen because, when she had a weapon in her hand, she was fierce and cruel.

– Bartolomeo Cerretani

If Lucrezia Tornabuoni led from behind the scenes, Caterina Sforza, ruler of a small but strategically located state in what is today Emilia-Romagna, seized center stage. The political philosopher Niccolò Machiavelli, who had a keen appreciation for intrepid and canny leaders, recounts a telling anecdote about Caterina in the midst of an attempted coup that began with the assassination of her husband, Girolamo Riario. The conspirators had taken her children as hostages, and the countess – having negotiated her way back into the Rocca di Ravaldino, the city's fortress – emerged on the battlements. Cutting a striking figure in her long gown, she did not, upon seeing her captive children, succumb to her opponents' efforts to exploit her maternal sensibilities. On the contrary: in Machiavelli's retelling, Caterina lifted her skirts, gestured pointedly between her legs, and retorted that she had the means to "make more": that is, more children and potential heirs (or avengers), rendering their threats useless.[1] Overturning her enemies' gendered expectations of her as a woman, mother, and female ruler, Caterina was victorious in this episode, earning the nickname "the Tigress" of Forlì – capable of sacrificing her young to maintain power – and going on to become one of Italy's most formidable leaders.[2] While Machiavelli may have embellished the story for dramatic effect, the account helped cement Caterina's persona as

DOI: 10.4324/9781003081807-4

a *virago* – a Renaissance term used to denote a woman of so-called manly political qualities, like courage, cunning, and ruthlessness – who had defiantly risked her children to preserve her state. A fifteenth-century celebrity, her rebellious spirit made her an enduring source of fascination to the public.

Said to have been a model for some of the most famous paintings of the Renaissance, including Sandro Botticelli's late-fifteenth-century *Primavera* (*Spring*) (see Figure 2.1), Caterina was born into the powerful Sforza dynasty of Milan, the northern counterweight to the Medici family in Florence.[3] The daughter of Galeazzo Maria Sforza (1444–1476), duke of Milan, and his longtime mistress, Lucrezia Landriani (b. circa 1440), Caterina was recognized as a legitimate Sforza child by her father and raised at court alongside her half-siblings from the duke's marriage to Bona Maria of Savoy (1449–1503). Like some women of her status, she studied Latin and literature, though not so extensively as her brothers. But her true passion was for hunting and the outdoors, and she lavished affection on the hounds she kept throughout her life. Through her stepmother, who maintained a medicinal garden near the Basilica di Sant'Ambrogio

Figure 2.1 Primavera (Spring), by Sandro Botticelli, c. 1480
(Uffizi, Florence)
Photo: Alamy

for the cultivation of "herbs, roots, flowers, seeds, and other things," Caterina was also introduced to the world of botanical medicine; later, she designed medicinal gardens of her own, where she grew plants and herbs used in tonics and cosmetics.[4] A half century later, Caterina's grandson, Cosimo I de' Medici (1519–1574), would establish Europe's first public botanical gardens in Pisa and Florence, designed by the naturalist Luca Ghini.

As a Sforza, Caterina had valuable political currency. Her marriage in 1477, at age fourteen, to Girolamo Riario (1443–1488) – a nephew of the sitting pope, Sixtus IV – was intended to bolster Sforza influence in Rome while ensuring papal interests in the Romagna. However, the wedding took place amid turmoil rather than celebration, for just a few months earlier, Galeazzo Maria had been assassinated as he entered the basilica of Santo Stefano for Mass. Even as Caterina left Milan behind to join her husband in Rome, the event foreshadowed the violence that would color her adulthood.

Although Girolamo reportedly – and fruitlessly – forbade his new bride to involve herself with politics, Caterina was welcomed into Rome's élite circles, thanks to the protection and patronage of Girolamo's kinsman, the pope. It was to curry favor with Sixtus that Girolamo, whose own political instincts were far less keen than Caterina's, became involved in the disastrous Pazzi conspiracy of 1478 – a failed coup that sought to bring down the Medici but succeeded only in rallying Florentines around a young Lorenzo de' Medici. Girolamo managed to escape, and the following year, Caterina gave birth to the first of their children, Ottaviano, followed by Cesare in 1480, and Bianca in 1481. Caterina and Girolamo had three more sons, born in quick succession: Giovanni Livio (b. 1484), named for the founder of Forlì; Galeazzo Maria (b. 1485), named after Caterina's father, and Francesco, called "Sforzino" (the "little Sforza," b. 1487), later Bishop of Lucca.

Even in these earliest years in Rome, long before Machiavelli would write of her exploits in Forlì, Caterina garnered a reputation for courage, political shrewdness, and a flair for the dramatic. In 1484, when Sixtus's death sparked civic unrest and looting across Rome, she was determined to protect her family from a potentially detrimental regime change. Clothed in a black velvet cap and an armored breastplate, Caterina – then seven months pregnant – took over Castel Sant'Angelo, the city's imposing citadel and occupied it for almost two weeks in an effort to force the cardinals to elect a successor favorable to the Riario

family. Only when Girolamo agreed separately – and without her consent – to accept 7,000 ducats (a sum rivaling the annual salaries of some
high-ranking government officials) in return for withdrawing opposition to the conclave did she vacate her post. In the wake of that crisis,
Caterina's reputation for tenacity followed her to the Romagna, where
she ruled alongside her husband and, later, as regent for her eldest son.

As the rulers of Imola and Forlì, Caterina and Girolamo – taking a
page from the Medici – funded public works and commissioned archi-
tectural and artistic projects to earn the goodwill of their subjects. They
fortified the defenses of both cities and created a large central piazza
in Imola, along with a personal residence and lodgings for important
visitors. In Forlì, their principal seat, they renovated another residence
adjacent to the Rocca di Ravaldino, calling it Paradiso, or "Paradise."
Caterina installed an enclosed garden near the Rocca, where she grew
vegetables, flowers, and medicinal herbs, and built a park along the
southern border, where she kept "wild animals of every type" and
fruit-bearing trees. Compared to other cultural centers of the time, the
Riario-Sforza court was smaller and largely agricultural; the aristocratic class was composed of only a handful of noble families, together
with a burgeoning professional élite. While it may have been more
difficult to attract the artists and intellectuals who flocked to richer
venues such as Urbino or Florence, Girolamo and Caterina worked to
project an image of magnificence, surrounding themselves with luxury
items. Sixteenth-century inventories of Caterina's possessions include
fine textiles and a silver dining service, along with brocade and velvet
gowns, gold-trimmed purses, and rings set with precious gems.

It was likely during this largely peaceful period that Caterina began
to develop an interest in alchemical experimentation, a subject of enormous interest to early modern princes. Rulers across Europe, from the
Hapsburg emperor Rudolf II to Philip of Spain, were intrigued by its
potential uses in metallurgy and warfare. The practical aspects were
particularly attractive to those in power, applicable as they were to
lucrative pursuits such as glassmaking, tanning, the manufacture of
saltpeter used in gunpowder, and the textile industry (in the fifteenth
century, the Medici held a monopoly on the sale of alum, used as a dye
fixative), but alchemical principles were also used in the production
of medicines, perfumes, and cosmetics. Today, historians of science
consider many elements of early modern alchemy as precursors to the
field of chemistry. Caterina was interested in its varied applications,
experimenting with salves and tonics to treat headache and toothache;

a general anesthetic "to protect those undergoing surgery from pain" and cosmetic products like hair dye, depilatories, and a beauty water to make "a woman of sixty . . . appear to be twenty."[5] She collected recipes that promised political or financial gain, such as a counterfeit finish to add "a reddish tint to any metal, giving the appearance of twenty-four carat gold." She sought out formulas for poisons and their antidotes, and even the elusive "quintessence," said to provide eternal youth and bring back the dead. She was not alone in these efforts: men and women across Europe engaged in alchemy, from the ill-fated Anna Zieglerin in Germany, executed when she failed to produce the fabled philosopher's stone as promised, to the more successful Isaac Newton in England, the father of modern physics. Caterina collected her recipes in a massive manuscript she called *Experimenti* (*Experiments*), a foundational source for the history of Renaissance science and medicine (see Figure 2.2). For Caterina, the pursuit of alchemical "secrets" was also a tool with which to build and cement profitable relationships with friends and allies by offering her knowledge as a gift, as she did to her brother-in-law Maximilian I, the Holy Roman Emperor from 1508 to 1519, and many others. Indeed, a well-known portrait of Caterina painted in the early 1480s by the Florentine Lorenzo di Credi appears to highlight this aspect of her persona, depicting her holding a pot of jasmine blooms, known for their therapeutic uses (see Figure 2.3).

But despite her skill at both alchemy and diplomacy, Caterina's political world was one of factions and bitter enmities – and there was no shortage of opponents to Sforza-Riario power. Girolamo was especially resented for his cruelty as well as his unpopular taxation policies: after several bungled attempts, he was finally assassinated on April 14, 1488. In an attack described by eyewitnesses, members of the rival Orsi family surprised Girolamo in the frescoed Hall of Nymphs in Forlì's government palace, where he granted audiences. Seizing their moment, they stabbed him repeatedly with a sword in front of his guards before flinging his lacerated body into the piazza: a gruesome echo of the failed Pazzi plot that Girolamo had once helped engineer against the Medici. Thanks to Caterina's bravado in the wake of the assassination – that defiant display on the fortress ramparts described by Machiavelli – she managed to retain both military and popular support. But she was ruthless in retaliation, raising "holy hell" against the conspirators, as one contemporary put it.[6]

Over the next years, Caterina was constantly engaged in political intrigue and warfare: as a woman, governing alone, she was subject

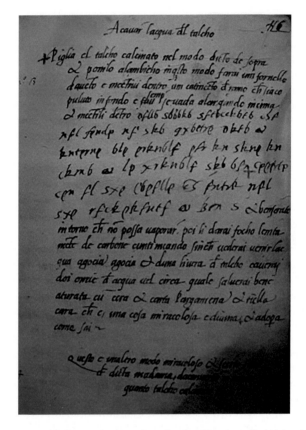

Figure 2.2 Partially encrypted page from Caterina Sforza's medical-alchemical
manuscript, *Experimenti (Experiments)*

Private archive

Photo: courtesy of author

not only to constant challenges to her power but also to insinuations
about her character. As regent for Ottaviano, her eldest son who had
not yet come of age, Caterina solidified her power through a combination of force and diplomacy. She established alliances, engaged in
marriage negotiations for her children, and oversaw the training of her
militia, all as the balance of power in Italy continued to shift as France

Figure 2.3 Portrait of a Young Woman with Jasmine, Lorenzo di Credi, 1485–1490, believed to depict Caterina Sforza

(Pinacoteca Civica, Forlì, Italy)

Photo: Alamy

and Spain vied for dominance over the peninsula. But Caterina's new relationship with Giacomo Feo (1471–1495), brother of the warden of Ravaldino, roiled the waters. When she secretly wed Feo and bore another child, Bernardino (b. 1492), some feared that she would grant him political power to the detriment of Ottaviano, the legitimate heir. These misgivings led to new plots, and, in 1495, Giacomo too was murdered as he returned on horseback from a hunting expedition. The grieving Caterina again took quick and merciless action against the perpetrators, this time striking back at their families and even killing their children to ensure that her message was clear: any challenge to her authority would be crushed. "The countess has dealt cruel punishment to anyone she can," wrote one contemporary, lamenting that "all of Romagna is crying out to heaven."[7] Suspicious of her own son's role in the plot, Caterina placed even Ottaviano under house arrest.

Her vengeance came with a cost, for what might be acceptable from a male prince as the price of power was deemed unnatural, even monstrous, from a woman. Support for Caterina began to erode among the citizenry, and it seems that she herself had misgivings. In 1496, she sought counsel from the fiery Dominican friar Girolamo Savonarola, who advised her to engage in charitable works to atone for her sins. She followed his advice, making donations to religious institutions and reestablishing political stability. In 1497, after making a profitable arrangement to supply grain to Florence, Caterina embarked on a new relationship with the agent who had been sent to Forlì to negotiate the deal. Her marriage to Giovanni de' Medici, known as "il Popolano" ("of the people") (b. 1467) – a wealthy businessman from a lesser branch of the famed Florentine family – was a more peaceful one; their son, Ludovico di Giovanni de' Medici (1498–1526), would become the renowned "Giovanni dalle Bande Nere," commander of the "Black Bands" mercenary force (so named for the mourning colors they donned in memory of the Medici pope Leo X), the finest company in Italy. But the marriage was short-lived. Plagued by gout (a condition that afflicted many of the Medicis), Caterina's third and last husband died of natural causes in 1498 while seeking treatment at the thermal baths in Bagno di Romagna.

A widow once more, Caterina had little time to mourn. The following year, she faced the fight of her life – the first she could not win. In 1499, Louis XII of France invaded Italy and ousted Caterina's uncle, Ludovico Sforza (1452–1508), as duke of Milan. The king entered the Lombard city accompanied by the Italian mercenary captain Cesare Borgia, son of the notorious Rodrigo Borgia (Pope Alexander VI) and brother to the famed Lucrezia. The scandal-plagued Borgias were known for their single-minded pursuit of influence, and the pope hoped to profit from France's gambit by expanding the papal territory and creating a state for Cesare in the Romagna. As commander of his father's armies and assisted by infantry and cavalry supplied by France, Cesare – whose calculating exploits were admired by Machiavelli in *The Prince* – set out to seize Imola and Forlì from Caterina; besieged by these united forces, Caterina waited in vain for reinforcements from her own allies. Trapped in Ravaldino, she penned an urgent plea for aid to her agent in Florence. "Send us three round, glass balls with small holes," she wrote, "large enough to hold two quarts, and also twelve sea onions – the ones they call squill – and the sooner you can send these things the more grateful I'll be."

Though mysterious, her request was not an idle one: the bulb of the red sea squill contains chemicals capable of causing intense vomiting and heart malfunction in humans; its derivative scilliroside is used today in commercial rat poison. After decades of gathering "secrets," Caterina now marshaled all the tactics at her disposal as she faced down thousands of invading troops, hoping to poison her enemy (or, perhaps, take her own life). But it was in vain. Vastly outnumbered, she and her troops managed to hold out for weeks before the fortress was breached, and they were forced to surrender. Their efforts evoked wide admiration: as Isabella d'Este, the duchess of nearby Mantua, observed, "if the French condemn the cowardice of [Italian] men, they must at least praise the daring and valor of Italian women."[8] A ballad by Caterina's contemporary Marsilio Compagnoni inspired by the episode imagines her exclaiming, even on the verge of defeat, "Oh, fearful Italians,/if you hear my story,/you will arm yourselves in passion/to win honor and glory."[9]

Caterina was delivered from the custody of the French commander, Yves d'Allegre, into the hands of Cesare Borgia in exchange for a large ransom. After boasting of raping Caterina – to the horror of contemporaries, who noted the "injustices done to the body of our poor and unfortunate countess"[10] – he paraded her back to Rome, ostensibly as a "guest" of the pope. Despite her ordeal, Caterina refused to renounce her claims on Imola and Forlì and was condemned to solitary confinement in the same Castel Sant'Angelo she had once occupied so defiantly. After a year of imprisonment, Caterina finally gave up her regency – but she did not give up her ambitions. Instead, she set up house in Florence, where she had sent her children for safety on the eve of Cesare's invasion. She entered into (and eventually won) a lengthy legal battle with her Medici in-laws, the family of her late husband, over the custody and patrimony of her youngest son, Giovanni, while working at the same time to secure the safety and prospects of her older children. She continued to engage in charity and nurtured connections with the Dominican convent of Annalena and the Benedictine convent of Le Murate, where she sought refuge on occasion as a boarder and where she was eventually buried. Caterina continued to seek a return to power, though she did not succeed. Her aspirations would instead be realized through Giovanni and his own son, Cosimo (1519–1574), who became grand duke of Tuscany (succeeding Alessandro de' Medici) after Emperor Charles

V restored Medici rule to Florence in 1530 – a shift that transformed the Republic of Florence into a hereditary monarchy and enlarged Medici territory well beyond its parameters under the de facto prince Lorenzo de' Medici and his influential mother, Lucrezia Tornabuoni.

If her political life suffered daunting setbacks, Caterina's scientific interests flourished in this final period of her life. She continued to collect "secrets" until her death from pleurisy and liver disease in 1509; her apothecary, Ludovico Albertini, from whom she procured materials, complained that she left behind a considerable debt. "[I]t didn't seem appropriate to mention it," Albertini wrote, "but the illustrious Lady – bless her memory – owed me 587 florins, and more, . . . as my account books clearly show."[11] Though these bills went unpaid, Caterina's testament distributed what wealth and possessions remained among her sons, also making provisions for two granddaughters as well as her servants and domestics, singling out in particular a "Mora Bona," possibly a servant or freed slave of African descent in her employ.[12] To her Medici son, Caterina bequeathed her volume of *Experiments*.

Keenly aware of the many factors that paved the road to power, Caterina Sforza was an active participant in her own political self-fashioning. Confounding conventional notions about women, femininity, and motherhood, she crafted a dramatic public persona as an independent and indomitable leader, outwitting rivalry, rebellion, and political intrigue with brilliance and sometimes brutality. Her interest in alchemy – a means to augment authority and prestige, as well as a practical tool to help manage the courtly household – inspired a legacy of scientific inquiry that lived on through her descendants: her grandson and great-grandson, the Medici grand dukes Cosimo I and Francesco I (1541–1587) would construct alchemical *studioli* and laboratories, and in the early eighteenth century Anna Maria Luisa (1667–1743), last in the direct Medici line, compiled medical-alchemical recipes much as her ancestor had.

Caterina's legend endured beyond the sixteenth century. She was a symbol of independence and resistance in the time of the Italian Unification in 1860, when an audience hungry for stories of regional heroes spurred a spate of biographies and presumed identifications of Caterina's likeness in portraits by a variety of Renaissance masters. For the Marxist political theorist Antonio Gramsci, she was an allegory of history itself, enduring through personal tragedy to face down her oppressors. Her story continues to resonate in popular culture today, with innumerable retellings in novels, plays, videogames – like the globally successful *Assassin's Creed* franchise –, films, and television series. Bold and independent, sometimes cruel and always resourceful, the iconoclastic Caterina Sforza lived by her own rules.

3 Isabella d'Este (1474–1539)

Diplomat and Tastemaker

among all the women in Italy, it was said that [Isabella] was the first lady of the world.

– Niccolò da Correggio

In Titian's iconic portrait, Isabella d'Este, marchioness of Mantua, emerges from a dramatic black background (see Figure 3.1). Her intelligent gaze, regal bearing, and luxurious attire – featuring a *zibellino*, a fashionable sable pelt, draped over one shoulder – radiate the power, determination, and elegance for which this intriguing and influential Renaissance woman, whose fame rivaled that of her contemporary Caterina Sforza, was known. Already sixty-two by the time of Titian's idealized and youthful likeness, Isabella was tied through blood and marriage to the most powerful dynasties of the sixteenth century, placing her at the very heart of the early modern political world. In addition to overseeing state affairs with her husband and defending the city in his absence, Isabella was an astute diplomat, a prodigious collector and patron of the arts, and a fashionista whose innovative style was imitated throughout Europe. She was also a prolific letter-writer, and her astonishing correspondence, numbering nearly sixteen thousand surviving letters, provides an intimate glimpse into her life at a bustling Renaissance court.

Born into privilege in the northern city of Ferrara, where Ludovico Ariosto would compose his famous paean to his Este patrons, the chivalric poem *Orlando furioso* (*The Frenzy of Orlando*), Isabella spent her girlhood in one of Italy's most vibrant cultural centers. As the eldest daughter of Duke Ercole I d'Este (1431–1505) and Eleanora d'Aragona of Naples (1450–1493), her future was determined early on: a well-planned marriage would bring added power, influence, and security to the house of Este. At six, Isabella was betrothed to Francesco II

DOI: 10.4324/9781003081807-5

Figure 3.1 Portrait of Isabella d'Este, by Titian, c. 1534–1536
(Kunsthistorisches Museum, Vienna)
Photo: Alamy

Gonzaga (1466–1519) of Mantua: they exchanged letters and gifts until their marriage by proxy when the bride reached fifteen. Isabella's siblings would be contracted into similarly strategic marriages: in a double wedding in 1491, Beatrice d'Este (1475–1497) wed Ludovico Sforza of Milan (1452–1508), while Alfonso d'Este (1476–1543) married Ludovico's niece, Anna Sforza (1476–1497) (and, after her death, took Lucrezia Borgia as his second wife). The festivities were orchestrated in part by Leonardo da Vinci, the artist, polymath, and sometime-diplomat who was in Ludovico's employ throughout the 1490s.

Political marriages like these were the primary mode by which the Este – and other dynasties – ensured survival, fortifying a web of influential and far-reaching connections. In preparation for their future roles, the Este progeny were educated in a wide range of subjects. Isabella was especially drawn to the study of classical history and literature; her enduring fascination with antiquity later inspired her avid collecting practices, leading her to seek out artifacts and *objets* in the ancient Roman style. She also learned the other courtly arts required for life at a Renaissance court, like dancing and singing, and became an accomplished musician, playing the violin-like *lira da braccio*. Even as a girl, Isabella was described as intelligent and inquisitive, with a keen eye for beauty – descriptors that would follow her as she aged.

Isabella's marriage in 1490 to Francesco Gonzaga, a well-known condottiere, or military captain, who by then was commander-in-chief of Venice's armies, strengthened the alliance between the two powerful families. The bride brought to the union not only her influential name and a substantial dowry of 25,000 ducats (far beyond what was typical for a noblewoman of the period) but also, as soon became evident, a formidable gift for diplomacy and government, along with an exacting artistic sensibility.[1] Upon her arrival in Mantua, an ancient Lombard city strategically located between Milan and Venice, Isabella took up residence on the main floor of the Ducal Palace of San Giorgio, turning two rooms into a *studiolo* and a *grotta*: private spaces for writing, study, and displaying the pieces she collected. While most women of her élite status commissioned primarily religious works, Isabella admitted to an "insatiable desire for all things ancient": she possessed such treasures as a Cupid attributed to the fourth-century-B.C.E. Greek sculptor Praxiteles and instructed her agents to remain always "on the alert for any beautiful and ancient bronze medals and other excellent things."[2] She amassed paintings and thousands of other items, from gems and coins to curiosities such as clocks, cameos, medallions, and a "unicorn's horn" thought to possess healing powers. An inventory made after her death listed over 1,500 items in Isabella's collection.

Soon pregnant with her first child – a daughter, Eleonora, born in 1493 – Isabella fostered a courtly environment at Mantua similar to what she had known in Ferrara. She gathered around her artists, writers, and musicians, and visited frequently with friends and family, like Beatrice (now duchess of Milan) and her new sister-in-law, Elisabetta Gonzaga (1471–1526) – whose court at Urbino, another important Renaissance center, is memorialized in Baldassare Castiglione's 1528 *Libro del Cortegiano* (*Book of the Courtier*). Isabella's circle included her old friend Ariosto, who mentioned her no less than three times in his poem and praised her as "liberal and magnanimous" – likely in gratitude for her help securing the patronage of her brother, Cardinal Ippolito d'Este (1479–1520); and the writer Matteo Bandello, who called her "supreme among women."[3]

Isabella's love of music endured: she hosted concerts and was among the first to employ women as professional singers, an unusual practice that would become more common in Italy in later decades. But her special passion was art, and, under her direction, beginning in 1492, the plain walls of her *studiolo* were transformed into a splendid display of mythological, allegorical, and religious scenes, along with paintings that celebrated the Este and Gonzaga names. Soliciting contributions from some of the era's most important artists, including Andrea Mantegna, Pietro Perugino, and Lorenzo Costa, Isabella was closely involved in the design process, choosing the story or "invention," and stipulating the measurements of each piece (see Figure 3.2).

Figure 3.2 Minerva Expelling the Vices From the Garden of Virtue, Andrea Mantegna, c. 1492–1502, from the studiolo of Isabella d'Este

(Louvre Museum, Paris)

Photo: Alamy

Though she likely had other *studioli* in mind as models, perhaps those she had seen in Ferrara or when visiting Urbino, Isabella was the first woman to implement so complete a vision for this interior, private space. Determined and imperious, Isabella was not above twisting arms to get what she wanted, on one occasion threatening to imprison the artist Giovanni Luca Liombeni "in the bridge dungeon" if he did not finish his work on the *studiolo* quickly.[4] She tried – and failed – to enlist the participation of the renowned Giovanni Bellini in her vision, who was unwilling to accept her detailed direction: in the words of one of Isabella's agents, the humanist and supreme literary authority of early-sixteenth-century Italy Pietro Bembo, the painter did not like "to be given many written details, which cramp his style."[5] Nonetheless, word of Isabella's marvelous rooms spread through Europe, making them a *de rigueur* stop for visiting dignitaries. Decades later, after Francesco's death in 1519, Isabella would move to new apartments in the palace's Corte Vecchia (Old Court), designed by Battista Covo. There, too, she commissioned new marble entrances from the great sculptors Tullio Lombardo and Gian Cristoforo Romano as well as allegorical paintings by Correggio.

Attentive not just to her surroundings but also to her own image, Isabella was always on the hunt for a flattering self-portrait (complaining that one likeness had made her look too heavy), and she approached Leonardo, whose earlier preparatory drawing of the marchioness holding a book had met with her approval (see Figure 3.3). In a letter dated May 14, 1504, Isabella wrote to the artist to outline her wishes, employing the royal "we" used by rulers to project authority: "When you were [in Mantua] and you did our portrait in charcoal, you promised that one day you would do one in color."[6] Though Leonardo could not honor her request for a likeness, others, including Titian, were happy to oblige, such that Isabella even joked, "I am afraid I shall weary . . . all Italy with the sight of my portraits."[7] Many decades after her death, the Flemish artist Peter Paul Rubens, copying another portrait by Titian (now lost), depicted Isabella garbed in rich red velvet and pearls the size of grapes, her corpulent figure still exuding luxury and authority almost a century later.

Isabella's interest in collecting extended into many areas. Claiming an appetite for beautiful things, she was a tireless shopper and sought the best in everything from fine fabrics, gloves, and jewelry to tableware, books, musical instruments, and other luxuries, amassing in particular a large collection of ceramics. She had a meticulous eye for

Figure 3.3 Sketch of Isabella d'Este by Leonardo da Vinci, c. 1499–1500

Louvre Museum, Paris

Photo: Alamy

fashion, furnishing her agent with detailed instructions for purchases, and was known for signature looks such as her elaborate *capigliara*, the beaded hairstyle on clear exhibit in Titian's well-known portrait. Isabella possessed the enthusiasm for experimentation that flourished in many Renaissance courts, devising and creating her own perfumes for which she sought out certain flowers and animals prized for their musk. She was famed for these unique scents, often sending them as gifts to friends and important acquaintances. Her interest in collecting, however, had a more grotesque side and extended to the trafficking of people. Isabella claimed to prize the "race of little dwarfs" she kept as jesters, in particular a woman she referred to as "her" Delia – whose daughter she proposed to send as a gift to Renée of France, the wife of Isabella's nephew, Ercole II d'Este (1508–1559) in Ferrara.[8] Isabella's letters also reveal her concerted efforts to acquire African children – whose black skin was seen as "exotic" in Renaissance culture – for her court, much as she sought out objects she considered beautiful or unique. Though she elsewhere evinced compassion for children, her concern did not extend to those who were enslaved: in one missive, for instance, dated June 14, 1491, she ordered her agent to scour Venice for a certain "Moorish" orphan to bring back to Mantua, provided she is "pretty, very black, and meets with our approval." Other letters refer to the purchase of African children in the same breath as jewelry that Isabella has ordered and list the price she is willing to pay for them.[9]

Isabella's influence as the marchioness of Mantua was not limited to the cultural realm: she was deeply interested and increasingly involved in all areas of public life, from administrative matters and agricultural management to policy and diplomacy. Though her marriage with Francesco was often difficult, she and her husband had a highly collaborative political relationship: they were partners not just in the domestic sphere – although Isabella was almost continuously pregnant until 1508, ultimately bearing eight children – but also in the daily governance of the city. If her partnership with Francesco was characterized by cooperation, Isabella also took an independent role in overseeing Mantua's affairs, even during some of its most turbulent periods.[10] When Francesco's military obligations took him away from the city in 1495, for example, Isabella was quick to assure him of her command at home, writing on June 30:

> Your Lordship may be calm of heart and think only of your military undertaking, for with the counsel of these experienced gentlemen I will govern the state in such a way that it will suffer no disturbance or damage, and all will be done to the benefit of its subjects. And if you should hear or read of disorder, and you have not heard it from me, you may assume that it is a lie. For because I have ordered that not only the officials, but all the subjects may speak to me any time they want to, nothing can happen for which provisions against disorder are not made before it can occur.[11]

Isabella's words resound with authority: nothing happened in Mantua without her knowledge.

Nor did Isabella always share her husband's shifting political and diplomatic positions. After years of service to the Republic of Venice, Francesco was dismissed from his position as captain-general of the Venetian forces. Although he hoped to regain the post, Francesco accepted a position as commander of an army comprised of troops from the Holy Roman Empire and its ally Milan, which was led by Isabella's former brother-in-law, Ludovico Sforza. When the French invaded Italy in 1499, forcing Ludovico to flee, Francesco pragmatically offered his aid to the king of France, Louis XII. But Isabella remained initially loyal to Milan. Having traveled there to seek protection for Mantua, she even offered asylum to refugees from the French-occupied city – including to Cecilia Gallerani, Ludovico's former mistress, famously painted by Leonardo, and two of her brothers. Isabella met personally with the French king, who expressed admiration for her persuasive diplomacy. Some historians suggest that the differing allegiances of Isabella and Francesco may have been strategic: a canny way to keep multiple negotiation paths open while navigating rapidly changing political conditions.

When Francesco was captured and held hostage in Venice some years later, in August 1509, Isabella again ruled in his stead, this time as official regent of Mantua. In this period of crisis, she assumed control of the city's military forces and successfully defended Gonzaga territory from foreign threat, negotiating a peace treaty that provided for Francesco's safe return. In a letter from that year, dated August 8, she wrote to his fellow captain Count Ludovico della Mirandola assessing the situation and explaining the measures she has taken:

> [A]lthough we are beside ourself and unable to think, we nonetheless have not neglected to take necessary measures either for the safety of our state or for the liberation of our lord. We have sent our men to the pope, the emperor, and the king of France. All that remains is that for our particular contentment Your Lordship stay at the border of this state until we are quite sure what our enemies will do.

The very next day, Isabella wrote to reassure the "vicars, podestà [mayors], and commissioners of Mantuan territories" of her firm hold on the state:

> [E]ven we – though we are very disheartened by [Francesco's capture] – are not so bereft of spirit and counsel that we are not aiming to do what is possible to preserve this state in its entirety. We have already made many provisions, and we have sought the powers of

His Most Christian Majesty, the emperor, and of His Holiness, our lord, to aid and favor us and our affairs whenever we are in need. We place such hope in them that not only do we have sufficient spirit to keep this state unharmed, we also promise the speedy liberation of our aforesaid lord.

Even as Isabella's letters exude leadership, her tone reflects the delicate ground she navigated as a woman. It deftly conveys the feminine dismay at Francesco's plight that would be expected of a wife and mother, while at the same time emanating the competence and authority of a head of state.

Though Isabella and her husband were productive co-regents, Francesco had an infamously roving eye. It was widely rumored that after meeting Lucrezia Borgia (whom Isabella once accused of taking an inordinately "long time to rise and dress in order to win eyes away" from the other court ladies) in 1502, he carried on a passionate romance with her.[12] While those accusations were probably unfounded, his exploits caused tensions in the marriage. When Francesco's health began to deteriorate from the syphilis he had contracted as early as 1496 – a sexually transmitted disease rampant in Renaissance Europe – the matrimonial relationship chilled, though the estrangement may have resulted as much from Francesco's discomfort with Isabella's superior political skills than from hers with his sexual transgressions. Whatever the reason, Isabella embarked on a series of diplomatic missions that took her away from court, traveling throughout Italy as an ambassador for Este, Gonzaga, and Sforza interests and providing valuable intelligence to Francesco back in Mantua. It was in large part thanks to Isabella's efforts that Mantua was raised to the status of a duchy in 1530; she also succeeded in obtaining a prestigious cardinalate for her son, Ercole Gonzaga (1505–1563). After Francesco's death, Isabella became regent of Mantua while her eldest son Federico II Gonzaga (1500–1540) was still too young to rule; much like the mother of the "magnificent" Lorenzo de' Medici of Florence, Lucrezia Tornabuoni, Isabella's role as the power behind the proverbial throne was widely recognized and she was sought out as a valuable channel in political matters. In 1525, Isabella purchased from her son the title to Solarolo, a fiefdom near Imola, in order to govern it in her own right, though she did so largely in absentia.

Isabella's diplomatic efforts continued as she traveled throughout Italy. She remained intent on promoting her family's interests and stayed very much in the public eye, exchanging gifts with heads of state including King Henry VIII of England. In 1527, Isabella was in Rome as the mutinous troops of the Holy Roman Emperor Charles V unleashed a terrifying assault upon the Eternal City on May 6, a spasm of violence and looting that became known as the Sack of Rome. Some see this moment, and the shifts in power it presaged, as the beginning of the end of the Renaissance. Pope Clement VII took refuge in the Castel Sant'Angelo as mayhem reigned in the streets; meanwhile, in dramatic evidence of the influence and respect she commanded, Isabella's Roman residence was among the few left unscathed – in fact, she was able to shelter some two thousand people within its walls. With her youngest son Ferrante Gonzaga (1507–1557) fighting for the emperor and Ercole (1505–1563), now cardinal, on the side of the papacy, Isabella, as always, had all angles shrewdly covered.

In the aftermath of the Sack, Isabella returned to Mantua, where over the next decade she continued to advise Federico, now the marquis, while transforming her famed ducal apartments into a veritable showcase and continuing to administer the state business of Solarolo. She often took an interest in the well-being of the women of her state, intervening on numerous occasions on behalf of her ladies-in-waiting, widows involved in property disputes, and victims of abuse. However, when a prized musician at her court, Bartolomeo Tromboncino, murdered his unfaithful wife, Isabella sought clemency for him on the grounds that "he had legitimate cause to kill [her] and since he is such a good and talented man." It seems there were exceptions to her support – especially when her own convenience was at stake.

In her final years, Isabella oversaw the construction of Santa Maria della Presentazione, a convent in Mantua, and remained deeply involved in the lives of her children and grandchildren. Thanks to her expert management of both private and state affairs, she remained firmly at the center of the Renaissance political and cultural world. So connected was she to the interrelated realms of governance, diplomacy, leadership, art, literature, and music that her relative, the Renaissance poet Niccolò da Correggio (1450–1508), dubbed her the "first lady of the world."[13] Isabella died in Mantua in February 1539; she was buried at the convent of Santa Paola, where her daughter Ippolita (1503–1570) resided as a nun.

The iconic Isabella d'Este continues to capture the attention of new audiences. Much of her copious correspondence has been translated into English, and she is the subject of numerous biographies and novels, as well as digital initiatives that offer interactive recreations of her multifaceted world. With her wide-ranging interests, Isabella was a true "Renaissance woman," with her finger firmly on the pulse of sixteenth-century politics, art, and culture.

4 Lucrezia Borgia (1480–1519)

Entrepreneur From Italy's Most Controversial Family

What can I tell you . . . of Lucrezia Borgia,
who with beauty, grace, honest virtue,
and enormous fortune flourishes
like a new plant in fertile soil?

– Ludovico Ariosto

Lucrezia Borgia, the golden-haired daughter of Rodrigo de Borja (Italianized as Rodrigo Borgia, 1431–1503; later Pope Alexander VI) and future sister-in-law of Isabella d'Este, was the subject of both admiration and wild rumors in her lifetime and long after her death. Born into the tumultuous world of Roman politics and power, her biography is shrouded in questions. Was she a passive pawn in the ambitious aspirations of her father – who, as Niccolò Machiavelli observed with reluctant regard, "never thought of anything, but how to deceive men" – or was she a shrewd political actor in her own right, purported to have worn a hollow, poison-filled ring to dispatch her enemies?[1] Was her close relationship with her brother, the ruthless Cesare Borgia (1475–1507) who vanquished Caterina Sforza at Forlì in 1499, truly incestuous or did the gossip that circulated about them stem from anti-Spanish malice? Speculation swirled, too, about the mysterious "Infante Romano" ("Roman child"), born while she was sequestered at a Roman convent. Was Lucrezia indeed the mother – and, if so, who was the father?

Sensational insinuations like these, fueled by resentment and xenophobia, have clouded the historical legacy of Lucrezia Borgia, long regarded as a victim – whether innocent or complicit – of her famous family's outsized designs on power (see Figure 4.1). In reality, the picture is more complex. Intelligent and educated, an adept diplomat and

DOI: 10.4324/9781003081807-6

Figure 4.1 Idealized Portrait of a Young Woman as Flora, by Bartolomeo
Veneto, c. 1520, sometimes identified as Lucrezia Borgia

Städel Museum, Frankfurt

Photo: Alamy

able administrator who presided over a vibrant court at the northern
Duchy of Ferrara, not only did Lucrezia play a critical role in the Borgias' political machinations, but she was an autonomous figure with a
talent for business enterprises. In the later part of her life, she initiated
reclamation and hydraulic works projects that transformed parts of Ferrara's swampy environs into arable and profitable land – bold ventures
whose scope is virtually unique for a woman of her time, and which
provided her with an unusual measure of economic independence.[2]

Born in Subiaco, an ancient hill town outside Rome, Lucrezia was
the illegitimate daughter of the Spanish-born Rodrigo, whose election to the papacy occurred amid rumors of simony. Her mother was

Vanozza dei Cattanei (1442–1518), a Roman innkeeper who was Rodrigo's long-standing mistress, though she herself married several times and lived separately. Rodrigo was made a cardinal by his uncle, Pope Callixtus III. But he led a notoriously secular life, punctuated by romantic and sexual entanglements and a general aura of debauchery. In addition to Lucrezia, Rodrigo fathered three sons with Vanozza: Cesare, future duke of Valentinois; Giovanni or Juan (b. 1476), count of Gandia; and Goffredo, or Jofré, prince of Squillace (b. 1481 or 1482). After his election to the papacy, Rodrigo legitimized Lucrezia and her brothers, openly recognizing them as his own and making Cesare a cardinal while still in his teens; all four became key players in his plans to amass dynastic power. Having worn cardinal's robes for over forty years, Rodrigo was well aware of the obstacles to advancement faced by his family, still considered interlopers in the Holy City. It would take an ambitious program of intrigue, alliances, political stratagems, and judicious marriages to achieve the Borgia goals.

As a young noblewoman, Lucrezia received a humanist education: at first under the tutelage of Vanozza's third husband, Carlo Canale, and later while living with Rodrigo's cousin, Adriana de Mila (d. post-1502), in a palace near the Vatican; joining the household was Adriana's daughter-in-law, the beautiful Giulia Farnese, widely rumored to be Rodrigo's new favorite and a close friend to Lucrezia. In addition to acquiring such traditionally feminine skills as embroidery, dance, and music, Lucrezia learned to keep meticulous accounts, read Latin and Greek, appreciate poetry, and compose verse of her own, though none survives. She was multilingual, fluent in her family's native Castilian as well as in Catalan, Italian, and French, and furthered her religious education through frequent visits to the Dominican convent of San Sisto, along the famed Via Appia, Rome's oldest and most important road.

It was said by some that Rodrigo adored his young daughter excessively, but this affection hardly impeded his plans to exploit her for Borgia benefit. In seeking a politically and socially advantageous match for Lucrezia, he was no different than many other Renaissance fathers – though his unvarnished determination to harness his personal and political capital for his family's advancement raised eyebrows. The worldly and charismatic cardinal found that his religious office presented few impediments to his plans, and in fact enticed prospective suitors with the promise of influence and power. Rodrigo's first impulse was to use Lucrezia to strengthen an alliance with Spain. At the age of ten, she was briefly betrothed to two Spanish noblemen: first to Cherubino Joan de Centelles, brother to the count of Valencia, and then to Gasparo Procida, count of Aversa. But as the political winds began to shift, Rodrigo, now pope, decided to seek a more expedient Italian match for his daughter. He found just the candidate in Giovanni Sforza (1466–1510), Count of Cotignola and Vicar of Pesaro, whose first wife had died a few years earlier. A union with Giovanni would provide a valuable connection to the powerful Milanese house of Sforza – and, in the process, repay Cardinal Ascanio Sforza, who had supported Alexander in the papal election. Still a child, Lucrezia underwent a proxy marriage to Giovanni on June 12, 1493; her wedding contract, which provided a dowry of 31,000 ducats – more substantial even than that of Isabella d'Este in the same years – stipulated that the thirteen-year-old bride remain in Rome for another year before consummating the marriage. After an official wedding ceremony in the Vatican celebrated before her father, Lucrezia – in part to escape an outbreak of the plague – followed her husband to Pesaro, where she spent two years at the city's small but sophisticated court.

At fourteen, Lucrezia exhibited a talent for the diplomatic skills useful to a Renaissance noblewoman. She remained closely allied to her Borgia family and sent regular updates from Pesaro to her father. Employing the florid language characteristic of Renaissance correspondence, she assured Rodrigo in a brief letter of 1494, "how well I have followed your commandments, finding everything just as it should be; such that Your Holiness can rest easy, for things are going well." Promising to remain "always alert," as instructed, she commended herself to her father and signed herself, "Your unworthy L[ucrezia]"[3] (see Figure 4.2). From the very start of what would turn into decades of conflict between France and Spain over control of the Italian peninsula known as the Italian Wars, Lucrezia also followed the news from Rome. In June 1494, grasping the danger posed by the designs of the French king Charles VIII on Naples – where the Borgias, always playing both sides, had close ties to the ruling family from Aragon – Lucrezia urged her father to flee (the French took Naples the following February). She also used her influence at the Vatican to seek favors and positions for friends and courtiers.

As the political landscape changed again, however, so did Pope Alexander's plans for his daughter. While Lucrezia's Sforza in-laws in Milan had sought security in an alliance with France, Alexander concluded that without Aragonese support, Rome – and, with it, the Borgia fortunes – were in peril. An alliance with Giovanni Sforza was

Figure 4.2 Autograph letter of Lucrezia Borgia to her father, Pope Alexander
VI, August 21, 1494

Archivio Segreto Vaticano
Photo: Alamy

suddenly of little worth to Alexander, who had also grown suspicious
of his son-in-law's true loyalties. The pope had already taken a step
toward strengthening connections with Spanish Naples through the
marriage of Lucrezia's brother Goffredo to Sancia d'Aragona (1478–
1506), illegitimate daughter of Alfonso II of Naples. Now, just two
years after celebrating Lucrezia's nuptials in the Vatican, Alexander
abruptly called for their annulment on the basis of non-consummation,

insisting that his daughter was still a virgin. This claim was widely disputed, not least by the bridegroom, who had reportedly fathered children during his first marriage and resented the implications of the assertion. The slight to his masculinity – and to the dynastic lineage – was an affront to the entire house of Sforza, and the episode gave rise to retaliatory accusations of an incestuous bond between the pope and his daughter. Disseminated by widely read sixteenth-century writers like Jacopo Sannazzaro, Giovanni Pontano, and Francesco Guicciardini, among others, the story has persisted for centuries, notwithstanding its clear roots in political rivalry.

Obedient to her father, Lucrezia took refuge in the familiar convent of San Sisto to await notice of her annulment, which came in December 1497, despite Giovanni's futile efforts to oppose it. As Alexander began negotiating a more advantageous match, she found herself embroiled in an episode that further fueled the dark stories about the Borgias. On a cold morning in February 1497, not far from the convent, two bodies were found drowned in the cloudy Tiber River: one was a Spanish servant to the Vatican, called Pedro or Perotto Calderón, the other Lucrezia's maid, Pantasilea. Not long after, whispers circulated that Lucrezia had given birth to a child while secreted away at San Sisto. The Borgia family denied it, but a baby, Giovanni – the "Infante Romano" – was in fact born in the Borgia household that year. Who was the father? Some claimed it was the murdered servant, Pedro; others, more darkly, pointed to Lucrezia's brother, Cesare, or even Alexander himself. Whatever the circumstances, three years later, in September 1501, Alexander would legitimize the child by secret papal bull, fueling rumors of the child's Borgia parentage (a prime example of the nepotism, or favoritism of relatives and allies – derived from the Latin root *nepos*, or nephew – for which he was infamous). Lucrezia herself saw to the child's support for the rest of her life.

Amid these dramatic developments, the Borgias were planning their next move. To further strengthen their relationship with Naples, it was decided that Lucrezia should now wed Alfonso d'Aragona (1481–1500), duke of Bisceglie and prince of Salerno. The eighteen-year-old Alfonso was an illegitimate son of King Alfonso II, but the match was still more prestigious than her first marriage had been – and happier. Lucrezia was reportedly won over by Alfonso's attentive manners and good looks, and their son, called Rodrigo for her father, was born in 1499. During this second union, Lucrezia's leadership abilities began to shine even more brightly. A year prior, Alexander had gifted Lucrezia with the title to the town of Nepi, in Viterbo, where she ruled as governor, followed by Sermoneta and other confiscated lands in Lazio. Now, while her husband was absent from Rome in 1499, Alexander entrusted Lucrezia with the task of governing Spoleto, part of the Papal States north of Rome. He was impressed with her performance, noting that she was gracious and persuasive, as befitted an effective leader.

But as Lucrezia was thriving, things turned darker for her new husband. Her ambitious brother Cesare – the model for Machiavelli's calculating prince in his eponymous political treatise of 1532 – had cast his lot with the French to help further his land grab in the Romagna, and an alliance with King Louis XII, whose power in Italy was growing, now looked like a more secure path for the pope. This time, it was Lucrezia's Aragonese husband who stood in the way. In 1500, Alfonso was murdered in cold blood: after surviving a stabbing near the Vatican a few days prior, he was strangled in his bed in the very papal apartments where he was supposedly under protection, as Lucrezia looked on – presumably in horror. Lucrezia fled Rome for her castle in Nepi, where she took to signing her letters as "Lucrezia Borgia, the unhappy princess of Salerno."[4]

Lucrezia refused a series of proposals for new marital alliances until 1500, when she finally agreed to a plan to wed Alfonso I d'Este (1476–1534), son of the Ferrarese Duke Ercole I d'Este and brother to Isabella d'Este, the marchioness of Mantua. This third and final marriage bolstered the status of the "outsider" Borgia clan through the connection to an ancient, noble family, while the affiliation with the strategically located anti-Venetian state of Ferrara brought added security. Suspicious of the scandalous rumors that continued to follow the Borgias – like the now-debunked story of the "Banquet of Chestnuts" featuring fifty courtesans – the Este initially resisted the match. However, reassured by reports that the proposed bride was charming, pious, intelligent, and "all good humour and gaiety," they acceded to pressure from the French and the prospect of an enormous dowry from the new bride: now some 200,000 ducats, almost ten times what she brought to her previous match, along with a guarantee of papal favors.[5] In 1502, Lucrezia made her way north, accompanied by seven hundred Roman, Spanish, and Ferrarese courtiers, soldiers, servants, and entertainers. She was greeted by dignitaries – among them her sister-in-law Isabella, who noted with reluctant admiration the bride's fine dress of "wrought gold with a crimson satin ruffle," sable-lined cape, and "gold cap" – and her entrance to the city was celebrated by writers like Ludovico Ariosto. Later, Ariosto would praise Lucrezia in his famous poem *Orlando furioso* (*The Frenzy of Orlando*), a veritable encyclopedia of sixteenth-century aristocratic society, noting her "beauty, grace, [and] honest virtue."[6]

Though whispers continued to follow Lucrezia – including improbable rumors of an affair with Isabella d'Este's husband, Francesco II Gonzaga of Mantua, still repeated in some accounts today – she had embarked on a more stable and autonomous chapter of her life. Over the next years, she bore seven children, including Ercole (1508–1599), later duke of Ferrara; Ippolito (1509–1572), future Archbishop of Milan and cardinal; and Leonora (or Eleonora, 1515–1575), a nun, musician, and composer. Lucrezia could finally turn the astute political instincts she had acquired as a Borgia to the business of overseeing her own court, governing in her husband's absence, and growing her personal wealth through innovative economic ventures. Though she would only officially become duchess once her father-in-law, Duke Ercole, died, she encouraged the vibrant cultural atmosphere at Ferrara by patronizing humanists, poets, and musicians. Among these was Pietro Bembo, champion of the Tuscan language and author of the era's most influential literary treatise, the 1525 *Prose della volgar lingua* (*Prose of the Vernacular Tongue*).

Lucrezia struck up an ardent friendship with Bembo, a frequent visitor to Ferrara. They began a correspondence that would last for years: three centuries later, the poet Lord Byron judged theirs to be "the prettiest love-letters in the world."[7] Much has been written about this epistolary "love affair," and, indeed, their letters, some of which employ ciphers for discretion, are deeply affectionate, even passionate. Whether or not their friendship ever transgressed the stylized conventions of courtly friendship, Lucrezia extolled her "affinity" with Bembo as a "gospel everlasting."[8] In turn, Bembo showered Lucrezia with praise, claiming "yours is the radiance which makes me burn," and lamenting any absence from her; in 1505, he dedicated his poetic dialogue on love, *Gli asolani* (*The People of Asolo*) to the beautiful duchess. The friendship was a source of consolation as Lucrezia grieved several miscarriages and mourned the loss of her father in 1503. Alexander and Cesare had taken ill in Rome with a suddenness that fueled talk of poison; her brother survived, but their father did not. Francesco Gonzaga later claimed to Isabella d'Este that seven devils had been spotted lurking about the pope's deathbed – which clearly "proved" that Rodrigo had achieved the papacy through a satanic pact.[9] With Borgia power in question, the Este court declined to mourn the unloved pontiff.

Bembo, however, offered his dear friend some words of condolence. Painting a mournful picture of Lucrezia lying bereft in a "darkened room" and "black gown, so tearful and distraught," he urged her to adopt the resolve demanded by her position. "Though you have now lost your very great father," he wrote, "this is not the first blow which you have suffered at the hands of your cruel and malevolent destiny. Indeed, your spirit by now should be inured to shocks of fate, so many and so bitter have you already suffered."[10] Astutely, Bembo also reminded Lucrezia not to show any weakness, adding, "Do not to allow anyone to assume that you bewail not so much your loss but what may betide your present fortunes." It was useful advice, for these tribulations were followed by others: Cesare's fall from grace upon the election of the anti-Borgia Pope, Julius II, and subsequent death by ambush in the Pyrenees after fleeing Italy; the death in 1512 of Lucrezia's twelve-year-old son, Rodrigo; and the loss of her mother Vanozza in 1518.

As the Borgia star waned, however, Lucrezia's only grew stronger and her diplomatic and entrepreneurial skills blossomed. She persuaded her husband to support Alexander's successor, Julius – Cesare's enemy – while it was expedient for Ferrara; later, she pawned her jewels – perhaps even her legendary "poisoned ring" – to help support Ferrara's war with Venice and the Papal States. During Alfonso's long wartime absences, Lucrezia shouldered responsibility for governing Ferrara, communicating with her husband through encoded letters and managing the requests and needs of the people with "skill and good will." An agent of Isabella d'Este reported:

> She improves every day in my esteem; she is a very intelligent woman, astute, and you need to have your head on straight [to deal with her]. I regard her as a wise woman, and this not my view alone, but that of the entire company.[11]

In 1518, another dispatch noted, "the Signora Duchess does not lack courage and [conducts] the examination of accounts every day of one sort or another, to the great satisfaction of the troops."

Freed from obligations to her Borgia kin, Lucrezia pursued plans of her own. While many Renaissance women are remembered for their political roles, literary production, or significant patronage of the arts, Lucrezia was an intrepid entrepreneur. Intent on enhancing her personal wealth, she did not focus on the typical princely projects that promised to enhance the magnificence of the city but deplete its finances, as her husband did, though she did have a palace built on Corso Giovecca in 1515–1518 as a personal retreat. Instead, she sought out investment opportunities that would positively impact the natural landscape around Ferrara while generating revenue to provide financial stability. Chief among Lucrezia's efforts was a series of reclamation projects aimed at making arable large areas of wetlands. Many of these initiatives occurred during Ferrara's wartime years from 1509 to 1513: for example, Lucrezia negotiated to undertake one such effort at Diamantina, a marshy expanse to the West of the city, in exchange for half of the owner's holdings there. Because the completion of hydraulic works at Diamantina greatly increased the value of the property, both parties benefitted from the deal. In another instance, Lucrezia arranged to purchase an incomplete monastery with the intent of transforming it into a convent. She deferred payment on it, managing instead to absolve the debt by draining and improving the lands around it, cultivating them or transforming them into pasture, and splitting the proceeds with the abbey. Lucrezia's forays into hydraulics were unrivaled for decades.

Centuries of legends that cast Lucrezia as either the passive victim of her family's appetite for power or an eager accomplice who readily engaged in plotting and poisoning have obscured her real influence. From Rome and Spoleto to the court of Ferrara, Lucrezia Borgia proved herself a political survivor who was as skilled in leadership and governance as any male – or female – counterpart; with her ambitious and innovative entrepreneurial projects, she eclipsed many of them. She also had a deep religious commitment, expressed through her patronage of, and occasional sojourns in, convents, correspondence with the nuns of Le Murate in Florence (where Caterina Sforza was buried), and consultations with learned friars. As a teenager, Lucrezia had been depicted in the guise of Saint Catherine of Alexandria for a fresco series in the Borgia Apartments in the Vatican, highlighting her piety; when she died, she was buried in the habit of a Franciscan tertiary, a lay order.

Though there are few definitive portraits of the captivating, complex Lucrezia, a handful of presumed likenesses from the Renaissance era hint at the wide spectrum of perceptions about her. On the one hand, Bartolomeo Veneto's *Idealized Portrait of a Courtesan as Flora* (shown earlier), one of the most well-known, depicts her with flowing golden hair (a lock of which is preserved, like a relic, in a jeweled case in Milan's Ambrosiana library), crown of laurels, and exposed breast: the painting has been variously interpreted as a nod to Lucrezia's sexualized, provocative reputation, or as simply a personification of Spring and idealized feminine beauty. On the other hand, a portrait by Dosso Dossi (c. 1519–1530) in the National Gallery of Victoria, Melbourne, long thought to depict a male sitter, is now thought to portray Lucrezia during her later years in Ferrara (see Figure 4.3). Dressed in fine, dark cloth and holding a dagger in reference to the Roman Lucretia,

Figure 4.3 Lucrezia Borgia, Duchess of Ferrara, portrait attributed to Dosso Dossi, 1518

National Gallery of Victoria, Melbourne

Felton Bequest, 1966

Photo: National Gallery of Victoria, Melbourne National Gallery of Victoria, Melbourne who fatally stabbed herself to preserve her own virtue and her family's honor, the figure is sober and self-assured – another side of Lucrezia, the capable, confident princess. Over the centuries, Lucrezia Borgia's story has continued to inspire countless novels, films, and other adaptations – from Victor Hugo's nineteenth-century play and Gaetano Donizetti's bel canto opera *Lucrezia Borgia*, to a spate of television series – reminding us to be attentive to the way history is written, to see past the admittedly dramatic flourishes through to the real-life legacy of its female figures.

5 Bona Sforza (1494–1557)

The Italian Queen of Poland

*[Italy] tempers the bitterness of all her present woes with the sweet memory
of such valiant ancestors and of your most happy birth. And if she could
have kept you for herself – a precious treasure granted her by the heavens,
which was instead released to the fortunate kingdom of Poland – truly Italy
would have no reason to yearn for the time when she was once lady of the
land and not, as she is now, servant of the people.*

– Ludovico Domenichi

In April 1517 – the same year that Martin Luther nailed his *Ninety-Five Theses* to a church door in Wittenberg, Germany, igniting the Protestant Reformation – the twenty-three-year-old Bona Sforza of Milan was married to Sigismund I, King of Poland and Grand Duke of Lithuania (see Figure 5.1). The lavish event offered the "most celebrated and splendid spectacle" of the Renaissance, in the words of the sixteenth-century author Matteo Bandello, eclipsing the nuptials of Lucrezia Borgia some twenty years before. The marriage of the young noblewoman – by now the sole legitimate heir to the powerful Duchy of Milan – sparked the Italian imagination, focusing new attention on a distant land known primarily for its export of furs, tapestries, and horses. It also placed a woman at the helm of the largest kingdom in Renaissance Europe, one of special importance due to its geographical position at the crossroads of East and West. Under the Catholic Jagiellon monarchy, the kingdom of Poland – which included parts of what is now Ukraine, as well as peripheral counties of Russia, Belarus, and Romania, and had a direct border with the Ottoman Empire – was a bulwark against the Turkish threat that preoccupied Italy, already jolted by the invasion of Otranto in 1480. Now, in the turbulent years of the Reformation, it would come into relief against

DOI: 10.4324/9781003081807-7

the backdrop of religious conflict that was unfolding between Protestants and Catholics throughout Europe. Though its Catholic monarchs issued anti-Reformation decrees, under Bona and Sigismund Poland was considered a haven of tolerance for religious refugees of various faiths in comparison to other states, where religious wars raged.

The future queen of Poland was born in Milan in 1494, another fateful date that marked the descent of French forces into Italy. It was the start of the so-called Italian Wars that would stretch into the mid-sixteenth century, as France, Spain, and a shifting array of allies vied

Figure 5.1 Detail, woodcut of Bona Sforza in Justus Ludwik Decjusz, *De vetustatibus Polonorum liber I. De Jagellonum familia liber II. De Sigismundi regis temporibus liber III* (Kraków: Hieronymus Vietor, 1521), 60

for control over the Italian peninsula. It was also a year stained by the political violence that dogged the Sforza clan, with the assassination of Gian Galeazzo (b. 1469), father to Bona and brother to Caterina Sforza, less than two decades after Bona's grandfather, Galeazzo Maria (b. 1444), had met the same fate. Galeazzo Maria's murder in 1476 had led to the installation of Gian Galeazzo, then just seven years old, as the new duke, but in name only. Almost immediately, an uncle – the notoriously ambitious Ludovico Sforza (1452–1508) – stepped in as regent, effectively wresting all power from his young nephew. In 1480, Gian Galeazzo was given special dispensation from Pope Sixtus IV to marry a cousin, Isabella of Aragon (1470–1524), daughter of King Alfonso II of Naples. Their wedding included a special operetta with scenery and costumes designed by Leonardo da Vinci, then in the service of Ludovico. But they were quickly pushed aside at Ludovico's court and constrained to live as virtual prisoners in nearby Pavia. Thus, when Gian Galeazzo died under suspicious circumstances at twenty-five, the historian Francesco Guicciardini observed that it was "was widely believed throughout Italy that he had died not through natural illness . . . but had been poisoned": nor "was there anyone," Guiccardini was quick to add, "who doubted that if it had been poison, it had been administered through his uncle [Ludovico Sforza]'s machinations."[1] Isabella, Bona's mother, initially returned to live with her children in the Sforza Castle in Milan, under the guard of a suspicious Ludovico who separated her from her son. But, fearing for her safety, she and her daughters moved in 1500 to Naples, which was still ruled by her uncle, Federico d'Aragona (1452–1504). They were briefly imprisoned at the Aragonese Castle on the island of Ischia when Federico was deposed the following year. Bona's mother began signing her letters "Isabella: unique in misfortune."

But Isabella was a unique political force herself. Her situation improved when she was granted the titles of Duchess of Bari and Princess of Rossano. A cultured woman who loved music and literature, she presided from Bari's medieval castle over a vibrant court frequented by poets like Niccolò Antonio (or Colantonio) Carmignano, who would later follow Bona to Poland. Isabella saw to it that her daughter received a well-rounded humanist education that included Latin, poetry, and theology. By observing her mother's effective navigation of a constantly shifting political landscape, however, Bona received something more useful still: a first-hand foundation in the principles and practicalities of statecraft that would serve her well in later years.

In Bari, Bona was showered with praise for her beauty, intelligence, and charm. Local poets composed sonnets in her honor, while a popular Spanish romance of 1513, *Question de amor (On Love)*, offered a thinly disguised account of the goings-on at court, including Bona's rebuff of a hopeful suitor. Of course, there was no possibility that Bona would marry for love: like most élite women of the Renaissance, her lineage and position made her too valuable a political commodity. Isabella was determined to make an advantageous match for her daughter and considered proposals from a variety of candidates. At the urging of the Hapsburg emperor Maximilian I, Bona's uncle by marriage, Isabella eventually agreed that Bona should wed the widowed Sigismund I of Poland (1467–1548), nearly twenty years her senior. Maximilian hoped this arrangement would benefit the Hapsburgs and check the power of the Jagiellons in East Central Europe, though Bona would thwart that prospect with the anti-Hapsburg policies she eventually implemented. As part of her dowry, which included jewels, gold, silver, and an enormous gilded wooden bed, Bona brought with her the impressive sum of 10,000 ducats. In turn, the position and prestige she would acquire as queen was inestimable. The union signaled the beginning of Bona's political life, opening a new chapter not only for her but also for Italy's cultural engagement with its eastern neighbor.

The marriage was performed in Naples on December 6, 1517, with a Polish proxy standing in for the king. Polish and Italian luminaries were in attendance, among them Bona's cousin, the celebrated poet Vittoria Colonna, who arrived clad in scarlet and gold and performed a special Hungarian dance.[2] Sixteenth-century chroniclers recorded the wedding in detail, from the bride's elaborate blue silk gown, jeweled necklace, and elaborately braided hair, to the rich wedding feast that included roast pigeon, rabbit, and chestnuts cooked in white wine and honey.[3] The voyage to Kraków did not commence until several months later; it was said that Bona feared the cold and therefore postponed the journey to February. An account of her departure from the port of Manfronia composed by Suavius Parthenopeus (a pseudonym for Carmignano), painted Bona as an innocent Italian maiden ("vergine latina"), undertaking a perilous journey to a faraway, foreign land, though in reality Kraków was already a well-connected European cultural center.[4] Suavius's account also highlighted Isabella's grief at bidding farewell to her daughter: a maternal sacrifice offered for the good of Italian interests. In Suavius's rendering, Bona is a passive political tool, rather than an independently powerful agent, yet in Poland she would show herself to be a capable and efficient ruler.

Escorted by an entourage of hundreds, Bona was greeted warmly as she stopped along the way. When the group finally reached Kraków, they were welcomed by a cannon salute and the presentation of a poem composed for the occasion by Andrzej Krzycki, a correspondent of the great Dutch scholar Desiderius Erasmus. As the wife of the last king in the Jagiellon royal line, Bona was expected to ensure its continuation through her male offspring. Pregnant almost uninterruptedly for the next seven years, Bona would bear four daughters – Isabella (1519–1559), Sophia (1522–1575), Anna (1523–1596), and Catherine (1526–1583) – and two sons, of whom only one survived to adulthood: the future King Sigismund Augustus, born in 1520.

At Wawel Castle, a complex in the heart of Kraków where Polish royalty traditionally resided, Bona gathered around her diplomats, agents, artists, and physicians. The Polish poet and diplomat Johannes Dantiscus was a chief advisor to both king and queen, and Bona's attendants included more than a dozen Italian governesses, ladies-in-waiting, and maids. Many of these came from illustrious noble families and went on to marry Polish men, an informal policy that led to an even fuller integration of Italian and Polish worlds. Preferring the cuisine of her native land, Bona employed Italians in her kitchen and is often credited with introducing the fruits and vegetables of the Mediterranean to the Polish diet – though it is likely that this process occurred naturally as a result of increased cultural contact throughout Europe. Italian architects and sculptors at the royal court included Francesco Fiorentino (Francesco of Florence) and Bartolommeo Berecci, who undertook the reconstruction of Wawel castle according to Renaissance principles of design, including its arcaded courtyard, the earliest surviving example of the form in Central Eastern Europe. Fiorentino executed the Olbracht tomb in the Wawel Cathedral, considered to mark the beginning of the Golden Age of Polish sculpture, while Berecci designed the famed Sigismund Chapel built in 1517 (see Figure 5.2).

Like Isabella d'Este, the stylish marchioness of Mantua, the queen's artistic interests extended to tapestries, fashion, and intricate jewelry. She employed a number of goldsmiths and the royal couple commissioned self-portraits in amulets and intaglios, including a famous cameo crafted by the Veronese artist Gian Giacomo Caraglio and a set of medallions by Giovanni Maria Mosca, known as Il Padovano.

Figure 5.2 View of Wawel Castle with Sigismund Chapel
Kraków, Poland
Photo: Alamy

Reflecting the growing links between the countries, further enhanced by the large number of Polish students traveling to Italy, Italian became the language of Bona's court, though she also devoted herself to learning Polish. Under her reign, the humanist culture of sixteenth-century Italy continued to take hold in Poland through writers and scholars like Kyrzcki, Mikołaj Rej, and Lukasz Górnicki, who adapted Baldassare Castiglione's Renaissance handbook, *Il libro del Cortegiano* (*The Book of the Courtier*), to a Polish setting. Scientific thought flourished, with many Poles studying medicine and science in Italy, especially at the University of Padua; the astronomer Nicolaus Copernicus, who had been a student at Padua himself two decades before Bona's arrival in Poland, published his world-changing model of the cosmos, *On the Revolutions of the Celestial Spheres*, in 1543.

As queen, Bona wielded her political and economic power to expand Poland's strategic access to the Baltic coast, reinforce Poland against Hapsburg influence, and support an alliance with France in the hope of recovering her native Milan from French dominion. She sought to establish good relations between Poland and the Ottoman Empire, including through diplomatic correspondence with Suleiman the Magnificent's imperial consort, the influential Hurrem Sultan, also known as Roxelana. Many of Bona's policies were aimed at reinforcing royal power and authority according to an Italian princely model: she worked toward these goals by promoting her supporters to important positions, creating a loyal magnate class, and attempting to increase the revenue from her land holdings. But her efforts led to tensions with the powerful Polish nobility, who saw her as a negative, calculating figure, a foreigner driven by self-interest.

By contrast, fascination with Bona only deepened in Italy, where she was no longer seen as merely a charming innocent but, instead, a model of queenship and virtue and a shining symbol of Italian cultural and political influence. A 1542 poem dedicated to Bona by Giovan Battista Nenna, a compatriot from Bari, praises her as the epitome of princely qualities, possessed of "infinite providence, the highest justice, . . . wise counsel, clemency, mercy, devoutness, faith, liberality, greatness of soul, humanity, doctrine, and learning." The writer and editor Lodovico Domenichi dedicated the first part of his 1544 *Rime* (*Poems*) to her, presenting her as both maternal and noble, a unifying figure destined to mitigate "the bitterness of [Italy's] present woes." Even the acid-tongued Pietro Aretino, known as the "scourge of princes," sought Bona's patronage by casting her as a national icon, if qualified by her gender: "the light of Italian women" and "the hope" of Italy itself.[5] Bona had come to represent a complex spectrum of tropes: powerful queen, virtuous wife, generous patron – and the incarnation of a politically inviolate Italy that had never really existed, subject as it was, for centuries, to external and internal struggles for control of the peninsula.

Due to its size and diverse ethnic population, Poland was the most religiously pluralistic country in early-sixteenth-century Europe. To an even greater extent than relatively tolerant cities like the duchy of Ferrara in Italy, which harbored evangelists and Protestants under Duchess Renée de France in the 1530s, Poland drew many religious refugees to its borders. Though the royal court was Catholic, the kingdom of Poland was known throughout Europe for its comparative openness to various religious confessions: it was a reputation that did not go unnoticed by Italians, particularly those connected to heterodox circles. Bona's confessor, the Franciscan Francesco Lismanini, later declared himself a Calvinist, while her personal physician, Giorgio Biandrata professed antitrinitarian beliefs. Bona's own religious views are difficult to pin down. The Jagiellon monarchs passed laws against heresy, but these were rarely carried out – though Bona did preside over the execution of Katarzyna Weiglowa for apostasy in 1539. She possessed a copy of the sermons of Bernardino Ochino, the Protestant reformer and exile who counted many Italian noblewomen among his followers, including Vittoria Colonna, and who would seek refuge in Poland in the 1560s, when Bona was no longer queen and the tide was about to turn against foreign dissidents. In Venice, the heterodox writer Ortensio Lando presented Bona as a model not just for queens but for all women in a 1548 anthology of letters filled with evangelist sentiment, again affirming that the Catholic queen was perceived by at least some of her compatriots as being sympathetic to reformist views.

If her religious opinions were opaque, Bona's political instincts were evident. A shrewd political strategist, she secured the throne for her only son with a *vivente rege* coronation, performed while he was still a child and the sitting king was still alive. An able administrator, she continued to exert significant influence on the formation of the Polish state and its economic stability after the king's death in 1548. But her actions stirred up distrust and animosity among the nobility, who saw her efforts as a challenge to their own power and were even less willing to accept the authority of an outsider – and a woman – once she no longer ruled alongside their Polish king.

Trouble brewed not only as the result of a growing power struggle with the Polish élite but also from tensions with the newly elected King Sigismund II. Just as Bona had tried to arrange politically useful matches for her daughters – Isabella was married to King John of Hungary, Catherine to King John III of Sweden, Sophia to a duke – so too had she hoped that her son would marry a princess of France or Italy, strengthening links to those dominant powers. When Sigismund instead revealed a secret marriage to the Lithuanian-born Barbara Radziwiłł (1520/3–1551), Bona could not conceal her disapproval and refused to attend Barbara's coronation. She softened her stance when Barbara fell ill, sending a letter promising "to recognize and honor Her Majesty [Barbara] as a daughter and beloved daughter-in-law" and hoping for her immediate recovery, but the situation deteriorated rapidly – as did Barbara's health. When Barbara died shortly thereafter, probably from cancer, rumors swirled that the dowager queen had poisoned her. Though the accusation was unfounded, Sigismund did little to dispel the whispers that fuel Bona's so-called black legend even today.

Unhappy with her increasing political marginalization, Bona determined to return to Bari. The situation had to be handled delicately, for there was opposition on the part of both the nobility, who suspected she was seeking to export her immense personal wealth from Poland, and her son, King Sigismund, who feared it would threaten his hereditary claims in Italy. Bona thus framed her departure as a temporary visit to tend to her health at the famed baths of Monteortone, near Padua. Her interest in preventive and therapeutic medicine was well-known, as she and Sigismund had employed numerous physicians and pharmacologists at court, and water cures were popular among early modern élites, making her justification convincing. Nonetheless, to ensure good faith, Bona also left her son with a substantial monetary gift and a magnificent jeweled ring called La Stella (The Star) in exchange for permission to depart. She left Warsaw on February 1, 1556.

After the tensions in Poland, Bona must have been relieved to make her way back to Italy, where she was still very much admired and was greeted with fanfare. Her progress, which led her first through the Veneto, was treated as a state visit, an elaborate, carefully orchestrated affair punctuated by ceremonial moments. At Padua, for example – part of Venetian territory and the first stop on her procession – she passed beneath a triumphal arch featuring the heraldic devices of the Sforza, Aragona, and Jagiellon families along with images depicting Justice, Strength, Liberality, and Prudence. The Venetian Senate made a gift to the queen of "forty barrels of malvasia wine, a thousand pounds of various kinds of white wax torches and candles, two cases of fine sugar," and a variety of sugared confections, nuts, and spices including "carnation, cinnamon, ginger, and nutmeg."[6] Venetian and Paduan nobility in gilded carriages drawn by white horses came out to meet her. Bona's own regiment included her chief steward, outfitted in black velvet and a heavy golden chain around his neck; her ambassador, Arturo Pappacoda; and his brother, the courtier Gian Lorenzo. The fanfare continued in Venice where, amid music and fireworks, the Bucenturo – a ceremonial boat used for state occasions – ferried the queen along the Grand Canal. Onlookers crowded the windows of palazzos hung with tapestries, and the canal itself was so thick with gondolas that one could "easily have jumped from Giudecca to San Nicolò with no danger of getting wet," as one spectator imagined of two landmarks on opposite sides of Venice's Giudecca canal. The spectacle of Bona's welcome was memorialized in poems and speeches, including an oration offered in her honor by Venice's most venerable humanist, the aged Cassandra Fedele.

From Venice Bona made her way south to Bari, where she spent the next two years presiding over her court, much as her mother had. But the political landscape, always treacherous, soon shifted once more. In 1556, envoys of King Phillip II of Spain attempted to persuade Bona to relinquish the Duchy of Bari and Rossano to the Hapsburgs; predictably, Bona refused, but she agreed to loan Phillip a staggering 430,000 ducats (the so-called Neapolitan Sums) to help him fund troops against France in the hopes of ousting them from Naples. It was an enormous amount, which the King had no intention of paying back. Instead, he bribed Pappacoda, the same trusted advisor who had accompanied Bona through the Veneto, to poison her and put the matter to rest (see Figure 5.3). Although the details around the episode remain

Figure 5.3 Poisoning of Queen Bona, Jan Matejko, 1859

Kraków, Poland

[open access]

murky, Bona's sudden illness in November 1557 was grave and unexpected. After writing a hurried deathbed will urged on and witnessed by Pappacoda and favoring Phillip, Bona recovered briefly, long enough to revise the will and make her son her main beneficiary. She died a few days later, in an echo of her Sforza father's fate some sixty years before. The deaths of several others in Bona's circle around this time also remain unexplained but were similarly suspicious.

King Sigismund passed away fifteen years after his mother, leaving no heir. Instead, Anna Jagiellon, the only daughter whose marriage Bona had not succeeded in arranging, was elected Queen of Poland and Grand Duchess of Lithuania in 1576, co-ruling the enormous state with Stefan Batory (1533–1586), whom she married at the unusually advanced age of fifty-two, since Polish law did not permit an unmarried woman to rule. It seems fitting that the legacy of Bona Sforza, one of the most powerful queens in early modern Europe – her death came just a year before Elizabeth I ascended to the throne in England – endured not through her son but, instead, though her daughter, who reigned for a decade. It was Anna who oversaw the construction of an elaborate marble tomb in her mother's memory in the Basilica of San Nicola in Bari, where it can still be seen today. Culturally influential and politically astute, Bona's queenship ushered in an era of diplomatic, commercial, and intellectual exchange across Europe, providing an illuminating example of female leadership and reflecting the interconnected political and cultural networks of the early modern world.

Part Two

Poets, Reformers,
and Courtesans

6 Vittoria Colonna (1490?–1547)

Divine Poet, Michelangelo's Mentor

Love engulfed me in a flame so noble
that – though it has died – it burns in me still;
nor do I fear a new passion, for the power
of that first flame extinguishes all others.

– Vittoria Colonna

Atop rocky Ischia, a rugged volcanic island in the Bay of Naples, sits the imposing citadel that was home for long stretches to one of the greatest poets of the Renaissance. The "divine" Vittoria Colonna, as her admirers called her, was the first woman in Italy to have a volume of poetry published in her lifetime. She cultivated an irreproachable literary persona as a devoted wife and chaste widow, motivated to write first by conjugal love and later by grief and growing spiritual fervor, an image that resonated deeply with her sixteenth-century audience. A presumed portrait of Vittoria by Sebastiano del Piombo encapsulates this carefully calibrated persona. We see a woman clad in rich but demure garments, a small volume before her – opened to one of Vittoria's own sonnets (see Figure 6.1). With one graceful hand, the sitter points down at the page; with the other, she gestures toward herself, but directs her gaze at the viewer rather than the text. The portrait conveys intelligence, dignity, and modesty: the very tightrope on which, as a woman writer, Vittoria tried to find her balance. Yet the full picture of this Renaissance figure is more compelling still: in addition to being a complex and original poet, she was also a skillful diplomat and a decisive, independent woman who charted her own course in literature and in life. Profoundly spiritual, she engaged closely with reformist religious circles and forged an intense friendship with the Florentine artist Michelangelo Buonarroti, as much his mentor as his muse.

DOI: 10.4324/9781003081807-9

Figure 6.1 Presumed portrait of Vittoria Colonna by Sebastiano Luciani (Sebastiano del Piombo), 1520–1525

(Museu Nacional d'Arte de Catalunya, Barcelona)

Vittoria was born, most likely in 1490, in the town of Marino southeast of Rome. The Italian Wars were on the horizon: a protracted struggle between Europe's major powers – primarily France and Spain – for control of Italy that would directly impact her life. The Colonna family counted a pope and several cardinals among its ancestors, including the same Giovanni Colonna (c. 1298–c. 1343–1344) famously memorialized by Francesco Petrarca (Petrarch), whose iconic fourteenth-century collection of love poetry informed Vittoria's own. As the daughter of Fabrizio Colonna (1460–1520), a military captain who fought for the king of Spain and appears in Niccolò Machiavelli's 1521 treatise *L'arte della guerra* (*The Art of War*), and Agnese da Montefeltro (1470–1523) of the refined court of Urbino, Vittoria's connections to the world of Renaissance high culture ran deep. She was instructed in literature and other humanist subjects, as well as in the traditionally feminine pursuits deemed necessary for a future wife and mother.

Plans for a politically advantageous marriage to Ferdinando "Ferrante" Francesco I d'Ávalos (1489–1525), marquis of Pescara, were laid when both parties were children: the d'Ávalos family had Aragonese roots, and the union thus aimed to cement an alliance between the Colonnas and the Spanish rulers of Naples. They married on Ischia on December 27, 1509. At nineteen, Vittoria captivated her contemporaries, as she would for decades to come. Writing almost twenty years later, the historian Paolo Giovio cataloged her many charms, noting her graceful dancing, her skilled horsemanship, her striking use of pearls and gems to adorn her hair, her beauty.[1] Notably, Giovio went on to praise not only Vittoria's "feminine" skill in household management but also her competence in governance and military affairs: her advice was routinely sought out by her father and husband. Most importantly, however, it was Vittoria's literary brilliance that distinguished her above all others.

Vittoria and Ferrante made their home in Naples until Ferrante – whose lineage compelled him to support the Spanish and papal forces cooperating in the Holy League against the French – was called to war. It was the beginning of a series of long and frustrating separations. Rumors of Ferrante's infidelities abounded, but more concerning to Vittoria was the fact that she had not given birth to an heir, as was expected of a woman of her status: "Our bodies were sterile, but our souls fecund," she wrote in a celebrated sonnet.[2] She awaited Ferrante's return in the company of his cultured aunt, the dynamic Costanza d'Ávalos (1460–1541), who had defended Ischia against French forces for months and was in return named its governor by the Holy Roman Emperor.

Costanza's court was frequented by poets like Jacopo Sannazaro, Luigi Tansillo, and Bernardo Tasso, father to the celebrated late-Renaissance poet Torquato. In this company, Vittoria first took up her pen in response to her husband's absences. Her earliest known work is an epistle addressed to Ferrante, composed when both he and her father were captured by the French after the rout of Ravenna in 1512. Vittoria assumes the posture of a classical heroine like those depicted in the *Heroides* of the classical poet Ovid, spurred to write by passion and yearning. Although Ovid had to imagine the pain of his fictional women, for Vittoria poetic expression merged seamlessly with lived experience. "My august lord," she wrote, "among how many doubts and fears I am miserably living, among how many harsh scourges! I was not expecting such torment and pain from you; for if the heavens had been favorable, the rich spoils would not have been lost."[3] Her eloquent complaint was grounded in real concerns: without the protection of a husband, a woman alone, even one in Vittoria's elevated position, faced challenges and uncertainties in this turbulent era.

Though Vittoria framed her verse within the acceptable and unthreatening themes of marital love and fidelity, she was keenly aware of the pitfalls faced by women writers. She never pursued publication, cultivating instead an attitude of indifference toward literary recognition. But her poetry was shared, even at this early stage, in manuscript form, and her command of the dominant Petrarchan style drew praise in Italian literary circles. Petrarch had found inspiration in the distant figure of Laura: a symbolic beloved who leads the poet to explore his own complex interiority and emotions. Blonde, angelically beautiful, and unattainable, "Laura" was the spark that moved Petrarch to burn and freeze – as he described his torments – for love. His example inspired hundreds of imitations – many of them unsuccessful. Vittoria adapted Petrarch's style and thematics brilliantly, but she was no mere acolyte. In assuming his paradigm, she entirely inverted it, becoming – as a woman poet – the active authorial voice, while her real-life husband replaced Petrarch's symbolic, idealized woman as an object of desire.

In 1525, Ferrante, now captain of the imperial army in Italy, was wounded at the Battle of Pavia. He died in Milan from complications caused by his injuries before Vittoria could reach him. The loss, after more than a decade of marriage, added new urgency to Vittoria's writing. In sonnets that mirrored her abruptly changed reality, Vittoria now cast herself as a devoted widow destined for permanent mourning – and, indeed, following Ferrante's death she sought a life of spiritual contemplation, renouncing fine clothing and luxuries. Still adopting the vocabulary of Petrarch – love as fire and precious burden – Vittoria insisted that she would remain perpetually faithful to Ferrante's memory, immune to any new passion: "Love wrapped me in a flame so that – though it has died – it burns in me still." She would never remarry, the fire of her first attachment "so strong it extinguishes all others." Her passion is at once powerful and restrained, bound firmly by the "knot" of conjugal love:

> So rich a bond ties me to that fine yoke,
> That my heart disdains all lesser chains.
> It feels no longer either hope or fear,

Since one fire burnt it, one knot bound it tight.
A single pungent arrow afflicts my breast
So that it keeps alive the immortal wound,
And shields all other love from entering.[4]

In other moments, by contrast, Vittoria's poems for Ferrante are infused with a subtle eroticism. There is an undeniable physicality to her evocation of the "beautiful scars" that mark Ferrante's body, telling the story of his military exploits; elsewhere, she compares her longing for him to the adventures of the mythological Jupiter with Leda, Danäe, and Europa.[5] But as Vittoria's piety deepened over time, her focus shifted from earthly love lyric to religious devotion and the figure of Ferrante gave way to a new beloved: Christ. The early verse directed at her husband thus marks the beginning of a poetic journey that would culminate in Vittoria's mature spiritual sonnets.

But before then, Ferrante's death had left Vittoria a widow at thirty-five and, with no children from her marriage, independently wealthy. This status made her a valuable asset to her family – who were likely keen to see her make an advantageous new union – but it also granted her a measure of autonomy enjoyed by few Renaissance women, and she was not eager to give it up. After Ferrante's death, Vittoria sought refuge in San Silvestro in Capite, an eighth-century convent in the heart of Rome. If her arranged marriage had been typical for a woman of her status, her steadfast refusal to repeat it was quite unconventional. But her plan to embrace religious solitude was forcefully opposed, including by Pope Clement VII himself, who hoped to profit from any new arrangement involving the powerful Colonnas that might yield alliances benefiting the interests of the Papal States. The cloister would negate such a possibility, and so he instructed the nuns of San Silvestro to prevent Vittoria from taking vows.[6] With the political situation worsening and tensions flaring between papal and Spanish forces, still vying for control of the peninsula, Vittoria returned instead to Ischia, barely escaping the calamitous Sack of Rome that saw the city plundered by imperial troops in 1527. Despite the Pope's obstruction of her desire to retreat into religious life (and even as some of her Colonna kin supported the emperor over the papal states in the conflicts of the next years), she would nonetheless maintain good relations with the Vatican, occasionally serving as an intermediary between these competing interests and proving herself as adept a diplomat as a poet. From this point forward, she led an itinerant and independent existence, moving between the environs of Rome, Naples, and Ferrara, with occasional – though always impermanent – returns to the convent life she longed for.

As Vittoria's poetry continued to circulate over the next decade, her name became increasingly renowned. She forged relationships with major figures in the literary world, including Pietro Bembo, a key proponent of Renaissance Petrarchism whose seal of approval carried enormous weight. Bembo argued that an antiquated Tuscan dialect, derived from Florence's three literary "crowns" – Dante Alighieri, Giovanni Boccaccio, and Petrarch – should be the basis for a vernacular literary language to rival Latin. Bembo's endorsement of Vittoria was cemented by Ludovico Ariosto, who enshrined Vittoria in his poetic review of sixteenth-century Italian society, *Orlando furioso* (*The Frenzy of Orlando*), as one who has "won immortal fame/with her sweet style – no sweeter do I hear." Like Bembo, Ariosto highlighted Vittoria's devotion to her husband's memory, finding in her poetry an expression of praiseworthy, socially permissible feminine devotion:

> She is Vittoria and justly crowned,
> As one to victories [*vittorie*] and triumph born.
> Where'er she walks, the laurel-leaves abound
> And diadems of fame her brow adorn.[7]

Vittoria readily collaborated in this literary identity, which brought her a degree of widespread respect virtually unheard of for women writers in this period. When Baldassare Castiglione, author of the genteel guide to courtly life, *Il libro del Cortegiano* (*The Book of the Courtier*), grumbled in his 1528 introduction that Vittoria had preemptively circulated his manuscript without permission, the complaint only added to the perception of her as a literary insider, privy to the latest happenings.

In 1538, Vittoria Colonna's book of *Rime* (*Poems*) finally appeared in print. The first collection of poetry to be published by a woman in Italy, it was a sensation. In the fashion of Petrarch, whose *canzoniere*, or poetic "songbook," was divided between compositions written for Laura before and after her death, Vittoria's volume, too, weaves together poems written "in vita" (while Ferrante was alive) and "in morte" (after his death). Though infused with Petrarchan language and imagery, her writing demonstrates a unique sensibility that is entirely her own, as she strives to reconcile love and loss:

> My heart was nourished by a lively hope
> Planted and tilled in such noble soil
> That its fruit promised to be pleasant and rich.
> Then Death uprooted what was flowering.
> My loving thoughts gathered at the shore,
> Transformed from serene day to darkest night,
> The sweet nectar became bitter poison;
> This was the only good not stripped from my mind.[8]

The widow's love for her spouse and simultaneously her painful memory of lost happiness take center stage. Her marital affection will be transformed into another kind of passion surpassing physical human bonds: as Ferrante's words "resonate in celestial harmony," Vittoria's love becomes a splendid, "bright blaze," and she wonders, "How will it be to see him without flesh?" The lines mark a progression toward an increasingly intense religious devotion.

Cementing her already considerable fame, the *Rime* went on to more than a dozen editions over the next decade, reaching a far wider readership than Vittoria's manuscript poetry had. To underscore that she wrote not to pursue "masculine" glory but, instead, "feminine" devotion and piety, the volume included another image of the author – no longer the elegant noblewoman of Sebastiano's portrait of the 1520s but now a chaste widow, head covered by a veil and a crucifix before her (see Figure 6.2). Vittoria continued to distance herself from all these editions, adopting a disinterest in public recognition that was considered appropriate for women. Yet her volume was so popular that by the end of the century she had become not just the first woman to have a book of her own poems printed but also the most widely read – and imitated – woman writer of the era.

Even as her fame grew, Vittoria would continue to explore her spirituality more deeply, an evolution that profoundly impacted her literary style. Over the course of the 1520s and 1530s, she had become increasingly involved with the networks of religious reform that sprang up in Italy around figures such as the Spanish religious writer Juan de Valdés and the Capuchin preacher Bernardino Ochino. This community also included the humanist Pietro Carnesecchi; the former papal nuncio

Figure 6.2 Title page of Vittoria Colonna, *Rime* (Venice, 1540)

Pier Paolo Vergerio the Younger; Marcantonio Flaminio, known for the *Beneficio di Christo* (*Benefit of Christ*), a central text of reformist thought in the period; Cardinal Reginald Pole of England; and Michelangelo. Such circles actively courted the participation of influential noblewomen. Among them were Giulia Gonzaga, who hosted a salon and corresponded with Carnesecchi; Caterina Cibo, duchess of Camerino; the reform-minded Renée de France, duchess of Ferrara; and Marguerite, queen of Navarre, whom Vittoria called a cousin and to whom she once sent an elaborate gift manuscript of her poems. In these years before the Counter-Reformation and an ensuing crackdown on religious debate, the Catholic Church had not yet clearly delineated the boundaries between orthodoxy and heresy. Reformers were afforded protection by the good reputation of their female followers, especially widows like Vittoria.

The theology of Valdés and like-minded Catholic reformers promoted a relationship between the individual and God independent of the mediation of the Church. Sometimes called Spirituali, the reformers came close to the Lutheran doctrine of *sola fide*, forgiveness ("justification") "by faith alone": good Christians will choose to lead an upright life because of their faith, but charitable works are meaningless in terms of salvation. The intensely personal nature of this relationship appealed to Vittoria profoundly. In 1544, she assembled a slim volume of devotional reflections in the form of letters that were reprinted in an anthology published by Paolo Gherardo and addressed to an unnamed recipient, most likely Ochino. So deep was her piety that, in 1537, she even considered a pilgrimage to the Holy Land but was persuaded against it in light of the fragile health from which she had suffered for years. Instead, she made her way to Ferrara to the court of Renée de France, who offered refuge to many heterodox thinkers, including the Protestant theologian John Calvin. There, Vittoria heard Ochino preach in person. Deeply moved, she composed in 1548 a volume of religious poetry, *Rime sacre e morali* (*Sacred and Moral Poems*). Though Vittoria's contemporaries murmured about her religious views, her connections to these reformist networks would be called into question only after her death, for example, during the inquisitorial prosecution of Carnesecchi, who was beheaded and burned as a heretic.[9]

It was against this backdrop that Vittoria's celebrated friendship with Michelangelo took root: they probably met for the first time in Rome in the early 1530s and their correspondence continued into the 1540s. Michelangelo, then working on the Sistine Chapel *Last Judgement*, made drawings and poems for Vittoria, embracing her as a spiritual mentor as well as a muse. Though intense, their attachment was platonic, based on intellectual and religious esteem and transcending traditional gender roles or romantic connection. In a famous sonnet, intended to offer high praise by characterizing Vittoria in masculine rather than feminine terms, Michelangelo refers to her as "a man within a woman," while in a letter written after her death, he calls her "my great friend," deliberately employing the masculine word for "friend" (*amico*).[10] To commemorate their bond, Vittoria prepared a manuscript of her spiritual sonnets for Michelangelo, compiled in

1540. In contrast to the gift she offered to Marguerite, this volume was plain, with no illumination or adornment: the title page includes neither her last name nor the epithet "divine" that so often accompanied it in print. The poems, only seventeen of which had been previously published, touch on *sola fide*, predestination, and God's love. No poetry for Vittoria's deceased husband is included; instead, the poet's focus is exclusively on Christ, who has supplanted Ferrante as the object of her attention.

Vittoria's innovative and intense style by now transcended the Petrarchism of her earlier poetry, as she linked her writing to Christ's passion:

> may the holy nails now be my quills,
> and may his precious blood now be my ink,
> may my paper be his lifeless sacred flesh
> so that I may record what he suffered.[11]

Evocative and powerful, her words conjure an almost tangible vision of the Crucifixion. They call to mind the intensity of Michelangelo's own devotional artistry, seen vividly in his representations of the Virgin cradling her crucified son, the pietà tableau that was so dear to him. In fact, in one pietà drawing attributed to Michelangelo, the features of the Virgin are thought to resemble Vittoria's own. Michelangelo shared at least three devotional drawings with Vittoria, including a *Christ on the Cross*, which – as she wrote with a deliberate play on words – "crucified in my memory whatever other pictures I have ever seen, nor could one imagine a design better made, more alive or more beautifully executed" (see Figure 6.3). Such exchanges illuminate the deep influence these two central Renaissance figures exerted upon one another, each supporting and deepening the other's piety.

Steadfast in her independence and devotion, Vittoria spent the final years of her life as she had long wished to, ensconced within convent walls at Sant'Anna de' Funari in Rome. When she died in 1547, Michelangelo was at her side: He memorialized the moment in a sonnet that lamented, "Nature, that never made so fair a face,/Remained ashamed, and tears were in all eyes."[12] Though Vittoria affected a distance from the circulation and dissemination of her work, she had lived to see more than a dozen editions of her poetry in print and achieved an iconic literary status that persists today. Embraced as the literary matriarch of a new lineage of women writers, she was praised as the "unique

Figure 6.3 Michelangelo's *Crucifixion*, c. 1538–41; presentation drawing given to Vittoria Colonna.

(British Museum, London)

Photo: Alamy

glory of our present age" by poets of the era such as the acclaimed Veronica Gambara, and influenced many others with her unique brand of spiritual Petrarchism.[13] Well into the seventeenth century, women writers would aspire to that highest of distinctions: to be compared to the "divine" Vittoria Colonna.

7 Lucrezia Gonzaga (1522–1576)

Epistolary Icon and Religious Dissident

*I try to spend most of my time reading and studying, not because this is a
medicine that can cure all that is wrong, but at least to escape the despair
that weighs upon me so heavily. . . . But if my fortune will not change of its
own accord or that of others, I will change it myself.*

– Lucrezia Gonzaga

The case of Lucrezia Gonzaga – domestic violence survivor, religious
reformer, and author of a book of letters written to affirm "the glory of
women" – vividly reflects how sixteenth-century ideas about gender
converged with literary tastes and new religious currents. Born in the
town of Gazzuolo in Lombardy, the dramatic events of Lucrezia's turbulent marriage, which her contemporaries followed with fascination,
brought her fame well beyond the borders of her natal city, while her
religious ideals that bordered on the edge of heresy placed her in the
orbit of other reform-minded women poets like Vittoria Colonna.

A minor branch of the powerful Gonzaga dynasty, Lucrezia's family
hovered on the peripheries of their ruling kin in neighboring Mantua:
a flourishing center of Renaissance art governed in the early sixteenth
century by Francesco II Gonzaga and the formidable Isabella d'Este.
At the age of eight, Lucrezia was orphaned, along with her six siblings, by the deaths of their parents, the condottiere Pirro Gonzaga of
Bozzolo (1490–1528) and Camilla Bentivoglio (1480?–1529), within
only a few months of one another. The double loss was a hard blow,
and Lucrezia was uprooted from her home and entrusted to her uncle,
Aloisio Gonzaga (1494–1549) – a captain for hire like her father –
in Castel Goffredo, north of Gazzuolo.

The court at Castel Goffredo was populated by a mix of military
and literary figures like Cesare Fregoso, a one-time commander for the

DOI: 10.4324/9781003081807-10

Republic of Venice, and the writer Matteo Bandello, Fregoso's secretary. Known for his masterful short stories, Bandello took immediate notice of Lucrezia's keen intelligence and began tutoring her in Latin, Greek, and rhetoric; later, he dedicated a series of celebratory poems to her. These years at Castel Goffredo were important for Lucrezia, providing her with the foundations for the literary life she would go on to build and instilling in her the value of study and writing as a salve to grief and hardship. For if Lucrezia's early life was marred by loss, her lot did not become easier. The story of her difficult marriage, abusive even by sixteenth-century standards, was the stuff of popular legend, while her steadfastness rendered her an icon of dutiful femininity. Yet Lucrezia manipulated these arduous circumstances to make a powerful entry into print and to voice, with impunity, religious views that diverged from Catholic doctrine – at least for a short time.

As reported in regional chronicles of the day, Lucrezia's uncle arranged for her to leave court to be married at fourteen. She was to wed Giampaolo Manfrone (1523–1552), known as "Fortebraccio" ("Strongarm"), a nickname derived from his membership in the *compagnia braccesca*, a division of mercenary "arms." A captain for the Republic of Venice, Giampaolo had a notoriously violent temper and a propensity for challenging rivals to duels. They lived briefly in Verona before settling uneasily in Giampaolo's palazzo in Fratta Polesine, later the site of Andrea Palladio's famous Villa Badoer (see Figure 7.1). In 1552, Ortensio Lando, a writer and editor who would become Lucrezia's literary collaborator and close friend, recalled her existence here as one of almost total solitude, confined to a "squalid tower," at the mercy of Giampaolo's irrational outbursts of jealousy and rage.[1] If Lando's description of Lucrezia's surroundings was tinged with exaggeration, his assessment of Giampaolo was accurate. Lucrezia's contemporaries disapprovingly noted the condottiere's pattern of striking his wife – in one instance for dancing at a party – and he was banned from Mantua after killing a servant. Lucrezia herself described him in a letter as "unbearable to his relatives, hateful to his neighbors, and hated by everyone else even before they met him," a man who "combined cruelty with an unbelievable arrogance."[2]

Continuing down an increasingly violent path, Giampaolo was arrested in 1546, five years after their marriage, for conspiring to murder Ercole II d'Este, the duke of Ferrara and son of Lucrezia Borgia, after suspecting an affair between the duke and Giampaolo's sister, Angela. The plot sent shockwaves through the entire region, and

Figure 7.1 Villa Badoer in Fratta Polesine, designed by Andrea Palladio
Photo: Alamy

even the Venetian Republic declined to intervene on their own captain's behalf. Although the would-be assassin was initially sentenced to death, his wife's entreaties – despite his abominable treatment of her – made such an impression on the duke that Giampaolo's sentence was commuted to life in prison. He would spend the next six years in a dank cell in the Tower of San Michele in Ferrara, writing increasingly frenzied letters to Lucrezia entreating her to secure his release. But to no avail: he died in prison in 1552, leaving Lucrezia with their two daughters, Isabella and Eleonora, and little else.[3] Following Giampaolo's death, Lucrezia was sent, on the authority of a male cousin, Vespasiano Gonzaga, duke of Sabbioneta (1531–1591), to a convent in Bozzolo; miserable and uncomfortable, Lucrezia repeatedly begged to be released.[4] Her pleas were eventually heard, for by the mid-1560s Lucrezia had returned to Fratta. The terms of Giampaolo's will stipulated that Lucrezia's dowry should be returned to her, so long as she continued to live "chastely" after his death and never remarry.[5]

Not only are the turbulent years of Lucrezia's marriage and its aftermath illustrative of the hardships she endured, but they also played a central role in shaping her engagement with cultural and religious currents. Women faced significant challenges to literary expression in early modern Italy. On the one hand, Renaissance literary tastes promoted women as facilitators of courtly conversation, as depicted in works like Baldassare Castiglione's *Libro del Cortegiano* (*Book of the Courtier*), printed in 1528. At the same time, however, a publication under a female author's own name often led to aspersions against her character or to derision for infiltrating a male cultural domain. Lucrezia took heed of other women who had successfully navigated this minefield, like the acclaimed poet Vittoria Colonna who cultivated an irreproachable persona as a pious wife and widow a few decades earlier. By presenting her literary activity as an effort not to achieve glory for herself but to obtain mercy for her husband, Lucrezia was able to avoid this common quagmire.

Her reputation had been and was still unimpeachable: given Giampaolo's notoriety, in both life and death, Lucrezia's support of him made her the epitome of female fidelity, while she was admired for her intellect in literary circles. In 1565, an anthology of poetry published in her honor cemented this exalted image with praise from numerous male authors and from the famous Neapolitan poet Laura Terracina. The volume included an elegant likeness, depicting Lucrezia as a decorous matron with a high, lace-edged collar and a direct, intelligent gaze (see Figure 7.2). With Giampaolo gone, a growing circle of writers and intellectuals now gathered at Lucrezia's residence at Fratta: no longer a lonely, confined place but, instead, a hub for literary and religious readings and discussion. This loosely knit group became known as the Pastori Frattegiani (Shepherds of Fratta) and included authors like Giovanni Maria Bonardo, Luigi Groto, Orazio Toscanella, Girolamo Ruscelli, and Lucrezia's champion, Lando. It was Lando who described Lucrezia as "the glory of women," a sobriquet echoed in the title of the letter-book she was soon to publish.[6] He saw in her a valuable partner for advancing his own agenda of cultural and religious critique, while she found in him support for her literary ambitions.

In the span of only a few years, Lando made Lucrezia a key character in several works he authored on female virtue and spirituality. He also included her in two anthologies of letters, a particularly fashionable sixteenth-century genre: the 1548 *Lettere di molte valorose donne* (*Letters of Many Valorous Women*), the first anthology of women's letters of the period, and the 1550 *Consolatorie* (*Letters of Consolation*).[7] Lucrezia was, in reality, an active correspondent, using her pen to plead her husband's case to authorities across and beyond Italy – going so far as to petition even the Ottoman sultan Suleiman the Magnificent – and keeping Giampaolo apprised of her efforts. With typical

Figure 7.2 Portrait of Lucrezia Gonzaga in *Rime di diuersi nobilissimi, et eccellentissimi auttori in lode dell'illustrissima signora, la signora donna Lucretia Gonzaga Marchesana*, edited by Cornelio Cattaneo (Bologna: Rossi, 1565)

(Biblioteca Nazionale di Firenze)

sixteenth-century formality, her frequent letters assured him that she was doing all she can "for the welfare and honor of Your Lordship"; to which a dejected and embittered Giampaolo responded, "Would to God that a great fire might engulf that house in Fratta and that the waters of the Po [River] drown what little is left to us."[8]

Letter-writing was a critical element of Renaissance communication with an infinite variety of functions, from the personal to the political. Those who were literate and had access to paper and ink composed their own letters; members of the élite often retained secretaries to take dictation and produce fair copies in a careful hand.

The rediscovery of Cicero's letters by the scholar-poet Francesco Petrarca, known in English as Petrarch, sparked a literary craze, but many Renaissance theorists considered epistolary writing an innately "feminine" genre, one guided, at its core, by emotion and spontaneity rather than art. Not only were such assessments based on broad and problematic assumptions about masculine and feminine literary voices, but they also overlooked the artificial nature of letter-writing – letters frequently underwent many revisions and were, increasingly, written for the express purpose of publication, with all the sincerity of a social media post today. Nonetheless, the perception of letter-writing as a feminine form of expression led to increased interest in women's letters as "authentic" exemplars of the genre. It is no surprise, then, that Lucrezia chose this form as the vehicle for her first – and only – solo-authored publication: the *Lettere della signora Lucretia Gonzaga . . . a gloria del sesso feminile . . . poste in luce* (*Letters of Lady Lucrezia Gonzaga . . . Published for the Glory of Women*), a 1552 collection of over three hundred missives covering a wide range of subjects (see Figure 7.3).

On the surface, Lucrezia's letters reinforce her persona as a wife dedicated to her husband despite his crimes: she is motivated to write by duty, not personal ambition. Many of her letters address Giampaolo's situation, beseeching such figures as Duke Ottavio Farnese of Parma, the famed naval commander Andrea Doria, two popes, and others for assistance. Lucrezia plays upon her vulnerable status as a woman and mother, noting that her children, like "little angels from heaven," join in her appeals, which remain fruitless and increase her desperation:

> I don't know what else to do; I don't know where to turn for help. I've written to popes and cardinals; I've implored the emperor, the king of France, the king of Bohemia, princes, dukes, duchesses, and marquesses. I've wearied the whole heavenly court with constant prayers, and I've caused it to be beleaguered by patriarchs, archbishops, archimandrites, deacons, canons, acolytes, monks, nuns, Beguines, hermits, cloistered nuns, and *convertite* [reformed prostitutes]. What else is there for me to do?[9]

While some of these printed missives may have had their origins in letters that Lucrezia sent, their artful rhetoric indicates that they were all revised for publication to highlight their author's literary skill.

To underscore this artifice, the volume is loosely divided in the fashion of Petrarch, whose poems for his beloved Laura were separated

Figure 7.3 Title page of Lucrezia's Gonzaga's *Letters*, 1552

(Rare Book Collection, Kislak Center for Special Collections, Rare Books and Manuscripts, University of Pennsylvania)

into the periods before and after her death; and of Vittoria Colonna after him, whose early poems were organized around the loss of her husband. The letters written while Giampaolo was alive often address him directly, urging him to draw on his faith in God for strength, while those composed after his death in 1552 position Lucrezia as a chaste widow, determined never to remarry – and who could blame her? Drawing on a tradition stretching back to antiquity, Lucrezia frames her writing as a form of consolation, explaining to her sister-in-law, Emilia Cauzzi Gonzaga (1524–1573), that it allows her to forget the unhappiness caused by her husband's actions and fate:

> I can find few remedies capable of freeing my heart from the many troubles that cloud it. . . . I try to spend my most of my time reading and studying, not because this is a medicine that can cure all that is wrong, but at least to escape the despair that weighs upon me so heavily . . . but if my fortune will not change of its own accord or that of others, I will change it myself . . . and if I cannot fight it with deeds, at least I can fight it with words and I give some vent to my grief by lamenting it.

By underscoring the acceptably "feminine" motivations for her writing, Lucrezia aimed to avoid the taint of "unfeminine" literary ambition.

In other letters, addressed to an array of friends, relatives, authors, and intellectuals, Lucrezia instead presents herself as an erudite cultural arbiter. She offers her judgment of works by influential writers like Girolamo Muzio, Francesco Robortello (author of the leading commentary on Aristotle's *Poetics*), and Terracina, whose verse she praises as "surpassing all possible praise." Her letters also abound with sage advice on weathering adversity with grace, fleeing vice, and placing faith in holy scripture. Together, Lucrezia's *Letters* paint an idealized portrait of the Renaissance woman: both lettered and virtuous, she is a model to be admired and imitated by others. Lucrezia's friend Lando, an experienced guide to the editorial market who helped her navigate the road to publication, reinforced this image in a parallel work he published the same year as her *Letters*: his *Due panegirici* (*Two Panegyrics*) includes a romanticized version of Lucrezia's story that casts her as a paragon of female loyalty and courage and the clear heroine to Giampaolo's villain. Lucrezia seems to refer to Lando's efforts when she thanks him in her *Letters* for his "little books that contain my ill-deserved praise" and "the many things you do in my honor."

Lucrezia's *Letters* mark a milestone in Italian literary history as the first "autobiographical" book of letters published by a living woman under her own name. Yet there is another facet equally important to the work's significance: the subcurrent of reformist views that runs through it. Deeply spiritual, Lucrezia became increasingly invested in the heterodox religious currents that percolated throughout Italy on the cusp of the Counter-Reformation: the courts of Ferrara, Mantua, Modena, and their environs were particular hubs of such Protestant-leaning thought. The movement of the Italian Spirituali promoted the tenet of *sola fide*, or forgiveness through faith alone; they gave precedence to the Gospels and prioritized the individual's connection to God, with a corresponding de-emphasis on the sacraments. These views could still be discussed openly in Italy (though not for much longer) and were embraced by many in Lucrezia's circle at Fratta. Just a decade before, in 1544, Lando had published a work under the name of another noblewoman, Isabella Sforza, exploring themes inspired by the 1543 *Beneficio di Cristo* (*Benefit of Christ*), a hallmark (and, by 1549, banned) text of the reformist movement. Capitalizing on the moral authority Lucrezia commanded by virtue of her patient response to her marital tribulations, Lando made her an interlocutor in his dialogue *Della consolatione et utilità che si gusta leggendo la Sacra Scrittura* (*On the Consolation and Utility of Reading Holy Scripture*), published in 1552, again the same year as her letters.

It is likely that Lando was seeking protection by linking himself to the social and political prestige of both Isabella and Lucrezia. However, such spiritual partnerships between men and women were common in sixteenth-century reformist circles, as we see in the case of Colonna, who explored similar ideas in dialogue with Michelangelo, or in that of Lucrezia's cousin, Giulia Gonzaga (1513–1566), the learned countess of Fondi who appears in the 1546 *Alfabeto cristiano* (*Christian Alphabet*) by the Spanish monk and religious refugee Juan de Valdés. Educated laywomen held a special kind of influence within such circles, where they were seen to merge humanist ideals with a nonintellectual, "feminized," and therefore less threatening spirituality (though some found that the intensity of their religious views made life in Catholic Italy untenable – like Olimpia Morata, the scholar and exile who moved in the same circles as Lucrezia and Lando but eventually fled for Protestant Germany).[10]

As reformist ideas spread, the vernacular letter-book became a vehicle to advance them. Many of the letters included in Lucrezia's collection evoke the teachings of the charismatic preacher Bernardino Ochino, the Dutch humanist Desiderius Erasmus, and other reformers of this period. In one letter, for example, Lucrezia explicitly affirms the doctrine of *sola fide*:

If you wish to be a Christian, you needn't make constant pilgrimage to all the holy sites your primary goal. Not that I condemn such a goal, but I tell you truly that faith is the only door to Christ, and it is better to study his scripture that was inspired by his spirit.[11]

She is as authoritative a judge in spiritual matters as she is on other subjects, confidently claiming in another letter, "[Y]ou will say that not only does Lucrezia Gonzaga know how to use a needle, but she is also a good judge of preachers." Lucrezia was open about her views and unafraid to express them in print, for she did not consider herself to be at odds with Church doctrine. However, a decade later, as the Counter-Reformation gained steam, she would find herself at the periphery and, ultimately, the center of several Inquisition trials. In June 1567, she was herself tried on suspicion of heresy; thanks to her social status and connections, she was released after making her recantation under oath – as Galileo Galilei would do three quarters of a century later. Several months later, Lucrezia expressed dismay about the experience in a letter to her sister, Isabella, writing, "I was amazed and astonished to be named in such a matter, since I am in fact quite removed from such thoughts and practices."[12]

Lucrezia died in 1576. She had never remarried, nor did she publish another book after her *Letters*. For centuries, scholars perpetuated the common historical bias toward women writers by assuming the *Letters of Lucrezia Gonzaga* to be the work of Lando, ignoring both her documented activity as a letter-writer in active correspondence with many people, including those who appear in the collection, and the fact that she was recognized by her own contemporaries as the author. The literary interplay between Lucrezia Gonzaga and Lando – their mutual admiration and praise, the guest appearances they make in one another's works – does not detract from her role as author. Instead, it reveals how sixteenth-century literary texts were often produced from the cooperation and influence of individuals linked by common literary, cultural, and religious views. By supporting and benefiting from one another so publicly, Lando and Lucrezia reinforced their own literary personas, broadened their audience of readers, and amplified their urgent message of religious reform. But with her *Letters*, Lucrezia boldly put her name to her story, taking ownership of its telling and subverting gendered notions of wifely devotion to step into the literary spotlight – for her own sake, and "for the glory of women."

8 Olimpia Morata (1526–1555)

Humanist and Heretic

> *Since letters transcend all human concerns, what women's spindles and*
> *needles . . . could pull me away from the sweet Muses? I have sealed my*
> *ears against such womanly lures, just like Ulysses at the rock of the Sirens.*
> – Olimpia Morata

If poets like Vittoria Colonna and Lucrezia Gonzaga tested the edges of religious reform, the life and writings of the humanist writer and religious reformer Olimpia Fulvia Morata were indelibly marked by the upheaval of the Protestant Reformation, set in motion a decade before her birth by Martin Luther. Olimpia (or Olympia) was born in Ferrara, just two years before the entrance in that city of Renée of France – the Calvinist wife of Duke Ercole II d'Este whose spirit of religious exploration would help shape Olimpia's own. Situated along the Po River in Emilia Romagna, Ferrara was a cultural magnet that attracted some of the most important artists, musicians, playwrights, and poets of the Renaissance: from Dosso Dossi, Andrea Mantegna, Ludovico Ariosto, and Torquato Tasso to the women of the famed concerto delle donne, an ensemble that featured the virtuosa Tarquinia Molza. After decades spent embroiled in the Italian Wars that engulfed much of the Italian peninsula, Ercole's marriage to a daughter of the king of France, Louis XII, brought added prestige to the walled city of Ferrara. (See Figures 8.1 and 8.2).

Renée's arrival also brought new religious currents. Under her influence, Ferrara became, in the words of one Italian ambassador, a haven for "Lutheran bandits from France," like the poet Clément Marot, whose verse translations of the Psalms would be adopted by Protestant congregations.[1] The duchess hosted the Protestant

DOI: 10.4324/9781003081807-11

Figure 8.1 Portrait of Martin Luther by Lucas Cranach the Elder, 1529

(Uffizi Gallery, Florence)

Photo: Alamy

theologian John Calvin, as well as Antonio Brucioli, known for his controversial translation of the Bible into Italian that landed on the Index of Forbidden Books (a list of works considered dangerous to the Catholic faith, instituted by the Church in the sixteenth century and abandoned only in the twentieth). The magnetic preacher Bernardino Ochino was in Ferrara in 1537, drawing huge crowds of listeners to his sermons, among them Vittoria Colonna and other Italian noblewomen with reformist sensibilities. Renée's activities confounded the duke, who grew increasingly uncomfortable with the religious environment she cultivated and eventually compelled her to renounce her Protestant beliefs.[2] It was in this atmosphere of debate and dissent that Olimpia,

OLIMPIA FULVIA MORATO
(Da un vecchio dipinto a fresco.)

Figure 8.2 Portrait of Olimpia Morata in Virginia Mulzazzi, *Olimpia Morato: Scene della riforma* (Milan: Bortolotti, 1875)

[open access]

invited to court as a companion and tutor to Renée's daughter, Anna d'Este, would spend her formative years. The religious climate she encountered there changed the course of her life.

The daughter of Fulvio Pellegrino Morato (1483–1548) – a humanist scholar deeply interested in religious reform himself – and Lucrezia Gozi, the studious Olimpia grew up amid learned conversation. Fulvio had himself served as a tutor for members of the Este family, and he now saw to it that his own daughter was instructed in Latin and Greek, which she could read, write, and speak fluently. By the time she was thirteen, Fulvio was coaching Olimpia on proper pronunciation in anticipation of her public recitations, reminding her that "Delivery, if it does not have all of its ornament in pronunciation, scarcely shines by other means."[3] Though the sixteenth century saw an overwhelming flourishing of vernacular poetry, Olimpia's orientation as a Latin humanist – the intellectual movement propelled by a new interest in the classical world – led her to focus not on love lyric, like other well-known female poets, but on works in Greek and Latin, from Xenophon to Cicero and Lucretius. In one early poem composed in Greek and probably dating to her first years at the court of Ferrara, Olimpia describes her passion for learning, which she prizes high above the traditional pastimes prescribed as appropriate to women:

> And I, though born female, have abandoned feminine things:
> yarn, shuttle, thread, and basket.
> I admire the flowery meadow of the Muses,
> and the pleasant choruses of twin-peaked Parnassus.
> Let other women delight in other things.
> These are my glory, these my delight.

Her feminist sentiment echoes the exhortations of a previous generation of illustrious women humanists, including Isotta Nogarola, Laura Cereta, and Cassandra Fedele, all of whom wrote works in Latin defending the intellect of women.

So sharp was Olimpia's mind and so great her aptitude that she was dubbed a prodigy and celebrated by other humanists in Ferrarese circles: among these was Celio Calcagnini, a friend of her father and an influential scholar with reformist interests who had served in the retinue of Queen Bona Sforza of Poland before coming to Ferrara. Beyond the original poetry she composed in this early period, Olimpia produced commentaries on ancient texts and drafted translations, including Latinizations of two stories from Boccaccio's vernacular classic, the mid-fourteenth-century *Decameron*. By her early teens she was in Ferrara, where she cemented her reputation with a public reading of Cicero's *Stoic Paradoxes*, conducted in Latin before a select audience at Renée's villa outside the city. Olimpia's performance earned accolades, with one admirer calling her a "miracle." It was a high – but highly gendered – compliment, suggesting that her intellect was uncommon in a woman.[4]

Renée's villa, nicknamed Il Consolando ("Consolation"), served as a site not only for literary events but also for clandestine religious activities. The audience for Olimpia's bravura display thus included an array of French, German, and Italian Protestants and reformers to whom the duchess had offered protection. It was not Olimpia's first exposure to the new religious spirit. Her father had undergone a shift in his own religious beliefs during his own time in Ferrara and, by 1532, was lecturing on Luther, Desiderius Erasmus, and Huldrych Zwingli in a school he opened in Viterbo, outside of Rome. By 1539, Fulvio was openly discussing Calvin's 1536 *Institutes of the Christian Religion*, which the Church had labeled a threat to orthodoxy. Another of Fulvio's friends, the itinerant humanist Celio Secondo Curione, was a defender of Luther who would become a central figure in Olimpia's life, and Olimpia's teachers at Ferrara included two German Protestants, the brothers Chilian and Johannes Senf (or Sinapius), who would connect her to a web of reformist thinkers across northern Italy. In addition to studying Aristotle, Ptolemy, and Euclid, Olimpia became well-rehearsed in the Old and New Testament and the Psalms of the Protestant theologians in the initially tolerant environment of Renée's court.

In 1546, Olimpia returned home temporarily to tend to her ailing father. Even away from Ferrara, her Protestant beliefs only intensified. But, when she subsequently sought to return to Renée's court after Fulvio's death two years later, she found the atmosphere much changed. Anna d'Este had left Italy for France to marry Francis, duke of Guise, and the reformers to whom Renée had once offered hospitality were now gone. Under the scrutiny of the Roman Inquisition – a system developed by the Catholic Church to prosecute heresy and challenges to religious doctrine – Ercole did not wish Ferrara to be a target. To head off any suspicion, he introduced a special court at Ferrara to make an example of figures like Fanio Fanino, a follower of Ochino who was arrested and executed despite efforts from Renée and her circle to save him. With Renée's influence circumscribed and Anna away in France, Olimpia protested that she had been "abandoned by my lady and received only in the most humiliating manner" and that she no longer had the freedom to study the Bible openly. Immediate and intimate access to scripture was a key tenet for reformers, who, flouting Catholic doctrine, advocated for the individual Christian's personal dialogue with Christ and argued that the Bible should be translated into vernacular languages for believers who lacked Latin literacy, as Brucioli had done in Italian. Olimpia's father had argued that "the entirety of our Holy Scripture should be . . . made available so that every artisan, worker, boatman, and laborer, young old, noble and common, may discuss and ponder it."[5] In her own letters, Olimpia especially encouraged her women friends to read scripture aloud at home regularly, with household and servants gathered around. Such democratizing spiritual activities went against Catholic doctrine, threatening the authority of the Church.

Fallen from favor in the changed climate of the ducal court and mourning her father, Olimpia shouldered the responsibility of caring for her mother and siblings even as she continued to study. Despite the abrupt transition, she did not regret losing "the brief, fleeting, and transitory things" she had once desired in Ferrara, such as literary fame and recognition. On the contrary, she declared, "God has kindled my desire to live in that heavenly home in which it is more pleasant to live for just one day than to spend a thousand years in the courts of princes."[6] By now, Olimpia was in her early twenties and on the brink of another major change in circumstances: she had fallen in love. In 1549, she married Andreas Grunthler (c. 1518–1555), a Bavarian medical student she had met in Ferrara, in a Protestant ceremony. In her letters, Olimpia tells Andreas "[Y]ou can't believe how madly I love you," and calls him "the man who is dearer to me than life." Their partnership was reflective of the Lutheran sentiment that marriage should be based on companionship, mutual support, and shared religious commitment (indeed, Olimpia described her husband as "a man who greatly enjoys my studies"), rather than the more common arrangement for many women in Renaissance Italy that aimed primarily to solidify and enhance socioeconomic status.

Faced with increasing hostility to reformist ideas in Italy and the very real threat of the Inquisition, Olimpia and Andreas decided to make their way to Germany, where they could find greater religious freedom. Andreas went first, to seek work; Olimpia missed him terribly and wrote, "I'm sad that you've left me and will be away for so long. . . . I swear by all that's holy that there is nothing dearer or sweeter to me than you." Eventually, she, too, crossed the Alps into Switzerland and continued on to join her husband in the newly Protestant town of Schweinfurt in Bavaria. She left her mother and sisters behind in Italy but brought her eight-year-old brother, Emilio (b. 1542), with her. Olimpia had no children of her own, but later she would also assume the care of the daughter of her old tutor, Johannes Sinapius, whose wife had died. In Schweinfurt, Olimpia and Andreas found the freedom they sought, however briefly. Andreas secured a position teaching medicine, while Olimpia continued to study and write. She missed her family, as her letters admit, but it was the price of living in "pure religion," free from the rites of Roman Catholicism.

Olimpia composed some of her most significant works in this period, including a Latin *Dialogue between Theophila and Philotima*, in which she reflected on the power of faith in overcoming adversity: "There is no one who merely wishes to live piously in Christ who does not endure the bitterest griefs and miseries and daily bears his cross." To her old family friend Curione, now an exile in Basel, she confided that she had no intention of ever going back to Italy and the authority of the pope: "You must know how dangerous it is profess oneself a Christian there where the Antichrist has so much power," she wrote, concluding "I would rather go to the ends of the earth than return." She instead rejoiced in the opportunity to read Protestant texts freely, and established connections with other Italian exiles in Germany, including the former papal nuncio Pier Paolo Vergerio the Younger, whom she begged to translate Luther's *Greater Catechism* into Italian.

Though she lamented the difficulty of relying on letters to exchange news, Olimpia was an avid correspondent in the humanist tradition, tackling weighty religious issues such as predestination and salvation in her letters along with more personal topics and family concerns. She often positioned herself as spiritual guide, especially to her female acquaintances and relatives, sending Luther's works to her longtime friend Lavinia della Rovere in Ferrara; to her sister Vittoria, she sent a copy of Calvin's *Institutes*. Writing in 1555, she implored Anna d'Este, now duchess of Guise, to intervene on behalf of the condemned heretics in France, "the men who are being burned there" who, Olimpia insists, "are innocent and are undergoing so many tortures for the sake of the gospel of Christ." It was to little avail; the persecution of Protestants in France had grown even more severe after the 1551 Edict of Châteaubriant, and the staunchly Catholic Guise family would remain mired in the French Wars of Religion that raged into the 1590s.

Olimpia's experience highlights the ways in which her own intellectual formation and eventual religious conversion took shape. More broadly, it shows how humanism, particularly humanist correspondence, helped circulate religious thought that challenged Catholic doctrine. Throughout Renaissance Italy, women – like Vittoria Colonna and Lucrezia Gonzaga, who both passed through the same court of Renée di France as Olimpia – played an important role in the spread of Italian evangelism, lending the protection of their own aristocratic status to the movement and embedding their support of its ideals into their poetry and prose. Unlike Olimpia, however, these women wrote in Italian, rather than Latin. Their literary goals in many cases overshadowed their religious commentary, which was coded and covert, intended for an exclusive, trusted group of like-minded friends. They did not identify themselves as Latin humanists, and sometimes even criticized humanism as a diversion from religious devotion. Olimpia herself was initially connected to such circles: in 1548 she was included in anthology of letters attributed to reformist women edited by Ortensio Lando, who was welcomed at Renée's court and who actively promoted several women associated with Italian evangelism.

Later, Olimpia, too, mused that her own literary ambitions and early fame as a humanist were perhaps distractions from the true work of reform:

> I have been lauded to the skies because I read so many authors, but I know my ignorance. I have been in danger of forgetting God. I fell into such error that I thought human affairs subject to fate and that God does not cure mortal ills.

Yet the dissemination of reformist ideas depended on a network of thinkers able to communicate across national and linguistic boundaries. Latin was both the universal language of humanism and the lingua franca of Protestant reformers. Olimpia, who saw herself as part of both communities, wrote and lectured in Latin, adopting it even in her personal correspondence. Though only fragments of her writings have survived, in the course of her twenty-nine years she composed dozens of Latin letters to friends and prominent Protestant theologians and at least two Latin dialogues, in addition to her poems and translations into Greek and Latin. Her adoption of Latin as well as her itinerant existence made Olimpia part of the Republic of Letters – a wide network of intellectuals that stretched throughout Europe. Olimpia contributed to this web of exchange by writing openly of her religious convictions, insisting, "[W]e will hasten with oar and sail to the place where we are allowed to profess ourselves openly as Christians [that is, Protestants] and not to have to use the ceremonies of the popes." She wrestled with thorny theological questions such as predestination but avoided the infighting between Lutherans and Calvinists over doctrinal subtleties, stressing instead the importance of obedience and hope.

In 1551, events took a dramatic turn. In the wake of Luther's death in 1546, Germany was convulsed by religious conflict and political instability. Olimpia became a direct eyewitness to the horrors of war

Figure 8.3 Olympia Fulvia Morata with the burning Schweinfurt in background
Photo: Alamy

when Albrecht II Alcibiades, margrave of Brandenberg-Kulmbach, sought to create his own state in Franconia. Entering Schweinfurt, where Olimpia and her husband were still living, his troops barricaded themselves inside the city, inflicting misery on its inhabitants even as they were besieged from the outside by Albrecht's foes in the Margraves' War (see Figure 8.3). Amid the prolonged conflict, disease spread; Andreas, as a physician, was made to provide medical care and soon fell ill himself but later recovered. Olimpia described the conditions to Curione, recounting, "Often at night you would have thought the whole town was about to go up in flames. We had to hide out in a wine cellar." She went on to describe how they narrowly escaped being burned alive in a church where they had planned to take shelter, and their subsequent flight from the city, in which they were "stripped of our clothes" and left with "nothing but a linen tunic." In another letter, Olimpia recalled, "I lost my shoes and had no stockings for my feet.

I was forced to flee over rocks and stones," and that, covering more than ten miles the first day, "I often said to myself, I am going to die. I can't go on any longer."

The refugees found temporary shelter in the town of Hammelburg, not far from Schweinfurt, with Olimpia arriving like "the queen of the beggars . . . with bare feet, unkempt hair, tattered clothes (which weren't even mine but had been given to me by a woman on the way)." Though she too was now ill with fever, the townspeople refused to allow the couple to remain more than a few days, fearing repercussions for sheltering them. Olimpia and Andreas continued on, finally arriving to the southwestern city of Heidelberg, where Andreas found a new position teaching medicine. Amid all her travails, Olimpia felt most keenly the loss of her books in the flight from Schweinfurt. Coming to the rescue, Curione promptly sought replacements from his editorial contacts throughout the region. But Olimpia would never fully recover her health. By 1555, she sensed that her days were limited. The realization added urgency to a final letter to Curione, to whom she sent copies of her poems, apparently expecting him to publish them for her: "This may be the last letter you will get from me. My strength is gone. I have no appetite for food. I am racked by congestion and fever. . . . Heidelberg seems deserted because of the plague. I am sending you the poems I was able to remember [that is, rewrite] after the destruction of Schweinfurt." She was not yet thirty.

Not only had Olimpia lost her library in the flight from Schweinfurt; most of her writings had also perished. After her death on October 26, not long after her last exchange with Curione, it was Andreas who collected what remained. He sent it to Curione, who indeed proceeded to publish Olimpia's letters and poems, along with the fragments Andreas provided. Fittingly, Curione dedicated the first edition of her writings, printed in Basel in 1558, to Isabella Bresegna, an early follower of the Spanish reformer Juan de Valdés who, like Olimpia, had sought religious freedom in northern Europe. Curione praised Olimpia as a woman "on whom God seemed to have conferred all the endowments of genius," and positioned her as both an icon of female intellect and virtue, and a heroine of the Reformation:

> Entire volumes have been devoted to famous women, and everyone reads them. And yet in these books how few women do we read of who to their erudition added chastity of morals, and even fewer who added true study of religion and a love of divine letters?

Curione's edition showcased Olimpia's connections to humanists and theologians and included her letters to her husband and five women. A second edition in 1562 was dedicated, even more ambitiously, to Queen Elizabeth I of England. Two more followed, cementing Olimpia's legacy as perhaps the greatest female scholar of the sixteenth century. The French writer Catherine des Roches praised her, as did the Dutch polymath Anna Maria van Schurman, while in Germany she was singled out for recognition in works by, among others, Johan Peter Lotichius and the Calvinist historian Melchior Adams, who put her on the level of Erasmus and Nicolaus Copernicus.

In Olimpia Morata, a model of humanist erudition and emblem of reform ideology, the two great movements of the early modern era – the Renaissance and the Reformation – were fused. As the embodiment of the ideal learned, Christian woman praised by Erasmus, Olimpia combined intellectual inquiry with religious commitment, demonstrating devotion to learning and courage of conviction as she moved between the unsettled spaces of early modern Italy and Germany. The writings she left behind, either saved or reconstructed after the siege of Schweinfurt, ensure her legacy as one of the most important intellectuals of the Renaissance and a fervent supporter of the Protestant reform.

9 Laura Terracina (1519–c.1577)

Bestselling Author, Defender of Women

> *Now let us dedicate ourselves to learning,*
> *and make space for our neglected voices,*
> *so they are not so quiet*
> *that they cannot be heard above the writings of men.*

— Laura Terracina

If Vittoria Colonna was the most celebrated woman poet in sixteenth-century Italy, the prolific Laura Bacio Terracina was the most widely published. Adapting the stylistic framework of established male poets to her own ends, she turned her pen to personal themes – including her desire for literary recognition – as well as political commentary and the critique of social ills, especially those affecting women. In keeping with the Renaissance fashion for verse in the style of the fourteenth-century poet Francesco Petrarca, or Petrarch, Laura Terracina adopted Tuscan Italian as her mode of expression. But she was Neapolitan by birth, raised in the seaside town of Chiaia on the Tyrrhenian coast. Of noble origins though not among Naples's ruling families, the Terracinas had gained title to their eponymous lands in southern Italy in the thirteenth century in exchange for supporting the powerful Colonna family against the papacy. Their subsequent pro-French activity resulted in the additional acquisition of the territory of Bacio (or Batio) and, when they switched their allegiance away from France to the Spanish rulers of Naples, Laura's father Paolo Terracina was made a baron by Ferdinand II, briefly king of Naples. While this nimble approach to shifting political winds served the family well, the political conflict and instability left a clear mark on Laura, who composed political verse in a Spanish royalist vein but, at the same time,

DOI: 10.4324/9781003081807-12

described the world around her as "off-kilter" and "senseless," one in which "every virtue is abandoned."[1]

Bucking the better-trodden paths for Renaissance women, Laura was a career poet, marrying only later in life, when she was nearly forty, and publishing continuously. There is no record of her having children. She received a modest education at home, along with her two brothers, Mariano and Giacomo, and sister Dianora; what she lacked in learning, she acquired on her own or with guidance from members of Naples's literary community. Certainly, her poetic gifts were recognized from a young age. Even Laura's famous compatriot, the "divine" Vittoria Colonna, knew her compositions, dubbing them "poems that gild our warlike century," and another prolific and well-respected poet, Laura Battiferri, was also an admirer.[2] By 1545, she had become one of only a handful of sixteenth-century women to be granted academy membership when she was admitted to the Neapolitan Accademia degli Incogniti (Academy of the Incogniti), a learned society that met to converse on cultural topics and to read, compose, and circulate verse.

Under the classical name Febea – from Phoebus Apollo, the god of poetry, and the name given to Diana, the goddess of the moon – Laura honed her craft as well as her connections. She composed verses in praise of nobles and forged friendships with fellow academicians like Luigi Tansillo, a Petrarchan poet with links to the court of Naples. Tansillo compared Laura to the great female poets of Ancient Greece and to the "modern women whose great names resound,/to such a degree that famous men cannot outdo them." In 1546, the editor Lodovico Domenichi included her work in an important poetic anthology.[3] But it was Marc'Antonio Passero, a bookseller with connections to the university and the cultured élite of Naples, who was the first to encourage Laura, now twenty-eight, to put out her own volume of poetry. That volume, simply titled *Rime de la signora Laura Terracina* (*Poems of Lady Laura Terracina*), was printed in Venice in 1548, ten years after Vittoria Colonna had become the first living Italian woman to see her poetry in print (and in fact contains two sonnets on Colonna's death). Laura later acknowledged Passero's support, writing: "You push me, oh noble Passero/To publish my many errors."[4]

Ostensibly at the advice of her editor Domenichi, Laura's 1548 collection was dedicated to Count Vincenzo Belprato of Anversa, with whom Laura exchanged warm verses. In the Petrarchan style, her volume concluded with a religious poem addressed to the Virgin Mary.

But most components eschewed religious themes for real-world issues and were addressed to influential figures from Laura's immediate circle, including women from prominent Southern families like Maria and Giovanna d'Aragona and Isabella Colonna. It was a deft example of poetic patronage-seeking. Laura would gain increasing skill in this kind of professional networking in order to promote her writing while at the same time safeguarding her reputation as a respectable woman. She largely evaded the familiar cultural minefield that often equated women's free artistic expression with a lack of virtue.

That Laura – and her editor – felt confident she would succeed in balancing on this knife edge is suggested by the woodcut likeness positioned prominently in subsequent editions of her work. Only a decade earlier, an edition of Vittoria Colonna's poems had depicted its female author as an older widow of unassailable chastity, carefully highlighting her religiosity rather than her femininity. By contrast, the image of Laura, designed by Enea Vico at the behest of the intellectual Anton Francesco Doni, presents the poet as an attractive young woman with an engaging, slightly quizzical air; her wavy hair is plaited and gathered up in a net. Her garments are simple but becoming, and she gazes to one side as if in conversation (see Figure 9.1). Marketing the poet's femininity as a novel selling point rather than a liability, the image is captioned: "A rare wonder of the world." Though some sixteenth-century contemporaries remarked on Laura's beauty, she largely avoided any hint of scandal as she made her entry into the male-dominated world of print.

Also aiding in this balancing act between feminine virtue and poetic ambition were Laura's frequent expressions of modesty – she often referred to herself as "ignorant" or "unpolished" – and the fiction that it was her editor's decision to publish her work despite her own "womanly" aversion to such a public display of ambition. This was a common protective claim of women writers. But Domenichi admitted that he had the author's approval, writing, "I am certain that, since I received these poems thanks to her, I have her tacit permission to do with them as I wish."[5] This constructed reticence would diminish as Laura assumed an increasingly overt and public hand in the publication of her work.

Laura's verse was met with enthusiasm: by the time her second volume appeared, in 1549, she had been included in an important compendium of women poets assembled by Domenichi that included selections by Colonna, Veronica Gambara, and others. In it, Domenichi called her

Figure 9.1 Portrait of Laura Terracina, by Enea Vico (engraving), 1550
(Rijksmuseum, Amsterdam)
[open access]

a "Laura among Lauras": that is, both an object of celebration, like
Petrarch's iconic beloved Laura, and the architect of her own fame,
like Petrarch himself.[6] Additional collections followed, featuring verse
by Laura and in dialogue with other poets and acquaintances: her *Rime
seconde* (*Second Book of Poems*) was financed by a former academi-
cian and printed in Florence in 1549, and three more collections were
published in 1550, 1552, and 1558. Along with her poems praising
friends and patrons were others that offer a glimpse of her acerbic wit;
in one example, bemoaning the duplicity of modern "gentlemen," she
quips that she regrets having mistaken a jackass for a "fine steed."[7] But
it was Laura's next effort – inspired not by Petrarch but instead by one
of the most successful and beloved books of her own day, Ludovico

Figure 9.2 Nineteenth-century engraving by Gustave Doré of a battle scene
from Ariosto's *Orlando furioso*, canto XXIV

Photo: Scala/Ministero per i Beni e le Attività culturali/Art Resource

Ariosto's *Orlando furioso* (*The Frenzy of Orlando*) – that caused the
most excitement (see Figure 9.2).

Ariosto's enormously popular chivalric romance tells the story of a
medieval knight, Orlando (from the medieval French poem, *The Song
of Roland*), who goes mad from lovesickness for the elusive object
of his desire, Angelica. Composed of forty-six cantos in *ottava rima*,
energetic eight-line rhyming stanzas, the poem intertwines multiple
romantic, heroic, and comic threads with the author's commentary
on contemporary society. The *Furioso* inspired numerous offshoots,
but Laura's 1549 *Discorso sopra il principio di tutti i canti d'Orlando
furioso* (*Commentary on the Opening of Each Canto of the* Orlando
furioso) is unquestionably one of the most intriguing. As early as her
first volume of poetry, Laura had been interested in Ariosto's example,

including in it four poetic laments written in the voices of various characters from the *Furioso*. Now, with her *Discorso*, she adopted Ariosto's iconic poetic framework as a platform for her own austere observations on social, historical, and political themes. It was a remarkably canny move: by linking her work explicitly to Ariosto's bestseller (which had itself caused a stir with its praise of women writers), she was guaranteed an audience. Her *Discorso* – which includes components addressed to an array of men and women, including Michelangelo Buonarroti, then working on St. Peter's Basilica in Rome – would prove Laura's most popular work by far, reprinted more than twenty times by the end of the century. It was also her most overtly feminist work, offering a clear-eyed critique of male literary privilege and women's corresponding erasure from history (see Figure 9.3).

In a feat of technical bravura, the forty-six cantos, or sections, of Laura's *Discorso* are intricately linked to the first stanza of each of Ariosto's cantos. Taken together, the final lines of the stanzas in each canto replicate the entire opening stanza of each corresponding canto in Ariosto's *Furioso*. Known as a "cento" – a rearrangement of passages taken from other authors – this impressive technique was often associated with women: from the fourth-century Roman Proba who based a Christian poem on Virgil's *Aeneid*, to Colonna, who wrote from the verse of Petrarch. The particular form employed by Laura, built around the eight-line stanza or octave, was derived from Spanish models, but rendered even more complex by the subtle and often witty changes she enacts to alter the meaning of Ariosto's original verses – for example, shifting the gendered endings of certain words.

Often, her emendations serve to comment explicitly on issues of gender: women's literary achievement, the violence to which they are subjected, and the unfair social conventions that burden them disproportionately. Laura clarifies that she has not attempted to mimic Ariosto's lines but rather to "accompany" them "*in a woman's voice/*to make them more pleasing and playful." Though she claims her effort was meant as a diversion, "to escape boring idleness," the requisite note of self-deprecation cannot conceal the serious nature of her social critique and feminist counsel.[8] Despite her light words, Laura had serious criticisms to level against Renaissance society. Her outrage at the injustices inflicted upon women is so great that it threatens to leave her voiceless, as she writes in the introduction to her fifth canto: "I would like to speak, but fury mutes my words,/for I am the only one to defend our sex."[9] Of all the species in the natural world, only men wage war

Figure 9.3 Title page of Laura Terracina's commentary on Ariosto's *Orlando Furioso* (Venice, Appresso Domenico Farri, 1567)

against women, and Nature herself: "From where do you derive such a right," she asks, "to draw your naked sword, or perhaps a dagger,/and turn the earth red with blood by beating her so fiercely?"

Her eleventh canto, which bears a generalized dedication to the "Insatiable Lustful," begins with Laura's condemnation of sexual vice and a perceived decline in morals, which invites her desire to "seal

tight these eyes and these ears, too,/forever, and not only for a year."
Yet her focus again narrows, as she notes that women suffer most from
this climate of moral decay, while men profit by a double standard that
allows them to trumpet their sexual conquests:

> How many matrons, and how many wayward maidens
> do you lead in shame to death?
> How many innocent and pure young virgins
> go sorrowfully to meet their fate?
> How many cries rise up from them to the stars
> because of your desire, so crazed and strong?
> Yet you each continue blithely on –
> and seldom do you feel the sting.

It is a powerful condemnation, one that strips open the complicit, intersecting forces that conspire against women.

Among the most compelling cantos in Laura's *Discorso* is the
thirty-seventh, which addresses the problem of women's learning and
their exclusion from the pages of history. It is certainly no accident that
this canto opens with pointed praise of Laura's contemporary, the celebrated Veronica Gambara – another well-known poet and intellectual,
whose example Laura urges others to emulate:

> Oh, if only there were many more women in the world like you,
> to rein in the arrogant male writers
> who publish against us, at breakneck speed,
> cruel verses, full of poison.

Renaissance libraries overflowed with misogyny, from Aristotelian
arguments about biological differences used to subordinate women to
men, to manuals for new wives preparing them for obedience to their
husbands. Laura instead echoes Ariosto's assertion that the erasure of
women's achievements by the envious and insecure male writers who
serve as the record-keepers of history could yet be reversed. "I certainly do not believe," she insists,

> that the writers who have
> written pages blaming us and offered scant praise,
> have mastered the job so well and with such art
> that nothing can be done to fight their deceit.

And, where Ariosto offers, by way of corrective, examples of male writers who praise women, Laura argues that even when men praise women, it is only out of self-interest or literary fashion. Women must thus give voice to their own experience, and to each other's: "for if women/had been able to write as much themselves,/perhaps male writers would not have silenced" their accomplishments.

Addressing women readers directly, Laura begs them to set aside their traditional pastimes and focus on learning:

Oh, if only women would give up needle, thread, and cloth
and take up the weight of study,
I think they would do some real damage to you writers.

But because so few women heed this call, she laments, "scant fame crowns our heads."

Though there are not many women who "toil day and night" to write, she continues, "brilliant" women must not be discouraged but instead set an example for others:

Drop your needles, be eager
to make a habit of pen and paper,
for you will make yourselves no less glorious
than those of whom I am complaining.
Now apply yourselves to your reading,
with the greatest diligence and care.

Where Ariosto urges women to focus on their customary "feminine" work, Laura reiterates that they should set themselves on intellectual work instead:

Now let us dedicate ourselves to learning,
and make space for our neglected voices,
so they are not so quiet
that they cannot be heard above the writings of men.

With this forceful call to intellectual arms, Laura positioned herself within a nascent tradition of feminist writing that stretched from earlier works, like the French Christine de Pizan's *Book of the City of Ladies* of 1405, well into the seventeenth century, with the Venetians Moderata Fonte, Lucrezia Marinella, and Arcangela Tarabotti.

Laura's interest in speaking to and about women and the issues they faced never diminished, though it took different forms. In 1561, she published a consolatory work dedicated to the widows of Naples, *Settime rime sovra tutte le donne vedove di questa nostra città di Napoli* (*Seventh Book of Poetry, Concerning All the Widows of This Our City of Naples*), intended to offer all the "ladies and gentlewomen" in the city who "are grieving the death of their husbands" some comfort "through my words."[10] Laura herself had by this time married her relative Polidoro Terracina. To judge by the poetic record of their union, the marriage was not always a happy one – seemingly marred by Polidoro's jealousy – but Polidoro, likely seeing a profitable opportunity, took an interest in Laura's literary career. In 1567, she put out a second book of commentary on Ariosto's *Furioso*, now based on the second stanza of each of Ariosto's cantos, noting that her husband had been pressed by the publisher, Luigi Valvassori, to "compel" her to do so.[11] But perhaps due to the increasingly restrictive climate of the Counter-Reformation, her focus had shifted. Between 1570 and 1572, Laura was in Rome, focusing instead on religious poetry but died before she could publish a ninth volume. Over two hundred of her unpublished poems are collected in a 1577 manuscript now at the Biblioteca Nazionale in Florence.

Laura Terracina saw herself as a gifted but underappreciated poet, a woman writer facing particular obstacles to pursuing her craft. She lamented that her talent was unappreciated and that her encomiastic poetry did not always produce the desired effect:

> Why do I go on cultivating the green laurel
> to crown other heads with unworthy honor?
> Why do I continually exhaust my mind and heart,
> if the world values only silver, and not gold?
> In the end, what can I hope to reap from my labors,
> but contempt, envy, and dishonor?
> Why do I consume my days and hours
> in beleaguering Apollo and his chorus of muses,
> if those who my poetry decorates and honors
> praise me to my face only to fiercely
> tear me apart, along with my writing and my words?[12]

Astute and determined, she nonetheless achieved enormous success in her lifetime. While her animated, highly topical poetry did not achieve the heights of prestige or depth of artistry that accompanied the aristocratic Vittoria Colonna, Laura published more actively and more prolifically and wielded greater control over the editorial process. She became increasingly more comfortable with expressing dissatisfaction when editors did not live up to her expectations, for example, complaining openly of errors introduced to her *Discorso* by Domenichi's editorial partner, Lodovico Dolce. She was also progressive in her deliberate use of dedications to attract patrons, a key method for securing protection and a financial return on her publications. She clearly recognized the benefits to be gained from such careful attention to the production of her books. When her sixth volume of poetry was published in Lucca without her permission in 1558, she complained that she had been twice cheated: deprived of not only the profits from the book itself but also any gift she might have received from its dedicatee as an expression of thanks, had she been given the opportunity to secure one.

Using her understanding of the literary market and its mechanisms to craft a successful career, Laura turned her attention not just to religious and Petrarchan themes but also to political subjects like the continued power struggle between France and Spain in Italy. Of even greater interest to Renaissance readers, she also called for the recognition of women's achievements, defending their intellect and their honor. Her moralizing commentary in the *Discorso* was so popular that it was often adopted in the classroom (where many teachers assumed the author must have been a man), replacing the more risqué Ariosto, who included episodes of magic, romance, and seduction.[13] Her reputation and influence extended beyond Italy, particularly to Spain, where the seventeenth-century Spanish playwright and poet Lope de Vega would mention her with admiration on several occasions, for example, in his plays *The Widow from Valencia* from around 1600 and the 1632 *Dorotea*. A key figure for understanding Renaissance poetic tastes and editorial practices and the particular challenges and opportunities they presented for women writers, Laura Terracina – following her own advice that women must "make space" for their self-expression – helped lay the groundwork for women's literary voices to be heard.

10   Veronica Franco (1546–1591)

Celebrity Courtesan

I'll share with you my heart, open in my breast,
so long as you don't hide your own from me,
and I'll revel in pleasing you;
and if you think I am prized by Phoebus
as a poet, in the works of love
you'll find me prized by Venus even more.

– Veronica Franco

At the height of the sixteenth century, Veronica Franco – the most renowned courtesan in Venice – took a different path to literary fame than Vittoria Colonna or Laura Terracina. Bustling, cosmopolitan Venice was famous for its courtesans: beautiful, highly educated, sophisticated women who commanded large fees for their intellectual as well as sexual attentions. Writing in 1611, the English traveler Thomas Coryat estimated their number at over 20,000 (in reality, there were closer to 12,000), and posited that the "allurements of these amorous Calypsos" were so compelling that "the fame of them has drawn many to Venice from some of the remotest parts of Christendom to contemplate their beauties and enjoy their pleasing dalliances."[1] Coryat observed that courtesans had supplanted their more proper counterparts in public life, openly gracing the city's palazzos and piazzas while its wives and daughters remained hidden away at home. He also astutely noted that the Venetian Republic benefited from the tax it shrewdly levied on courtesans.

Despite his hyperbole, Coryat's comments touched on a paradox at the heart of Venetian gender politics. Known as the Serenissima Repubblica, a "most serene republic" undisturbed by the internal conflict and foreign invasions that wracked the rest of Italy, Venice prized its reputation for independence and justice. Yet the women of Venice,

DOI: 10.4324/9781003081807-13

beyond the disproportionally large number of women in its many convents, were subject to restrictive gender norms aimed at "protecting" their honor and good reputation. Patrician women, in particular, lived largely cooped up, Coryat wrote, "within the walls of their houses," except for on special occasions such as weddings, "the christening of a Jew," or "late in the evening rowing in a gondola." While in reality Venetian noblewomen did move around their neighborhoods, though less freely than working women, they did not participate widely in the social gatherings and intellectual salons for which the city was celebrated. The absence of "respectable" women from public cultural life left a void that was filled by courtesans, who did not have to abide by the same conventions. In fact, the term "courtesan" – as opposed to *meretrice*, used to denote a woman who only sold sex – derives from the Italian *cortigiano*, or courtier, describing the male attendants and advisors who served at court (*corte*) in the orbit of the local ruler. Courtesans were sometimes depicted wearing men's garments under their own rich gowns, an erotically charged fashion statement that hinted at these blurred boundaries (see Figure 10.1a-b).

Veronica Franco skillfully navigated the complex undercurrents of power faced by women – and courtesans in particular – in a patriarchal society. If modesty and chastity were held to be necessary virtues for Renaissance women, courtesans inhabited a more fluid space. On the one hand, it was a space rich in possibility: the opportunity for education, self-expression, sexuality, wealth, even literary fame. Veronica's livelihood depended on her intellect and artistry as much as her appearance, and she cultivated connections to influential men who supported her literary aspirations. But the courtesan's life, though free of some of the constraints faced by married women, had a dark side: the risks and unequal power dynamics inherent in sex work, the threat of abuse and disease, and financial uncertainty. Veronica's poetry embraces female sexuality and authority without looking away from the difficult realities of her profession, and the arc of her rise and fall is emblematic of the Venetian courtesan's complex status. Her success burned bright, but brief.

The courtesan's trade often passed down through families. Veronica's mother, Paola Fracassa, is named, along with her daughter, in a catalog of courtesans in Venice that circulated in 1565, where she is listed as Veronica's intermediary, collecting the fees Veronica charged for her services.[2] Mother and daughter were living together in the *sestiere*, or district, of Santa Maria Formosa; Paola died by 1570. Veronica's family belonged to the Venetian class of *cittadini*

Figure 10.1 A–B Woodblock print of a Venetian courtesan from Pietro Bertelli's *Diversarum Nationum Habitus* (Clothing of Different Countries), 1591

originari, native-born citizens who were part of the republic's professional class, a background of which she was proud. As a girl, she managed to avail herself of the education afforded by private tutors to her three brothers; she was also trained in music, an important skill for a courtesan, whose job entailed entertaining clients and friends by playing and singing. Briefly married to a doctor, Paolo Panizza, in a probable arranged union in the 1560s, Veronica separated from him and maintained her own household, which grew to include the children she would have with the Venetian nobleman Andrea Tron and Giacomo di Baballi of Ragusa (now Dubrovnik). Shown in a portrait by Tintoretto wearing sumptuous garments, her red-gold hair framing her face and one breast just slightly exposed in a pose typical for courtesans (she would later thank the artist for so skillfully having "imitat[ed], even surpass[ed]" her natural likeness), the elegant and talented Veronica quickly attracted the admiration of Venice's élite (see Figure 10.2).

Figure 10.2 Portrait of Lady, by Tintoretto (16th c.), presumed as Veronica Franco
(Worchester Art Museum, Massachusetts)
Photo: Alamy

Veronica's friendship with Domenico Venier, a politician and influential cultural patron who hosted a literary salon and promoted other women writers like the Venetian Moderata Fonte and the celebrated Roman courtesan Tullia d'Aragona, was important to her success: he would become one of her greatest allies, championing her literary endeavors. Also key to Veronica's rise to fame was her encounter with Henri III of Valois, briefly the monarch of the Polish-Lithuanian Commonwealth, where Bona Sforza once ruled. Henri passed through Venice in 1574 on his way back to claim the French throne, spending a night with Veronica as part of the welcome prepared for him by the city. The visit was ostensibly secret, but Veronica later advertised it as evidence of her exceptional status and success in the volume of letters she published in 1580. She also wrote two sonnets about the event, recounting how Henri, having arrived at her "poor dwelling" without fanfare, was so lovestruck that he kept a miniature portrait of her, done "in enamel and paint," as a memento.³ Though the meeting was meant to bolster Venice's political interests by currying favor with an important visitor, Veronica turned it to her own advantage.

Like the term itself, the role of the courtesan, whose clients belonged to the city's most powerful echelons, was akin in certain respects to that of the male courtier. Sexual activity aside, both provided entertainment to the Venetian élite, and both depended on patronage for their own economic security. For both courtesans and courtiers, literary talent provided a competitive edge. Veronica saw writing – and especially publishing – as a way to promote herself, shape her own image, and showcase her intellect and principles as an "honest courtesan," along with her beauty and sex appeal. Through print, she could also rebuke those who slandered her.

In 1575, Veronica published a volume of poems in *terza rima*, or three-line rhyming stanzas. Invented by Dante Alighieri in the early fourteenth century to recount his journey toward Paradise, the form was rarely used by Renaissance poets – especially not with Veronica's boldly sensual and wholly un-Dantesque voice. Composed as *capitoli* – lengthy poetic letters to friends, lovers, patrons, and even critics – the poems highlight Veronica's sexualized image as a courtesan-writer capable of jousting with the brightest literati in Venice. "If you think I am so prized by Phoebus/as a poet," she writes in one, "in the work of love/you'll find me prized by Venus even more" (see Figure 10.3). At the same time, her *capitoli* also challenge negative perceptions of the courtesan as venal and lacking moral character by underscoring

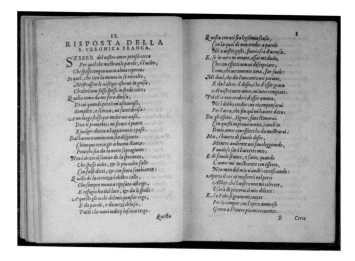

Figure 10.3 Poem (capitolo II) from Veronica Franco's *Rime* (Venice, 1575)

(Rare Book Collection, Kislak Center for Special Collections, Rare Books and Manuscripts, University of Pennsylvania)

her values: unflagging fidelity to those she esteems and loves, concern for the well-being of other women, and a deep identification with her native city. By claiming kinship to Venice, "high ruler of the sea,/lofty virgin, inviolate and pure," Veronica argues that she, too, is possessed of the same qualities of virtue and independence.[4] She does not deny her trade or sexuality; instead, she establishes her own ethical code within a framework that allows for both sexual passion and integrity – a radical expression of female agency in Renaissance Italy.

Veronica's expression of autonomy is clear in her second *capitolo*, in reply to Marco Venier, her lover and Domenico's nephew. It is not enough to talk about love, she insists. She also expects her suitors to be honest and constant and her relationships to be partnerships of equals:

> when, fatigued and annoyed by fictions,
> you show me your love in deeds,
> I will assure you of mine in the same way.
> I will show you my heart open in my breast,

> once you no longer hide yours from me,
> and my delight will be to please you.

Subverting the characterization of prostitutes as immoral and avaricious, Veronica insists that the "honest courtesan" is motivated by loftier virtues than money, for she is not "greedy for gain,/for that vice is not concealed in my breast." Love and passion, she maintains, are what matter to her, not financial gain:

> And what I now request from you
> is not that you express your love
> for me with silver or gold;
> for to make a deal with a gentleman
> in order to extract a treasure from him
> is most improper if one's not entirely venal.
> Such an act doesn't suit my profession.

In an effort to defy negative characterizations of the courtesan, Veronica also draws on the imagery of chivalric literature – widely appreciated by Renaissance audiences and populated with knights, ladies, and courageous battles – as a framework for her exchanges with both lovers and foes. Her thirteenth *capitolo* was written after a misunderstanding with an unnamed partner, perhaps Marco, and employs the language of combat to defend the honor of her heart: "No more words! To deeds, to the battlefield, to arms!" The field of war for this lovers' quarrel, however, is the bedroom, where Veronica – recalling past trysts – moves from a call to arms to a proffer of peace, forged in passion:

> Do you wish for the field, the secret inn,
> that hardhearted and deceptive once watched
> over so many of my now bitter delights?
> Here before me now stands the bed
> where I took you in my arms and which still
> preserves the imprint of our bodies, breast to breast.

Why not put aside weapons, she asks, and take "the path opened to a love match in bed?" In that case, she assures her lover, she would follow him, though it would not be an act of surrender:

> I would yield to you in no way at all.
> To take revenge for your unfair attack,

I'd fall upon you, and in daring combat,
as you too caught fire defending yourself,
I would die with you, felled by the same blow.

This frank, physical language, with its open discussion of female desire, is virtually unique among sixteenth-century women poets in Italy: it is more overtly sexual even than the poetry of Veronica's near-contemporary Gaspara Stampa, to whom she is sometimes compared.

Veronica's open embrace of her sexual and literary authority, together with her increasing celebrity, earned her enemies as well as admirers, particularly among male courtiers who saw her as a threat in the competition for patrons – like Maffio Venier, Marco's cousin. In the 1570s, Maffio circulated several obscene and misogynistic poems about Veronica composed in Venetian dialect, including one that punned on her name to call her a "*ver unica* [truly unique] whore."[5] She was infuriated not only by the slander but also by the damage such accusations could wreak on her reputation and, therefore, her livelihood. She responded fiercely. Women in general, not just courtesans, she declares, are placed at deliberate disadvantage by patriarchal society, which – fearing their power – deprives them of the education she invokes as "weapons and training." What if women were to turn the tables?

Again employing the imagery of war, Veronica now warns that, if given the proper tools, women would "fight you to the death"; and, to prove it, "among so many women I will act first,/setting an example for them all to follow." Continuing the metaphor, she challenges her detractor to a duel in defense of "all women," but, this time, her weapons are literary, not amorous. Pointedly ridiculing Maffio's reputation as a dialect poet – a far less lofty endeavor, she implies, than writing in Dante's Italian, the prized literary language of Renaissance Italy – she graciously allows him to select the "arms" or idiom with which they will wage poetic war:

The sword that strikes and stabs in your hand –
the common language spoken in Venice –
if that's what you want to use, then so do I;
and if you want to enter into Tuscan,
I leave you the choice of the high or comic strain,
for one's as easy and clear for me as the other.

Playing on chivalric notions about male and female roles, she declares that it is "not a brave knight's gallant deed . . . to strike without warning an unarmed woman," and warns her antagonist that, if he does not respond to her challenge, "I will say that you feel great fear of me."[6]

If Veronica's poems are passionate, her letters, published five years later, strike a more measured tone. Evocative of classical epistolary models and central to her campaign to take control of her public image, they include a dedication to a high-profile Church figure, Cardinal Luigi d'Este of Ferrara, and an opening letter to Veronica's former client Henri, now king of France, accompanied by the pair of sonnets she wrote for him. Part self-promotion and part self-defense, the letters highlight her literary and moral authority. Veronica offers sage advice on the trials of grief and misfortune, congratulations on the birth of a friend's child, greetings to influential patrons, and discussions of future literary projects. She again underscores her identity as a Venetian citizen, linking herself to an idealized republic that saw itself as "not a subservient city, but a noble one," a "city that is truly an immaculate maiden, unstained by injustice, and never offended by enemy force."

As in her poems, Veronica's letters make no effort to conceal her profession, though here she does not linger over its occasional pleasures or freedoms. Instead, she offers a powerful discussion of the qualities necessary for a woman to succeed in so difficult and dangerous a trade. In a letter to a woman who is considering raising her daughter to be a courtesan, Veronica offers this clear-eyed assessment of the courtesan's life:

> [E]ven if fate should be completely favorable and kind to her, this is a life that always turns out to be a misery. It's a most wretched thing, contrary to human reason, to subject one's body and labor to a slavery terrifying even to think of. To offer oneself as prey to so many men, at the risk of being stripped, robbed, even killed, so that one man, one day, may snatch away from you everything you've acquired from many over such a long time; to give oneself over to so many, to eat with another's mouth, sleep with another's eyes, move according to the will of another, always risking the shipwreck of one's faculties and life – . . . believe me: of all worldly tribulations, this is the worst.

No matter how successful she may be, Veronica has come to realize, the courtesan remains dependent on the whims of her clientele, without true autonomy over her body or her choices: her independence is an illusion. To push a daughter into this profession blindly, therefore, would be to "slaughter in a single blow your soul and your reputation, along with your daughter's." Instead, she offers to find a place for the girl in the Venetian Casa delle Zitelle (Home for Unmarried Maidens), which provided shelter to selected women whose families could not support them. Veronica's concern for women's economic security was genuine, reflected in the provisions she made in her will for women servants and prostitutes wishing to leave the trade and in her proposal to the Venetian government to establish a refuge, similar to the Zitelle, for married women in need. Her awareness of the constraints and dangers faced by women in Venetian society is reflective of a feminist sensibility that was shared by Veronica's contemporaries, Moderata Fonte and Lucrezia Marinella – though, perhaps because they inhabited very different social worlds, they do not appear to have known each other.

Veronica's comments about the precarious nature of sex work proved prescient. When plague broke out in Venice in 1575, the year her poems were printed, vulnerable figures like courtesans became easy scapegoats for a city reeling from illness. The presence of the Inquisition in Venice – the tribunal established by the Roman Catholic Church to suppress heresy – was also exerting an increasingly sobering effect on the city and its culture. In 1580, when her letters were published, Veronica was accused by Ridolfo Vannitelli, the tutor of one of her sons, of performing magical incantations. As trial records show, Ridolfo was motivated by personal antipathy, deeply resentful of Veronica's influence among the city's most powerful men.[7] Proving as capable in legal argument as she was in literary expression, Veronica was freed after mounting her own defense, supported once again by her ally Domenico Venier. Yet the damage was done: not yet forty years old, she had fallen from favor. By 1582, Veronica was living in the sestiere of San Samuele, which housed many of the city's poorest prostitutes. She died nine years later, without publishing anything more.

Veronica Franco's fame traveled well beyond Venice, thanks in part to her own efforts: the French essayist Michel de Montaigne, for example, noted that she had sent him "a little book of letters of her own composition" soon after its publication.[8] Also writing from France, the Italian poet and playwright Muzio Manfredi thanked Veronica for a sonnet she sent him and inquired about an epic poem she was apparently planning, but never published. Veronica's verse was included in Luisa Bergalli's important anthology of women poets in 1726 – the first of its kind – and nineteenth-century biographers revived her compelling life story. With her strong literary voice and unabashed embrace of female desire and sexuality, Veronica Franco's lyric and letters comprise a major contribution to the Renaissance literary tradition, and her work has continued to captivate readers over the centuries. Several biographies are devoted to her, and she is the subject of a 2001 play by the feminist writer Dacia Maraini. The 1998 film *Dangerous Beauty* depicted Veronica's story in romanticized terms that focused largely on her relationship with Marco Venier and culminated inaccurately, in true Hollywood style, with the men of Venice leaping to Veronica's defense at her Inquisition trial. The realities of Veronica's life, as her own writings tell us, were far more complex than these romantic depictions, but the legacy she leaves through her poems and letters still resonates, compelling us to reassess our notions of what women's lives – and careers – looked like in the Renaissance.

Part Three

Musicians, Composers, and Performers

11 Gaspara Stampa (1523–1554)

Renaissance Sappho

> *From my burning passion,*
> *something unique is born*
> *that seems to have no equal in any other woman.*
>
> – Gaspara Stampa

Venice was a city of music, from the calls of gondoliers navigating its maze of canals to the sound of nuns' voices spilling out from its churches. Like poetry, music was a central part of sixteenth-century culture, and for a *virtuosa* like Gaspara Stampa – a gifted singer and one of the most significant poets of the Renaissance – it promised an entrée into the upper echelons of society. This "new Sappho," as she came to be known, composed powerful, expressive verse, often setting it to music and accompanying herself on an instrument as she recited it.[1] Her writing upends familiar models by embracing female passion and desire and centering her own voice as musician and poet. Gaspara's story suggests an alternative model for women's creativity and autonomy beyond typical Renaissance roles: a life outside the lines, guided by artistic expression rather than social dictates.

For sixteenth-century women, music, like poetry, presented both opportunities and pitfalls. To play or perform music was to navigate a delicate terrain shaped by social and cultural norms regarding "appropriate" feminine activity and anxieties about female honor and chastity. To speak – or sing – raised fears of social and sexual accessibility. Writing in 1541, the eminent author Pietro Bembo noted that playing a musical instrument was "a thing for vain and frivolous women"; others took even more extreme views, like a choirmaster at Venice's San Marco church who opined, "Never is there found a woman so

DOI: 10.4324/9781003081807-15

rare nor so chaste that if she were to sing she would not soon become a whore."[2] The spectrum of opportunity for musical women in Gaspara's adopted city of Venice was bookended by two extremes. On one hand, Venice was famous for women's religious music, though under certain controls. Nuns lifted their voices in prayerful song while concealed behind a grille that separated them from the congregation, and Venetian *ospedali grandi* – charitable institutions that housed all-women choirs – also trained girls in music but modeled themselves on convents to safeguard the reputations of women performers. On the other hand, musical proficiency was an important tool in the arsenal of Venetian courtesans, especially the most élite and best educated: the acclaimed poet Veronica Franco played the lute, and many courtesans were noted singers.

Yet not all female musicians fell neatly into these categories. As Gaspara's case illustrates, some were neither nuns nor courtesans – nor even wives – but instead practiced music and achieved recognition as composers and performers on their own terms. It would be decades before the rise of professional women singers and composers like the Venetian Barbara Strozzi – a development spurred by the success of the all-women *concerto delle donne* in Ferrara in the 1580s that featured Tarquinia Molza of Modena – or the advent of commercial opera. Nonetheless, Gaspara, who composed poetry and gained recognition for her exceptional voice, made a life for herself as part of Venice's vibrant cultural milieu, eschewing the conventional parameters for women.

That her path was not predetermined by marriage or the convent was made possible not only by Gaspara's talent but also by her family, who shared a common devotion to music and learning. Her father, Bartolomeo Stampa (active 1522–1526), was a goldsmith based in Padua; her mother, Cecilia, a native of Venice. The family had distant ties to nobility but not the attendant expectations of prestigious marital alliances – or hefty dowries – for its daughters. Along with her siblings – Baldassare (d. 1544), a promising writer, and Cassandra (d. post-1576), also a singer – Gaspara was educated at home in humanist studies including Latin and literature. It is clear from her poetry that she was well acquainted with both classical models and canonical Italian poets: Ovid's Latin *Heroides*, a series of love laments voiced by abandoned heroines, became an important model for her writing, as did the obsessive love poetry of Francesco Petrarca (Petrarch). When Bartolomeo died around 1529, Cecilia moved the family to Venice, where they settled in the parish of Saints Gervasio and Protasio (now San Trovaso) in the neighborhood (or, in Venetian parlance, *sestiere*) of Dorsoduro and Gaspara and Cassandra were tutored in voice and lute.

The convivial and cultured Stampa household was a musical and intellectual hub. Baldassare, whose presence as de facto "paterfamilias" offered some social protection to his unmarried sisters, was gaining recognition as a poet. His friend Francesco Sansovino, a prolific writer and author of an important history of Venice, was a frequent visitor, along with other notable literary figures like the editor Ludovico Domenichi and the writers Giovanni Betussi and Sperone Speroni. All three Stampas were admired for their talents, but Gaspara's musical gifts garnered particular attention. In his 1545 *Lettere amorose* (*Love Letters*), Girolamo Parabosco, organist at the Basilica of San Marco, described her voice as "angelic" and possessed of such "sweet harmony that it . . . awakened spirit and life in the coldest stones."[3] Two years later, her music teacher, the French musician and composer Perissone Cambio (c. 1520–c. 1562), prefaced his book of popular secular music with a dedication to her:

> Noble lady . . . it is well known by now – and not only in this fortunate city, but almost everywhere – that no woman in the world loves music as much as you do, nor possesses it to such a rare degree. And thousands upon thousands of fine and noble spirits attest to this who, having heard your sweet harmonies, have given you the name of divine siren.[4]

When Baldassare died suddenly at the age of nineteen, members of the circle that had sprung up around the Stampa siblings joined the sisters in grief. Some, like Sansovino, made a point of embracing and supporting Gaspara in particular as they mourned her brother. In his dialogue *Ragionamento . . . d'amore* (*Discussion on Love*), Sansovino recalls how Baldassare had held Gaspara "in the greatest esteem": "many times he praised your intellect and steadfastness to me." Professing admiration for both sisters, he urges Gaspara to avoid the snares of romantic love and to "continue in your worthy studies, avoiding any distraction from your goal."[5]

Highlighting Gaspara's keen literary judgment as well as her musical ear, Sansovino dedicated two more works to her. The first was an edition of Giovanni Boccaccio's mid-fourteenth-century pastoral romance *Ameto*, in which Sansovino praises Gaspara's "perfect discernment" in interpreting this icon of the Italian literary canon. The second, a lecture on Giovanni della Casa – author of the celebrated Renaissance etiquette manual, the *Galateo* – brought Gaspara into the orbit of some of the most important names in Renaissance poetics. By situating her amid established male figures – including the patrician Domenico Venier, patron of Venice's literati and friend to Veronica Franco and other women poets – Sansovino implicitly recognized her as a cultural mediator in her own right. Gaspara found herself at the heart of an influential group of writers actively shaping the cultural landscape of Venice, a number of whom had musical interests and careers beyond literature. Some in this group were particularly interested in promoting women as writers and readers of vernacular literature. The mounting surge in popularity of Italian over Latin for certain kinds of works, coupled with the continued spread of print, made the editorial world more accessible to women than ever before, and female writers and readers were proving a valuable resource and market.

Though we lack many details about Stampa's performances, it is evident that she created her own verses for musical settings, preferring to have lyrics and ideas ready so that she could "write them down and sing them."[6] Given the intertextual resonances of Gaspara's poetry with Petrarch's, it is likely that she also performed settings of Petrarchan *canzoni*, a popular longer lyric form, and like many Renaissance singers, she improvised on stock melodies and performed solo arias. The relationship between music and poetry was symbiotic: as Gaspara's success as a singer bolstered her reputation as a poet, she began circulating her work in manuscript form. By 1552, the well-connected writer Lucrezia Gonzaga would describe Gaspara – in a letter to their mutual friend Ortensio Lando, a writer and promoter of women authors – as a "virtuosa," marveling also that she had read one of Gaspara's sonnets "more than a thousand times."[7] As if to protect her against the potentially scandalous implications of singing – or writing – for women, Gaspara's supporters emphasized the exemplary purity of her nature: one, comparing her favorably to the ancient poet and lutenist Sappho, described her as "equal to the Greek in her own Tuscan idiom,/she is more chaste, just as she is more beautiful."[8]

It was in this environment (perhaps in Venier's salon) that Gaspara first crossed paths with Collaltino di Collalto, the aloof count who would become the object of her single-minded passion and the inspiration for some of her most famous lines. Symbolically dating their encounter in 1548 to Christmas, Gaspara imbued their meeting with hidden meaning, linking the instant of "rare good fortune" in which the handsome Count "made himself a nest and refuge in my heart" to the spiritual gravity of the moment in which Christ issued from the "virginal womb."[9] Though close in age and part of the same intellectual circle, the lovers were separated by a gulf in social status and Gaspara was well aware that the liaison could never lead to marriage; still, their tumultuous affair lasted three years (see Figure 11.1).

Gaspara played on this imbalance in her poetry, characterizing herself as "lowly" and "abject" in contrast to the noble Collalto, whose name signifies "lofty hill" in Italian. Like her model, Petrarch, who used the figure of his beloved "Laura" as a springboard for exploring his own psyche in verse, Gaspara mined the emotional nuances of her relationship with Collaltino for literary ore, which she expressed

Figure 11.1 Portrait of Collaltino di Collalto in Luisa Bergalli's *Rime di Madonna Gaspara Stampa* (Venice: Francesco Piancentini, 1738)

Photo: Alamy

in musical, often openly erotic lines. Often, she alludes to Petrarch directly: her nostalgic recollection of a peaceful moment, which begins "Chiaro e famoso mare" ("Clear and shining sea"), for example, deliberately echoes Petrarch's famous canzone "Chiare, fresche, et dolci acque." When she despairs over Collaltino's absence, or his coolness to her, she adopts Petrarch's familiar language of dichotomy: "I am made of fire, and you of ice,/you are free, and I am in chains."[10]

Embracing the Petrarchan model offered clear advantages. As the predominant style for sixteenth-century poetry, it offered those with the ability to imitate it an opportunity for immediate acceptance – especially important to a woman writer seeking fame in a male-dominated sphere. Yet there were some critical differences in Gaspara's poetic voice. Petrarch wrote about an idealized, objectified *woman* who existed not only to inspire his poetry with her beauty but also to spur him, after her death, to denounce the pursuit of literary glory and turn instead from earthly to divine love. A typical Petrarchan verse describes Laura's flowing blond hair, graceful form, and passively angelic demeanor. By contrast, Gaspara, in the very act of writing, undid the conventional position of the male poet. In her poetry, a woman gazes upon the *male* object of desire and catalogs his attributes in realistic detail, urging the "ladies" who read her verse to

> picture a man of sweet and pleasing looks
> who's young in years but mature of intellect,
> an image of glory and valor.
> His hair is blond, his skin a lively color,
> he's tall of build, broad-shouldered and broad-chested,
> and finally in every way he's perfect –
> just (woe to me) a little cruel in love.

It is Gaspara who also eagerly pursues Collalto, in a reversal of the typical gender positions of Renaissance poetry.

Unlike Petrarch, Gaspara openly seeks literary recognition. In his celebrated opening sonnet that begins, "You who hear in scattered rhymes the sound of those sighs with which I nourished my heart," Petrarch characterizes his love for Laura as youthful foolishness for which he now feels shame. He writes to seek "pity, not only pardon" from his audience and renounce earthly love for divine.[11] But Gaspara, though echoing Petrarch's poetic vocabulary, does not renounce passion as youthful folly. Rather, she embraces it as a path to literary glory, as well as acceptance by those of higher station:

> You who hear in these troubled rhymes,
> in these troubled and these dark accents,
> the sound of my amorous laments
> and sufferings that vanquish all others' –
> wherever valor is esteemed and prized,
> I hope to find glory among the well-born:
> glory and not only pardon, for what
> gives rise to my laments is so sublime (see Figure 11.2).

Her words are in direct dialogue with Petrarch's sonnet. However, Gaspara wants not pity, but instead for her audience to recognize her experience as unique and envy the intensity of her love:

> And I hope some woman will be moved to say:
> "Most happy she, who suffered famously
> for such a famous cause!
> Oh, why can't the fortune that comes
> from loving a lord like him be mine,
> so such a lady and I might walk side by side?"[12]

While Petrarch's relationship with Laura existed only in poetry, Gaspara's romantic entanglement with Collaltino was almost certainly real, but it, too, was in many respects invented for the page. She often casts it, for example, in a deliberately classicizing light. The languid hills around the Collalto castle of San Salvatore become the pastoral backdrop to their love, and she adopts a classical name for herself according to the custom of literary academies: Anassilla, derived from Anaxum, the ancient name for the Piave River that flowed through Collaltino's estate. By detailing the ecstasies and humiliations of love – as it seems Collaltino by turns welcomed and then rejected her attentions – Gaspara showcased her own authority as a lover and author, her example unequaled by any other. Though Collaltino, by her account, was fickle and often cruel, Gaspara's passion and even her pain fuel and inspire her writing. She revels in love's torments as that which sets her apart from other women, claiming, "Grief no one will believe if they've not felt it!/Alas, that I alone defeat the infinite."

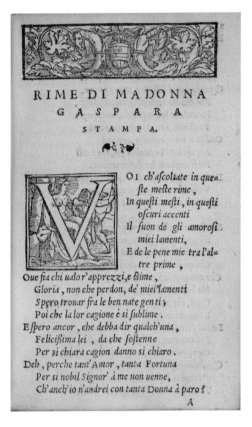

Figure 11.2 Title page and opening sonnet of *Rime di Madonna Gaspara Stampa* (Venice: Plinio Pietrasanta, 1554)

The affair with Collaltino ended after only a few years, sending Gaspara into a deep depression. But it marked the end of neither her poetry nor her passion. She continued to write, chronicling a new relationship with the Venetian Bartolomeo Zen – named only in an anagram – and mentioning a third man, referred to only as "Guiscardo." In one of her most famous sonnets, which later became an anthem of the Romantic era, Gaspara compares herself to a salamander, said to thrive in fire.

> Love has fashioned me so I live in flame.
> I'm some new salamander in the world,
> and like the animal who also lives and dies
> in one and the same place, no less strange.
> These are all my delights, and this my joy:
> to live in burning and never feel the pain,
> nor do I ask him who reduced me to this state
> to pity me, much or a little.

Though exhausted by desire, she cannot live without it, and must always seek it out:

> Hardly was that first passion spent
> when Love lit another, and what I've sensed thus far
> suggests this one's more alive, more forceful.
> Of this consuming love I won't repent,
> as long as he who's newly taken my heart
> is satisfied with my burning and content.[13]

Gaspara's ardent voice resonated with her audience. With its mix of influences from Petrarch to Ovid, Sappho, and the Latin poet Catullus, her poetry was uniquely powerful, while also grounded in literary tradition. She was accepted into the Accademia dei Dubbiosi (Academy of the Doubtful) in 1550, though such literary circles rarely admitted women: a reflection of the wide regard in which she was held. Though her fame was increasing, her promising career, like her brother's, was cut tragically short. After an illness in 1553, Gaspara died in Venice on April 23, 1554, at only thirty-one (some later raised the specter of suicide or even poisoning, but the culprit was a more mundane case of fever, perhaps influenza).[14] She left behind two daughters from her relationship with the Venetian nobleman Andrea Gritti, and over three hundred poems.[15] Of these, only three were published in her lifetime, while the others had circulated in manuscript form. In addition to love lyric, she had composed on a range of other subjects, from religious sonnets to poems addressing friends and admirers, male and female, or written to commemorate special events.

Of the three Stampa siblings, only Cassandra remained. Almost immediately upon Gaspara's death, Cassandra set to work gathering and organizing her sister's compositions. In 1554, she published them in an edition printed in Venice by Plinio Pietrasanta. The loosely chronological order of the poems as they are traditionally read, chronicling the stages of Gaspara's affair with Collaltino, is therefore due in part to Cassandra's efforts to impose a narrative structure on the work, while the early-twentieth-century editor of Gaspara's poems, Abdelkader Salza, later intervened even more significantly, re-ordering the poems into two sections as a truly Petrarchan *canzoniere*, or collection, in order to suggest a movement – even less authentic – from passion to remorse and separating the love poetry out from that on other themes.[16] The most recent edition of Gaspara's poetry, edited by Jane Tylus and Troy Tower in 2010, restores Cassandra's original sequence.

Cassandra claimed to have put the volume together at the insistence of her sister's many admirers; its dedication to Giovanni Della Casa, together with an appendix of poems in praise of Gaspara, reflects the serious interest and esteem her work inspired. Nonetheless, following Cassandra's edition, Gaspara's poetry fell into oblivion until the eighteenth century, when a distant descendant of Collaltino, Count Antonio Rambaldo di Collalto, commissioned a new one from the noted Luisa Bergalli (who in 1726 had included Gaspara in the first anthology of Italian women poets to be edited by a woman).[17] He also commissioned an engraving of Gaspara on the design of Daniel Antonio Bertoli. Depicting her with a laurel crown and a lyre at her side, it evoked once more for posterity Gaspara's virtuosity and the intimate connection between music and poetry (see Figure 11.3).[18] Even so, Gaspara's verse would have to wait almost two hundred years more for its next public foray.

Gaspara Stampa's modern legacy has been complex, due in large part to the attention paid to her biography and love story at the expense of her poetry and music. Bergalli's early-eighteenth-century edition romanticized the episode by painting Gaspara as a victim of passion and speculating that she had committed suicide when Collaltino married, launching the enduring myth of the poet as the tragic heroine so admired by Ranier Maria Rilke and other Romantic poets. Salza, on the other hand, enveloped Gaspara in a cloud of controversy by focusing on her moral character over her literary merit and suggesting that she had been not a faithful lover but, instead, a professional courtesan; to further the point, he paired her with the famous courtesan-poet Franco

CASPARA STAMPA
Clarior ingenio, forma
...que sui
virtutis amore,
nulla fuit, nec erit

Figure 11.3 Portrait of Gaspara Stampa in Luisa Bergalli's *Rime di Madonna Gaspara Stampa* (Venice: Francesco Piancentini, 1738)

(Beinecke Rare Book and Manuscript Library, Yale University)

[open access]

in his 1913 edition. Ignoring the cultural nuances of sixteenth-century Venetian society and hypothesizing that only prostitution could explain Gaspara's "free" way of life, he sought to cast her story as one of error and redemption, a more titillating version of Petrarch's poetic cycle.

For decades, the debate over whether Gaspara was a courtesan overshadowed her stature as a foundational figure in Renaissance poetry. By the 1980s, however, literary historians had begun to see her poetry not as a simple diary of amorous relationships but rather as a carefully crafted literary product and a valuable resource for understanding the intertwined arts of music and writing among early modern women.[19] The romantic myth persists; the nineteenth-century poet Gabriele D'Annunzio famously quoted Gaspara's phrase "To live in burning and never feel the pain," and her story has been featured in a spectrum of fictionalized accounts and artistic works. Today, however, she is appreciated in all her complexity as a musical *virtuosa* and one of the finest and most original poets of the Renaissance.

12 Tarquinia Molza (1542–1617)

Virtuosa and Philosopher

It is resolved that Tarquinia Molza be numbered in the ranks of [Rome's] most noble citizens with the title 'Unica,' never before bestowed on anyone, in recognition of her singular virtues and merits.

– Decree of Roman citizenship granted to Tarquinia Molza

Like Gaspara Stampa before her, the musician, poet, and philosopher Tarquinia Molza excelled in a variety of arts from an early age. The sixteenth-century historian Carlo Sigonio reported that Tarquinia – born in his hometown of Modena in Italy's Emilia-Romagna region – scorned feminine activities like sewing and embroidery, and always had a book tucked away in her sleeve. When her mother, Isabella di Antonio Colombi, wasn't looking, Sigonio wrote, Tarquinia would impatiently take out the hidden book and, "laying down the needle, commence reading."[1] According to this account, which Sigonio embellished to underscore what he considered to be Tarquinia's "masculine" intellectual drive, her mother despaired at this disobedience.

But Tarquinia's father Camillo (1513–1558) – son of the respected poet Francesco Maria Molza (1489–1544), a friend of the famed Vittoria Colonna – was pleased by his daughter's intellectual precocity. He arranged for her to be tutored by Giovanni Bertari (also called Poliziano), the erudite priest he retained to instruct Tarquinia's brothers, and by the mathematician Antonio Guarini. Tarquinia's education was thus far more extensive than typical for a girl of her middle-class echelon, encompassing rhetoric, natural philosophy, mathematics, and astronomy, as well as languages and literature. Her commonplace book with notes and fragments of her writing survives today in a manuscript in Modena and includes passages in Hebrew and a translation of a

DOI: 10.4324/9781003081807-16

dialogue by the ancient Greek philosopher Plato, along with transcriptions of her grandfather's Latin poetry.

Camillo died in 1558, having just returned from Venice where he was overseeing a new edition of Francesco Maria's poetry, leaving the Molza family in financial distress. Tarquinia's mother scrambled to provide for her children. On June 16 of that year, Isabella wrote to Camillo's former employer Cardinal Alessandro Farnese in Parma, a wealthy Renaissance duchy to the northwest of Modena, begging him to help provide for her daughter, who "has a good disposition and excellent potential," and her brothers Lodovico and Nicolò.[2] Soon after, with a modest dowry of 500 *scudi*, Tarquinia wed Paolo Porrino (1535–1579) – a relative of the poet Gandolfo Porrini (1510–c. 1565) who had been a friend of her grandfather – in a ceremony in Modena's San Lorenzo church. But she remained as devoted to study as ever, reading the works of Plato and Aristotle and composing Latin verse as well as sonnets and madrigals – a poetic form especially popular throughout the sixteenth and early seventeenth centuries and often set to music. The composers Marc'Antonio Pordenone, Paolo Isnardi, and Giovan Leonardo Primavera would all create arrangements for Tarquinia's verse (see Figure 12.1).

As Tarquinia's reputation grew, her home became a meeting place for literati. Torquato Tasso, author of the influential epic *Gerusalemme liberata* (*Jerusalem Delivered*), first printed in 1581, composed several poems for her, including one that began, "Tarquinia, if you contemplate the beautiful turnings of the heavens," gesturing to her interest in the observing the starry night sky. In these respects, Tarquinia's experience echoes that of her contemporary, the celebrated Margherita Sarrocchi. Both were poets and polymaths who hosted salons from the residences they shared with their husbands, both corresponded with Tasso, and some of Tarquinia's earliest verse was published in a 1575 anthology that also included Margherita's.[3] Tasso admired both women and marveled of Tarquinia, "[Y]ou have read everything, and you remember all of it!"[4]

Tarquinia returned Tasso's esteem, addressing to him passionate declarations of affection and sorrow upon parting:

And so you, oh my soul,
wish to leave me here,
bereft of you, who are my life?
Oh, cruel assassin,

Figure 12.1 Portrait of Tarquinia Molza in a seventeenth-century anthology
of women philosophers (*Effigies fœminarum de poesi philosophia
alisque litteratum disciplinis . . .* Venice, 1652, 67)

(Archivio dell'Accademia di Belle Arti di Venezia)

with what miserable destiny
do you lead me toward death?[5]

Though ardent, Tarquinia's verse for Tasso displays an emotional
intensity typical of many sixteenth-century poems, and characteristic
of many of her other compositions. Her poems directed to women are
similarly fervid, with an evocative use of erotic language and striking
imagery – as in these verses for a female recipient:

The tears on your face,
that day, my lady, were

like candid pearls against a scarlet veil,
and I cried out, "Alas, what are you doing, you eyes?
Would you burn me with your emotion?[6]

Inflected with contrasts borrowed from the vocabulary of the preeminent fourteenth-century poet Francesco Petrarca (Petrarch) – Angela's crystalline tears against her flushed cheeks, the coupling of love and despair – Tarquinia's lines transform the traditional Petrarchan model to position herself, a woman, as both poet and admirer, and Angela as her "beloved." Similar inversions – and subversions – occur in the other verse by Tarquinia addressed to female interlocutors and set to music. In these instances, as was customary, the woman singer would appear to adopt a masculine rhetorical stance, though there is some debate as to whether Tarquinia's written texts originally employed feminine adjectival endings that would have made a same-sex connotation explicit. Thus, while the fluidity of Tarquinia's lyrical "I" opens up the possibility of fluid sexuality, it also reflects a broader context of sixteenth-century poetic and musical mores. Tarquinia was not the only woman of the period to address love lyric to another woman: the impassioned poems for Margaret of Austria written by Laudomia Forteguerri of Siena, for example, were renowned, and similarly ambiguous. The spectrum of sexuality was as diverse in the Renaissance as it is today, but the lines between stylistic bravura and autobiographical expression can be difficult to define.

Along with composing poetry, Tarquinia continued to study harpsichord and singing – complementary interests that also recall the example of Stampa, the Venetian poet and *virtuosa* who died a decade after Tarquinia's birth. For Tarquinia, however, music became a full-fledged career. Her instructors included a tutor known as "Modonino" (perhaps Bartolomeo da Modena, whom she could have met through the influential Farnese family) as well as Francesco Cadarino, Giovanni Maria Fiammenghi, and Alfonso della Viola, the singing master at the Este court in Ferrara. She became expert in the guitar-shaped viola da mano, clavier, and lute and in setting her own verse to music. Word of her exceptional voice spread. By the age of twenty-six, Tarquinia had so enchanted the duke of Ferrara, Alfonso II d'Este, with her performance of a Petrarchan sonnet that the duke begged her to sing it at least "four or six times."[7]

Not yet forty when her husband Paolo died, leaving her a widow in 1579, Tarquinia insisted that she would never remarry. To underscore her adamance, she adopted her own emblem, a kind of personal logo that combined words with an enigmatic picture to convey a complex idea. Emblems were hugely popular in Renaissance culture, and Tarquinia's featured a dangling vine hanging from a fallen oak, accompanied by the Latin motto "Non sufficit alter" ("None other suffices"), perhaps adapted from the sixth canto of Virgil's Latin epic, the *Aeneid*. She accompanied the image with a poem elaborating that, like the single vine that Fortune deprives of its "indispensable support," from now on she too would sustain herself alone:

> nor shall I ever lean on another,
> in plains or knolls;
> for as shelter from the angry storm,
> no other will do.[8]

Tarquinia had good reason to embrace her widowed state. Childless and her husband's sole heir, she could live a comfortable and socially acceptable life as a widow, dedicating herself to study while also cultivating her growing reputation as a musician and singer. She was also becoming increasingly interested in natural philosophy, a broad umbrella of scientific inquiry that included the study of the cosmos.

In many ways, music and natural philosophy went hand in hand: Neoplatonic philosophers like Marsilio Ficino, for example, who translated Plato's corpus into Latin in Florence in the mid-fifteenth century, posited a profound connection between musical harmony and planetary order. Around 1575, shortly before her husband's death, Tarquinia struck up a friendship with the writer Francesco Patrizi da Cherso, a philosopher and humanist deeply influenced by Ficino. In conversations and letters, they discussed the nature of the heavens and the concept of the music of the spheres. In a letter dating to 1577, Patrizi expounded to Tarquinia on ancient and medieval notions of the cosmos, distinguishing between the physical aspects studied by natural philosophers and abstract metaphysical and theological concepts. "More recent astronomers say that above the starry [heaven] there is another heaven, which they call crystalline," Patrizi wrote, adding that "and above it the theologians place the Empyrean," where God resides[9] (see Figure 12.2).

In another letter, as they discussed the practical complexities of planetary revolution, Patrizi suggested visualizing the Moon as a body "implanted in the epicycle [the geometrical model in which the Moon,

Figure 12.2 Portrait of Francesco Patrizi in his *Discussiones peripateticae* (Basel, 1581)

Photo: Alamy

Sun, and planets each move in a uniform speed around a circle] like a nail or a knot in a piece of wood," and carried along by that epicycle, "which has its own motions," or variable path.[10] This formulation was a radically different interpretation of planetary movement that required rejecting the then-canonical notion of physical planetary spheres and that planets were fixed in orbits.[11] Both correspondents would have known the new sun-centered model proposed by the Polish astronomer Nicolaus Copernicus – whose *On the Revolutions of the Heavenly Spheres*, published in Nuremberg in 1543, would be condemned by the Church as heretical in 1610. They would have also been familiar with the responses from the Danish astronomer Tycho Brahe and others that attempted to reconcile the Copernican model while still retaining the Earth at the center of the universe. Like Brahe, Patrizi's own view was geocentric, but he used mathematics to posit the existence of a finite material world surrounded by an infinite, light-filled void: an endless Empyrean. Through many such discussions, the two correspondents queried, proposed, and debated varied and sometimes competing theories of the cosmos. In this way, Tarquinia helped Patrizi formulate and refine the views he would express in later works.

Patrizi knew the respect Tarquinia commanded in Modena, where he also lived for a time. Inspired by their conversations, he made her the star character in his dialogue, *La filosofia amorosa* (*The Philosophy of Love*), written in 1577 but never completed. Organized into four parts and modeled on Plato's famous *Symposium*, the work presents Tarquinia as a miraculous, unique figure, a central character who embodies the Platonic ideal of love as unity and wholeness. Combining every male and female virtue, which exist in her in perfect harmony, Patrizi's fictional "Tarquinia" evokes Plato's idealized androgyne: her temperament is a seamless blend of "feminine and masculine" qualities mixed together "in a way that is beyond comprehension and ineffable."[12] A divine muse whose perfection is complete, she stands in not only for Love itself but also for Diotima, the character from the *Symposium* offered by Plato as the ideal female philosopher.

Patrizi's dialogue is populated by writers, philosophers, and musicians, whose lavish praise of Tarquinia links her philosophical sophistication to her musical talent: with her angelic singing, she is said to imitate God's own creative power. These male speakers compare "La Molza" to each of the nine Muses: she exemplifies erudition in the liberal arts, physical sciences, and mathematics, and possesses a profound knowledge of the universe, thanks to the astrologically favorable circumstances of her birth and her otherworldly connection to music's divine harmony. Influenced in particular by the planet Saturn, associated with knowledge and wisdom, Tarquinia is said to have an "infinitely marvelous ear": her musicality transcends language itself and inspires those who experience it to better themselves and their world.

An indirect presence in the first part of the work, Tarquinia later takes an active speaking role, assuming the Aristotelian perspective to Patrizi's Neoplatonist character. Asserting after Aristotle that self-love (*philautia*) is the foundation of all forms of love, her persona traces "all kinds of love and well-wishing" to their origins in "love for ourselves" – an early articulation of the now common idea that in order to love others, we must first love ourselves. A third interlocutor named "Paolo" – to evoke Tarquinia's husband, who died shortly after the dialogue was written – professes bewilderment; he attempts to refute her argument with counterexamples, such as widows who grieve for their deceased spouses, as the actual Tarquinia herself would later profess to do. A final chapter was intended to resolve this debate, perhaps by reconciling the Aristotelian and Platonic positions, but remained unfinished. Tarquinia's starring role in Patrizi's dialogue indicates that she was esteemed in philosophical as well as musical circles by the 1570s. Others also enshrined her in literary form – including Tasso, who titled a philosophical dialogue *La Molza ovvero l'Amore* (*Lady Molza: Or, On Love*) in her honor. Here, Tarquinia, "possessed of ingenious wisdom and adorned by wide reading and great learning," serves as the arbiter of competing theories of love. A rare manuscript preserved in Modena's Biblioteca Estense, purports to record lectures she herself gave on the subject.[13]

By 1581, Tarquinia had been elected to the learned Accademia degli Innominati (Academy of the Nameless) in Parma, an indication of her prestige. At the same time, however, after becoming embroiled in a legal dispute with her former in-laws over the estate of her deceased husband, she determined in 1583 to leave Modena for Ferrara, where she had long-standing connections to the court of the Este court. If Tarquinia's fame before now had rested largely on her activities as a poet and philosopher, this new chapter solidified her reputation as one of Italy's most celebrated female performers of vocal music. Duke Alfonso, who had so admired Tarquinia's singing in 1568, had an enduring interest in women's singing practice and the embellished "luxuriant" madrigal for which Ferrara – and Tarquinia herself – would become known. Entering the service of Alfonso's third wife, the teenaged Margherita Gonzaga, Tarquinia became involved with the fledgling *concerto delle donne* (or *concerto delle dame*): an innovative and influential ensemble of women vocalists and musicians drawn from among Margherita's ladies-in-waiting (not unlike Margherita's all-women *balletto delle donne*, a dance ensemble formed in the same years). The acclaimed group included the harpist Laura Peperara (or Peverara); Livia d'Arco, playing the *viola da gamba*, a bowed, stringed instrument prevalent in the Renaissance; and on lute Anna Guarini, daughter of the poet Battista, who was tragically murdered by her husband in a jealous rage a decade later. The composer and organist Luzzasco Luzzaschi, who set Tarquinia's verse to music as early as 1571, served as concertmaster. Celebrated for her technical virtuosity and command of "all three modes of singing: the Italian, Spanish, and French," Tarquinia took an official role training and supervising the musicians in addition to performing with them, in exchange for a yearly stipend, lodging, and other support.[14]

Playing for select audiences at court – recitals so special they were referred to as "musica segreta," or secret music – the ensemble was lauded for its innovative, highly ornamented style of singing, in which Tarquinia excelled. The concerto delle donne made Ferrara the center of the musical world in the 1580s and influenced the work of composers such as Claudio Monteverdi. More broadly, it revolutionized the role of women in music, shifting from an amateur model that cast music as a courtly pastime for noblewomen who "happened to sing," to one in which middle-class women joined the court precisely because of their musical talent (see Figure 12.3).[15] It would gradually lead to the professionalization of music for women as an occupation

Figure 12.3 A concert of women, Venice, 1520s

(The National Gallery, London)

Photo: Alamy

in which they could build independent careers. The influence of Ferrara's concerto delle donne resonated throughout Italy, with rival ensembles cropping up in other courts: for example, in Medici-ruled Florence, where the operettist Francesca Caccini and her sister, Settimia, a noted singer, performed with their father's "concerto." In the early seventeenth century, Barbara Strozzi of Venice was arguably the last female singer to adopt the florid vocal style of the concerto delle donne, but the path to music as a profession was now open to women in Italy.

Protected by her proximity to court – and perhaps because she did not openly seek publication of her poetry, an ambition that often led to tensions for learned women – Tarquinia up to this point had preserved an immaculate professional and personal reputation, even without the protection of a second marriage. However, as the decade drew to a close, scandal simmered when she was accused of an affair with the composer Giaches de Wert. Wert had served as the director of music at the court of Mantua before coming to Ferrara, accompanied by a controversial history that included a wife embroiled in a nefarious plot to murder her lover's wealthy uncle. Unlike Tarquinia, Wert did not come from nobility, and it was likely the difference in social status between the presumed lovers more than Wert's disreputable associations that scandalized urbane Ferrarese society. Though Tarquinia denied an alliance, attributing the rumors to professional jealousy on the part of another musician, she was forced to leave court.

Returning to Modena, Tarquinia put the gossip behind her and continued a rich engagement with intellectual and musical life. She likely continued to write, though no poems from this period survive. A surviving inventory of Tarquinia's personal library reflects her wide reading in these final years: she possessed volumes in Greek, Latin, and Italian, including works by Aristotle, Plato, and the great Roman orator Cicero, as well as Lucretius's influential *On the Nature of Things* and several multilingual dictionaries.[16] In 1600, more than a decade before her death, the sixty-five-year-old Tarquinia – who had never lived in Rome – was declared an honorary citizen of the city based on her "singular virtues and merits" – the first woman to receive this recognition. The honor speaks to the scope of her celebrity: as one of her early modern admirers exclaimed:

Who doesn't know, at least by reputation, of the exceptional and wide-ranging merit of Signora Tarquinia Molza of Modena? . . . in her erudition and command of the three languages, Greek, Latin, and the vernacular, it is no exaggeration to say that she rivals the most learned men of our time.[17]

Tarquinia Molza died in 1617 and is buried in Modena's Cathedral. In her will, she made a provision granting modest dowries of 200 lira to three young women each year to help them marry. The rest of her estate she left to her sisters and the charitable institutions of her natal city. With her brilliant command of poetry, music, cosmology, and philosophy, Tarquinia's legacy is a powerful reminder of the vital connections between Renaissance intellectual and creative worlds, and of how freely women participated in them.

13 Isabella Andreini (1562–1604)

Diva of Stage and Page

If ever someone should read my forgotten stanzas,
don't fall for their pretended passions:
I am used to playing imagined loves on stage,
with contrived emotion.

– Isabella Andreini

In the spring of 1589, as women singers like Tarquinia Molza flourished in Este Ferrara, Medici Florence was in a flurry over the impending nuptials of Grand Duke Ferdinando de' Medici to his French bride, Christine de Lorraine. Extravagant festivities were planned, including rival performances by two of Italy's reigning divas of the stage: Vittoria Piissimi of Rome and Isabella Canali Andreini of Padua. Both actresses were linked to the Gelosi troupe (the Zealous), where Piissimi first gained accolades before performing with the Confidenti (the Confident) and Uniti (the United) companies. Isabella joined the Gelosi in 1578, following in Piissimi's footsteps as the principal love interest, or "prima donna innamorata" – the starring female role that gave rise to the term "prima donna," still used today – in the company now led by her husband, Francesco Andreini (1548–1624). Each woman had her own following, and their Florentine appearance was billed as a competition of theater's greatest female icons. Who would take the prize?

Judging from a description of the event offered by one contemporary spectator, the diarist Giuseppe Pavoni, Isabella shined brightest. Performing the role for which she was best known, *La pazzia di Isabella* (*The Madness of Isabella*), she mesmerized her audience with her portrayal of a woman who, betrayed in love, descends into madness, and is returned to sanity by a magic potion. Largely improvisational, the role called for Isabella to transform onstage from an elegant,

DOI: 10.4324/9781003081807-17

learned lady who employs the elegant parlance of fashionable love lyric, to a disheveled, semi-clothed madwoman who demonstrates her inner turmoil by speaking in multiple languages, including Spanish, Greek, and French (in honor of the bride), and mimicking her fellow actors. Isabella's complete metamorphosis thus required an extensive command not only of a variety of idioms but also an ability to inhabit both her own role and those of the other men and women on stage. As Pavoni observed, "in the performance of her Madness," Isabella demonstrated "her sane and learned intellect," leaving her audience "murmuring and marveling so that as long as the world lasts, her beautiful eloquence and worthiness will always be praised."[1] And indeed this artistic versatility – the ability to move fluidly between characters and emotional states, between genders and genres – was the hallmark of this most famous actress of the Renaissance, who built a parallel literary career to ensure her legacy.

A hugely popular form of improvisational sketch theatre, *commedia dell'arte* was born in Italy in the sixteenth century, reaching its apex in the seventeenth and spreading to France and throughout Europe. It relied on *scenari*, broadly outlined plotlines featuring stock characters – from the greedy "Pantalone" to the Harlequinesque trickster "Zanni" – with distinct attributes, behaviors, and costumes. With the exception of those playing the Innamorati (Lovers), actors typically donned masks that lent an abstract, often buffoonish quality to their expression, a mediation later echoed in the chalky face paint of nineteenth-century French mimes (see Figure 13.1). Within these fixed parameters, *commedia dell'arte* troupes mounted performances that were satisfyingly familiar to audiences while also allowing for original flourishes, regional specificity, and individual virtuosity: that is, the ability of certain stars, like Isabella, to stun and enchant spectators.

Isabella infused the role of the *innamorata*, the attractive ingénue whose love story drives the plot, with depth and comic instinct, presenting herself as the epitome of learned femininity by adopting a refined Tuscan Italian and often reciting poetry or singing. Her approach was deliberate. Though women were central to the development of *commedia dell'arte* – the first record of a female actor, a certain "Domina Lucrezia of Siena," dates to 1564 – women onstage were often viewed with suspicion. One sixteenth-century chronicler opined that both the men and women of *commedia dell'arte* troupes were dissolute but that the women in particular "are always, or nearly always, without morality." They were "frequently prostitutes," the observer added, echoing

Figure 13.1 Commedia dell'arte troupe (Isabella Andreini and the Gelosi), Flemish, late 16th c.

(Musée Carnavalet)

Photo: Alamy

a common accusation of women who took public roles, whether as actors, singers, musicians, or published authors; and their beauty, "elegant mannerisms and clothes," and suggestive dancing and singing "excites the spectators' libido."[2] Isabella navigated such stereotypes by curating her public image to highlight not only her dramatic talent and erudition but also her "traditional" feminine virtue as a devoted wife and mother.

The first European actress to acquire social and cultural respectability along with celebrity, Isabella, unusually, further molded this identity by publishing literary works. A portrait by Paolo Veronese dating to the early 1580s reinforces the persona she sought to project: depicted in three-quarter length, Isabella gazes into the distance, one hand resting on a partially opened book to mark her place (see Figure 13.2). She wears an elegant gown, with puffed sleeves and a ruched collar but no jewelry or other markers of social status. The overall effect is one of genteel propriety and taste rather than extravagance – even the sprightly little dog beside her is a spaniel, a breed fashionable at European courts. A closer look, however, suggests subtle allusions to her profession: from the dark drapery behind her, echoing a stage curtain, to her jacket-like bodice, a masculine garment with

Figure 13.2 Presumed portrait of Isabella Andreini, by Paolo Veronese, c. 1585–1588
(Musée Thysesen, Madrid)
Photo: Alamy

theatrical associations that gestures to Isabella's fame for performing
androgynous roles.[3]

How did Isabella Andreini come to command the stages of Europe –
and its presses? We know little of her early years, except that she was
born in 1562, perhaps to Venetian parents although she called herself
Paduan. Her family was not aristocratic, but her education was sufficient
to propel her ascent to star performer and published poet. In 1576, at
fourteen, she encountered Flaminio Scala – author of some of the most

well-known scenarios in *commedia dell'arte* – and joined his Gelosi troupe. Immediately, she began to refine the role of the *prima donna innamorata*, performing for audiences throughout Italy and France. By 1578, she had married Francesco Andreini, a fellow actor who developed the role of the braggart, Capitano Spavento (Captain Fright), and became director of the Gelosi in 1589. Their union would prove long-standing and productive, both personally and professionally. They worked and toured together, with Isabella serving a central role in managing the troupe's activities and negotiating its performances while also raising their seven children – one of whom, Giovan Battista (1576–1654), would become a well-known actor himself, founding the Compagnia dei Fedeli (Company of the Loyal). To set themselves apart from their rivals, the Gelosi made the notions of virtue, honor, and fame central to their brand, and Isabella underscored these qualities in her own persona.[4]

Onstage, Isabella drew on the poetic traditions and genres that dominated sixteenth-century literary culture to reaffirm her cultured image. Next on the horizon was authorship. In 1588, she published her first literary work, *Mirtilla* (*The Blueberry Bush*), a pastoral play. Popular with Renaissance audiences and often performed for marriage festivities, such plays were usually formulaic, recounting the romantic tribulations of shepherds and nymphs – menaced by a sexually aggressive satyr – before ultimately resolving in happy, socially sanctioned marriages.

Though a comic character, the satyr was explicitly misogynistic, and his efforts to take the nymph by force were a critical part of the plotline. *Mirtilla* was the first pastoral drama to be published by a woman and, Isabella, who had an insider's understanding not only of the generic characters and plot points but also the techniques to effectively block and represent character and action on stage, turned such tropes on their head. Her *Mirtilla*, which includes a part written for her "rival" Piissimi, is a feminist rewriting of the traditional pastoral sequence, in which the shepherd rescues the nymph. Instead, it features the nymph Fillide saving herself and turning the tables on her would-be attacker, the satyr. Using the language of conventional love poetry to seduce her aggressor, Fillide ties him to a tree under the pretense of protecting herself from his overpoweringly "manly" ardor; she then inflicts upon him a series of eroticized humiliations that nullify him as a sexual threat. Finally revealing her trickery, Fillide cries out with delight, "Now you see that I've been playing with you! . . . Oh, now you see that I've got you: stay there, humiliated, just as you deserve, for I'm leaving you!"[5] With this shrewd subversion, Isabella's *Mirtilla* rejects female subordination and, instead, offers a witty and powerful triumph of women's ingenuity.

Though *Mirtilla* was well received, Isabella felt it failed to display the full range of her erudition.[6] But it was only the first step on her carefully orchestrated literary trajectory. She had been composing verse for over a decade, and her compositions were anthologized in several collections, often alongside celebrated male poets.[7] But she truly established herself with the publication of her first volume of *Rime* (*Poems*) in 1601, dedicated to a cardinal, Cinzio Aldobrandini, and printed with her engraved likeness and an endorsement from the influential scholar Erycius Puteanus. Coupled with her admittance that year to a prestigious literary society – the Accademia degli Intenti (Academy of the Resolved) of Pavia – the volume introduced Isabella to a far broader audience of readers. Its three-hundred-plus poems elicited praise from influential poets like Gabriello Chiabrera and Giovan Battista Marino. In a contest sponsored by Aldobrandini, her verse was judged second only to that of the celebrated Torquato Tasso.

Like her *commedia dell'arte* roles, Isabella's poetry also presented a multilayered picture of the author. The dedicatory letter to her *Rime* has the modest, self-effacing tone typical of many Renaissance women's collections. But Isabella centers her identity as a woman writer by emphasizing her productive maternity. Her poems are her offspring, and as such she must love and care for them in their imperfections as well as their felicities. Her take on such literary "maternity" offers a unique twist: she is not only mother to these poetic lines but "Father, Mother, and Nursemaid to these, my children."[8] On stage, Isabella was renowned for her skill in playing both men and women. In her poems, too, she similarly merges femininity and masculinity, signaling the socially constructed nature of these categories. This fluidity is showcased in the introductory sonnet, which alerts the reader to the artifice of both theater and literature:

If ever someone should read my forgotten stanzas,
don't fall for their pretended passions:
I am used to playing imagined loves on stage,
with contrived emotion.
I have set forth the Muses' lofty inspirations
with lies and false words,
where my fictive sorrows sometimes I bewail,
or sometimes sing my fictive delights.[9]

Underscoring Isabella's links to the stage, the "feigned passions" of the poet are likened to those of the actress, and the physical and imaginative spaces – or "scenes" – of the stage are explicitly invoked: the "fictive sorrows" and "fictive delights" to be presented in the rest of the collection, which includes sonnets, madrigals, and sestinas, as well as love poems offered from both male and female perspectives.

Exposing love as a poetic conceit, Isabella peels back the underlying layers of dramatic illusion and evokes the blurred lines between the improvisational nature of *commedia dell'arte* and the work of scripted performance, or between "Nature" and "Art":

> And, as in the theater, in varied style
> I now have played a woman, now a man,
> as Nature would instruct, and Art as well,
> So in green April, following once more
> my star of fleeting years, with varied style
> I have penned at least a thousand pages.

Just as the spectators who witness a theatrical performance must not be drawn in by its fictions, Isabella warns, so too must the reader of her poetry remain alert. Her poems are intended to reveal – not conceal – the craft behind her role as both *prima donna innamorata* and author, as well as the artistic ambition that drives her to "follow her star" according to her own original and "varied style": phrases which, while declaring her own versatility, directly echo the famous "canzoniere" of the fourteenth-century poet Petrarch, the model for Renaissance lyric. Like those of other women poets, including Gaspara Stampa and Tarquinia Molza, many of Isabella's poems were set to music, in her case, by Donat'Antonio Spano, Pietro Paolo Torre, and other composers.

Following the publication of her volume of poetry, Isabella continued to revise the volume with an eye to an expanded edition. She also began planning a book of letters, a genre considered *de rigueur* for an established writer. If she described writing poetry as difficult work and observed that she "sweated with the effort" of composing verse, letter-writing was esteemed best when completely unmediated by art ("guided only by Nature"), especially when a woman was the author.[10] Though the distinction was spurious – published letters, like poetry, were the result of skill and revision – the pretense made letters an especially popular genre for women writers who, according to Renaissance literary theory, must be more closely inspired by emotion and instinct than men. As the dedicatory letter to the collection makes clear, however, Isabella had no illusions about the challenges she faced as a woman writer. Fame, though a worthy goal, was arduous and costly, even for men. She distinguished herself from other women whom she described as "choosing" traditional feminine pastimes over literary glory, "those women who – even though they learn about their many female predecessors who gained fame and immortality through study – nonetheless wish only to attend to . . . the embroidery needle." Isabella, by contrast, boasted "a most ardent desire to learn, which I have nourished with all my power."

Like her poems, Isabella's letters are notably theatrical in nature: composed for publication, rather than actual correspondence, they are often based on her dramatic monologues. Some center on love, the theme for which she was known onstage, but others are polemic in nature and even evoke the feminist tones of her earlier *Mirtilla*. In one letter congratulating a noble father on the birth of his daughter, Isabella also chides him for not celebrating as he would have for a son, who could have inherited property and would have spared the family the increasingly large dowry daughters required to be married according to their station. Prominent female humanists like Isotta Nogarola, Cassandra Fedele, and Laura Cereta had discussed the negative consequences of this gendered social economy in their Latin works composed in the late fifteenth and early sixteenth centuries; here, Isabella uses the philosophical reasoning fashionable in élite sixteenth-century literary culture to make her point. Feminine beauty is the reflection of the beauty of the soul, she writes, in the tradition of Renaissance Neoplatonism, reminding her correspondent to delight in God's will:

I learned with the greatest pleasure that your wife . . . has given birth to a very beautiful daughter, who as she grows in beauty (as is to be expected) will be perfect in both body and soul, as corporeal beauty is a clear reflection of the beauty of the soul . . .: but as happy as I was to have heard of this birth, I was equally distressed by your most unjustified sadness. I heard that you are greatly disappointed because a daughter was born to you, as if by being a girl she was not of your own flesh, blood, and bones, just like a boy would have been. And is it possible that a man of such great experience as you would not choose joyfully to embrace all that is given by God the most wise, the Maker of all things?

In closing, Isabella seizes the opportunity to offer a roll call of learned women in antiquity, exclaiming: "Don't you think that they could call themselves wholly fortunate, those fathers of the eternally famous Corinna, Sappho, Erinna, Aspasia, Diotima, Praxilla, Almathea, Manto, Arete, Carmenta, and innumerable others, who not only rivaled, but surpassed men?" Unparalleled in her own professional and artistic achievements, she highlights a long lineage of women's accomplishments, urging others to "follow their star" as she has done.

In 1604, returning from a tour in France where the Gelosi had performed for King Henry IV and his wife, Maria de' Medici, of the powerful Florentine dynasty, Isabella died just outside Lyons, perhaps from complications of a miscarriage. She was pregnant with her eighth child. In a measure of her celebrity, a memorial medallion bearing her effigy was struck; inscribed on the reverse was the Latin phrase *AETERNA FAMA* ("eternal fame") (see Figure 13.3). But her literary legacy continued to evolve. The following year, Francesco, picking up where his wife had been forced to leave off, quickly brought out an expanded commemorative edition of her *Poems*.[11] With the help of their son Giovan Battista, Francesco went on to curate his wife's writings, overseeing not only this 1605 edition of her poems but also, in 1607, the volume of *Lettere* (*Letters*) she had begun assembling before her death. This would prove her most popular publication, reprinted four times over the next century. In 1606, Giovan Battista published a book of poetry in his mother's memory, titled *Pianti d'Apollo* (*Apollo's*

Figure 13.3 A–B Commemorative medal by Guillaume Dupré depicting Isabella Andreini

Tears); while in 1617, Francesco published *Fragmenti di alcune scritture* (*Miscellaneous Writings*), containing theatrical dialogues performed by Isabella on stage. Their efforts ensured that Isabella's name would not be forgotten.

Though the Gelosi disbanded soon after Isabella's death, her literary and dramatic personae went on to many afterlives. The stock "female lover" in *commedia dell'arte* is now known as "Isabella" after her, and many of the scenarios she perfected are still performed by theater companies across the globe today. The most famous actress of her generation, Isabella was instrumental in bringing a more expressive and perceptive vein to Italian *commedia dell'arte* and to theatre in general, which moved progressively toward a focus on individual expressiveness. A multifaceted talent who built her career moving between Italy and France, Isabella Andreini left a lasting mark on the world of theater and played a major role in the development of the theatrical diva.

14 Francesca Caccini (1587–post-1641)

Opera's Star at the Medici Court

Let me tell you about the incredible virtuosa Cecchina. . . . Not only did this talented woman . . . produce marvelous operas, but she also composed and improvised beautiful odes and elegant Latin verses, accompanying herself by singing or playing . . . in all the big cities, before the greatest princes: Rome, Paris, Turin, Padua, Verona, Venice, Genoa, Parma, Modena, and Bologna. . . . No one can surpass or even come close to her wonderful compositions, for as a composer she stunned the brightest lights of Florence.

– Cristofano Bronzini

Some two decades after Isabella Andreini's bravura performance for the Medici, the Florentine Francesca Caccini was born into an exciting and rapidly evolving musical world, one distinguished by expanding opportunities for women and the advent of opera. Though her admirer and biographer Cristofano Bronzini records that she was initially more interested in studying rhetoric, philosophy, and geometry than music – to which she turned "only as a pastime, and to please her father" – Francesca became a renowned *virtuosa* and professional musician at the grand-ducal court, and the first woman to compose an opera. Her father, to whom Bronzini alluded, was Giulio Caccini Romano (1551–1618), a composer, tenor, and renowned singing teacher credited with developing "a new kind of music, a singing without song."[1] As a member of the innovative Florentine Camerata (from the Italian *camera*, or chamber) – a group of intellectuals, poets, and musicians that included Vincenzo Galilei, father of the astronomer Galileo – Giulio played an important role in the dissemination of the new monodic music or *stile recitativo*: the expressive solo song, in which the singer adopts the rhythms and cadence of regular speech, that developed into operatic recitative and is associated with the beginning of the Baroque era.

DOI: 10.4324/9781003081807-18

Francesca's mother was Lucia di Filippo Gagnolandi, a skilled singer who also performed at the Medici court until losing her post when the grand duke Ferdinando I succeeded to the throne in 1587 and did away with the "indulgences" of his predecessor.

Lucia died five years later, but her two young daughters – Francesca and her sister Settimia (1591–c.1660), also a noted singer – inherited her talent. Francesca, in particular, had an exceptional breadth of musical aptitude: in addition to her accomplished singing style, she mastered multiple instruments, including the guitar, harp, harpsichord, lute, and theorbo, a long-necked, lute-like instrument that came into fashion in the late sixteenth century. The Caccini household was populated by Giulio's students and by the artists and poets who orbited the Medici court. Though the family was not noble, Giulio was ambitious for his children and arranged for Francesca, described by contemporaries as intelligent, witty, and hungry for knowledge, to receive instruction in a wide range of subjects in addition to music and voice. Like Tarquinia Molza of Modena and many female musicians of the previous generation, Francesca also composed poetry in both vernacular Tuscan and Latin, and her career in music was made possible by the training and support she received at home.

Giulio's aspirations for his daughters were fueled by practical concerns as well as paternal pride. A colorful, even notorious figure in Renaissance Florence known for his mercurial temper, tumultuous love life, and big ambitions, Giulio – who had at least ten children to support, including one, Pompeo (1577–1624), from a previous relationship – recognized an opportunity in his children's talents. The success of the *concerto delle donne* in Ferrara, the secular musical ensemble of women musicians that emerged at the d'Este court in the early 1580s, performing for élite audiences, had inspired imitations at other princely courts; in fact, Giulio too had previously directed a *concerto di donne* in Florence under the grand duke Francesco I and his consort Bianca Cappello.[2]

Whereas the Ferrarese ensemble comprised noblewomen hailing from aristocratic families, who were considered court ladies rather than salaried musicians, Giulio created his own concerto featuring his family: his daughters Francesca and Settimia; Pompeo; his second wife, singer Margherita della Scala; and others from his household, sharing a bond not of nobility but of kinship and Florentine birth. This majority-female ensemble performed chamber music and other entertainment for the Medici court, including two of music history's first operas, *Euridice* (*Eurydice*) by Jacopo Peri and Ottavio Rinuccini and Giulio's own setting of Gabriello Chiabrera's *Il rapimento di Cefalo* (*The Abduction of Cephalus*). Both were presented in October 1600 for the marriage in Florence of Maria de' Medici, Ferdinando's niece, to Henri IV, king of France. Court diarists took note of Francesca's voice on these occasions, comparing her favorably to other famed singers such as the Roman Vittoria Archilei, with whom she occasionally performed.

In 1605, Giulio brought his singers (known as "le donne di Giulio Romano," or Giulio Romano's women) to France, where they again performed for Henri IV and his queen. Francesca – often called La Cecchina, a diminutive of her given name – continued to draw particular praise: the king called her "the best singer ever heard in France."[3] Francesca was now a star in her own right, though her path forward was not yet entirely hers to determine (see Figure 14.1). She was offered a salaried position at the French court: Giulio rebuffed it, perhaps due to his ties to the Medici or because he hoped for an even better arrangement. The following year, Giulio attempted to negotiate a position for Francesca in the Roman household of Margherita della Somaglia-Peretti, the sister-in-law to an important cardinal. That position would have provided Francesca with both a dowry and a stipend, potentially setting her up for a secure, and more conventional future, but Giulio rejected it too, and Francesca remained in Florence. It proved a pivotal juncture, however, for back in her native city, her professional career was taking off. Officially listed on the grand-ducal rolls as a salaried *musica* or professional musician, Francesca was earning a regular stipend and stood on the threshold of what one biographer describes as "the most fully professional, productive career any European woman musician had yet known."[4]

Francesca was lauded for her spectacular vocal skills – the breath control, trills, and *passaggi* or transitions that were the hallmark of a *virtuosa* singer. Her admirer Bronzini noted that "whether playing, singing or pleasantly talking, she worked such stunning effects in the minds of her listeners that she changed them from what they had been." As a Medici *musica*, she taught and coached other performers and began composing. She found important support among the Medici, forging one of the most significant relationships of her professional career with the grand duchess of Tuscany, Christine de Lorraine. The granddaughter of Henri II of France and the Florentine Caterina de' Medici, Christine had married the newly installed Ferdinando in 1589, upon the death – possibly murder – of the previous grand

Figure 14.1 Portrait of a Woman, by Palma Vecchio, believed to depict Francesca Caccini, c. 1518–1520

Musée Thysesen, Madrid

Photo: Alamy

duke, Francesco I. A great patron of the arts, the influential Christine perceived music and spectacle as tools through which to solidify her political authority (see Figure 14.2). This strategy became increasingly important as Ferdinando became infirm, leaving Christine the *de facto* ruler of Florence: her powerful role would endure through the reign of their son Cosimo II and, subsequently, her co-regency with Cosimo's widow, Maria Magdalena of Austria, which lasted from 1621 to 1628 and placed two women at the helm of one of Italy's major powers.

Figure 14.2 Christine of Lorraine, by Agostino Carracci, 1589
Photo: Alamy

In 1607, with Ferdinando already ill, Christine commissioned Francesca's first known work, *La stiava* (*The Slave*), composed as an entertainment for Carnival, the festivities preceding Lent. The text was scripted by another important figure in Francesca's life, Michelangelo Buonarroti the Younger, poet, librettist, and grandnephew to the artist of the same name. The well-connected Buonarroti had studied mathematics at the University of Pisa – where he met Galileo, also part of Christine's circle in Florence – and was a friend of the powerful Maffeo Barberini, later Pope Urban VIII. The plot of *La Stiava* – the first of several collaborations between Francesca and Buonarroti – centered on a Persian queen rescued from slavery by valorous Florentine knights, evoking the fraught history of Medici power and involvement in the Mediterranean slave trade.[5] The theme was in keeping with Christine's Islamophobia and expansionist Christian-political agenda and reflects the entanglement of Christian European anxieties about religious and racial difference. Still living at her father's house, Francesca composed the music in phases, completing it in less than a month. Though the music does not survive today, Buonarroti described it as "very beautiful" and the production itself – its elaborate costumes, mock battles, and solo and ensemble songs – is well documented. The role of the queen was sung by a man, signaling the growing interest in the use of *castrati* – castrated male singers prized for their unique voices – for opera. The elaborate production was intended, on the whole, to underscore the grand duchess's importance at the Medici court, as both a cultured patron and a political force.

In a reflection of Christine's interest in Francesca, she arranged in 1607 for her to be married to another Medici musician. Giovanni Battista Signorini (1573–1626) was a tenor who also taught music and coached performers, in addition to overseeing the Medici collection of musical instruments. They wed in November of that year in a ceremony in the Caccini home and Giulio paid the first installment of Francesca's dowry, though he would later notoriously try to renege on Settimia's.

The arranged match was convenient for both parties, though more so for Giovanni, who lacked both social position and means. For Giovanni, a partnership with a rising star like Francesca promised financial stability even beyond the dowry she brought to the arrangement – in his will, he openly acknowledged that she was the principal earner in the family and ceded to her all oversight of their daughter and her education. Though Francesca was the primary breadwinner, marriage provided that most crucial component for early modern women: respectability. Particularly for female singers and musicians, whose public performances of intimate emotions were seen as self-exhibition, the question of virtue and honor remained vexed, and a husband provided protection against gossip or rumors of unchastity. Though Francesca's successful career as a musician and composer was remarkably devoid of the hostility or defamation that men launched at many other female performers, she certainly understood the razor's edge of female reputation. We sense a hint of just how deeply it concerned her in her attitude to her own daughter, Margherita Signorini (b. 1623), who would also become a sought-after singer in her mother's footsteps: yet, when the Medici later invited Margherita to perform publicly in a staged comedy, Francesca refused on her behalf, insisting that such exposure could ruin her daughter's prospects for either a good marriage or a respectable future as a nun.

By the 1620s, Francesca was the highest-paid musician at the grand-ducal court, with a stipend of twenty *scudi* per month (to her father's earned sixteen): a testament to her talent and to the status associated with composing, as well as to the central role that music and spectacle continued to play in projecting princely authority.[6] After her compositional debut with *La Stiava*, she went on to contribute music to at least a dozen other entertainments written with official court dramatists: these included Rinuccini's 1611 *La mascherata delle ninfe di Senna* (The Masquerade of the Nymphs of Seine), Ferdinando Saracinelli's 1615 *Ballo delle zingare* (Dance of the Romani Women), Jacopo Cicognini's 1622 religious play *Il martirio di Sant'Agata* (The Martyrdom of Saint Agatha), and Buonarroti's comedies *La Tancia* (Tancia) from 1611, *Il passatempo* (The Pastime) from 1614, and *La fiera* (The Beast), from 1619. But her most famous – and only surviving – opera is *La Liberazione di Ruggiero dall'isola di Alcina* (*The Liberation of Ruggiero from Alcina's Island*). A seventy-five-minute "comedic ballet" in four scenes with text by Saracinelli, it was commissioned by Archduchess Maria Magdalena of Austria – Christine's daughter-in-law and Francesca's other major patron – as part of the celebrations for a visit to Florence by Prince Władisław Sigismund of Poland in 1625.

Like Christine, Maria Magdalena saw the political value in spectacle, and the *Liberation* offered an impressive display. Performed at the Medici villa of Poggio Imperiale south of Florence, it featured sorceresses, enchantments, a noble knight, a dragon, and twenty-four horses performing a choreographed "ballet," as was the fashion at European courts.[7] Inspired by the best-selling chivalric romance, *Orlando furioso* (*The Frenzy of Orlando*), published by Ludovico Ariosto in its final form in 1532, the story, with its dynastic and military undertones, would have been immediately familiar to its audience. Ruggiero, a knight, is imprisoned by the enchantress Alcina, and Melissa, her virtuous counterpart, must free him with a magic ring so that he can return to battle and found a ruling house. Francesca's opera employs tonal contrast to underscore the identity, characteristics, and motivations of each character: impulsive Ruggiero, moderate Melissa, sensual Alcina. Written in the "modern style" pioneered by Claudio Monteverdi, it uses a form of *recitativo* and did not employ castrato singers. The oldest known opera by a woman, the *Liberation*, was also one of the first Italian operas to be performed abroad, in Poland, befitting the occasion that prompted its commission.

The score for the *Liberation* was published in Florence in 1625, not long after its performance. But the versatile Francesca also composed

Figure 14.3 Fresco by Niccolò dell'Abate (sixteenth century), depicting Ruggiero in a scene from Ariosto's *Orlando furioso*

Pinacoteca Nazionale, Bologna, Italy/Mondadori

Portfolio/Electa/Bridgeman Images

hundreds of her own songs, many joined with her poetry. In 1618, she published her *Primo libro delle musiche* (*First Volume of Musical Compositions*), containing both sacred and secular vocal works, solos as well as duets for soprano and bass, styled as sonnets, madrigals, motets, canzonetti, and other poetic forms. While the first published book of music by a woman in the Western tradition was a collection of madrigals by the Venetian singer and lutenist Maddalena Casulana, printed in 1586, Francesca's volume, likely intended for pedagogical use, is among the largest and most complex of the era. Though she dedicated it to a Medici patron, Cardinal Carlo de' Medici, Francesca wanted it to serve as an acknowledgment of her father and his role in her professional training. In a letter to Buonarroti, she confided:

> If possible, I should like to name my father where I praise the virtuosi of Florence, in such a way that he would be honored by it, to speak of him as the master of the others, because I would not have it appear that I wished to depend on him through pride, but to acknowledge him as a master.[8]

Giulio died just months after its publication, but the volume offers insight not only into his influence on Francesca but also into her own approach to teaching music, which included furnishing extensive notation for vocal ornamentation. Musicologists note that the *Primo libro* serves as both an important record of Francesca's methods and an important source in the history of the *romanesca*, a harmonic-melodic formula used for sung poetry and instrumental variation that reached the height of its popularity in this era and features prominently in Francesca's collection.

Her husband's death in 1626 – just a year after the triumphant debut of her *Liberation* – was once considered the end of Francesca's musical career, due to a dearth of information about her activities after this point. Recent archival discoveries, however, reveal that this period signaled instead a new beginning, one that led her to the city of Lucca for the later part of the decade, before returning her to Florence again in the 1630s.[9] By 1627, in fact, Francesca was living in Lucca with her daughter and had remarried. Her second husband, Tommaso Raffaelli (d. 1630), three decades her senior, was a musician and music patron himself, deeply involved with the musical academies in Lucca, including the Accademia degli Oscuri (Academy of the Hidden) that included many Lucchese nobles. He appears to have valued and admired his bride's talent and likely enlisted her to put together new performances for the academy's 1628–1629 musical season. From aristocratic stock, Tommaso offered Francesca something her first marriage had not: a chance to ascend the ladder of social mobility. They had one son together and, when Tommaso died soon after, he left everything to Francesca, including a palazzo, a country villa, olive groves, and woods that produced chestnut flour. It was a wealth of independent property and income that Francesca had never known. Between 1630 and 1633, Lucca and other parts of Tuscany were hit by a severe outbreak of the plague and issued strict regulations on the movements and

Figure 14.4 Title page of Francesca Caccini, *Il primo libro delle musiche a una e due voci*, featuring Medici coat of arms (Florence: Zanobi Pignoni, 1618)

Photo: Biblioteca estense universitaria

[open access]

gatherings of its inhabitants in an effort to contain disease. There is no record of musical activity in this period by Francesca who, like other residents, was largely confined to her residence. But by 1634, she was back in Florence with her thirteen-year-old daughter Margherita and again on the Medici payroll. Despite her newfound economic security and social status as Tommaso's widow, Francesca's musical calling was as strong as ever – as were her Florentine roots.

With Ferdinando II (r. 1621–1670) now in power, Francesca reestablished her connections to the powerful Medici women. Still an influential force, the dowager grand duchess Christine moved primarily between her villa of La Quiete and the Florentine convent of Santa Croce, known as La Crocetta, in the center of town. Convents were home to many early modern noblewomen, not just those who professed vows: daughters were often sent to live in such women's communities until marriage; widows retreated there after losing husbands. Noble families often gravitated to the wealthiest convents, with the result that small groups of female relatives gathered within their walls, creating a kind of parallel world to that of the court. This was true of La Crocetta, where Christine's own daughters had resided, along with the young Medici princess Anna de' Medici and the future grand duchess Vittoria della Rovere. Life at La Crocetta bore little resemblance to the austerity associated with many convents: the ladies kept servants, entertained visitors, and enjoyed their customary rich clothing and jewels, instead of the simple habits of nuns. Music was an important part of life at La Crocetta, with frequent performances of spiritual comedies and other entertainments.[10] Living in nearby Borgo Pinti, Francesca obtained special papal license to visit freely with Margherita, who was also in demand as a singer. Mother and daughter would have performed privately for the convent's inhabitants and most likely taught music to the princesses. Francesca's professional musical career had again entered a new phase: one played out not in the semi-public spaces of elaborate court spectacle but, instead, in the semi-private, exclusively female spaces of Florence's most selective convent.

As the widow of a Lucchese nobleman and the mother of a noble son, Francesca was now a lady of some rank and determined to make provisions for her children's future accordingly. She was especially concerned with protecting her daughter's reputation and marriage prospects and continued to manage her estate in Lucca on behalf of her young son Tommaso (b. 1629). She also used her influence to advocate for other women: her letters, for example, show her fighting to protect her stepmother, Margherita, from eviction after Giulio's death. Her positive relationship with the Medici continued into the 1640s. Indeed, one of the final traces of her activity is a 1641 expression of support for her recorded by the secretary to Ferdinando II: "Francesca Caccini Raffaelli having long served us as a *musica*, to our extraordinary satisfaction and with particular fame for her singular value in that profession . . . lives under our protection."[11] There are indications that she planned to leave the service of the Medici later that year but, after that, her trail goes cold. She perhaps entered a convent or ended her days back in Lucca, with her son. Margherita never married and instead entered the convent of San Girolamo, professing vows and taking the name Suor Placida Maria; she lived there until her death in 1690, continuing in her mother's footsteps by singing, composing, and teaching. Tommaso sent his own daughter to board with Margherita for a period: named for their mother, Maria Francesca Raffaelli (1656–1733) also followed in Francesca's example and served as an attendant to Vittoria della Rovere who, like Christine before her, remained a political and cultural force long after the death of her husband, the grand duke, in 1670.

Prolific and influential, Francesca Caccini made her name at a critical moment in music history. Poised at the vibrant transition from the madrigals of the women's ensembles that flourished in the 1580s to the birth of opera, she composed the first known opera by a woman and created a rich body of work that paved the way for centuries of professional women in music. If female singers and composers faced suspicion and doubts about their social respectability and honor only decades earlier, Francesca's success and stature as the Medici's most esteemed *musica* showed that music could instead be a fulfilling and autonomous way of life. Today her music is widely performed and recorded, and her *Liberation of Ruggiero* has been revived across the globe.

15 Barbara Strozzi (1619–1677)

Trailblazing Composer

Had she been born in another era, surely she would have
have usurped or expanded the place of the muses.

– Gian Francesco Loredano

A passage in John Ruskin's *Stones of Venice*, the iconic nineteenth-century treatise on the city's art and architecture, lingers over a building in the Corte del Remer near the Rialto bridge. Ruskin's interest lay in the palazzo's graceful, pointed arches, but the small piazza where it stands hints at another important history: that of the multi-talented Barbara Strozzi, the most prolific and widely published female composer of secular vocal music of her day. Daughter of the poet and librettist Giulio Strozzi (1583–1652), Barbara lived in the Corte del Remer at the height of her musical activity. Several decades after Francesca Caccini made her mark on opera in Florence, Barbara Strozzi forged a remarkable career in this other major center of Renaissance music.

Her path was an unusual one for an early modern woman. Unmarried her whole life, she was educated by her father and trained in music; by her teens, Barbara was already enmeshed in Venice's flourishing musical and intellectual culture. Neither wife, nun, nor courtesan, Barbara dedicated her life first to performing and then to composing. She was one of few women known to have done so, her most significant predecessor being her near-contemporary Caccini. Though Venice is known as the birthplace of public opera – inaugurated at the Teatro San Cassiano in 1637 – Barbara composed in the more intimate genre of chamber music: chiefly cantatas and arias, standalone pieces for soloists, though she was remarkably flexible and wide-ranging in her activity. Defying historical trends for women, she composed mostly

DOI: 10.4324/9781003081807-19

secular music, but, even more remarkably, she pursued a strategic and extensive program of publication, ultimately ushering eight volumes of her compositions into print. In this respect, no other woman composer of the era – and few men – can rival her; in fact, her prolific output eclipses most Renaissance authors writing in any genre (among women writers, only Laura Terracina and Lucrezia Marinella compare). Barbara's outsized talent and independent, entrepreneurial spirit were buoyed by Venice's distinctive editorial market, academies, and innovative musical culture.

But as with many other female artists and musicians, early family support helped lay the groundwork for Barbara's future career. Though the circumstances of her birth are not entirely clear, Barbara was the daughter of Giulio Strozzi and his long-time servant, Isabella Garzoni (d. 1653), called La Griega or La Greghetta ("the little Greek," likely for her Greek origins). Such "informal marriages" – sometimes called concubinage and complicated by questions of gender, power, and consent – were common in Venice: Barbara herself was likely later part of such an arrangement. Giulio's 1628 will designated Isabella as his sole beneficiary, stating that her daughter should inherit in the event of Isabella's death. But a later version, dated to 1650, was revised to name as his heir "Barbara of Santa Sofia" – for the parish where she was baptized – explicitly claiming her as "my chosen [*elettiva*] daughter, called La Strozzi," though here he may also mean "adoptive."[1] The will indicates not only Giulio's acknowledgment of Barbara, to whom he entrusted his modest "Venetian effects," but also the fact that by this time she had taken – and was known by – his surname. Had he not done do, perhaps Barbara would have made her way instead in one of Venice's *ospedali*, institutions that provided refuge and education for orphans and others in need and were renowned for training women to perform sacred music.

Giulio was a central figure in the world of early modern opera. Born in Venice as an illegitimate son of the noble Strozzi family from Florence, he was immersed in Venetian musical life, providing librettos for most major composers working in opera in these early days of its development, including Francesco Manelli and Francesco Sacrati. He was also the author of a 1621 epic poem in praise of the city, entitled *Venetia edificata* (*Venice Edified*), which narrated its early history and incorporated praise of Galileo Galilei, just over a decade before the scientist's trial by the Roman Inquisition. His celebration of Venice continued in his librettos, most notably those for Sacrati's *La finta pazza* (*The Fake Madwoman*), one of the most popular operas of the century that in 1641 premiered at the Teatro Novissimo, the first building in Venice created specifically for opera performance. A supporter of female musicians, Giulio helped publish a work in praise of the production's star, the celebrated Roman diva Anna Renzi, printed in 1644.

Alongside his musical undertakings, Giulio was closely involved in Venice's literary culture, and the creative environment of the Strozzi household – a magnet for musicians, singers, composers, and writers – shaped Barbara's early life. Giulio nurtured her talent from an early age: she trained with the opera composer Francesco Cavalli and, by fifteen, was performing informally for gatherings at the Strozzi home. Her virtuosic soprano voice, flexible and capable of rapid and technically demanding passage work, drew such acclaim that, in 1635 and 1636, the composer Nicolò Fontei dedicated two volumes of solo songs to her – perhaps encouraged by Giulio, who provided many of the texts and was always ambitious for his daughter's success. Barbara has been sometimes identified in a portrait from these years by the artist Bernardo Strozzi (no relation), who also painted Claudio Monteverdi, as well as Giulio himself, and clearly presents his subject as a musician. Lightly grasping a *viola da gamba* in one hand – a bowed, stringed instrument played against the leg – with the other arm resting next to an open book of music, the figure faces the viewer (see Figure 15.1). The sensuality of the portrait, which depicts the sitter with tousled hair, deep decolletage, and a frank, direct gaze, has long sparked debate as to whether Giulio marketed his daughter not only as a *virtuosa* singer but also as a courtesan, the cultured, élite class of prostitute for which Venice was famous. Yet some musicologists point out that the portrait just as readily evokes representations of the Catholic virtue of *caritas* (charity), or of the virgin martyr Cecilia, patron saint of music.[2]

What is evident, however, is that Barbara, a teenager at the time of this portrait, was the target of accusations of unchastity: accusations that were seemingly inevitable for any woman, especially if unmarried, who dared assume a public role in early modern Italy, whether writing, singing, or composing. In a manuscript dating to these years, one anonymous satirist sneered to Giulio that it was a "fine thing to distribute the flowers after having surrendered the fruit," linking Barbara's musical performances ("the flowers") with her presumed sexually accessibility ("the fruit"); another insinuated that she had avoided becoming pregnant only because she was involved with a *castrato*,

Figure 15.1 The Viola da Gamba Player, believed to depict Barbara Strozzi, by
Bernardo Strozzi, c. 1630–1640

(Gemäldegalerie, Dresden)

Photo: Alamy

one of the castrated men valued for their high singing voices in early
modern Italy.[3] Such sexual innuendo was common currency among
Venetian litterati. Giulio may have seen the attention as added public-
ity for his daughter's musical talents, which he was keen to promote
– but Barbara, its target, surely felt differently.

Thanks to his association with several academies, from the Roman
Ordinati (Academy of the Orderly) – which also included the well-
known epic poet Margherita Sarrocchi – to Venice's influential and
iconoclastic Incogniti (Academy of the Unknown), Giulio understood
how such circles worked and knew their power to advance careers
as well as ideas. In the early 1630s, having survived a devastating

outbreak of the plague in Venice, he founded a spinoff of the Incogniti called the Accademia degli Unisoni (Academy of the Like-Minded), punning on the musical term "unison." The society provided, in part, a platform to showcase Barbara's creative talents and help launch her professional future. A 1638 work commemorating some of the activities of the academy, the *Veglie de' signori Unisoni* (*Gatherings of the Unisoni Members*), was dedicated to Barbara and attests to her role as unofficial host, judge, and performer at Unisoni meetings – which hosted a veritable who's who of Venetian culture, including Monteverdi, by then in his early seventies. The volume recounts, for example, Barbara's eloquent intervention in a comparison between "tears and song," in which the Unisoni debated the more powerful weapon in love: tears, because they are natural, or song, because it is artful. Perhaps unsurprisingly, Barbara supported the prevailing view that art, which improves on nature, must be the winner.

In attendance at the Unisoni gatherings were several members of the Incogniti, like Giovan Francesco Loredano, a leading figure in Venice's editorial landscape. The Incogniti, who ascribed to a libertine, anticlerical philosophy and were influenced by the elaborate style of the Baroque poet Giovan Battista Marino, had overlapping musical interests: many Incogniti, in fact, provided the *invenzioni* or plots or for the librettos that fueled the Venetian opera scene. Though their own attitudes toward and writings about women were often openly misogynistic, some of them also had a particular interest in promoting writers, including women, who shared their anti-establishment ethos. Arcangela Tarabotti – the polemical nun who wrote outspoken works that castigated fathers, church officials, and the Venetian state itself for their institutionalized abuse of women – was a particular favorite of Loredano, who took a similar interest in Barbara. In a published letter, he exclaims to a friend that had Barbara "been born in another era, surely she would have usurped or expanded the place of the muses."[4] Along with Giulio, the well-connected Loredano – king of the Venetian publishing scene – may have encouraged the 1644 publication of Barbara's first book of music, *Il primo libro de' madrigali* (*First Book of Madrigals*, referred to as Opus 1): it was the first of eight, marking the launch of Barbara's career as a professional composer, as well as her extraordinary publishing campaign (see Figure 15.2).

Like the feminist work published that same year by Loredano's other protégée Tarabotti, Barbara's Opus 1 was dedicated to Vittoria della Rovere, the grand duchess of Tuscany, suggested to both women

Figure 15.2 Title page of Barbara Strozzi's *Il primo libro de'madrigali* (Venice: Alessandro Vincenti, 1644)

by Francesco Zati, the Tuscan Resident in Venice from 1642 to 1652.[5] Known for her interest in music and previous support of women like Francesca Caccini and for her patronage of female convents, Vittoria was a strategic choice. Her approval promised recognition, respectability, protection, and the possibility of future commissions (she may, in fact, have inspired the subsequent dedication of Barbara's later Opus 5 to Vittoria's sister-in-law, Anna of Innsbruck, in 1656). Barbara's dedication to Vittoria employs common literary tropes of female modesty. She claims hesitancy to publish and seeks the protection of the powerful grand duchess to stave off the criticism she fears must follow: "I must reverently consecrate the first work which I, as a woman, publish all too boldly, to your most august name, so that under a golden oak it may remain sheltered from the lightning bolts of slander that await it"[6] (see Figure 15.3). Though less explicitly feminist than some of the more polemical works of the era, like those of Tarabotti or the Venetian writer Lucrezia Marinella, Opus 1 nonetheless situates itself squarely within the debate over women that was fashionable in seventeenth-century Venice. With this publication, Barbara hopes to gain recognition as a "new Sappho" and to establish her own authority as a professional composer.

While Barbara's fame to this point revolved largely around her reputation as a singer, following the publication of Opus 1, she began to gain recognition as a composer of chamber music. She continued to seek out influential patrons through her printed dedications (though

Figure 15.3 Portrait of Vittoria della Rovere, by Justus Sustermans, c. 1640–1645

(Villa medicea di Poggio a Caiano)

Photo: Alamy

it is unclear how useful they proved), from the Holy Roman Emperor Ferdinand II, dedicatee of Opus 2, to Nicolò Sagredo, the later doge of Venice, dedicatee of Opus 7. All in all, she would publish over one hundred compositions, primarily cantatas and arias, across multiple volumes, distinguishing herself also for her unique focus on preserving her own works in monographic publications – to a degree that surpassed her male counterparts. As Barbara's fame increased, she became progressively more self-assured. By the dedication to her fifth volume, published in 1655, she took a far more confident tone, claiming to be no longer "held back by feminine weakness than by any allowance made for my sex," and to "fly on lightest leaves, in devotion, to bow before you."[7] If Giulio had been involved in the publication of Barbara's first two collections, she continued to publish at a quick pace even after his death in 1652: her final work, *Arie (Arias*, Opus 8), appeared in 1664. Today, only Opus 4, thought to have been composed between 1654 and 1655, has been lost. By 1656, Barbara's compositions were also anthologized alongside those of male composers like her former teacher, Cavalli, in two printed collections.[8]

Historians of music describe Barbara's music as "singer's music," meant to advertise vocal talent, and observe that she likely performed much of it, though she herself notes that certain compositions were written with particular other singers in mind. Her pieces, most written for solo soprano, showcase the female voice, and most take love as a theme: desire, jealousy, delight, despair, and – allusively – sex. Set to Baroque texts that, in the tradition of Marino, often highlight small, sensual details – such as "Canto di bella bocca" ("Song for a Beautiful Mouth"), a duet from Opus 1, or "Begl'occhi" ("Beautiful Eyes") from Opus 2, which celebrates sparkling eyes, snowy breasts, golden hair, and coral lips – her music is by turns light and playful, dramatic and erotic. Though her subject matter at times purports to denounce women as sirens and temptresses – recalling the characterizations of Barbara's own critics and even her admirer Fontei, who compared the allure of her performance to the siren faced by Ulysses – her brilliant, often witty, musical ornamentation positioned her as a commanding musical presence. A standout among her many compositions, often cited as evidence of her uniquely intense and dramatic style, is her lament "Lagrime mie" ("My Tears") from the 1659 *Diporti di Euterpe (Euterpe's Amusements*, Opus 7). Combining a profound understanding of vocal technique with a powerful, unsettling evocation of anguish, the piece is set to a text that describes a lover's despair over his beloved, who has been imprisoned by her father; it opens with a virtuosic showcase of the soprano voice that flows through her vocal range and features trills that mimic tears.

Atypically for the era, Barbara's compositions are overwhelmingly secular and even include some narrative pieces, such as the one in both Opus 2 and Opus 3 based on Henri Coiffier de Ruzé, the French marquis of Cinq-Mars executed for treason in 1642. She published only one volume of sacred music, the *Sacri musicali affetti* (*Sacred Musical Sentiments*, Opus 5), but here too her music is sensual, intense, and lush – so much so that it was probably not designed to be performed in churches. In fact, Barbara did not perform in any of the public spaces for music in seventeenth-century Venice, like its opera houses. She preferred to limit herself to chamber music and the intimate private settings where it was usually performed, reserving her forays into the public sphere for print.

Like Gaspara Stampa, the poet and virtuosa active in Venice in the previous century who was also praised as a "new Sappho," Barbara – who may have composed poetry herself – eschewed more conventional paths for women to pursue her artistic vocation. However, she was involved for several years – and had four children with – Giovanni Paolo Vidman, a friend of her father's since at least 1638 and the dedicatee of his most famous libretto, written for *La finta pazza* in that period. The nature of their relationship is murky: one contemporary refers, in disconcertingly offhanded fashion, to Giovanni Paolo having raped Barbara, a comment seemingly at odds with the length and seriousness of their relationship. The letter-writer – unconcerned on this point – states only that Barbara was "celebrated as a singer, and also as a poet. . . . She was raped by the Count Vildman [*sic*], a Venetian nobleman."[9] Yet some early modern relationships did come about after rape, a consequence of oppressive gender norms governing female virginity that could leave a woman with no choice but to remain linked to her victimizer in an effort to recoup her reputation (as in the well-known case of the artist Artemisia Gentileschi), and long-term "concubinage" relationships, like that between Barbara's own parents, were not uncommon.

Whether the relationship was consensual or not, Giovanni Paolo appears to have made provisions for his children with Barbara before his death in 1648, despite being married to another woman, Camilla Grotta. Their son, Giulio Pietro, was born in 1641, and retained links to the Vidman family until the time of his death in 1719. Their daughters, Laura and Isabella, born in 1642 and 1643, entered the convent of San

Sepolcro in 1656; Isabella died soon after, but Laura took the name Suor Lodovica and professed vows in 1661. The legitimate Vidman daughters were cloistered in the wealthier convent of San Daniele, but it is interesting to note that Camilla – not Barbara – paid the spiritual dowries, or entrance fees, of Barbara's girls, citing her motive as "simple charity."[10] Barbara herself continued to rent a house from Giovanni Paolo's brother, Lodovico Vidman, in the Corte del Remer, suggesting an ongoing relationship with the wealthy family. Sometime in the spring of 1677 – some twenty years later – Barbara traveled to Padua, where she died after a three-month illness. She was buried in the Chiesa degli Eremitani, home to Andrea Mantegna's Ovetari Chapel frescoes.

The story of Barbara's composing career is one of paradoxes. She composed chamber music in a time and place in which opera reigned; she wrote sensual, erotic music that often appears on the surface to present women as sirens and objects of desire but gave voice to a strong feminist ethos through the composer's powerful creative agency. She was more prolific and published more works than many other composers – certainly more than any woman composer – of her day, and yet she did not perform in public. Today, by contrast, her music takes center stage, performed all over the world and preserved in dozens of recordings. She has been the subject of several fictionalized representations and even has a website and a dedicated Facebook account in her name with thousands of followers determined to keep her story alive. A proponent of the *seconda prattica* or "second practice" put forth by Monteverdi – the Baroque vocal style in which the expressive text dominates the music – and the composer credited by some for the development of the cantata genre, Barbara Strozzi defied early modern gender constraints to create dramatic, complex works that left an enduring stamp on the world of music. By pursuing an organized and deliberate program of publication, she not only made her name as a major musical voice in early modern Venice but also ensured that it would endure long into the future – and with it, the legacy of women in music history.

Part Four

Artists and Scientists

16 Sofonisba Anguissola (c. 1532–1625)

Portraitist to Kings

Sofonisba of Cremona . . . has worked at the complexities of design with more skill and better grace than any other woman of our time, for not only does she know how to draw, color, and copy from nature . . . but she has executed, by her own hand, very precious and beautiful works of painting.

– Giorgio Vasari

In the *Libro del Cortegiano* (*Book of the Courtier*) – an idealized guide to Renaissance court life – Baldassare Castiglione notes that a *donna di palazzo* or "woman of the court" should have some knowledge of literature, music, and painting. For Castiglione, such an education enhanced the court lady's role as a hostess, so that "in her talk, her laughter, her play, her jesting, in short, in everything," she could be "very graceful" and entertain "appropriately, and with witticisms and pleasantries befitting her."[1] He thus praised a "modestly employed" acquaintance with painting for women, for the primary purpose of fostering a refined, amusing atmosphere. Yet the case of Sofonisba Anguissola, a salaried court portraitist and one of the most important artists of the Renaissance, demonstrates that Renaissance women could and did go well beyond Castiglione's limited recommendation, forging enormously influential careers in art as well as in music, literature, and other areas. Sofonisba's talent was widely recognized in her own time, and today she is considered one of the most significant painters of the sixteenth century. Prized by high-ranking patrons in Italy and beyond, she was sought out as a teacher by men and women alike.[2]

Hurdles to pursuing art as a profession were numerous and daunting for early modern women. On top of navigating concerns about the appropriate form and extent of education for women, women were largely excluded from the typical practices and venues of art

DOI: 10.4324/9781003081807-21

instruction like apprenticeship and working from nude models. The lack of opportunity to obtain broad technical experience made it more difficult for women to attain expertise in large-scale religious or historical narratives – prestigious subject matter that promised the most lucrative commissions, but which also required a deep knowledge of both anatomy and composition. As a result, women artists often turned to domestic subjects more readily accessible to them. This much was true of Sofonisba's early career. Yet, in other key respects, Sofonisba forged an entirely new path for female artists, training outside the home with two prestigious male painters in Cremona before embarking on a career on the roster of Philip II of Spain. Beyond her gift for portraying others, Sofonisba was also one of the most prolific and innovative self-portraitists before Rembrandt, who made the self-study a central part of his oeuvre.

The eldest of seven, Sofonisba was born in the prosperous city of Cremona in northern Italy. Famous for its textiles and, later, as the birthplace of the violin-maker Antonio Stradivari, Cremona came under Spanish rule in the 1530s after years of struggle for dominance between Spain and France, when Sofonisba was still a girl. The Anguissola family traced its noble origins back to Byzantium: the surname Anguissola derived from the asp pictured on an ancestor's shield. They lived in the Via Pellegrino Tibaldi, near the site of an ancient battle between the Romans and Carthaginians, a heritage echoed in the children's names: Sofonisba was named for the ancient noblewoman of Carthage who poisoned herself to protest the Roman victory, and her brother, Asdrubale (1551–1623), for a Carthaginian general, Hasdrubal Barca. Sofonisba's sister Minerva (b. 1548/49), was a writer and scholar, while the others – Elena (c. 1534/5–1584), Lucia (1536/38–c. 1565), Europa (1542/43–1572), and Anna Maria (1555/58–1611) – also studied painting, though they did not achieve Sofonisba's fame.

Amilcare Anguissola (b. 1494) – a devout, civic-minded Cremona native and largely unsuccessful entrepreneur – and his wife Bianca Ponzone, the daughter of a count, saw to it that Sofonisba and her siblings studied Latin, Greek, music, literature, and art. For Sofonisba and her sisters – as was true of other Renaissance artists and writers – this familial support was essential, for it allowed them to enrich and expand their potential through an education not always available to women otherwise. Even more importantly, recognizing Sofonisba's talent from a young age, Amilcare took the unusual step of allowing her to apprentice with a local painter. Though apprenticeship was a conventional path for men to acquire artistic training and connections, it was highly unusual for women, who were bound by social norms governing feminine virtue and respectability. To paint from life or train professionally outside the home was deemed unnecessary to a future as a wife and mother, and even disreputable. Female artists were far more likely to apprentice informally, with a family member, and draw inspiration from the domestic world around them.

The Anguissola family saw beyond such strictures – perhaps Amilcare, whose economic fortunes were declining in these years, saw in his talented daughter a solution to the family's increasing impoverishment. Regardless of his motivation, Sofonisba and her sister Elena apprenticed for three years with Benardino Campi, a young Cremonese artist known for his portraits and religious paintings in the naturalistic Lombard tradition, developing the fundamental principles of *disegno* (design) and composition. When Campi left Cremona for Milan, Sofonisba took on the task of tutoring her sisters in painting. By 1550, she had entered the workshop of Bernardino Gatti (known as Il Sojaro), who was a former student of the Parma master Correggio and who produced frescoes for the Cathedral of Cremona and other churches in the region. Gatti mentored her for several years.

Sofonisba's early double portrait from the late 1550s, *Bernardino Campi Painting Sofonisba Anguissola*, attests to her regard for her first teacher's mentorship but also demonstrates that the student had eclipsed the teacher (see Figure 16.1). Revealing Sofonisba's capacity for vividly naturalistic portraiture – as well as her particular interest in self-portraiture – it depicts Campi positioned before an easel, upon which rests a canvas bearing Sofonisba's own likeness. While the image could be interpreted as a gesture of acknowledgment – a recognition of Sofonisba as Campi's "creation," as one contemporary described her – subtle elements in this portrait-within-a-portrait point to a more complex array of meanings.[3]

First, though the painting presents "Sofonisba" or, rather, her semblance, as the "object" of the painting and the focus of Campi's gaze, it is, in actuality, Sofonisba herself who is doing the painting – calling into question the relationship between subject and object and, more broadly, on the objectification of women in artistic representation. Campi, meanwhile, gazes back over his shoulder at the artist and the viewer, who is thus drawn into this destabilization of artistic convention. Along with a paintbrush, Campi wields a mahlstick, a steadying instrument associated with less mature artists that Sofonisba depicted

Figure 16.1 Bernardino Campi Painting Sofonisba Anguissola, by Sofonisba
Anguissola, c.1559

(Pinacoteca Nazionale, Siena)

Photo: Alamy

herself holding in some of her earlier self-portraits, another suggestion
that the student has overtaken the teacher. A 1996 restoration of this
painting revealed under layers of paint a *pentimento,* a visible correc-
tion made by the artist, showing "Sofonisba" wearing a red-and-gold
gown later toned down into a sober black garment and reaching out to
take the brush from her former teacher's hand. The image of Sofonisba
that rests on Campi's easel is larger than he is, suggesting her dominance, and at the same time less compellingly rendered, again implying that he has been surpassed by his protegée.[4] The double portrait is
thus not only visually stunning but also replete with complexities of
meaning regarding the place of the woman artist, a strikingly modern
and self-referential commentary on art and subjectivity.

Figure 16.2 Boy Bitten by a Crawfish, by Sofonisba Anguissola, c. 1554

(National Museum of Capodimonte, Naples)

Photo: Alamy

Following these early apprenticeships, Sofonisba traveled to Rome in 1554 to sketch and paint. An anecdote from this period recounts her meeting with the great Michelangelo Buonarroti, then at work designing the dome of Saint Peter's Basilica. After seeing a drawing that Sofonisba had made of a smiling girl, Michelangelo, recognizing her talent, challenged her to produce a more difficult subject: a weeping boy. Sofonisba promptly drew her brother, Asdrubale, as the *Boy Bitten by a Crawfish*: an image depicting both a weeping boy *and* a smiling girl (see Figure 16.2). The sketch brims with life, humor, and energy. A friend of Michelangelo's was so impressed that he later sent it as a gift to the grand duke of Florence Cosimo I de' Medici, with a note that explained, "I believe that it may stand comparison with many other drawings, for it is not simply beautiful, but also exhibits considerable invention."[5] Years later, the drawing would catch the attention of the Baroque master Caravaggio, inspiring his 1597 painting, *Boy Bitten by a Lizard*. Michelangelo continued to take an interest in Sofonisba, maintaining contact with the Anguissola family after she had returned to Cremona and occasionally sending sketches for her to work from. In a letter of May 1557, Amilcare Anguissola asked Michelangelo to send Sofonisba a drawing "that she may color it in oil, with the obligation to return it to you faithfully finished by her own hand." Amilcare added his profound thanks to the great artist for "the honorable and thoughtful affection" he had shown Sofonisba, whom Amilcare himself had always "encouraged to practice the most honorable art of painting."[6] The following year, Amilcare again expressed delight that Michelangelo, "such an excellent gentleman, the most virtuous above all others, deigns to praise and judge the paintings done by my daughter Sofonisba."

Sofonisba often painted her parents, siblings, and other members of the household – and herself. Vibrantly lifelike, her self-portraits are also typically austere, conveying a consistent, deliberate image of feminine modesty and decorum to the viewer. She frequently portrays herself as dressed in dark clothing, at once elegant and demure. Sofonisba was renowned for her expert handling of fabric and texture: a simple velvet jacket, framed by a high-necked white lace collar, is so richly rendered that one can almost feel it. Her hair is pulled back from her face in a plain but flattering braid, and she wears few or no jewels, though she skillfully painted other subjects adorned in them. Her distinctive eyes are arresting and wide set, fixing the viewer in their steady gaze, and in her signature she often adopts the Latin term *virgo*, "virgin" or "unmarried maiden," as if to underscore her feminine purity and honor even as she boldly claims the public space of self-portraiture as her own. In a self-portrait dating to 1554, for example, she holds a small book clearly inscribed with her signature: "The virgin Sofonisba Anguissola made this with her own hand" (see Figure 16.3). Sofonisba also used religious imagery to invoke such associations. In another self-portrait dating to 1556, she depicts herself in the act of painting the Madonna and Christ child, thus underscoring her feminine piety together with her painterly skill.

Sofonisba also made important contributions to genre painting – portrayals of everyday life – a style that would come into vogue much later. She produced a number of lively, natural depictions of quotidian scenes inspired by her family, which eventually caught the attention of artist and historian Giorgio Vasari, who included only one woman, Properzia de' Rossi, in the 1550 edition of his famous *Le vite de'più*

Figure 16.3 Self-Portrait, by Sofonisba Anguissola, 1554

(Kunsthistorisches Museum, Vienna)

Photo: Alamy

eccellenti pittori, scultori e architettori (*The Lives of the Most Excellent Painters, Sculptors, and Architects*) but several more in his 1568 edition, among them Sofonisba. In a visit to the Anguissola home in 1556, Vasari took note of one painting of the family in particular, pronouncing that the figures it displayed were "truly alive" and "wanting in nothing save speech." This was *The Chess Game* from 1555 (shown in the Introduction to this volume), a vivid and delightful picture in which Sofonisba depicted her younger sisters at play; it remains today one of her best representations of female friendship and most famous works.

Chess was a popular Renaissance pastime. The rules of the game had undergone significant changes in the late fifteenth century, resulting in a speedier game and, notably, the increased stature on the board of the queen, now more powerful than the king. Other paintings of the period also depict chess games, but only Sofonisba's shows it being played by a pair of women. Lucia, to the left, has won the game, and seems to share her triumph with the viewer (and the artist), while Europa raises a hand in submission. Meanwhile, Minerva, probably around seven years old here, offers the mischievous grin of a younger sister delighted by this good-natured competition. To the right, an older woman – perhaps a chaperone or servant – looks on with interest – or perhaps consternation at being drawn away from her other duties. Together, the chain of their gazes leads the viewer's own eye through the image, ultimately calling attention to the unseen artist recording the scene. It is a commentary on not only the intellectual achievement evident in a skillful game of chess but also the way in which the Anguissola sisters learned from and supported one another in terms of their artistic growth.[7] In some ways, this idyllic grouping of women, which places female friendship, alliance, and intellect at the fore, is evocative of the Edenic garden of women imagined a century later by the Venetian Moderata Fonte in her feminist treatise of 1600, *The Worth of Women*. Paintings such as *The Chess Game* or another evocative genre painting by Sofonisba from around 1559, *The Portrait of Minerva, Amilcare, and Asdrubale Anguissola*, offered intimate, psychologically complex explorations of Sofonisba's family and homelife. Such works were likely not intended for the market: as Vasari noted, they hung in the Anguissola home. It was only in the next phase of her career that Sofonisba turned to the official state portraiture that would further fuel her reputation.

Under imperial control, Sofonisba's hometown of Cremona abounded in Spanish influence. The Anguissola family had long-standing ties to the Spanish court, and the Duke of Alba, Fernando Álvarez de Toledo, who met Sofonisba in Milan in 1558 and admired her artistic skill, recommended her for a post in Madrid as lady-in-waiting to the teenaged third wife of Philip II, Isabel de Valois, sometimes called Elisabeth de France (1545–1568). The move marked a turning point in her career. During her fourteen-year residency in Spain, Sofonisba painted subjects ranging from Philip's wife, sister, and son to the king himself, and received an annual stipend.

Sofonisba's portraits of the royal court are animated by her signature gift for handling fabric and texture, the rich garments and jewels that adorn her subjects almost jumping off the canvas. Sofonisba also

Figure 16.4 Minerva, Amilcare, and Asdrubale Anguissola, by Sofonisba
     Anguissola, c. 1559

Nivaagards Malerisamling, Niva, Denmark/Bridgeman Images

reportedly tutored Isabel and her daughters, the Infanta Catalina (or
Catherine) Micaela (depicted clutching a pet marmoset) and Isabella
Clara Eugenia. Sofonisba worked closely with the painter Alonso
Sanchez Coello during this period – indeed, a portrait of Philip once
thought to be Coello's is now attributed to Sofonsiba – and her reputation continued to grow. She was now in great demand. In a letter to her
former tutor Campi, written from Madrid in 1561, Sofonisba explained

that she had just completed a portrait of the queen, and was occupied with making one of the king's sister for the pope: "Therefore, my dear teacher Bernardino," she wrote, "you can see that I am busy at painting." Archival records from this period abound with references to the "Cremonese woman who paints," and indicate that both the king and his wife held her in great esteem.[8]

When Isabel died following a miscarriage in October 1568, Sofonisba was devastated. The two women had grown close; after the queen's death, one observer noted, "Lady Sofonisba says she no longer wants to live." Wishing to recognize Sofonisba's long service, Philip took an interest in her future. He arranged an aristocratic marriage for her, which took place five years later, and provided her with a dowry. The groom was Fabrizio Moncada (c. 1535–1579), a Sicilian nobleman at the Spanish court. In certain respects, Sofonisba's trajectory resembles that of the singer Tarquinia Molza and, even more closely, the composer Francesca Caccini. Like these near contemporaries – artistic, self-sufficient Renaissance women – Sofonisba had risen to a salaried position at court, finding financial stability and moving up the ladder of both social and professional success through her proximity to a powerful monarch. As in Francesca's case, Sofonisba's powerful patrons secured for her a marriage they deemed advantageous, but, also as with Francesca, Sofonisba ultimately forged her own path, and it was her husband who benefitted disproportionately from the success of his professional wife. Soon after the wedding, Sofonisba and Fabrizio, who was then governor of Paternò (near Catania), returned to Sicily, but she continued to receive a royal pension, and to paint. By now, she was the primary financial support for her entire family: Amilcare was dead, and Asdrubale had squandered any inheritance he once had.

Within five years, Sofonisba's husband from this arranged marriage died when his ship was attacked by pirates near Capri, leaving her a widow at age forty-seven. She had no children to support, but Fabrizio had died without making a will; Asdrubale traveled to Sicily to assist in her subsequent inheritance dispute with his family. Though she planned to return to Cremona with Asdrubale, fate intervened. As Sofonisba journeyed by sea to her natal city, she fell in love with Orazio Lomellino, captain of one of the ships. Despite efforts to dissuade her from a union considered beneath the "quality of her house," Sofonisba was undeterred, responding that "marriages are first made in heaven and then on earth."[9] She and Orazio married quickly and settled in his native Genoa with Orazio's son from his first marriage,

Giulio Lomellino, who would become so close to his stepmother that he later named his daughter after her. Orazio supported his wife's painting career as she built new connections to the artistic community in Genoa over the next three decades. Sofonisba retained her ties to the Spanish court by hosting guests like Isabella Clara Eugenia, Isabel's daughter, and became a highly sought-after teacher, such that the painter Pietro Francesco Piola, who studied with her for many years, "could boast of having been the disciple of the most famous woman painter in Europe."

Around 1615, when Sofonisba was nearly eighty, Orazio's business interests prompted a final move to Palermo. There, Sofonisba continued to paint into her nineties, producing some devotional paintings in addition to her signature self-portraits (her last, in which she appears much older but still elegantly dressed in her customary black, dates to 1620). By now famous throughout Europe, Sofonisba received visitors like the Flemish painter and portraitist Anthony van Dyck, who sketched her likeness in July 1624. Believing her to be ninety-six years old at that point, though she was only ninety-two, he noted her continued mental acuity and steady hand despite her failing vision and declared that the useful guidance she offered made him understand that "she was a painter from nature and very skilled."[10] Van Dyck's subsequent portrait of Sofonisba is the last one made of her; she died in Sicily the following year.

Calling his wife "great among mortals," Orazio buried Sofonisba at the Church of San Giorgio dei Genovesi in Palermo. To mark what would have been her hundredth birthday seven years later, he commissioned an inscription for her tomb:

> To Sofonsiba, my wife, . . . who is recorded among the illustrious women of the world, outstanding in portraying the images of men. Orazio Lomellino, for the loss of his great love, in 1632, dedicated this small tribute to so great a woman.[11]

Today there are approximately thirty-five extant paintings attributed to Sofonisba, with dozens more whose attribution remains inconclusive, and her work hangs in major galleries across the globe, from Bergamo to Baltimore and from Milan to Madrid. Though only a portion of her works survive, Sofonisba's influence is undeniable. She produced more self-portraits – a prestige genre of the Renaissance – than most other European artists, male or female, of her day. She was admired by Michelangelo and her portrait depicting Isabel de Valois with a *zibellino*, or jeweled pelt, was among the most widely copied paintings in Spain, including by the famed Peter Paul Rubens. Vasari considered her one of the finest painters of her time.

Sofonisba's career opened the door for women artists to come: in 1570, the Bolognese Mannerist painter Lavinia Fontana noted that both she and Irene di Spilimbergo, another talented sixteenth-century Italian artist who studied under Titian, had "set [their] heart on learning how to paint" after seeing a portrait made by Sofonisba.[12] Along with these admirers, Sofonisba's artistic successors include Barabara Longhi, Fede Galizi, and Artemisia Gentileschi. Today she is exhibited across the world and has been featured in major exhibitions: in 1994 ("Sofonisba e le sue sorelle" ["Sofonisba and Her Sisters"] in Cremona), 2020 (at the Museo del Prado in Madrid, paired her with Lavinia Fontana), and, most recently, the 2022–2023 solo show "Sofonisba – History's Forgotten Miracle," a collaboration of the Danish Nivaagaards Collection and Rijksmuseum Twenthe. Sofonisba is also showcased regularly in exhibitions focusing more broadly on early modern women. Painter to kings, queens, and high-ranking patrons throughout Europe, Sofonisba forged an international and groundbreaking career.

17 Lavinia Fontana (1552–1614)

Pioneering Professional Artist

*Among those who shine today in painting is Lavinia Fontana, the great
wonder of nature: a noble painter, as unique in the world as a phoenix.*

– Giulio Cesare Croce

As Sofonisba Anguissola was making her name as court painter to the
king of Spain, Lavinia Fontana was launching a career in art from Bologna, home to the oldest university in the West. Art historians point to a
unique "Bolognese phenomenon" of early modern women artists that
was encouraged by the cultural climate of *La Dotta*, the Learned City:
a phenomenon that encompassed figures like Properzia de' Rossi, the
early sixteenth-century sculptor said to have taught herself by carving
peach stones. In fact, more women artists were active in Bologna –
where Saint Catherine de' Vigri, patroness of painting, was venerated –
from the fifteenth to the eighteenth centuries than in any other Italian
city, eclipsing even Rome, Venice, and Florence.[1] Artistic patronage in
Bologna – located in the heart of Italy's Emilia-Romagna region – was
also diverse, with collectors from a varied socioeconomic spectrum
that itself included many women.

Elsewhere in Italy, women artists were typically connected to either
court or convent. One of the first known female painters in Renaissance Florence, Plautilla Nelli, was a Dominican nun memorialized
in the 1568 edition of Giorgio Vasari's famous historical study, *Le vite
de' più eccellenti pittori, scultori e architettori* (*The Lives of the Most
Excellent Painters, Sculptors, and Architects*); while the patronage
of Philip II helped Sofonisba Anguissola vault to fame. In Bologna,
which did not have an élite court culture, Lavinia found by contrast
the conditions to forge an independent, autonomous career as a professional painter – a rarity for a woman artist in Italy. She worked

DOI: 10.4324/9781003081807-22

on commission, amassing an influential clientele in and beyond Bologna and competing with men for prize assignments. By the end of her career, she had produced a remarkable number of paintings – some 135 known works – ranging from portraits and altarpieces to the genre of mythological paintings that she pioneered for women artists.

Born to Prospero Fontana (1512–1597) and his wife, Antonia de Bonardis, of a respected publishing family, Lavinia was educated and accomplished. Little is known of her earliest years, but her father – a well-known Mannerist painter who worked alongside Vasari on the frescoes in Florence's Palazzo Vecchio – ran an art school in Bologna and provided Lavinia and her sister, Emilia, with the most common form of artistic training open to early modern women: working in the family studio. Lavinia received instruction from Prospero and his pupil Ludovico Carracci, an influential artist of late-sixteenth-century Italy. She also took advantage of her city's academic culture by enrolling at its university – open to women since the thirteenth century, when Bettisia Gozzadini studied and taught law there. In 1580, having also studied literature, mathematics, and music, Lavinia earned her degree. The Fontana family moved in well-connected circles that included scholars, nobles, bankers, and Church officials – networks that would prove invaluable as Lavinia launched a professional career. By her early twenties, she had begun taking on commissions, painting portraits for friends of her father at the University, like the humanist Carlo Sigonio (an associate of the *virtuosa* Tarquinia Molza), and the physician Girolamo Mercuriale. She depicted them with the tools of their trades: letters, papers, and a quill for Sigonio, pictured before his desk; an open anatomy book for the learned Mercuriale.

Self-composed and focused, Lavinia – like her near-peer Sofonisba – was highly attentive to her own self-presentation and produced several self-portraits. The earliest surviving example, made in 1577, shows a dark-haired young woman seated at the spinet, an instrument associated with female decorum and social position, in a pose in which Sofonisba had also depicted herself some two decades earlier. Prospero, who took an acute interest in his daughter's career, may have seen in the noble-born Sofonisba a successful model for female artists and actively encouraged Lavinia to follow her example by creating similar images. As in Sofonisba's painting, here too the artist/subject gazes steadily out at the viewer, radiating assurance. Her position at the spinet evokes both her feminine virtues – women of the élite class to which Lavinia aspired were expected to possess some musical skill – and her cultured background (see Figure 17.1). Where Sofonisba overwhelmingly tended

Figure 17.1 Self-Portrait at the Spinet, by Lavinia Fontana, 1577

(Accademia di San Luca, Rome)

Photo: Alamy

to depict herself in her customary modest black garments, however, Lavinia paints herself wearing red – the color of Bolognese brides – her bodice richly embroidered and studded with pearls, her face framed by a lace collar. A servant further symbolizing the sitter's status hovers in the background, bearing a book of music. The Latin inscription in the top corner of the canvas – again echoing Sofonisba's self-representation – underscores Lavinia's chastity, reading: "The *virgo* [virgin or unmarried maiden] Lavinia of Prospero Fontana has represented this likeness of her visage from the mirror in the year 1577."[2]

In fact, this self-portrait in bridal red was made for Lavinia's soon-to-be father-in-law, Severo Zappi, senator of Imola. In an unusual marital agreement, Prospero – who clearly recognized both the artistic and financial potential his talented daughter represented for the Fontana family's welfare – sought a husband who would be supportive of

Lavinia's career. He had found his ideal candidate in Severo's son, Gian Paolo Zappi (c. 1555–1615), a minor nobleman and artist who trained in Prospero's studio. This unconventional agreement, dated February 14, 1577, substituted the traditional dowry that most Renaissance marriage contracts required of the bride's family with Lavinia's potential future earnings from her art. It also stipulated that Gian Paolo move to Bologna and that the couple live in Prospero's house, turning over the income from Lavinia's commissions to support the Fontana family. They abided by the terms of the contract, with Gian Paolo taking on – again, unusually – the position of intermediary and agent for his wife and perhaps also assisting in the workshop. Occasionally, Lavinia signed her paintings with her husband's surname, adding "Zappi" to "Fontana." Gian Paolo also helped care for their family as it grew, for Lavinia was now a working mother who maintained an active professional career despite having eleven children at home, though only three would outlive her. All in all, by Renaissance standards, theirs was a modern marriage.

By the 1580s, Lavinia was specializing in portraits of Bolognese noblewomen, who served as some of her earliest and most loyal patrons. She had a naturalistic style and an exceptional gift for depicting the female form, whether alone or in complex groupings that ripple with the undercurrents of familial dynamics. In many cases she formed deep attachments with her subjects, apparently even naming her daughters after them – as in the case of Laudomia, recorded as born and baptized in 1588 following Lavinia's painting of Laudomia Gozzadini discussed later – and inviting them to serve as godmothers, as for Costanza, born in 1595 and named for Costanza Sforza Boncompagni, Duchess of Sora, whose portrait Lavinia had made the previous year.[3] Lavinia was unmatched in her ability to capture the richness of textiles in paint: the elaborate brocades and beadwork, lace, gold stitching, and gems that adorned her sitters' fashions and displayed their wealth and status. In her early painting, *Portrait of a Noblewoman* – completed around 1580, shortly after Lavinia's own marriage – she employs a rich, dark background to focus attention directly on the figure of the Bolognese bride, again dressed in traditional red. The artist renders the young woman's gown in minute detail: from the delicate pattern on her stiff overdress to the lustrous pearls that ornament her neck and hair. A marten pelt, another symbol of the sitter's high social status, hangs from a jeweled belt at her waist, while the little dog she caresses, a common feature of Lavinia's portraits, symbolizes marital fidelity and injects a warm playfulness into the composition.

Another important family group painting from this period was commissioned in 1584 by the noblewoman Laudomia Gozzadini, perhaps to assert the legitimacy and patrimonial rights of the two Gozzadini sisters, daughters of the late senator Ulisse Gozzadini (though Ginevra Gozzadini, on the left, was also deceased by this time). Rich in proto-feminist undertones, the imposing painting – measuring a life-size eight by seven feet – highlights the authoritative presence of the sisters over their spouses, who fade into the background in their dark garments. Laudomia, shown in the customary bridal red, was engaged in an inheritance dispute with her estranged husband and brother-in-law, the executors of Ulisse's estate. By depicting the women in their finery and opulent wedding jewelry and by underscoring their connection to their long-deceased father – also present in his senatorial robe – Lavinia cleverly reminds the viewer of her patron Laudomia's importance as Ulisse's daughter (see Figure 17.2). As in other portraits

Figure 17.2 The Gozzadini Family, by Lavinia Fontana, 1584

(Pinacoteca Nazionale, Bologna)

Photo: Alinari Archives/Art Resource

by Lavinia, both sisters gaze directly and confidently at the viewer, perhaps a reflection of the active role Bolognese women tended to play in society.

A final example from Lavinia's many portraits of noblewomen, dating to a later phase of her career, is her striking image of Bianca degli Utili Maselli in Rome, with six of her children. One of Lavinia's finest paintings, it exudes psychological depth and tenderness in its intimate and meticulous rendering of its subjects, from the distinctive auburn hair they share to their coordinated brocade outfits and dynamic expressions. The children whisper among themselves as their mother gazes out with an enigmatic expression, one hand on the shoulder of her daughter and the other holding Lavinia's signature lapdog. This portrait of a young mother with her children is made more poignant still, knowing that Bianca died shortly after its completion, between 1604 and 1605, following the birth of her nineteenth child (see Figure 17.3).

Along with pictures of noblewomen, Lavinia also produced more portraits of children than any other painter in Bologna of the period, inflected with flashes of insight into the experience of childhood,

Figure 17.3 Portrait of Bianca degli Utili Maselli and Her Children, by Lavinia Fontana, 1604–1605

Photo: Alamy

together with her customary exquisite attention to detail. Her portrait of the twelve-month-old Ippolita Savorgnani of 1583, for example, presents a serious, adult-looking child dressed in the opulent garments of her social class – but the way she clutches a small dog in her right arm evokes her youthful energy and impulsivity. Lavinia painted newborns swaddled in their cribs, as well as portraits of boys, again with beloved dogs or with books indicating their developing intellectual maturity. A standout among Lavinia's portraits of children is her rendering of Antonietta (Tognina) Gonzales, painted between 1594 and 1595, featuring a young girl who, along with her siblings, suffered from a condition that caused an excessive growth of hair all over the body (see Figure 17.4). A subject of intrusive curiosity, Antonietta resided at the court of Isabella Pallavicina, the marchesa of Soragna; Lavinia may

Figure 17.4 Portrait of Antonietta Gonzales, by Lavinia Fontana, c. 1583
Manuel Cohen/Art Resource, NY

have first encountered her in Parma.[4] Though it may seem unconventional, the portrait was in keeping with a broader Renaissance interest in the "marvelous" – and, more darkly, the "monstrous." The natural philosopher Ulisse Aldrovandi made a study of the Gonzales family for his *History of Monsters* published in 1642, and other artists, like Agostino Carracci, also painted them. Lavinia, however, who depicts her subject with sparkling, intelligent eyes and noble dress, holding a leaf of paper inscribed with a brief biography, imparts a particular sensitivity and warmth that highlights Antoinetta's humanity over her otherness. Regardless of her sitters' social position or difference, Lavinia's portraits display them in their individuality, complexity, and humanity, inviting the viewer to imagine their stories.

Though Lavinia first gained fame as a portraitist, renowned for her ability to capture both the materiality and interiority of her largely female clientele, she began to branch out into religious painting, traditionally the realm of men. Along with the intellectuals associated with its university, Bologna was home to the archbishop Gabriele Paleotti, a Counter-Reformation leader and author of the 1582 *Discorso intorno alle immagini sacre e profane* (*Discourse on Sacred and Profane Images*), which called upon art to perform a moral and didactic function. Paleotti was interested in promoting the visual arts as a tool for disseminating the teachings and values of the Catholic Church, and his support of Lavinia, whom he met through Prospero, paved the way for a critical stage in her professional career. In 1584, Paleotti commissioned Lavinia to paint an altarpiece for the city of Imola, the *Madonna of the Assumption of Ponte Santo*. She was the first woman to receive so public a religious commission, and other assignments followed. Among these was another from Paleotti in 1593 for the *Assumption of San Petronio*, for which she was paid a sum rivaling those commanded by the most famous male artists of the era, including Caravaggio. Lavinia's 1581 *Noli me tangere*, a tender, affective depiction of Mary Magdalene kneeling as she recognizes Christ after his resurrection, hangs today in Florence's Uffizi gallery: the painting was part of the collection of Don Antonio de' Medici, son of the grand duke of Tuscany. In 1589, Lavinia was commissioned by Philip II of Spain, patron of Sofonisba, to paint *The Holy Family with the Sleeping Christ Child*, an altarpiece for a church in Madrid that would extend her reputation well beyond Italy. Like her secular portraits, Lavinia's devotional paintings also display close attention to detail and profound psychological complexity.

Lavinia's religious paintings brought her new attention and powerful new patrons, including several popes. A major triumph came in 1600, a Jubilee year in which the Catholic Church offered special remission of sins, causing pilgrims to flock to Rome. Lavinia was hired to make the altarpiece for a new Dominican chapel dedicated to the recently canonized Saint Hyacinth of Poland, a prestigious commission that brought visibility and affirmed her equal footing with male artists. A few years later, in 1604, Lavinia and her family settled in Rome at the invitation of Pope Clement VIII himself, a high honor for any artist – and a rare one for a woman. It was in this period that Clement VIII commissioned Lavinia to produce one of her largest and most well-known public pieces: a twenty-foot altarpiece, *The Martyrdom of Saint Stephen*, made for the Church of San Paolo Fuori le Mura (a fire in 1823 destroyed both the basilica and its artworks). A favored painter of the papal court, she continued to paint portraits, including both Clement VIII and Paul V garbed in papal vestments.

Perhaps influenced by Rome's monumental ruins, Lavinia's style started to shift in the early 1600s. For instance, she began to feature powerful heroines in her paintings, like the Queen of Sheba, whom Lavinia depicts in Renaissance costume, and Judith holding the head of Holofernes, a popular and dramatic Old Testament subject for Renaissance and Baroque artists that would be powerfully revisited by Artemisia Gentileschi. Her new direction may also have been influenced by the heroic poetry that was in fashion – like Torquato Tasso's influential Christian epic of 1581, *Gerusalemme liberata* (*Jerusalem Delivered*) – inspiring her to take on such larger-than-life female subjects. Lavinia was showered with honors in Rome, where she spent the last decade of her life. Gregory XIII appointed her Portraitist in Ordinary, the chief painter to the pope, and she became, in 1603, the first woman inducted into the Accademia di San Luca, one of the oldest academies for painters.

Not only was Lavinia one of the first women to receive commissions for large-scale religious works to be hung in churches and private chapels, but she also portrayed the female nude – an unprecedented subject for a female artist. Though male artists frequently painted the unclothed female form – an accepted object of the desirous male gaze – women did not, for reasons of propriety as well as the lack of opportunity to paint from live models. Many scholars wonder how Lavinia managed it at all – or if she resorted to using herself as a model. Lavinia's historical and mythological paintings, a genre she pioneered for women artists over the next stage of her career, feature graceful and intimate Venuses and other allegorical female figures, as in the two versions of *Minerva Dressing* she produced in 1612 and 1613 (see Figure 17.5). The 1613 version – her last surviving work – was painted for Camillo Borghese, then Pope Paul V, a longtime patron and friend she had known in Bologna. While the 1612 version depicts Minerva enveloped in a transparent veil, the 1613 painting shows the goddess nude, her instruments of war strewn at her feet. Though indisputably sensual, the figure can also be interpreted as a non-sexual image evoking philosophical themes of Platonic love and peace, connecting to a higher spiritual wisdom and beauty. By

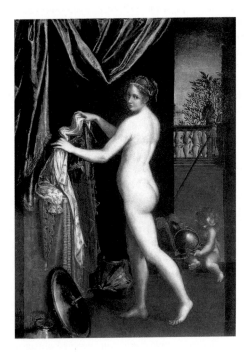

Figure 17.5 Minerva Dressing, by Lavinia Fontana, 1613

(Galleria Borghese, Rome)

Scala/Ministero per i Beni e le Attività culturali/Art Resource, NY this interpretation, the painting manages to navigate the moralistic Counter-Reformation resistance to "lascivious" images, presenting Minerva as a chaste, virgin goddess despite – or because of – her nudity, which is modest in its natural purity.[5]

On August 11, 1614, when Lavinia died in Rome, where she was buried at the church of Santa Maria sopra Minerva, she had produced more paintings than any other woman of her century, though not all of them survive and only a portion are signed. A true trailblazer, she was exceptionally adept at forging a varied array of patronage relationships, from Bolognese noblewomen to Roman clerics and even popes. Though she did not operate a workshop or train any successors directly, she made a deep impact on the women artists who came after her, from Artemisia to Elisabetta Sirani, another Bolognese painter active in the seventeenth century. In both her extraordinary success and her prodigious output, Lavinia rivaled even Caravaggio for his typical title of "the most famous painter in Rome."

Lavinia Fontana was the subject, with Sofonisba Anguissola, of a major exhibition in 2020 at the Museo del Prado in Madrid, and the focus of a solo show at the National Gallery of Ireland in 2023. Works continue to be attributed to her, like the recent discovery of a portrait of the Bolognese musician Lucia Bonasoni Garzoni with a score of music. The painting, which attests to Lavinia's strong ties to the women of Bologna as well as to the rich and complex connections between women, art, and music, was recently acquired by the National Gallery in Washington, DC. Such efforts to increase the representation of women artists like Lavinia Fontana in the collections of major museums are a fundamental step in the project of reinscribing women into the history of Renaissance art.

18 Artemisia Gentileschi (1593–1656?)

Fearless Painter, Feminist Icon

You'll find the strength of Caesar in this woman's soul.
– Artemisia Gentileschi

The image – among the most recognizable in Baroque art – is riveting (see Figure 18.1). A woman plunges a sword into the neck of a bearded man awakened, too late, from sleep. Emerging from the shadows, her face is stony with resolve; his contorts in horror as he twists away, blood spurting and staining the sheets. A second woman holds him down, assisting her mistress whose sleeves are pushed up to reveal muscular forearms: it takes all their strength, united, to complete the murderous deed. The figures are Judith, her maidservant Abra, and Holofernes, from an Old Testament story in which the Jewish heroine delivers Israel from Assyrian invaders by seducing and slaying the enemy king. The artist is Artemisia Gentileschi, celebrated for her naturalistic paintings that brim with energy and tension, bathed in chiaroscuro – shadow and light.

More intensely dramatic than the paintings of Sofonisba Anguissola and Lavinia Fontana, Artemisia's gory depiction of Judith killing Holofernes is the work with which she is most closely associated today. It invites myriad psychoanalytical and feminist readings, especially when interpreted in conjunction with events from her own life: notably, her rape as a teenager in Rome, a trauma preserved for history in the sensational trial that followed. Artemisia's Judith is indisputably powerful and alive, and it is the artist's original invention to depict the two women – Judith and Abra – as working in partnership.

At the same time, Artemisia's painting cannot be reduced to mere autobiography. Though her assault and its highly public aftermath left an indelible imprint, an overly autobiographical interpretation of her

DOI: 10.4324/9781003081807-23

Figure 18.1 Judith Slaying Holofernes, by Artemisia Gentileschi, c. 1620
(Uffizi Gallery, Florence)
Photo: Alamy

work threatens to overshadow Artemisia's true agency and achievement. *Judith Slaying Holofernes* can be read not only as a response to
rape but also as a political allegory, a story of female courage in defense
of homeland, or a broader expression of feminist unity. More generally, the Judith story was a popular subject of late Renaissance art, and
Artemisia was measuring herself against other models. She was certainly familiar with the version painted some years earlier by the famed
painter Caravaggio, a master of the tenebristic style Artemisia would

deploy to stunning effect; her interpretation takes Caravaggio's example and pushes it to the bounds of dramatic realism. We might better understand Artemisia's *Judith Slaying Holofernes* not as a "defensive psychological reaction by a female victim" but as an active gesture of "pictorial revenge . . . a playful, imaginative expression of retribution [Artemisia] was due."[1] A brilliant and original artist – possessed of great range, as a slew of recent scholarship and new attributions continues to reveal – Artemisia was complex and multifaceted. She was a shrewd businesswoman and active member of the cultural and political circles of her day, a mother, wife, lover, and an independent woman.

To understand Artemisia's remarkable career, we must start in Rome, where she spent her earliest years. Artemisia was born on July 8, 1593, to the well-known painter Orazio Gentileschi (1563–1639) and his wife Prudenzia di Ottaviano Montoni (c. 1575–1605). Still a child when she lost her mother, Artemisia grew up in a household populated by men: her five brothers, her father, and his friends and clients. Like other female artists of the Renaissance, Artemisia's training in art started at home: in Orazio's workshop, she studied color, composition, and perspective. She took chaperoned excursions to view the splendid works of art that adorned Rome's buildings and churches: Santa Maria Maggiore, Saint Peter's, and the Palazzo Quirinale. She may have even had an opportunity to encounter the renowned Lavinia Fontana, who settled in Rome in 1603; indeed, it has been suggested that Fontana's success may have spurred Orazio to encourage his own daughter to pursue art as a career.

The Gentileschis were artisans, and Artemisia received little or no formal schooling. In the trial proceedings of 1612 she would claim – perhaps to bolster sympathy for her case – "I don't know how to write and can only read a little," though in reality she wrote quite well and often wove references to Italian poetry into her later letters.[2] Still, what she lacked in organized education, she gained through other means, acquiring cultural literacy through exposure to art, music, theater, and listening to the fashionable verse of Francesco Petrarca (Petrarch) and Ludovico Ariosto recited aloud.[3] Caravaggio was a frequent visitor during Artemisia's childhood, before fleeing Rome in 1606 after killing a man in a brawl. Artemisia would not cross paths with him after her youth, but his artistic influence – or her determination to outdo him – remained with her.

Artemisia was seventeen when she painted her "matriculation work": an iconic rendering of another popular Old Testament subject, *Susanna and the Elders* (see Figure 18.2). Though it was a common

Figure 18.2 Susanna and Her Elders, Artemisia Gentileschi, c. 1610
(Schönborn Collection, Pommersfelden)
Photo: Alamy

subject for the period – depicted by other major artists including Peter
Paul Rubens and Tintoretto – her version of the voyeuristic tableau, in
which a young wife is spied on by two elderly men who try to black-
mail her and then accuse her of adultery, imbues it with new perspective and heightened tension. Artemisia's Susanna is visibly anguished,
twisting away from the men who intrude on her. Portraying objectification and trauma from the victim's perspective, the painting declares
women's resistance to sexual aggression a legitimate subject for artistic representation.[4]

By 1611, when Artemisia was eighteen, Orazio was working with
Agostino Tassi, an artist skilled at frescoes and perspective. Orazio
hired him to tutor Artemisia. As would later come out court, Tassi was a

predator with a shocking criminal history that included sexual violence and murder. In a premeditated attack, organized with an accomplice who also harassed her repeatedly, Tassi assaulted and raped Artemisia one day in 1611, then coerced her into a sexual relationship that went on for months. He was abetted by one Tuzia, the Gentileschi family's longtime tenant, who had befriended the motherless girl and often chaperoned her outings around Rome. Tuzia allowed Tassi access to the house and did nothing to intervene: at the trial, Artemisia accused Tuzia of acting as a "procuress." As Artemisia also recounted at the trial, after the rape she had no choice but to cling to Agostino's false promises of marriage. Such was the common scenario for victims of rape in Renaissance Italy, an act of violence that was rarely prosecuted – unless the victim was a virgin, for not only was virginity considered the core of a woman's honor, but it was also a commodity with real economic value for her family on the Renaissance marriage market. In fact, only when it became clear that Tassi had no intention of marrying Artemisia did Orazio press charges, nine months after the assault.

At the heart of the ensuing proceedings was the question of Artemisia's "honor." Had Tassi truly deflowered her, or was she unchaste? Remarkably, the full transcript survives, allowing us, across the centuries, to hear Artemisia's own voice. She recounts in excruciating detail her efforts to defend herself by scratching her attacker, pulling his hair, and throwing a knife at him: "I might have killed him," she testified, if he hadn't shielded himself. She describes the pain caused by the rape itself. And though Artemisia was the victim, she submitted to an intrusive physical exam and to *sibille*, metal rings tightened around her fingers – a form of torture, particularly damaging for a painter – to prove the veracity of her testimony. Throughout it all, Artemisia repeats, "It is true, it is true, it is true," as she relives the attack.

Agostino's violent past came tumbling out during the proceedings, but he eventually went free, as offenders too often did. Meanwhile, Artemisia – now a reluctant celebrity, her name forever associated with the trial – sought a new beginning, far from Rome, and perhaps also from her father, who had been slow to defend her and was most concerned with the financial impact to himself, as well as from Tuzia, who had abetted the crime. Florence, a booming cultural center under the Medici grand dukes, called to her as it had many Renaissance artists – but how to set up a new life for herself there? A strategically planned marriage to a Florentine citizen offered a solution. In 1613, a year after the trial, Artemisia left Rome as the bride of Pierantonio Stiattesi

(b. 1584), an apothecary probably related to the Giovan Battista Sti-attesi who had been a sympathetic witness for Artemisia and offered damning testimony about Tassi – including the fact that he was already married when he made his spurious promise of marriage to Artemisia, and had hired contract killers to murder his wife. While Artemisia's marriage was planned in part to restore her reputation after the trial, it is likely that she, eager to make her mark in Florence as an artist, also sought the arrangement in hopes of gaining entrée to local patronage networks.

Artemisia wed Pierantonio in Rome in late November 1612. The marriage contract included a substantial dowry of 1,000 gold *scudi*, half to be disbursed at a later date, a sum from which the groom was free to borrow providing that Artemisia gave her consent. The stipula-tion gave the bride an unusual degree of power; from the beginning, it seems, Artemisia controlled their financial affairs. Pierantonio agreed to invest the dowry in support of Artemisia's painting career. Though he never used the money to open his own pharmacy, as he once planned, his apothecarial training was likely useful in helping his wife prepare pigments and varnishes – a valuable skill in both vocations, which had once belonged to a single professional guild in Florence. Their arranged marriage was not a love match, and, in fact, they would eventually separate, maintaining separate households. But Pierantonio assisted his wife by collecting payments and helping to seek out clients as her fame and commissions increased over the next years. During her seven-year residence in Florence, Artemisia also became a mother. Three of her children died in infancy – one after just eight days – and only one survived to adulthood: a daughter, Prudentia (sometimes called Palmira, born around 1618), named for Artemisia's own mother.

Such deep personal sorrows, on top of the ordeal she had suffered in Rome, undoubtedly marked Artemisia. Yet her Florentine period was artistically transformational. She and her husband set up house in Via Santa Reparata (formerly Via Campaccio) with Pierantonio's father, Vincenzo (c. 1547–1615), living rent-free amid its gardens and fruit trees. Though historians commonly characterize these as years of penury and poor business decisions, recent scholarship points instead to Artemisia's astute navigation of Florentine patronage networks and her exploitation of its culture of credit – the city was, after all, home to the Medici, originally a major banking family – to build up her clien-tele.[5] Artemisia ascribed to the philosophy of "dressing the part." She borrowed funds to invest in a lavish wardrobe, including expensive silks and satins for dresses and cloaks that Vincenzo, a tailor, may have helped fabricate, knowing that the right appearance would attract well-heeled patrons who valued such things. She likely featured many of these garments, like her instantly recognizable mustard-colored dress, in her paintings. Artemisia also sought to benefit from the patronage – or, more properly, matronage – fostered at the Medici court by Christine de Lorraine and her daughter-in-law Maria Magdalena of Austria, who collectively governed Tuscany from 1621 until 1628. These powerful rulers offered their support to many other creative women, including the composer Francesca Caccini. In a sign of her growing stature, Cristofano Bronzini added Artemisia to his collection of biographies praising other women in the Florentine circle, like the writer Lucrezia Marinella, whom Artemisia may have later encountered in Venice.[6]

Michelangelo Buonarroti the Younger, a writer who collaborated with Caccini on several court operas for the Medici, took Artemisia under his wing as well. He gave Artemisia her first major commission, for the Casa Buonarroti honoring his revered great-uncle, the great artist and sculptor Michelangelo, which still stands in Florence's Via Ghibellina today. Her magnificent *Allegory of Inclination* from 1616, for which she was paid more than twice the other male artists decorating the ceiling, depicted a nude female figure holding a magnetic compass: a nod to Galileo Galilei, also in residence at the Medici court (see Figure 18.3). Graceful and seductive, the figure is a celebration of female strength and the creative spirit; her facial features and tousled hair are said to evoke Artemisia herself, who often used her own likeness as a model in addition to those of other well-known women in Florentine circles, like the actress Virginia Ramponi Andreini, daughter-in-law of the famed diva Isabella Andreini.[7] Few women depicted the nude female form – Lavinia Fontana is considered the first in Italy. To do so, especially if based on the artist's own body, was unusual, even scandalous: so much so that, some seventy years later, in the frequent practice of the stricter moral climate of the Counter-Reformation, a descendant of Buonarroti commissioned the painter Baldassare Franceschini (known as Il Volterrano) to cover the figure up with a strategically placed drape and veil. A 2022–2023 exhibit and restoration project, "Artemisia Svelata/Artemisia Unveiled," at the Casa Buonarotti, examined these changes to Artemisia's original rendering.

On the heels of this public success, in 1616, Artemisia joined Florence's Accademia delle Arti del Disegno (Academy of the Arts of Drawing) – the sole female member of the society founded in

Figure 18.3 Allegory of Inclination, by Artemisia Gentileschi, 1615–1617

(Casa Buonarroti, Florence)

Photo: Alamy

1563 – and set up a new workshop in Borgo Ognissanti, not far from the Medici estate of Palazzo Pitti. Artemisia produced other significant paintings during these Florentine years, including *Judith with Her Maidservant* from around 1613 to 1614, another Old Testament scene, and the *Penitent Magdalene* from around 1617 to 1620, probably commissioned by the Medici grand duchess with whom it shared a name. The story of Judith slaying Holofernes was never far from Artemisia's mind: she painted a second version between 1620 and 1621 and would produce other variations on the theme throughout her career.

By 1618, Artemisia, who changed residences numerous times while in Florence, was no longer cohabiting with Pierantonio, though they were still linked by their joint financial interests. The Medici grand duke Cosimo II was now commissioning her works, but controversy continued to follow her. Her involvement with a wealthy Florentine nobleman, Francesco Maria Maringhi, was a mixture of business and romance and caused tongues to wag, though the relationship was probably carried on with the tacit approval of Pierantonio. Letters exchanged between Artemisia and Maringhi uncovered only in 2011 alternate between declarations of passion – in one, Artemisia exclaims, "I am yours so long as I still draw breath," and swears she will remain celibate if she cannot be with her beloved – and remarks about commissions, supplies, and other practicalities.[8]

Adding to the clouds gathering around Artemisia was a dowry dispute with Orazio, who refused to hand over the remaining 500 *scudi* owed of her dowry. In 1620, Pierantonio filed a lawsuit against his father-in-law for payment. Artemisia, meanwhile, facing increasing cashflow problems along with backlash to her relationship with Maringhi, began to consider leaving Florence. After contemplating a trip to Bologna, a city famously welcoming of women artists, she attempted an initial flight to nearby Prato with one of her brothers but was forced by government officials to return to Florence because of her outstanding debt. Taking another tack, Artemisia pleaded with the Medici grand duke for permission to visit Rome on family business. After entrusting the contents of her workshop to Maringhi to safeguard them from her creditors, she finally arrived in Rome, with Pierantonio, on February 28, 1620.

Despite her assurances to her Medici patrons, Artemisia never intended to return to Florence. Instead, she immediately began arranging to have the items she had left behind sent to her. As in Florence, she again set up a comfortable, well-appointed house near the Church of Santa Maria del Popolo, which she described in a letter as "fit for a gentleman to see and to be in." Pierantonio concurred, writing in a separate exchange with Maringhi, that such a display of luxury was necessary since "if you want to get ahead, you need to make a show of good taste and demonstrate that you live in comfort," which "makes all the difference and you enjoy much more credit."[9] By 1624, census records describe Artemisia's household as comprised only of herself, two servants, and her daughter Prudentia; from this point on, Pierantonio disappears from her story.

Artemisia began a new chapter marked by travel and a broadening of her network of contacts and patrons. In Venice, she was welcomed by the city's cultural influencers, including Gian Francesco Loredano, founder of the literary Accademia degli Incogniti (Academy of the Unknown) and promoter of the singer and composer Barbara Strozzi. She also knew – perhaps directly – the feminist nun

Arcangela Tarabotti, whose brother-in-law, Giacomo Pighetti, owned one of Artemisia's paintings. She may have met other women intellectuals in Venice, like Marinella, a friend of Artemisia's own Florentine admirer Bronzino; in Genoa, where she is also thought to have traveled, she would have encountered – by reputation if not in person – the venerable Sofonisba. By 1622, however, Artemisia had returned to Rome, where she remained for the rest of the decade. Works from this period include her second treatment of Judith, the monumental 1625 *Judith and Her Maidservant* (see Figure 18.4). Less bloody but

Figure 18.4 Judith and Her Maidservant, (Artemisia Gentileschi), c. 1623–1625
(Detroit Institute of the Arts)
Photo: Alamy

no less dramatic than her earlier Judith, the tenebral painting employs dramatic lighting effects and striking positioning to create an ensemble that crackles with tension. Judith, bathed in candlelight, lifts a hand in warning, while Abra remains frozen beside Holofernes's body.

The third major stage of Artemisia's professional life saw her uprooting herself once more, this time for Naples. Still separated from Pierantonio and now employing her brother, Francesco (b. 1597) – also a painter – to assist with occasional business affairs, she professed to dislike the city, citing the "fighting" and "the hard life and the high cost of living." Yet she found it teeming with professional opportunity.[10] Ruled by Spain since the early sixteenth century, the city's Spanish viceroys were enthusiastic artistic patrons, and the Duke of Alcala had purchased several paintings from her in 1626. In 1630, Artemisia completed her first large altar painting, an *Annunciation*, probably commissioned for the Neapolitan church of San Giorgio de' Genovesi. Other paintings from this first period in Naples include Artemisia's powerful, dramatic images of female heroines such as Cleopatra and the Roman Lucretia.

By these years, Artemisia's reputation was international. In 1638, she was invited to the royal London court of Charles I and Queen Henrietta Maria, where Orazio had been court painter for over a decade. Father and daughter had been estranged for years – perhaps since the tensions and ensuing lawsuit over Orazio's refusal to furnish the remainder of Artemisia's dowry. England offered a chance at reconciliation, and a final opportunity to collaborate: up until Orazio's sudden death in 1639, some months after her arrival, Artemisia assisted him with ceiling paintings for the Queen's House in Greenwich. Charles was an avid collector of Italian art and acquired from Artemisia a number of works, including her celebrated *Self-Portrait as an Allegory of Painting*. Like works by other Renaissance women artists, the painting seems to challenge the tensions inherent between "woman" as both the subject and object of artistic representation. She is at once the painter and the personification of painting itself – depicted in an influential emblem book of 1603 by Cesare Ripa as a beautiful woman with tousled dark hair and expressive eyes. With sleeves rolled up and her dress covered by an apron, Artemisia's figure is poised in action, nearly twisting out of the canvas. If indeed a self-portrait, it would have been a very technically difficult pose to paint, probably requiring the use of mirrors on either side.

In 1642, not long after her arrival, fighting broke out in England, presaging the coming years of bitter civil war. Though she had been welcomed at the English court, Artemisia overcame her reservations to return to Naples, where she would spend the remainder of her life and where she produced paintings for a new patron, the Messina-based collector Don Antonio Ruffo. Several of these works depicted mythological figures like Galatea, Andromeda, and Diana, reflecting Artemisia's continued attention to the female form, though in a letter Artemisia complained of the "intolerable" price of hiring nude female models.[11] Artemisia's letters to her Sicilian patron confirm her sharp business acumen as well as her confidence in her own worth. When Ruffo tries to negotiate a lower fee, she responds with outrage that he dares treat her as a "novice," telling him that he will not be disappointed in her work and that he "will find the strength of Caesar in this woman's soul." As late as 1654, Artemisia was still accepting commissions. She died in 1656, perhaps from the plague that was sweeping through Naples.

Today, Artemisia Gentileschi is one of the most recognizable Baroque artists, celebrated for her dramatic compositions, striking use of color and shadow, and the psychological complexity of her works. Though she was renowned in her lifetime, her posthumous fame was not immediate. Historians began delving into her biography and oeuvre only in the early twentieth century, and feminist art historians above all have been integral to the "rediscovery" of Artemisia that has finally led to widespread acknowledgment of her impact. What took so long? As Linda Nochlin argued in a seminal 1971 essay, oppressive institutions – not lack of talent – have long conspired to keep women artists out of the canon.[12] As a female painter, Artemisia did not have the kind of large-scale workshop to guarantee followers or an entire movement, as Caravaggio did, closing one sure route to an enduring legacy. Yet she made a space for her prodigious talent, producing a significant body of work, and forged an international name for herself in a world dominated by men. New attributions to her continue to be made, such as a *Hercules and Omphale* discovered in 2020 in the wreckage of a Beirut mansion.

Artemisia's talent and grit have captured the popular imagination over the decades, from the fictionalized accounts of Anna Banti and Susanna Vreeland to director Agnès Merlet's controversial cinematic interpretation of 1997, titled simply *Artemisia*. Her paintings – particularly her versions of *Judith Slaying Holofernes* – are regularly evoked today as a kind of feminist shorthand against misogyny of all kinds. Two major exhibits of Artemisia's work have encapsulated the shift to embracing Artemisia as a major influence on late Renaissance art: in 2001, the Metropolitan Museum of Art in New York paired Artemisia's work with that of her father, Orazio; while the first exhibition dedicated to Artemisia alone, at the National Gallery in London in 2020–2021, placed the spotlight squarely on the artist herself. In 1649, Artemisia declared in a letter to a patron, "I will show you what a woman can do."[13] Now the world is finally catching up.

19 Camilla Erculiani (d. post-1584)

Pharmacist-Philosopher

Through my studies, I wanted to show the world that women, like men, are capable in all areas of knowledge.

– Camilla Erculiani

Stocked with colorful ceramic jars of spices and herbs, tonics for wellness and beauty, and even the minerals and pigments used by artists like Artemisia Gentileschi, Renaissance apothecary shops – the early modern equivalent to the pharmacy – bustled with activity. These multifunctional spaces offered both commerce and conversation. From behind a counter, an apothecary might measure out contents from neatly labeled containers, consult a hefty pharmacist's manual, or simply discuss the day's news with customers. Along with medicines, apothecaries sold groceries like sugar, oil, and honey, and other goods such as soaps and cosmetics, but they were much more than shopkeepers. They were skilled practitioners with specific expertise, literacy, and their own professional guilds – secular associations akin to modern-day labor unions that governed the arts and trades. Knowledgeable about the medicinal properties of plants and other materials, they dispensed remedies for all manner of ailments and often worked with physicians – and their ranks included women as well as men. There were a number of professional women apothecaries in the Venetian Republic in the sixteenth century; in many cities, nuns, too, were renowned for their convent pharmacies, producing and marketing their own elixirs (just as male monasteries across Europe manufactured spirits like Chartreuse or Trappist beer)[1] (see Figure 19.1).

It was at the Tre Stelle ("Three Stars") Apothecary in Padua that Camilla Greghetta Erculiani, the first Renaissance woman to publish a

DOI: 10.4324/9781003081807-24

Figure 19.1 Early Italian Pharmacy (left side of pair) with women assistants,
        Italian School, 1600–1699

(Science History Institute, Philadelphia)

[open access]

work of natural philosophy, made her living. The treatments she produced ranged from "simples" – herbs prescribed for everyday maladies
like toothache and headache – to the elaborate "theriac," a complex
panacea thought to protect against serious illness such as plague and
made from a jealously guarded recipe that included pulverized viper
flesh. Though Padua's professional guild was open to women, Camilla –
who described herself as a "speziala," or female apothecary – was not
a member. But from her shop near the Palazzo del Bo, the main seat
of the University of Padua that hosted the anatomist Andreas Vesalius
and the astronomers Nicolaus Copernicus and Galileo Galilei, she had
ample opportunity to exchange ideas with the students, professors, and
philosophers who populated the city.

From a literate though not élite background, Camilla managed to
acquire not only the apothecary's practical experience in medicine but
also a solid foundation in both Galenism – based on the four humors
described by the ancient Greek physician Galen, a foundation for
Renaissance medicine – and in Aristotelian natural philosophy, a pre-
cursor to modern science concerned with the problem of terrestrial and
cosmological change. She built an intellectual network that stretched
well beyond Padua and showcased her knowledge as well as her connections in her *Lettere di philosophia naturale* (*Letters on Natural Philosophy*), published in 1584 in Kraków, Poland, a work that addresses
topics like the material cause of the Biblical flood, the nature of rainbows, and astrological influence on human actions. While apothecaries occasionally published their recipes, primarily to attract a broader
clientele, it was unusual for a professional pharmacist, as opposed to

a learned doctor, to publish a theoretical work like this one, especially if the author was a woman – as Camilla was well aware. Dedicated to a powerful female figure with strong Italian connections – the illustrious queen of Poland, Anna Jagiellon – her *Letters* make a forceful and explicit case for the place of women in science. But many questions remain about Camilla and her book, which drew the attention of the Paduan Inquisition for its potentially heretical blurring of the boundaries between theology and science.

The daughter of Andrea Greghetti, a grocer and spice merchant, Camilla seems to have been destined for the pharmacist's life. Her first marriage, arranged by her father in the 1560s, was to the apothecary Alvise (or Alovisio) Stella, who owned a shop in the parish of Sant'Andrea in Padua, near the university.[2] Camilla's father invested money in Alvise's business, and she began working there with her husband. They had a son, Melchiorre, sometime before Alvise's death in the early 1570s. It has been suggested that the "Tre Stelle" denominating their business may have referred to the young family: Camilla, Alvise, and Melchiorre.[3] Unusually, when the widowed Camilla remarried – to Giacomo Erculiani (d. 1605), who had close ties to the medical students and faculty at the university – she did not give up the Tre Stelle but instead continued to run it with her new husband, with whom she had five more children.

Through her work at the Tre Stelle, Camilla gained valuable expertise and even created her own innovations to existing medicines. In her letters, she describes "toiling with our Galen" in order to write her own commentary on the "nature, property, and quality of the ingredients used in theriac" as a remedy for poison.[4] Profoundly curious, she read widely. Vernacular translations and summaries of Latin scientific works abounded in sixteenth-century Italy, making them available to a broader audience than ever before: Antonio Brucioli's translations into Italian of several works by Aristotle contributed significantly to this effort, though Brucioli himself became suspect after his translation into Italian of the Latin Bible landed on the Catholic Church's Index of Forbidden Books in 1555. Camilla corresponded with the Venetian nobleman Sebastiano Erizzo, who had translated Plato's dialogues into Italian, and she was also well acquainted with the works of Alessandro Piccolomini, a writer committed to making scientific knowledge accessible to readers – especially women – without university education. Piccolomini published several works of natural philosophy in Italian, including his widely disseminated *Sfera del mondo/De le stelle fisse* (*The Sphere of the World/On the Fixed Stars*) of 1540 that he dedicated to the Sienese poet Laudomia Forteguerri. Camilla refers to Piccolomini directly in her *Letters*, citing his 1554 *Seconda parte della filosofia naturale* (*Second Part of Natural Philosophy*) as evidence for her assertion that the elements of earth, water, fire, and air are finite rather than infinite. Though she maintains that her knowledge of the natural world comes from experience rather than deliberate study – knowledge she has derived "instinctively, without consulting Galen or Aristotle" – the breadth and complexity of her arguments belie this claim.

Apothecarial establishments were sociable, highly trafficked spaces that attracted an international clientele. In addition to providing health guidance and functioning as places to exchange gossip and news, they sometimes also served as hotbeds of religious dissent; through her encounters at the Tre Stelle, Camilla waded deeper into sometimes theologically sensitive debates over natural philosophy. She likely first encountered Georges Guarnier (or Giorgio Garnero) – a physician from Burgundy who studied in Padua and authored a Latin work on the plague – at the Tre Stelle: her collection contains two letters to him, along with his response. Guarnier refers to Camilla's second husband as his "patron" and, in 1577, requested a vial of the theriac that she and Giacomo had made during a plague outbreak in the Veneto. Camilla also debated natural philosophy with visitors from Poland like Martin Berzeviczy, the Polish chancellor to Transylvania who also appears in her volume. But throughout her *Letters*, her unorthodox interpretations of biblical events teeter on the edge of dangerous religious territory.

As Camilla began thinking about publishing on natural philosophy, the Polish visitors to the Tre Stelle encouraged her to seek support from their queen, Anna Jagiellon, "a great lover of knowledge" (see Figure 19.2). Camilla may have already known something of Anna, daughter of the Italian-born queen of Poland Bona Sforza; Bona had been welcomed with fanfare when she passed through the Veneto three decades earlier in 1556, greeted with an elaborate ceremonial arch in Padua and regaled in Venice with a public address by the esteemed humanist Cassandra Fedele. An anthology in honor of Anna's husband and co-regent, Stefan Batory, published in Venice in 1583, also brought Poland's Italian connections to the fore. Edited by Batory's physician, the Padua-educated surgeon Ippolito Zuccanello, the volume included contributions from Italian poets including the Venetian Moderata Fonte, who also wrote about natural philosophy.

Figure 19.2 Miniature of Anna Jagiellon of Poland, by Lucas Cranach the Younger, c. 1553

(Czartoryski Museum, Kraków)

Photo: Alamy

When Camilla published her *Letters* just a year later, she chose a printer in Kraków, rather than in Italy – despite Venice's prominence as the print capital of Europe – capitalizing on these transnational relationships. And she dedicated the work not to Poland's king but to its queen, a choice that underscored her feminist message. By publishing the fruits of her own studies, Camilla explained, "I wanted to show the world that women, like men, are capable in all areas of knowledge." Praising Anna's "goodness and wisdom," Camilla highlights famous women through the ages: her genealogy of learned women is updated from the catalogs of "women worthies" that had circulated in Renaissance Europe since the mid-fourteenth century, when Giovanni

Boccaccio composed his widely read anthology of famous historical and mythological women. In presenting her book to Anna, Camilla wrote humbly, she trusted that "in your generosity you will not disparage this small gift since it is from a woman who desires to shed glory on the women of her age, which is truly my desire."[5]

Though she hoped that Anna would welcome her offering, Camilla knew that she would face criticism for daring to publish a work of natural philosophy, especially one that made unorthodox claims about the origins of the world. Nonetheless, her dedicatory letter insists that nothing can thwart her determination to demonstrate women's value and reawaken them to their own intellectual potential. Significantly, Camilla would also have known Poland's reputation for religious tolerance – in contrast to the turmoil of the Protestant Reformation in much of Europe – which made it a haven for religious exiles and other free thinkers from Italy, where the Counter-Reformation was clamping down on religious dissent. In the 1560s, Giovanni Bernardino Bonifaccio, a Neapolitan follower of the Catholic reformer Juan de Valdés of Spain, proclaimed that Kraków offered "great liberty, I would say the very greatest, to think, deliberate, live, write and publish."[6] Camilla's decision to seek Anna as patron and protector was thus linked not only to the feminist framework of the *Letters* but also to her awareness that the work trespassed into precarious theological territory in the name of philosophical debate. In an era when the Church's power extended throughout Italy and into much of Europe, she had reason to worry (see Figure 19.3).

The sixteenth century was a "great age of Biblical science" in Europe.[7] Natural philosophers and physicians were intent on understanding and explaining natural phenomena described in the Bible. Camilla's *Letters* take up some of these debates, focusing principally on the origin of the flood described in Genesis that leads her to consider also the causes of rainbows and the influence of planets and stars on human actions and temperament. Most Renaissance philosophers concurred that the flood that sent Noah fleeing to the Ark was a fundamentally supernatural event, relating to God's punishment of humankind's sinfulness, not a naturally occurring phenomenon. Camilla, by contrast, attempts to explain the flood in physical, natural terms, as an imbalance of elements, leading to water overtaking earth. "Man could not live for eternity," Camilla writes, "because, as it is written in Genesis, man is made of the clay of the earth":

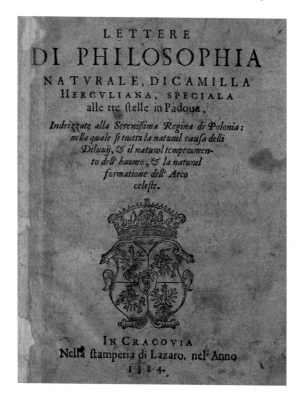

Figure 19.3 Title page of Camilla Erculiani's *Lettere di philosophia naturale* (Krakow, 1584)

(PAN Biblioteka Kórnicka, Kórnik)

[open access]

The Flood came because men had grown to be so many on Earth in number, and so great of bodily size and length of life, that after the sin the earth element was much diminished, since it was this element that gave the earth the greatest part of itself to those large bodies. Over many hundreds of years, the earth element was not returned to the earth, such that the Earth became so greatly diminished that it was necessarily swallowed up by the waters, which had contributed only a little part to these bodies.[8]

By this reasoning, even without original sin, humans would not have been able to live forever, because the Earth's balance of elements could not support it. Though Camilla was careful to clarify that her argument was scientific rather than theological, her inquiry itself was provocative. But, as her critics would soon ask, was it possible to strictly separate natural philosophy from theology? What repercussions might follow if such an approach – one that allowed for alternative explanations of divine events – were applied to other events described in the Bible, like the assumption of the Virgin Mary, or even the resurrection of Christ?

Camilla's discussion of rainbows – like the one observed by Noah after the flood – also relies on material rather than religious justification. Returning to her argument about the imbalance of elements, she writes:

> As for saying that the elements of the earth are not reduced, I say to you that those that are palpable undergo reduction, and especially the earth, as the great philosopher and astrologer Noah teaches us, truly and naturally, when he describes that certain and true sign of the rainbow in the sky, signifying that there will never again be a flood nor will the earth be swallowed by the waters, a sign that is truly worthy of such a learned man.

Camilla's explanation – that the rainbow arises from the Earth's shadow, which could only happen with a sufficient balance of the earth element – was an original notion, diverging from the traditional Aristotelian interpretation of the rainbow as a reflection of the sun. Her description of Noah in this passage as an "astrologer and philosopher" was also unconventional. The line between interpreting real-life events as the products of divine will or instead as the result of particular astrological combinations was contested in the late Renaissance – though what the Church truly cared about was not astrology but its own authority. To cast the biblical Patriarch as a reader of the heavens verged on heresy. The *Letters* venture even further into risky astrology through Camilla's analysis of the influence of the cosmos on human temperament and action. Though practiced even by astronomers like Galileo Galilei, and by priests and popes, certain forms of judicial astrology – employed for "divination," rather than simply to map or predict astronomical movement or events – were becoming increasingly suspect and would be condemned by papal bull in 1586, just two years after the publication of Camilla's *Letters*. Her arguments that the planets "distribute" (even though without exerting direct influence) certain elements that influence those born under their "rule" – creating the potential for either smooth or "star-crossed" lives or relationships – were therefore already suspect.

Camilla's *Letters* were printed at a transitional cultural moment in Counter-Reformation Italy, when it was still possible to discuss controversial ideas on the basis of philosophy and science but when the Church was beginning to scrutinize those who pushed the boundaries of orthodoxy. The heresy trial in 1633 of Galileo Galilei for teaching that the earth revolves around the sun – upsetting its traditional position at the center of the Catholic cosmos – and his subsequent recantation and house arrest would signal the apex of this struggle. Though Camilla attempted to avoid such unwanted attention by publishing her letters in more tolerant Poland, the *Letters* caught the attention of the Paduan Inquisition almost immediately, and she was summoned for a trial not long after, probably by 1586, to be questioned about her possible "heretical depravity."

Was she a heretic? While we do not have a direct record of her trial or its outcome, Camilla's lawyer, Giacomo Menochio of Lombardy, insisted that she was not. Menochio seems to have defended Camilla effectively, for there is no evidence of any further action against her, and her book was not placed on the Index. But Menochio did publish an account of his defense in 1604, which centered on the distinction – put forward by Camilla herself in the *Letters* – between science and faith. Like others before and after her – notably, Galileo – this line of reasoning maintained that philosophical arguments were different from theological belief: it was entirely possible to hold two seemingly opposite views at the same time, without challenging Catholic doctrine: a "double truth." Menochio noted that Camilla, who titled her *Letters* carefully, "did not speak theologically, but philosophically," and she herself maintained that she had acted on the legitimate basis of *libertas philosophandi*, the "freedom to philosophize." He made this distinction point by point for each argument she raised in her *Letters*, concluding emphatically that he saw "nothing that is so inimical to Catholic faith that it can be called heretical."[9]

It is poignant – or gloomily ironic – to note that, despite her dedicated efforts to promote women's equality, Menochio's ultimate defense of Camilla in her heresy trial ultimately rested not only on the assertion that philosophical thought did not encroach on theology – traditionally a weak argument – but also on misogynistic truisms about women, as if to diminish her importance or impact in the eyes of her accusers. Repeatedly referring to her volume as a "little book," Menochio wrapped up his case with a reminder that allowances must be made for women's mistakes, implying that their work is less serious than that of men and therefore less cause for concern. While Menochio's characterization may have helped secure Camilla's freedom – or perhaps the Inquisitors simply could not imagine that a female apothecary might be capable of generating truly controversial ideas – it was a glaring misrepresentation of her complex thought, her sharp grasp of natural philosophical texts and debates, and her imaginative, original mind. While it is tempting to imagine Camilla taking some grim satisfaction in the fact that her adversaries' own misogyny had paradoxically protected her, there is no evidence that she ever picked up her pen again – despite her comments in the *Letters* about works she was planning on sin and the nature of the soul.

Though Camilla Erculiani's case is the only known instance of a female natural philosopher being tried by the Inquisition in the sixteenth and seventeenth centuries, she was far from the only woman to engage in these pursuits. From pharmacy to philosophy, her activity exemplifies many of the ways in which women participated in scientific culture in the Renaissance, in practice and through publication. Working at the Tre Stelle apothecary, she gained practical, hands-on experience and connected with an international medical and intellectual community. Well versed in vernacular Aristotelianism as well as Galenism, she developed her own naturalistic philosophy that in many points revised or challenged established philosophical authorities. Building on a broader sixteenth-century movement to make scientific learning more widely accessible, she cast her *Letters* not only as a presentation of her own theories but also as a larger defense of women's intellect in general. Her *Letters on Natural Philosophy* are a significant contribution to the scientific culture of the Renaissance – and evidence of women's involvement in science long before better-known examples like the mid-seventeenth-century Elena Cornaro Piscopia, the first woman to earn a doctorate in Italy, or the famous Marie Skłodowska-Curie, who in 1903 became the first woman to receive a Nobel Prize in physics. As Camilla herself wrote in her *Letters*, by publishing her treatise she hoped to remind women of their own unlimited potential – to be a "cause of the reawakening of their intellects"– and spur her readers to recognize, more broadly, women's capabilities and contributions to scientific inquiry. Her ambition still resonates today, as women continue to be vastly underrepresented in STEM fields, and the central role of women in the history of science remains to be fully understood and appreciated.

20 Margherita Sarrocchi (c. 1560–1617)

Reader of the Stars, Galileo's Correspondent

> *Epic poetry requires a nearly universal grasp of the most important arts and sciences; not to mention engineering, sublime eloquence, and that marvelous, wide-ranging knowledge to which all our studies aspire: that is, the most holy natural philosophy, or what is commonly called "understanding of the world."*
>
> – Antonio Bulifon

Like Camilla Erculiani, Margherita Sarrocchi – a writer and friend of the astronomer Galileo Galilei – found herself at the heart of the increasingly fraught encounter of science, literature, and faith in late Renaissance Italy. A poet and polymath, she was described in a 1625 account by Cristofano Bronzini as

> A true *virtuosa*, and famous for her learning in all the most difficult areas of knowledge . . . accomplished not only in languages and poetry . . . but also in philosophy, theology, geometry, logic, astrology, and exceedingly well versed in many other noble sciences and skilled in *belles lettres*.[1]

Bronzini's praise of the multitalented Margherita – whom he claimed had even been offered an appointment at the University of Bologna – was widely echoed: her contemporaries regarded her mastery of both literature and science with awe, calling her "a marvel of the female sex" and praising the agility and originality of her mind.[2]

Margherita wove those interests together seamlessly, especially in her massive epic poem, *Scanderbeide*, inspired in its title and style by Virgil's famous *Aeneid*; hers was the first complete work in this enormously popular Renaissance genre to be published by a woman.

DOI: 10.4324/9781003081807-25

She also played an important role in defending the early discoveries of Galileo, who attended her salon in Rome and with whom she corresponded about astronomy, astrology, and epic poetry. Linked to some of the most important intellectual circles of her time, Margherita walked a careful line between the innovation of the Scientific Revolution and beliefs about the world that were deeply rooted in Catholic orthodoxy, a tension epitomized by Galileo's trial for heresy in 1633. Her experience sheds light on a moment when these cultural currents still coexisted, if uneasily.

Margherita is thought to have been born in the town of Gragnano in populous, Spanish-controlled Naples, then in economic decline but rich in cultural activity. Though information about her earliest years is scant, she came from a well-to-do family, but the deaths of both parents left her orphaned. In a twist of fate that would help shape her remarkable future, Margherita was entrusted to the care of the well-connected Cardinal Guglielmo Sirleto, custodian of the Vatican library and a figure of influence and authority in the Church; once, there had been talk of him becoming pope. Sirleto brought his ward to Rome, entrusting her to the nuns of Santa Cecilia in the Trastevere neighborhood. Convents commonly served as repositories for young women until they could be married, but the advanced education Margherita received there was far more unusual. As a celebrated linguist, scholar, and collector of ancient manuscripts, Sirleto saw to it that Margherita's studies continued well beyond what was typical for women, reading literature and natural philosophy and becoming so proficient in ancient languages that she could translate Greek texts into Italian.

Sirleto procured as her tutor the Neapolitan Luca Valerio, known for using the methods of the ancient Greek mathematician Archimedes as a basis for geometric calculations. Valerio would become the most important person in Margherita's life, a long-term intellectual partner and companion with close connections to the scientific world. It was Valerio who first introduced Margherita to Galileo, whose improvements to the telescope and subsequent discoveries – detailed in his 1610 *Starry Messenger* – shook the foundations of an earth-centered cosmos that had been accepted for centuries. Too, Valerio brought Margherita into the orbit of the members of the Roman Accademia dei Lincei (Academy of the Lynx-Eyed), the prestigious academy of science and philology founded in 1603 by Federico Cesi.

A quick study, Margherita composed poetry, penned commentaries on canonical Italian authors like the fourteenth-century Francesco

Petrarca (Petrarch), and wrote an essay on the theorems of the great geometer Euclid. At just fifteen, one of her sonnets was published in the 1575 anthology *Componimenti . . . per dame romane* (*Compositions for Roman Ladies*), an early nod of approval by Roman literary society. Margherita was one of only five women included, along with the poet and musician Tarquinia Molza, and drew comparisons to the doyenne of Italian verse, Vittoria Colonna. As Sirleto's protégée, she gained entrée to the powerful Colonna family. She was a frequent guest of Marcantonio II Colonna, an admiral who had triumphed at the 1571 naval battle of Lepanto pitting the Western Holy League coalition against the Ottoman Empire fleet, and his wife Felice Orsini, to whom she dedicated an early astrological poem. When she traveled with them back to Naples, an admirer noted, "There shines in the residence of the lords Colonna the exquisite intelligence of Margherita Sarrocchi, who has reached great heights of knowledge."[3] Her presence in a 1588 treatise on the waters of Ischia dedicated to Duchess Geronima Colonna of Monteleone, *De' remedi naturali* (*On Natural Remedies*), reflected her continued ties to the Colonna clan over the next decade. It also indicated her growing reputation in natural philosophy: her contribution, a sonnet praising the author, Giulio Iasolino, and his subject, positioned Margherita prominently alongside a cast of male medical writers. Now twenty-eight, her star was on the rise.

Gaining attention in Naples, Rome, and beyond, Margherita delivered public lectures and exchanged poetry with Torquato Tasso, who corresponded with a number of female poets and whose epic *Gerusalemme liberata* (*Jerusalem Delivered*), first printed in 1581, she admired. She was also closely linked to the influential Baroque poet Giambattista Marino, known for his elaborate style that combined language and imagery in unexpected ways, though they later fell out, likely over differences in poetic philosophy. She was active in "the public Academies of Rome" – institutionalized literary societies like the avantgarde Accademia degli Umoristi (Academy of the Humorous) and the more traditional Accademia degli Ordinati (the Orderly) – as well as those in Naples, where she was listed among the predominantly male membership of the Accademia degli Oziosi (the Idle).[4]

By 1588, Margherita had married Carlo Birago, from the northern Piedmont region. They had no children, though in 1599 Margherita took in the young son of Beatrice Cenci, a Roman friend who, after years of abuse by her father, Francesco Cenci, killed him and was executed for the crime – a tragic saga retold in literature, art, and music for centuries to come, including by Percy Shelley in 1819 and Alberto Moravia in 1958. Margherita's closest relationship, however, continued to be with Valerio, who remained her confidant and boarded for a time in the home she shared with Carlo. The gatherings Margherita hosted there attracted, in the words of Bronzini, "the most noble and virtuous spirits ever to live in or pass through Rome."[5] Among these were mathematicians, poets, church officials, and eventually, Galileo.

Margherita's first meeting with Galileo may have been at her salon or at one of various presentations in Rome during which Galileo demonstrated the power of his new telescope. On at least one occasion, she engaged him "with great ability . . . regarding the movements of the heavens themselves," using "erudite and well-reasoned arguments." Since Galileo's contemporaries noted that to "debate with Galileo, one must first have read Copernicus carefully, for otherwise one would seem ignorant," she must have been well-informed regarding the new theory of a sun-centered universe, although she likely still adhered to a geocentric view.[6] Her discussion with Galileo, who had not yet been ordered to cease teaching heliocentrism, would have been vigorous and helps illustrate the still fluid contours of seventeenth-century science, within which a Copernican astronomer and the female ward of a Vatican official could freely discuss the structure of the universe. Though there are other examples of learned women hosting salons in Renaissance Italy – we might think again of Molza in Ferrara, Lucrezia Gonzaga in Fratta, or of Sarra Copia Sulam in Venice – Margherita's salon had a unique focus on new scientific discoveries that placed her at the heart of debates about the cosmos.

By the early 1600s, Margherita, now an established poet, was immersed in the composition of her ambitious *Scanderbeide*. Lengthy and complex, epic poems wove together multiple, interlocking narrative threads and often celebrated patrons and ruling families. A genre that signaled the pinnacle of literary achievement, it was dominated by men like Ludovico Ariosto, author of a bestselling example that spurred a flood of spinoffs (including the popular adaptations by Laura Terracina), and the equally popular Tasso. Other women writers, like Tullia d'Aragona and Moderata Fonte, had tackled the form, but Margherita would be the first to publish a full-length poem. In its final form, the edition of 1623, her *Scanderbeide* consisted of twenty-three cantos, while an earlier, incomplete version, published in 1606, had only eleven (see Figure 20.1). Her example directly influenced

Figure 20.1 Title page of Margherita Sarrocchi's *Scanderbeide* (Rome: Andrei
    Fei, 1623)

later epics like the 1635 *L'Enrico* (*Enrico*) by the Venetian Lucrezia
Marinella.

Margherita's subject matter was inspired by the war waged between
Christians and Turks in Hungary from 1593–1606, and she chose as
her central protagonist Gjergi Kastrioti or Skanderbeg (1442–1468),

the Albanian prince who fought against the Ottomans and lends his name to the work. It was a popular topic for literary accounts: Scanderbeg's adventurous story included his capture by Sultan Murad II, conversion to Islam, return to the Christian faith, and command of an Albanian resistance effort supported by various Italian states and by the Pope. While scientific topics are not the primary focus of Margherita's poem, her interest in natural philosophy and cosmology is evident. As the dedicatory letter accompanying the poem explains, the epic poet is expected to have mastery, as Margherita does, of "all the most important sciences and arts."[7] Accordingly, her characters display knowledge of subjects ranging from agriculture and geography to hydrology, engineering, and astrology: in particular, the erudite sorceress Calidora, central in the incomplete version but cut from the 1623 edition, demonstrates a command of Aristotelian philosophy with "acute intelligence" and "penetrates, from the principle causes, the secondary, which produce different effects in us all."[8] Calidora's understanding of "the light and movement of the stars and the workings of nature" reflects the conviction, common to early modern scientific thought, that celestial bodies influence circumstances on earth through light and motion.

Renaissance astronomy and astrology were closely enmeshed: in fact, some of the earliest objections to Galileo's discoveries involved the potential impact that any newly discovered heavenly bodies might have on the zodiac. Despite warnings from the Church against impinging on divine will by using astrology to explain or forecast human events, Margherita and many others, including Galileo, shared an interest in it, often casting natal charts for friends and acquaintances. Margherita's friend Bronzini asserted, however, that her well-known belief in the "influence of the stars" remained strictly within the bounds of Catholic doctrine – used only to calculate the movements of planetary bodies – and did not deny free will.[9] It was an important clarification, since the doctrine of free will had been reaffirmed by the Council of Trent, held from 1545 to 1563, and was a central element in the conflict with Protestantism, which denied it and maintained salvation by grace alone. Like many areas of Renaissance science, astrology was a discipline in flux: while it was widely studied and practiced, too great an emphasis on determinism could cross into heresy. Only God, not astrologers, could predict human affairs.

If scientific discussion carried risk, literary culture faced its own minefields. One of the most hotly contested debates among sixteenth-century literary circles regarded which model for epic poetry should hold primacy: Ariosto's romance *Orlando furioso* (*The Frenzy of Orlando*), completed in 1532 and filled with magical flights of fancy and sensual enchantresses, or Tasso's marvelous Christian epic that corrals Ariosto's free-wheeling spirit into a moralizing Counter-Reformation ethos. Margherita's *Scanderbeide* adheres closely in many respects to Tasso's model, especially in its use of the "Christian marvelous": supernatural events propelled by a divine plan. Nonetheless, as she was preparing a second edition in 1611, Margherita sought the advice of a noted Ariosto enthusiast: Galileo, to whom Valerio had sent a copy of her poem in 1609. A writer as well as a scientist – his groundbreaking *Dialogo sopra i due massimi sistemi del mondo* (*Dialogue Concerning the Two Chief World Systems*) of 1632, promoting the heliocentric model, would be composed as a vernacular literary dialogue, not a scientific treatise in Latin – Galileo was an avid reader of epic poetry and had authored his own comparison of Ariosto and Tasso (see Figure 20.2).

Like many Renaissance women writers, Margherita was no stranger to criticism – her former ally Marino insulted her in print, comparing her to a chattering magpie, and others accused her of being too prideful in her accomplishments. She was therefore determined that her revised *Scanderbeide* should be above reproach and invited Galileo to read the draft critically, without fear of offending her, "so that you may note every little error; and believe me that I say this truly, and I will take all the criticism you offer as a sign of great goodness and great affection."[10] Though she was Neapolitan by birth and Roman by residence, Margherita – like many writers of the era – believed Tuscan Italian to be the most appropriate language for literature, and she also asked Galileo, a native of Tuscany who shared this view, to help her make it "as Tuscan as possible." Finally, she sought Galileo's advice on finding a well-placed dedicatee for the *Scanderbeide*, offering in return to mention him in the finished poem – though she never did so, perhaps due to the downturn in Galileo's fortunes after 1616, when the Inquisition condemned heliocentrism as heresy.

Margherita clearly recognized the value of an endorsement by Galileo, who was still a celebrity in the early 1600s, rather than a Church exile, but she was not alone in having something to gain from the relationship, He needed something, too: the support of the Roman scientific community to validate and promote his scientific discoveries. Almost as soon as Galileo's *Starry Messenger* was published in March 1610, both Margherita and Valerio were reading and praising

Figure 20.2 Portrait of Galileo Galilei, c. 1602–07, attributed to Domenico Robusti, c. 1605–1607

(Royal Museums, Greenwich)

Photo: Alamy

it: Valerio mentions it in a letter dated to 29 May of that year, in which he describes "signora Margherita Sarrocchi" as "no less [Galileo's] supporter than I am."[11] During his 1611 trip to Rome, Galileo continued to study Jupiter's satellites – which he named "Medicean" stars, for his Medici patrons – before rushing his observations into print in 1612 with the *Discorso sulle cose che stanno in sull'acqua* (*Discourse on Bodies in Water*); he also sent this work and his 1613 *Istoria e dimostrazioni intorno alle macchie solari* (*Letters on Sunspots*) to Margherita and Valerio. Galileo was concerned that his critics, using the telescope incorrectly, might not be able to perceive the movement of these satellites, and he was counting on Margherita and Valerio to defend his observations to others.

His confidence was well-founded, at least initially. In 1611, Guido Bettoli of the University of Perugia in Umbria sought Margherita's opinion on the newly discovered satellites:

> The marvelous discoveries one keeps hearing about regarding signor Galileo Galilei's telescope, or shall we say lens, which inspire everyone offer their opinion, spurs me to the presumption of writing to you, to ask you to favor me with your opinion, and since you are so perfectly learned in every area, I hope for a perfect account of the truth, since you too must have seen it for yourself a thousand times.[12]

Margherita responded with vigorous support of Galileo, avowing that

> everything they say about signor Galileo's discovery is true: that is, that there are four unfixed stars around Jupiter that move independently, always maintaining an equal distance from Jupiter, but not from one another; and I saw this myself through signor Galileo's telescope, and showed it to some friends, as the whole world knows.

Margherita kept Galileo apprised of the grumblings she was hearing, even sending him a copy of her letter to Bettoli so that he might see "everything that is going on." She also sent him a copy of her correspondence with a friar, also from Perugia, on the same subject, explaining to Galileo how she had responded with "the truth of [Galileo's] discovery of the stars, and praised your genius." She expressed frustration not only at the friar's doubts about Galileo's findings but also at his insinuation that, as a woman, her advocacy for Galileo's discoveries carried less weight: "It is quite true that the friar seems to have it in for me, and wants to bicker with me over words." But she refused to give in: "I've set better people straight than him," she concluded, "so I hope to do the same with him, even though I am a woman and he is a learned friar" (see Figure 20.3).

While Galileo sought the support of numerous prominent men in the scientific community, Margherita appears to have been the sole woman to receive his works prior to publication, with the exception of his daughter, Suor Maria Celeste, a nun in a Florentine convent, with whom he corresponded regularly.[13] Margherita's intellectual stature and powerful connections made her a valuable ally but, as a woman operating in a male-dominated environment, she faced hostility and

Figure 20.3 Letter of Margherita Sarrocchi to Galileo Galilei, October 12, 1611

(Biblioteca Nazionale Centrale, Florence, MSS Gal 2, cc. 12 r-v)

Su concessione del Ministero della Cultura/Biblioteca Nazionale Centrale di Firenze. Image should not be reproduced or duplicated in any way without permission.

suspicion as well as admiration. Some saw her as an interloper, and later even accused her of poisoning Valerio against the scientific community in Rome. Indeed, when Valerio, fearing repercussions for his close association with Galileo, attempted to resign from the Accademia dei Lincei, which stood by Galileo, Margherita was blamed.[14] But there is no evidence that she intervened with Valerio, nor is it clear what her own thoughts were on Galileo's situation. While there are no extant letters from Margherita to Galileo after 1616, it is uncertain whether one of them broke off the correspondence, or if their letters simply did not survive the subsequent decades when so many documents related to Galileo were destroyed by parties fearful of guilt by association.

The misogynistic shadow of Margherita's presumed "alienation" of Valerio from Rome's male-dominated scientific society – the Yoko Ono to Valerio's John Lennon – lingered into the mid-seventeenth century, when a comedic play by Giovanni Giacomo Ricci portrayed her not as a serious natural philosopher and epic poet but as a peripheral romantic interest for the male characters. But by the nineteenth century, she had been reclaimed by her native Naples as the heroine of a four-act drama by the Neapolitan Michele Cuciniello titled simply *Margherita Sarrocchi*. Her experience as a writer, correspondent, and cultural mediator offers a window into the key role played by women in the history of Renaissance science, a history comprised not just of single moments of exceptional discoveries but all the rich and complex relationships and scientific, literary, and religious exchanges that made these discoveries possible. Though their names may be less widely known than those of the male giants in the history of science, women like Margherita Sarrocchi, the epic poet who studied the stars and defended Galileo's earth-changing discoveries, played a crucial role in establishing the intellectual and critical environment of the Scientific Revolution.

Part Five

Renaissance Feminists

21 Laudomia Forteguerri (1515–1555?)

Queer Poet, Civic Hero

Anyone possessed of even the faintest shadow of her virtue should be admired. I will never believe that any spirit could be so barbarously and fixedly opposed to the freedom of one's city that upon witnessing her fierce defense of it, they would not have been overcome, humbled, and forced to retreat.

– Giovanni Betussi

The formidable Laudomia Forteguerri was a product of Siena, home to the Piazza del Campo – the famous brick-paved clamshell in the heart of the city – and to the Palio horse race still run there twice a year, a symbol of civic pride. A free-standing republic until its defeat by rival city-state Florence in 1555, Renaissance Siena was also renowned for its political and cultural vitality. It fostered literary salons and societies, and visitors were especially struck by the active role women played in intellectual and civic life. One seventeenth-century historian linked the high profile of Sienese women explicitly to their role in the republic's fight for autonomy, writing that they "learned to transcend the condition of sex" and were "equally as spirited in nocturnal debates with their courteous friends [such as academy meetings] as bold in conflicts during the day with enemies of the state."[1] Though this account did not mention her by name, the description aptly applied to Laudomia, who was celebrated for her poetry and praised by her contemporaries as the very incarnation of Fame.[2] In later decades, Laudomia would come to emblematize the republic's fierce – albeit futile – resistance to the designs of imperial-backed Florence. Though she left few traces in the historical record, abundant literary accounts present Laudomia, the mobilizer of the women of Siena who is often described, perhaps

DOI: 10.4324/9781003081807-27

anachronistically, as the first lesbian poet in early modern Italy, a woman who lived outside conventional boundaries.

Laudomia came from a noble family with deep Sienese roots. Her father was Alessandro di Niccodemo di Forteguerri; her mother, Alessandro's second wife, was Virginia di Giulio Pecci. Both the Forteguerri and Pecci families had been members of the Noveschi (Nine), the political élite that wielded significant power in Siena and still enjoyed the support of the Hapsburg Holy Roman Emperor Charles V, Archduke of Austria and King of Spain, who was locked in a power struggle against France. Linked by blood and marriage to other Sienese nobility like the Piccolomini and Petrucci families, they were connected to the city's innermost political and ecclesiastical circles.

Quick and curious, Laudomia studied canonical literary authors like Dante Alighieri and had a passion for science, especially astronomy – though, to her frustration, her instruction did not include Latin, making many scientific texts inaccessible. As for most women of her social class, however, the primary expectation for her future was not study but, rather, an advantageous marriage followed by motherhood. By 1535, not yet twenty, she had wed Giulio Cesare di Alessandro Colombini (b. 1507), from a Noveschi family like her own. They had three children – Olimpia Antonia (b. 1535), Antonia Anna (b. 1537), and Alessandro Antonio (b. 1539) – before Giulio died, leaving Laudomia a widow at twenty-seven. Two years later she married Petruccio Petrucci (1513–1592), a military captain from another influential Sienese clan. As was customary for widows in Renaissance Italy, Laudomia's children remained with her first husband's family. There were no further children from this second marriage. Laudomia and Petruccio lived alone with two servants during what would be, for them and for Siena itself, the calm before the storm. Soon, imperial forces would occupy the city and then align with Florence to besiege Siena, devastating the republic and its population.

At the forefront of Sienese cultural life in this period were academies like Gli Intronati (The Stunned), a society with a typically playful name that was formed in the mid-1520s to promote the liberal arts. After decades of destabilizing warfare – and the 1527 Sack of Rome by the imperial army that shocked all of Italy – the Intronati proposed to set aside political discussions and focus instead on literature and intellectual exchange. They welcomed women into their orbit, if not always their membership (the poet Laura Battiferri was the first recorded woman member, in 1560), inviting them to participate in gatherings, dedicating literary works to them, celebrating them in print, and, in Laudomia's case, promoting them as authors in their own right.[3] Much of what we know about Laudomia, in fact, comes to us through the writings of two Intronati members: the cousins Marcantonio and Alessandro Piccolomini, for whom Laudomia embodied the potential of women to participate powerfully in public life, given the proper tools and education.

Laudomia first takes literary center stage in Marcantonio Piccolomini's 1538 dialogue, titled simply *Ragionamento* (*Discussion*). Along with the Sienese noblewomen Girolama Carli de' Piccolomini and Frasia Marzi, Laudomia discusses topics like the nature of beauty and the relationship of the sexes, intrinsic elements of the early modern debate over gender roles known by the French term as the *querelle des femmes* ("the woman question"). Their conversation, which weaves together literature, philosophy, and theology, is an implicitly feminist endorsement of women's intellectual force and the importance of making women's voices heard. Soon the characters venture into even more controversial territory, discussing delicate and even dangerous religious topics like free will, a tenet of orthodox Catholicism that was being challenged in Italy by evangelist groups inspired by certain aspects of Protestantism. One such group – the Spirituali (Spirituals), who espoused that salvation was attained not through good works but by faith alone (*sola fide*, in Latin) – had strong links to Siena through reformers like the popular sixteenth-century Sienese preacher Bernandino Ochino. Though their views were at odds with Catholic doctrine, the followers of these evangelist circles included many women – like Vittoria Colonna and Lucrezia Gonzaga – who often expressed their sympathetic opinions in veiled writings. Marcantonio's dialogue sets up a literary triad in which Laudomia voices unorthodox positions on contentious issues like predestination and the existence or non-existence of Purgatory but is ultimately persuaded back to the orthodox stance by her friends, bringing the dialogue to an "acceptable" conclusion and preserving the good reputation of all participants. Marcantonio's dialogue, which entrusts Laudomia with a prominent role in so sensitive a subject, shows that, in the years preceding the Counter-Reformation, religious questions could still be freely debated in Siena, though the climate would soon grow more restrictive: by 1542, Ochino, then branded a heretic, would flee Italy for more tolerant Poland.

Alessandro Piccolomini was an even more fervent admirer of Laudomia. He commiserated especially with her frustration at women's lack of access to Latin, the traditional language of natural philosophy – the umbrella of subjects that developed into modern science. That concern prompted him to translate several scientific works from Latin into vernacular Italian in order to reach a female audience. It was to Laudomia that Alessandro dedicated his influential 1540 compendium on astronomy, *Sfera del mondo/De le stelle fisse* (*Sphere of the World/ On the Fixed Stars*), the first work to contain maps of all constellations then known and to indicate the relative luminosity of each star. In his dedication, Alessandro explains that he wrote the work in Italian for Laudomia's benefit because she "had not been able to feast her spirit on matters of cosmology, to which she felt more inclined than to any other subject." Not only will his vernacular manual enable her to study astronomy, Alessandro adds, but it will also deepen her already considerable understanding of Dante's *Divina Commedia* (*Divine Comedy*) – especially the theologically and cosmologically complex third canticle set in the heavens, *Paradiso* (*Paradise*), on which he once heard her expound "so subtly" that he still marveled at the memory.[4] For Alessandro, Laudomia's thirst for "worthy study" of "honorable" scientific disciplines called attention to inequities in women's access to education, a problem that would be discussed in depth by women writers later in the century. Her exemplary intellectual curiosity was cause not just for literary celebration but also for concrete action: the production of contemporary translations and summaries of otherwise inaccessible scientific works intended to help her and other women attain the knowledge that had been kept from them.

Along with an interest in natural philosophy, Laudomia also had a unique poetic voice. Six of her sonnets were published in Ludovico Domenichi's important 1559 anthology of women poets. One is addressed to the Pavian noblewoman Alda Torelli Lunati; the other five are inspired by Laudomia's devotion to the princess Margaret of Austria (later known as Margaret of Parma), the daughter of Charles V whom Laudomia met in the early 1530s (see Figure 21.1). The precise year of their meeting is debated: Alessandro, who delivered a public lecture in praise of Laudomia's verse before the Accademia degli Infiammati (Academy of the Inflamed) in Padua, placed it in 1535, when Margaret was en route to Florence for her first marriage, while others suggest a time closer to her second marriage in 1538 – but both women were very young, in or barely out of their teens. Their story, at least for

Figure 21.1 Portrait of Duchess Margaret of Parma, by Anthonis Mor, 1562

(Gemäldegalerie, Berlin)

Photo: Alamy

Laudomia, is a literary romance filled with longing, ambiguity, and silence.

Margaret's own story is a dramatic one. As the illegitimate but acknowledged daughter of the Hapsburg emperor who loomed large in Italy's fractured political landscape, her marriage was intended to enhance Charles's alliances. At age ten, Margaret was betrothed to the twenty-seven-year-old Alessandro de' Medici, duke of Florence (see Figure 21.2). A grandson of the famed Lorenzo the Magnificent who had presided over Florence during the golden age of Botticelli and Michelangelo, the duke had a political pedigree that stretched back generations, making him a precious asset to the imperial Hapsburg dynasty. Like Margaret, he was the product of an out-of-wedlock

Figure 21.2 Portrait of Alessandro de' Medici, Duke of Florence, by the work-
        shop of Agnolo Bronzino, 1555–1565

(Uffizi Gallery, Florence)

Photo: Alamy

union: his mother is believed to have been Simonetta da Collevecchio
(d. after 1534), an African woman in the Orsini household in Rome.
Sometimes called "Il Moro" ("The Moor") – a racialized term entangled with notions about ethnicity, religion, and social class that was
used throughout Renaissance Italy to indicate dark skin – the duke's
story is an important one for the study of both race and class at the
courts of early modern Europe.[5] But it was his rapid ascent to power –
ending the exile his family had faced after 1527 – that created the bitterest tensions with his other Medici relations. In a plot engineered
in part by Lorenzino de' Medici, a duplicitous cousin thereafter nicknamed Lorenzaccio (Lorenzo the Bad), the duke was ambushed and
assassinated less than a year into his marriage. In retaliation, Charles

secretly hired hitmen to kill Lorenzaccio and avenge the murder of his son-in-law.[6]

Whatever Margaret's feelings may have been for Alessandro during their fleeting union, she was clearly disinclined toward her next alliance just a year later. Margaret dressed in black widow's weeds to her wedding with Ottavio Farnese, duke of Parma, the fourteen-year-old nephew of Pope Paul III, and refused to consummate this second union for the next five years. European courts buzzed with gossip about Margaret's clear distaste for her spouse, whom she openly mocked in letters. The rumors died down when she eventually produced twin sons; still, she continued to live apart from her husband, preferring to maintain her own court in Rome. Though the famed Vittoria Colonna, who befriended her in these years, reportedly advised her to seek refuge in a convent, this option was not available to a woman of Margaret's political value.[7] Margaret remained married and later played an active role as governor-general of the Netherlands, a position to which she was appointed in 1559 by her half-brother, Philip II of Spain.

Margaret's solitary life and virtual estrangement from Ottavio made her the target of salacious speculation about her alleged sexual activities, with some anonymous Roman satirists accusing her of sodomy with her father-in-law and even with Pope Paul III himself.[8] The passionate verse that Laudomia dedicated to her, inspired by their brief encounter in Siena, fueled more gossip about Margaret's sexual orientation: one French commentator declared it "false" to say that Margaret "loved that beautiful lady [Laudomia] purely and with a holy love," and asserted that Margaret had instead attempted to "cover up her own lasciviousness." But many of Laudomia's contemporaries admired her poems and, like readers today, were intrigued by their multivalence. Did her sonnets reveal an affection that was romantic and even erotic in nature or, as many in Laudomia's own circle maintained, one that was chaste and literary, in keeping with poetic trends of the era that rediscovered both Socrates and Sappho? Perhaps her verse was simply a political stratagem, an attempt to gain the friendship and favor of the daughter of the powerful Holy Roman Emperor by using the currency of sixteenth-century patronage: passionate expressions of love that served to cultivate socially or politically advantageous relationships.[9]

The sonnets, which skillfully rework fashionable models of love poetry in a feminine – and feminist – key, lend themselves to multiple interpretations. When Alessandro Piccolomini presented one of them at his 1541 lecture before the Infiammati – a commentary subsequently published in a pirated edition in Bologna – he described how the two

women "immediately burst into the most fiery flames of love" upon
their first encounter. For him, such imagery evoked a love that was
sisterly, not sexual. For Agnolo Firenzuola, author of a philosophical
treatise on beauty, their love was the embodiment of Plato's famed
androgyne. "Those who were female in both halves" at their creation,
he wrote, "love each other's beauty, some in purity and holiness, as
the elegant Laudomia Forteguerri loves the most illustrious Margaret of Austria, some lasciviously, as in ancient times Sappo from Les-
bos."[10] But others, especially Margaret's detractors outside Italy, read
the poems in a sexual key, claiming that Margaret pursued Laudomia
"for her pleasures." Whatever their impetus, this literary expression of
love between two women, no matter how stylized or abstracted, put a
new spin on the conventional poetics still dominated by the love lyric
of the fourteenth-century Francesco Petrarca (Petrarch) – one bound to
cause controversy.

Laudomia skillfully played on these ambiguities, drawing on a variety of influences from the Sapphic poetic tradition to the earliest Italian poets and innovating the traditional literary phases of love – hope,
delight, despair – by applying them to a same-sex passion. In the first
of her surviving sonnets, she compares her beloved to the sun, while
the second bubbles over with Petrarchan images of "lovely flowers"
and "bright waters" as Margaret rules proudly and nobly "over famous
streams." Particularly admired, this composition was included by the
prominent publisher Gabriel Giolito in a 1546 poetic anthology. Only
in the third poem does Laudomia finally mention her beloved by name,
playing on the Italian meaning of "Margherita" as "daisy" and imbuing
her with the angelic valence of Dante's famous muse, Beatrice:

> Fortunate plant, so welcome in heaven,
> for nature invested all her sublimity in you,
> when it decided to create such beauty:
> I speak of my divine Margaret of Austria.
> I know well that she would never have left heaven
> except to show us celestial things.
> God sculpted her and created with his own hand
> this woman he so loved and cherished.[11]

Beyond the clear allusions to a medieval tradition in which the poet's
beloved is cast as an angelic being guiding the poet from earthly to
divine love, the sonnet is replete with political allusion. By calling

Margaret a "fortunate plant," Laudomia also evoked a favorite expression used to describe her friend's native country, "Felix Austria" (Fortunate Austria).[12] The poem thus ties Margaret – and, Laudomia hopes, Siena itself – to the Hapsburg empire in the expectation of receiving its favor.

Superior in all ways, a divine poetic being who also surpasses Laudomia in the social hierarchy, Margaret remains unattainable, and Laudomia is bereft in the final sonnet. "Alas my lovely Sun will not turn/her divine rays toward me:/shall I then live without my light and joy?" she laments, going on to wish for death rather than to "live in this world without her." Bewailing her distance from Margaret, she implores of "cruel fortune":

> why do you not allow my body to go
> where my heart goes?
> Why do you hold
> me in this cruel prison without hope
> of escape from woe?

The question is ambiguous – is their separation geographic or romantic, sexual or symbolic? – though the original Italian grammar unambiguously presents both the lover and beloved as women. Distraught, Laudomia tries to persuade Margaret to return her affection:

> turn your face to me now, for it's no
> glorious act to abase one of the female sex.
> Hear my words, how ready they are
> to beg you; for I ask only that you
> let me remain at my goddess's side.

Whether or not there was a romantic aspect to Laudomia's poetic relationship with Margaret, her "goddess," Laudomia's tribute breaks away from the typical, male-focused structure of early modern love poetry to center same-sex love. Evoking a fluidity of sexuality, hers is a queer poetics, though the term did not exist in the Renaissance.

If Laudomia's poetry for Margaret is intimate, it also evinces a broader feminist attitude. Her admonition that it is "no glorious act to abase one of the female sex" calls for women to unite in support, not turn against one another. That sentiment is apparent in Laudomia's civic and political activism, which cemented her enduring celebrity in Italy just as strongly as her unique poetic voice. In the early 1530s, when Margaret had first passed through the city, relations between Siena and Spain were still warm: with fireworks and festivities the republic welcomed the emperor, who promised to retain local governance. But by 1551, more than a decade after Laudomia penned her lines for Margaret, anti-Spanish sentiment ran high. In 1552, the Sienese republic finally expelled its imperial occupiers only to face a renewed assault against its autonomy by Florence, its rival aided by the Spanish crown, in a siege that endured for an agonizing three years. Siena was instead supported by France, which hoped to contain Florence and counter Spanish-imperial power, but the republic was ultimately crushed by Florence at the Battle of Marciano fought in the Tuscan countryside in 1554.

Surrounded by enemy forces, thousands starved in the ensuing siege. One witness described men and women "emaciated and gray-faced" from "continual hardship" and hunger, ravaged by sickness, while those who attempted escape were tortured or killed.[13] Despite the brutal conditions, the citizens fought back, martialing a valiant though ill-fated defense through which Laudomia made her most lasting mark. In December 1552, as the siege began, the women of Siena, led by Laudomia and two women companions, gathered outside the Porta Camollia, a gate toward the vulnerable northern wall of the city. Calling out "France! France!" to summon the help of their ally and their invaders' adversary, an army of 3,000 "Ladies, Gentlewomen, and Citizens," adorned with flags and insignia, carrying "Picks, Shovels, Baskets, and Bavins" in their arms and "baskets of earth" on their heads, rallied to fortify the wall and defend the city. Some, it was reported, had demolished their own houses to amass materials for the barricade.

These were not the timid, housebound women idealized in Renaissance comportment manuals, but bold, courageous leaders determined to defend their city, and their defiance inspired the men of Siena to follow them. So fierce were Laudomia and her compatriots that the general sent to Siena by Henry II of France in the aftermath of the episode, marveled, "I would rather defend Siena with only Sienese women to help me than defend Rome with the Romans of today."[14] Nonetheless, Siena, outnumbered and weakened by the protracted fighting, ultimately fell at Marciano – a victory for Florence that was memorialized by Giorgio Vasari in a massive fresco for the city's Palazzo Vecchio

Figure 21.3 The storming of the fortress near Porta Camollia in Siena, by Giorgio Vasari, 1570

(Comune di Firenze)

Photo: Alamy

(in turn given a central role in Dan Brown's sensational 2013 novel *Inferno*) (see Figure 21.3). The republic of Siena was absorbed, via agreement between the emperor and the Medici grand duke Cosimo I, into the Florentine grand duchy. Though her heroism could not save the city, Laudomia's story endured. By the time Italy was fighting for nationhood three centuries later, her legend had become part of Italian civic mythology, its feminist resonance enmeshed within nationalist implications.

Taken together, Laudomia's activity as a queer poet, advocate for women's education, and political activist paints the portrait of a woman who pushed back against prescribed gender norms and social roles: a woman who prized – and fought for – the right to live, learn, and love freely. Just as she challenged heteronormative conventions in her love poetry for Margaret of Austria, Laudomia – who studied, wrote, and participated in the public life of her native city – also exemplified the quest for women's freedom and access to knowledge. Today, visitors to Siena can discover the echoes of her legacy at the remains of the "Women's Fort" just outside the city's northern walls, so named in memory of Laudomia Forteguerri and the women of Siena.

22 Moderata Fonte (1555–1592)

Visionary of Women's Equality

Even though people say that women must be subject to men, this ought to be understood in the same way that we say we are "subject" to misfortunes, diseases, and all the other accidents that befall us in this life.

– Moderata Fonte

As the sixteenth century drew to a close, the Venetian writer Moderata Fonte – born Modesta Pozzo – set out to capture a conversation among seven women, gathered in an idyllic garden to discuss the social and political norms that governed women's lives. Her dialogue, entitled *Il merito delle donne* (*The Worth of Women*), remains today a strikingly resonant contribution to the development of feminist thought. Though light-hearted in tone, it poses serious questions about gender, power, and inequality that cut to the heart of patriarchy: who gets to write history? How have men managed to claim superiority for themselves? Why are sexism and misogyny enshrined as law and custom? The Renaissance debate over women's roles, nature, and capabilities known as the *querelle des femmes* had been raging throughout Europe for two centuries when Moderata wrote her dialogue – ever since Christine de Pizan, a Venetian-born writer at the French court, penned *The Book of the City of Ladies*, an early-fifteenth-century defense of women's intellect, reason, and morality that countered misogynistic literary representations of women. Italian writers took up the cause, debating the prevailing belief in male superiority established in antiquity and showcasing the virtue and erudition of women.[1] Shifting the discussion from a purely philosophical or theoretical realm and anchoring it in the everyday, Moderata went even further, daring to

DOI: 10.4324/9781003081807-28

ask: what would equality for women in Renaissance Venice look like in real, practical terms?[2]

Modesta Pozzo was born in Venice in 1555 – the same year that another important republic, Siena, home to the poet Laudomia Forteguerri, fell to Florence. The Serenissima Repubblica, or "most serene republic" of Venice, prided itself on its reputation for justice and its freedom from the political turmoil that afflicted Italy's other major powers. The self-designation was not entirely accurate, for Venice was governed by a rigidly patrician oligarchy, and women, excluded from political life, did not enjoy the same "serenity" as men. Nonetheless, the Venetian civic mythology informed the writing and worldview of Modesta, who deeply identified with her native city. Her parents – Marietta del Moro, and Girolamo Pozzo, a lawyer – were *cittadini originari*, "original citizens" in the educated upper middle class; both died when she was barely one year old and her brother, Leonardo (b. 1553), just three. Much of her biography comes to us through Giovanni Niccolò Doglioni (1548–1629), a notary and relative by marriage who eventually stepped in as Modesta's guardian and later published a brief account of her life as a preface to the 1600 *Worth of Women*[3] (see Figure 22.1).

There, Doglioni recounts that Modesta first boarded for several years in the Santa Marta convent, where she received a rudimentary education but charmed the nuns with her precocity. At age nine, she returned to the home of her maternal grandmother, Cecilia di Mazzi, and Cecilia's second husband, the lawyer Prospero Saraceni. Displaying an early thirst for knowledge – Doglioni states that she "excelled in everything she tried," from poetry to arithmetic – Modesta continued her studies, devouring all the volumes in Prospero's rich library and convincing her brother to teach her Latin by repeating his daily lessons from school. When Prospero's daughter, Saracena Saraceni, just a little older than Modesta, married Doglioni around 1576, Modesta joined their household. A well-connected writer with a strong interest in natural philosophy, Doglioni encouraged Modesta's literary talent and included one of her sonnets in his 1587 treatise, *L'anno* (*The Year*). In turn, a character in Moderata's dialogue evinces her regard for Doglioni, describing him as a "gentleman and great friend" and marveling, "What wisdom! That a mortal can decipher and distinguish each power of the heavens, each power below."

VERA MODERATÆ FONTIS EFFIGIES,
ÆTATIS SVÆ. ANNO XXXIIII.

Figure 22.1 Portrait of Moderata Fonte at age thirty-four, accompanying
    Il merito delle donne (Venice: G. D. Imberti, 1600)

(Rare Book Collection, Kislak Center for Special Collections, Rare Books and Manuscripts, University of Pennsylvania)

It was during this period, and certainly by 1581 when she published her first book, that Modesta Pozzo became Moderata Fonte.
Not only was the pseudonym a confident play on her given name –
evolving from "Modest Pool" to "Moderate Fountain" and emphasizing a tempered and refined quality prized by the intellectual fashion
of the time – but it also offered an added degree of protection. Like
most Venetian women of her social class, Moderata lived a private,
secluded life, her reputation carefully guarded. Though famous for
their elaborate fashions – including their chopines, or dramatically
tall clogs, and elaborate hairstyles, like the braided "horns" worn
by Moderata in the image that accompanied *The Worth of Women* –

Venetian noblewomen had limited participation in public life, considered unbefitting of their status. This created a vacuum that was often filled instead by the courtesans for which the city was famous: beautiful, highly educated escorts who sold conversation as well as sexual company. Some of the best-known Venetian women writers – like Veronica Franco and Gaspara Stampa – were closely associated with the more public worlds of courtesanry or music; even so, Gaspara sometimes shielded herself with the classicizing pseudonym "Anasilla." Moderata's close contemporary, the respectably married Lucrezia Marinella, published under her own name but took great pains to craft an untouchable persona of feminine virtue, and women writers – regardless of the name they wrote under – often claimed to have been prodded into publishing by others, rather than risk criticism for seeking to do so themselves. But for an unmarried woman of the citizen class, entering the public world of print courted controversy, even slander. A pen name, no matter how transparent, offered a veil of anonymity. Such concerns are evident in the dedicatory letter to Moderata's first published work, the chivalric romance *Tredici canti di Floridoro* (*Thirteen Cantos of Floridoro*), which declares she has adopted an "imagined name" in order to avoid "public censure"[4] (see Figure 22.2).

Dedicated to the grand duke of Florence, Francesco de' Medici, and his Venetian bride, Bianca Cappello, *Floridoro* takes inspiration from Ludovico Ariosto's poem, *Orlando furioso* (*The Frenzy of Orlando*, itself inspired by Matteo Maria Boiardo's fifteenth-century *Orlando Innamorato*, or *Orlando in Love*). Ariosto's Renaissance bestseller was produced in the early sixteenth century for the Este family, Ariosto's patrons, and the rulers of Ferrara. Like Ariosto's tale, Moderata's *Floridoro* is populated by knights, ladies, and sorceresses, but it takes place in ancient Greece and relates the adventures of prince Floridoro and his future bride, presenting them as the founders of another powerful dynasty, the Medici. Moderata infuses this traditionally male literary form with an early preview, rooted in a fantastical world, of the feminist stance she would adopt in the *Worth of Women*. Female characters, like the warrior Risamante, whose armor conceals her identity, or the wise enchantress Circetta, are strong, intelligent women and morally above reproach, capable in "arms" as well as "letters."

More explicitly, a famous verse from the fourth canto of the *Floridoro* offers a powerful appeal that serves as the nucleus of Moderata's

Figure 22.2 Title page of Moderata Fonte's *Tredici canti del Floridoro* (Venice, 1581)

thought and a potent expression of Renaissance feminism, later cited by Marinella in her own 1601 feminist manifesto:

> Throughout the ages, women have been endowed by Nature with excellent judgement and great courage, and they are born no less well fitted than men to display wisdom and valor, if properly trained and nurtured. And, indeed, if men and women share the same bodily form, if they are composed of like substance, if they eat and speak in the same way, why should they be thought to differ in courage and intelligence?

For Moderata, the answer is clear: if women have not achieved the same fame and glory as men and in equal numbers, it is because they have been discouraged from turning their energies "toward heroic and challenging deeds."

Though untapped, their potential is no less valuable for that. Borrowing the imagery of metallurgy, Moderata offers a forceful analogy, asserting, "The gold that lies buried in the mines is still gold, even though it is buried from sight, and when it is mined and worked, it is as precious and exquisite as any other gold." Women's intellect is inherently powerful, and with attention will shine as brightly as that of men. Though unfinished – in her dedication she projects at least fifty canti for *Floridoro*, rather than the thirteen that appeared in print, an ambition that would have outdone Ariosto's forty-six – Moderata's poem inspired other women writers, notably Marinella and Margherita Sarrocchi, who also undertook new feminist approaches to this genre traditionally overlooked by women authors.

Championed by Doglioni and others, *Floridoro* was a success. Moderata published two more works the following year: *Le feste* (*The Celebrations*), a short dramatic dialogue performed for the doge, Venice's highest political authority, and *La passione di Christo* (*The Passion of Christ*), which interspersed the familiar biblical story with interludes highlighting female figures at the heart of Christianity, such as the Virgin Mary and Mary Magdalene. In a sign of the accolades garnered by these early works, Moderata's verse was featured in a 1583 poetic anthology in honor of Stephan Bathory after his marriage to Anna Jagiellon, queen of the Polish-Lithuanian commonwealth and daughter of Bona Sforza.[5]

Amid these literary successes, in 1583 Moderata married Filippo Zorzi, a lawyer from a fellow family of *cittadini originari* selected by Doglioni. She was now twenty-seven, older than most Venetian brides of her social class. The union may have been delayed due to legal issues regarding Moderata's inheritance resulting from her parents' untimely death; marriages required often costly dowries – a fact decried in *The Worth of Women*, where one character wryly observes that if men instead paid dowries to women, "marriage would be a little more tolerable." Unusually, Filippo did sign control of his new wife's dowry back over to her shortly after their marriage.[6] Whatever the reason for the delay, it had provided the precious freedom to pursue her literary ambitions. After she married, Moderata's authorial efforts slowed, though they did not stop. Doglioni claims that Fonte composed "countless sonnets, canzoni and madrigals," mostly anonymously, and in 1592 she published a religious poem, *La resurrettione di Giesu Christo* (*The Resurrection of Jesus Christ*), prefaced by an admiring sonnet by her husband. But it is likely that the duties of marriage and motherhood took their toll. As the humanist Laura Cereta wrote a century earlier, time is a "terribly scarce commodity" for women intellectuals, "those of us who spend our skills and labor equally on families and our own work."[7] Moderata gave birth to two sons and a daughter over the next nine years, before dying of complications from the birth of her fourth child in 1592.

In the decade before her death, Moderata had begun working on her best-known book, *The Worth of Women* (see Figure 22.3). A conversation spread across two fictional "days," it covers a wide range of topics affecting women – from concerns about the men in their lives to health, education, beauty, and favorite recipes – and traces perceptive connections between Renaissance notions of gender and social roles and their impact on women's lives. The *Worth of Women* was written in the years before 1592, making it an early and highly prescient articulation of the Venetian feminism that would develop further in the seventeenth century, but was not published until after Moderata's death. The right occasion came with the controversial 1599 release of Giuseppe Passi's outrageously misogynist treatise, *I donneschi difetti* (*The Defects of Women*), a volume that marked the vitriolic apex of the literary battle of the sexes in Renaissance Italy. Moderata's manuscript, which so lucidly lays out the case for women's equality, was a perfect response to Passi and, in 1600, it was published with a dedication to the new duchess of Urbino, Livia Feltria della Rovere, by Moderata's daughter, Cecilia (b. circa 1585), and two sonnets by her eldest son, Pietro (b. 1584). The following year, another feminist rebuttal would follow, authored by Marinella.

Moderata's protagonists include two unmarried women, a newly-wed, two matrons, a widow, and a dowager. They discuss literature, medicine, and science along with the day-to-day concerns of Venetian women, from motherhood to financial worries and abusive husbands. Moderata's literary alter ego, the scholarly Corinna, unmarried by choice, often voices the explicitly feminist perspective ("sensible women," she notes, "leave their wicked husbands to avoid a living hell").[8] But no matter the topic at hand, all seven women collectively pose questions that steer the discussion to its heart: the oppression of women.

Figure 22.3 Title page of Moderata Fonte's *Il merito delle donne* (Venice: Domenico Imberti, 1600)

(Rare Book Collection, Kislak Center for Special Collections, Rare Books and Manuscripts, University of Pennsylvania)

The work begins with a celebration of female friendship as the women gather at the home of Leonora, a young widow with no plans to remarry. "To tell the truth," sighs the older matron Lucretia, "we are only really happy when we are alone with other women." As the characters begin to praise the merits of women, however, one interrupts the discussion to pose a simple but powerful question: if women are equal – even superior – to men, why do men continue to oppress women and act as their "superiors on every count"? Calling into question a long-standing argument against women rooted in the ancient philosopher Aristotle, which held that men were biologically superior and that women were "imperfect" or unformed versions of men, the response is straightforward. "This pre-eminence," Corinna answers succinctly, "is something [men] have unjustly arrogated to themselves." Not satisfied, Leonora, presses the issue, querying:

> If men usurp our rights, should we not complain and declare that they have wronged us? For if we are inferiors in status, but not in worth, this is an abuse that has been introduced into the world and that men have then, over time, gradually translated into law and custom, and it has become so entrenched that they claim (and even actually believe) that the status they have gained through their bullying is theirs by right.

Leonora recognizes that there is no biological or even theological basis for the domination of men over women – and that gender is culturally constructed to benefit some groups over others.

Corinna then extends the line of inquiry by asking why examples of male excellence and heroism predominate, while women's contributions to history go unsung:

> Do you really believe . . . that everything historians tell us about men – or about women – is actually true? You ought to consider the fact that these histories have been written by men, who never tell the truth except by accident.

It is a sharp observation about the ways in which history – and historiography – shapes power: who gets it, and who is excluded from it. Moderata's speakers have a remarkable ability to step back from their own lived reality and pose big, enduring questions about how inequities become entrenched in social reality.

In the second half of their conversation, the women turn from exploring the origins of gender inequality to an encyclopedic discussion of medicine, science, and the cosmos. They debate the causes of various natural phenomena like earthquakes, thunderstorms, and ocean currents, along with the properties of plants, herbs, and spices, their display of knowledge always remaining tied to their central theme. For instance, Leonora, marveling that water manages to rise high enough to feed mountain springs despite being a heavy element, concedes that in this respect water is like men, who though inferior and "heavy" by nature, still find the means to rise and rule – an example of Nature breaking her own laws:

> Just think of the way in which men, who are inferior to us and so should by rights stay below us, in a lowly and humble position, manage to rise above us and dominate us, against all reason and against all justice. So you shouldn't be surprised if water, too, though such a base element, is presumptuous enough to ascend to the level of mountains. At least water flows back to its natural level again, whereas men remain obstinately fixed in their stern position of eminence.

The women's discussions of natural phenomenon and medicine are multilayered, simultaneously providing practical information to the reader – like recipes for preparing fish or remedies for common ailments (rhubarb for fever, aloe for nerves, nutmeg for fertility), demonstrating the spectrum of women's knowledge about the world, and strengthening their arguments. As Corinna concludes, it would hardly be in men's interest to provide women with equal access to education, which would destabilize the existing social structure in which women care for men and men abuse them. It is a radical twist on Christine de Pizan's advocacy for women's education, which focused on the moral benefits – and a feminist facet to Niccolò Machiavelli's arguments about the systems of political power and class conflict. This early articulation of the systemic oppression of women stands at the origins of modern feminist social critique. Knowledge – about history, politics, natural philosophy, medicine – is central to gender equality. If women want to take control of their own future, they must first take control of their own education, their own health, and their autonomy.

Like other Venetian women writing before and after her, Moderata turned to Venice's own vision of itself as a free, independent, and inviolate city to bring into relief the subordinate and marginalized state of its women. Women, she argues, are more than their roles as daughters, wives, and mothers: they yearn for – and deserve – the opportunity to freely pursue education and intellectual pursuits, to make their own choices, and to receive the respect they are owed, just like men. The all-female cast of *The Worth of Women* dares to imagine a society in which women are fully realized as individuals outside of their relationships to and with men. Yet her speakers do not present themselves as revolutionaries. Unlike authors in subsequent years – notably, the fiery Arcangela Tarabotti – Fonte presents her characters in the *Worth of Women* as ultimately conciliatory, seeking not to upend the status quo but rather to point out injustices and contemplate a more equitable world.

Moderata was recognized in her own day as an important voice: writing in 1625, the biographer of early modern women Cristofano Bronzini praised *The Worth of Women* as "a most beautiful and learned prose discourse," and her views influenced some of the most significant feminist writers in early modern Italy.[9] Her assertion that women, when given the same educational opportunities as men, can succeed equally well at any profession or skill they choose, makes her one of the most important feminist thinkers of Renaissance Italy, and the questions she posed about power continue to resonate. Scholars and audiences have increasingly recognized the powerful political and philosophical legacy of her writing with regard to her views on women's equality and liberty – symbolized, in the walled garden where her dialogue unfolds, by a graceful statue of a woman holding the sun, an emblem of freedom – and *The Worth of Women* has been staged as a play by the Kairos Italy Theater Company, with performances at Carnegie Hall and New York University. In the twenty-first century, with women's equality and freedom still contested and their access to education still denied in some parts of the world, Moderata Fonte's intellectual clarity and courage are a reminder – then and now – that the first step to enacting change is to assess and question the world around us.

23 Lucrezia Marinella (1571?–1653)

Champion of Women's History

My desire is to reveal to all this dazzling truth: that the female sex is nobler and more excellent than the male.

— Lucrezia Marinella

Born in Venice less than two decades after Moderata Fonte, whose writings she knew and admired, Lucrezia Marinella added her own voice to the discussion. Contemporaries described the erudite Lucrezia, doyenne of the Venetian literary world, as "a woman of wondrous eloquence and learning . . . impossible to surpass," an expert in everything from "sacred compositions" to moral and natural philosophy.[1] Her career – which spanned eight decades – was exceptionally long, prolific, and varied, encompassing religious biographies, epic poetry, and a brilliantly argued vindication of women. Her writing reflects aspects of the moral, religious, and ideological environment of the Counter-Reformation – inaugurated by the Council of Trent convened between 1545 and 1563 in reaction to the Protestant Reformation. But it just as often tests those bounds, highlighting the contributions of women to the social and political fabric and proclaiming their equality and even superiority to men. Together with her compatriots Moderata Fonte and Arcangela Tarabotti, Lucrezia was a principal contributor to the development of early modern feminist theory.

An engraved likeness of Lucrezia by Giacomo Piccini (or Pecini) dating to 1652, just before her death, depicts a composed and refined figure with an inquisitive gaze and the laurels of a poet (see Figure 23.1). It elegantly evokes both the intellectual prestige and the decorum that Lucrezia cultivated in her literary persona. Born into a Venetian family of the educated professional class, Lucrezia was raised in learned

DOI: 10.4324/9781003081807-29

Figure 23.1 Depiction of Lucrezia Marinella, by Giacomo Pecini in a seventeenth-century anthology of women philosophers (*Effigies fae-
minarum de poesi philosophia alisque litteratum disciplinis . . .*
Venice, 1652, 63)

(Archivio dell'Accademia di Belle Arti di Venezia)

environment, gaining a particular familiarity with medicine and philosophy. While little is known of her mother, her father was Giovanni
Marinelli (Lucrezia employed the feminine version of his surname,
as was common for women of the period), a physician who published
works devoted to the medical and cosmetic concerns of women, as
well as a treatise on the Italian language. Lucrezia's brother, Curzio,
also a doctor, authored a work on pharmacology. When she eventually
married at a relatively late age for women of her class, it was to another
physician, Girolamo Vacca.

   Like other Venetian women of her social class, Lucrezia lived a
secluded life, but she enjoyed an unusual degree of intellectual freedom. She was not forced to enter a convent, nor did expectations for
her future role as wife and mother curtail her education. As the only

daughter in a household of physicians, she took advantage of her father's library. She learned Greek and Latin, read medical and biological texts, and studied classical poets and philosophers along with the major voices of the Italian vernacular tradition. Instructed in music as well as literature and philosophy, she played the lute and several other instruments. Giovanni died sometime before 1600, but the affectionate light in which Lucrezia casts fathers in her writing suggests that she credited him for her thorough education, and it was during these years at home that Lucrezia forged some of the most important literary connections of her career. Chief among these was the writer and physician Luigi Scarano, a family friend who took an early interest in her talents, publicly praising her poetry and her skill in dialectic, the practice of philosophical reasoning. It was likely through Scarano that the otherwise reserved Lucrezia established a foothold in the world of Venetian publishing – and it was to him that she would later dedicate her feminist treatise. At the same time, however, Lucrezia maintained her distance from some of the most influential literary forces in Venice, especially the libertine Accademia degli Incogniti (Academy of the Unknowns), notorious for their scandalous publications, which were frequently misogynistic and anticlerical.

From the ages of twenty-four to thirty-five, Lucrezia published six books in rapid succession. After her marriage to Vacca around 1601, there followed a long pause in publication between 1606 and 1624, a period that saw the births of her children, Antonio and Paulina, both mentioned in the will she made in 1645. But after two decades of literary silence, Lucrezia, now living near Venice's Arsenale shipyard, took up her pen once more. She would publish several more works before her death, making her the most prolific woman author in seventeenth-century Italy – some fifty years after Laura Terracina, the most published woman of the sixteenth century, made her mark on that earlier era of unprecedented participation by women in Italian print culture.

Erudite and devout, Lucrezia took to heart the Counter-Reformation notion that literature should promote Catholic doctrine and morality; in fact, most of her works are dedicated to religious subjects. While she is associated today with the bold arguments of her feminist treatise, she was most celebrated in her own day for her explorations of the lives of holy women like Columba, Catherine of Siena, and the Virgin Mary, though she also wrote in praise of male saints like Francis of Assisi. Lucrezia highlighted the power of these women as teachers, preachers, and spiritual icons central to Christianity. In her 1602 *Vita di Maria*

Vergine, imperatrice dell'universo (*Life of the Virgin Mary, Empress of the Universe*), written in the "poetic prose" of Renaissance epic, for example, Lucrezia's Mary takes an active role in guiding others toward salvation, preserving the story of Christ and even converting others to the Christian faith. While a surge of devotion to Mary in the late Renaissance emphasized her role as mother and co-redeemer of all Christians, Lucrezia's dynamic representation of the Virgin as the "empress" at the center of her own heroic narrative challenged in many respects the more submissive Mary typical of many other Counter-Reformation depictions. Lucrezia's *Maria Vergine* proved her most successful work, with multiple editions over the next decade.[2]

Lucrezia's contribution to the Renaissance *querelle des femmes* – the French term used for the "argument" over the virtues, capabilities, and proper role of women that had gripped Europe since Christine de Pizan composed her *City of Ladies* in France in 1405 – was thus a notable departure from her signature literary style. Like another feminist work by Moderata Fonte just a year earlier, Lucrezia's *La nobiltà et l'eccellenza delle donne, co' difetti et mancamenti de gli uomini* (*The Nobility and Excellence of Women and the Defects and Vices of Men*) was published in response to *I donneschi difetti* (*The Defects of Women*), a misogynist screed by Giuseppe Passi printed in 1599 (see Figure 23.2). A member of the Accademia degli Informi (Academy of the Formless) of Ravenna, Passi inveighed against women as lustful, corrupt, adulterous, and prone to vanity and gluttony, claiming that they "were the cause in all things of men's ruin." He drew on historians, poets, and theologians to justify his points, seeking to conquer his readers through an avalanche of examples, and even insinuated that women, lacking reason and virtue, did not belong to the same species as men at all – an argument that would return in Venice with a vengeance by the 1640s. Though Passi's diatribe teemed with outlandish characterizations of women's moral and intellectual inferiority, publishers – betting on a market of outraged readers keen to read its rebuttal – saw it as a commercial opportunity. This was especially the case in Venice, the capital of the European print industry, where editors and presses played a key role in shaping and profiting from hot-button cultural conversations – much as certain television, radio, and internet personalities today capitalize on stoking manufactured controversy and "culture wars."

Lucrezia's pointedly titled treatise advertising the "nobility and excellence of women" is a direct and open refutation of each of Passi's

Figure 23.2 Title page of Lucrezia Marinella, *La nobiltà et l'eccellenza delle donne, co' difetti et mancamenti de gli huomini* (*The Nobility and Excellence of Women, and the Defects and Vices of Men*) (Venice, 1601)

Rare Book Collection, Kislak Center for Special Collections, Rare Books and Manuscripts, University of Pennsylvania

accusations, employing philosophical proofs and examples drawn from ancient and modern history to debunk them entirely. Her central claim – that women are not just men's moral and intellectual equals but their clear superiors – injects a bold new twist into the *querelle*. Turning the two pillars of ancient philosophy to her advantage, Lucrezia uses Aristotelian philosophy to argue that men and women share the same human nature, and Neoplatonism to assert that female beauty reveals a superior degree of inner virtue. Her deft intertwinement of canonical sources with new feminist arguments is on display in the very first pages, where she declares that she will prove how women "surpass men" in "nobility," beginning with the words used to describe them.³ The idea that the names of things reflect essential qualities of their referents was common in Renaissance philosophy. In a tortured etymological argument, Passi had claimed that the origins of the Italian and Latin words for women – *donna*, *femina*, and *mulier* – revealed the innate evil of the female sex. Accepting Passi's methodology, Lucrezia agrees that names reveal the nature of things – and therefore, "Who will ever deny that the feminine sex is adorned with worthier and more illustrious names than the masculine sex?" Using Passi's own examples to draw diametrically opposed conclusions in favor of women's superiority to men, she concludes: "it can be seen that woman brings forth the ungrateful male, gives him life and soul, illuminates him with the splendor of divine light . . . and finally rules over him with a sweet, nontyrannical dominion."

With the stage set for a subversive philosophical tour de force, Lucrezia then makes her case by presenting a long lineage of women renowned for their intellect, from the ancient Egyptian astronomer Hypatia of Alexandria and the Greek philosopher Sosipatra of Ephesus to the fourth-century scholar and martyr Catherine of Alexandria. Pointedly, she adds modern examples to this pantheon, including the fifteenth-century scholars Cassandra Fedele and Isotta Nogarola; the poets Terracina and Vittoria Colonna; and many others, among them Marguerite of Navarre and Catherine Parr, the last wife of Henry VIII of England. If "women have the same reasoning souls as men, . . . and souls that are still nobler," Lucrezia argues, "why should they not be even better than men at learning the same arts and sciences?" In a direct reference to another work by Fonte, Lucrezia notes that women are excluded from education because "men, fearing to lose their authority and become women's servants, often forbid them even to learn to read or write."⁴ Though Lucrezia's catalog of famous women highlights only the examples she would have known from the Western tradition, it conveys a central message about recognizing a female intellectual genealogy, supporting and acknowledging women's achievements. Lucrezia argues that it is vital to make a deliberate record of women's excellence – in effect, to create the discipline of women's history – for "history books" have been authored by men for their own benefit. Why bother reading these existing accounts, she asks, "when their authors – being men who are envious of women's worthy deeds – do not talk about women's noble actions, but instead consign them to silence"?⁵ For Lucrezia, the roots of this envy lie in men's anger, "the origin of indecent accusations against women" – an anger that derives from men's inability to truly control women, no matter what mechanisms they put in place.[6]

Lucrezia's defense of women extends – as Fonte's did – to the quotidian aspects of their lives. Even their right to enhance their beauty – a "special gift" granted to them by God – is unjustly attacked by men, who condemn them for using cosmetics and skin tonics. Yet, she asks,

> Why should it be a sin if a woman . . . washes her face with delicate lemon juice and the water of beauflowers and privets in order to remove her freckles and keep her skin soft and clean? Or if with colombine, white bread, lemon juice, and pearls she creates some other potion to keep her skin clean and soft?

Why, she continues, should women not also bleach and curl their hair, if they like? Their outer beauty reflects the goodness of their soul. Men, by contrast, go to absurd lengths to hide their innate cowardice behind "artifice and tinsel."[7] Again, Lucrezia counters Passi's every attack with the argument of women's superiority.

While *The Nobility and Excellence of Women* is Lucrezia's most direct philosophical defense of women, she addressed these issues – if more subtly – throughout her literary career. Courting influential patrons with dedications to doges, duchesses, and other powerful figures, she published a wide variety of works in many different genres that feature strong, intelligent female protagonists. Her pastoral romance *Arcadia felice* (*Happy Arcadia*), of 1605; her 1618 reinterpretation of the classical Cupid and Psyche myth, *Amore innamorato, et impazzato* (*Love Enamored and Driven Mad*); and her mid-career epic, *Enrico, ovvero Bizanzio acquistato* (*Enrico, or Byzantium Conquered*) of 1635 present women as both moral and erudite, and implicitly question their lack of freedom and access to education. In *Arcadia*, for instance, the king's virtuous daughter Ersilia flees palace intrigue for peaceful Arcadia, where she disguises herself as a young man, "Ersilio," and distinguishes herself in games and sports. After this fleeting experience with the liberty that men take for granted, Ersilia's true identity is uncovered, and she is forced to return to her circumscribed life as a princess, a commentary on the social roles and norms imposed on women. Episodes of gender confusion and cross-dressing abound in early modern literature, from Ariosto to Shakespeare, but from the pens of women writers like Lucrezia they become windows into an alternative world in which women enjoy the same possibilities as men.

Two decades after this venture into Arcadia, Lucrezia turned her hand to another popular Renaissance genre: heroic poetry. Dedicated to Venice itself, her *Enrico* took inspiration from Torquato Tasso's prominent Christian epic, the *Gerusalemme liberata* (*Jerusalem Delivered*) first printed in 1581, and in turn from her contemporary Margherita Sarrocchi's *Scanderbeide*, composed after Tasso's model in 1623. Heeding Tasso's Counter-Reformation advice to combine historical episodes with "marvelous" adventures sparked by divine intervention, Lucrezia reinterprets a still relevant event from several centuries prior: the Fourth Crusade, which launched from Venice in 1202 and opened with the siege of Zara (a city in what is now Croatia) but failed to achieve its goal of retaking Jerusalem and ended instead with the sack of Constantinople. Lucrezia reframes the event from a distinctly Venetian angle that imagines the Christian crusaders sailing for Palestine before returning to assist in Byzantium and glorifies the role of the doge, embellishing his religious devotion over the more pragmatic interests that had in actuality fueled the endeavor (see Figure 23.3).

Though the hero of her story is ostensibly the crusading knight Venier, it is the brilliant sorceress Erina and her handmaid Altea who help the shipwrecked Venier understand the glorious past and future of the Venetian Republic and guide him back to his encampment. Unlike many of their counterparts in male-authored epic, who sow erotic confusion, Lucrezia's supernatural characters – who show Venier the world from a flying chariot – are both learned and chaste. Their passion is reserved instead for knowing the world: the vast geography of the globe, the moon's pull on the tides, and the composition of the Milky Way. But their knowledge respects accepted Catholic cosmology, for although such references indicate a familiarity with the new scientific discourse heralded by the astronomer Galileo Galilei, whose trial for heresy took place just a few years before the publication of *Enrico*, Lucrezia's characters still adhere to the earth-centered view of the universe approved by the Church, in line with her general orthodoxy.

The curious capstone to Lucrezia's career, however, was instead a 1645 treatise titled *Essortationi alle donne et a gli altri* (*Exhortations to Women and Others*), which has long perplexed readers with its seeming acceptance and even advocacy of traditional roles for women. In apparent contradiction to her stance in the *Nobility and Excellence of Women*, and to the active role ascribed to her other female characters, in this final work Lucrezia advises women to pursue a life of

Figure 23.3 The Crusaders Conquering the City of Zara in 1202, by Andrea Vicentino (Michieli), c. 1578

(Palazzo Ducale, Venice)

Photo: Bridgeman

seclusion and domesticity, shun literary activity, and content themselves with feminine pastimes such as weaving or embroidery. Now calling literary ambition "a useless effort" "of little comfort," Lucrezia appears to reject her own prodigious accomplishments over the course of her decades-long career. Was this a sophisticated play on an ancient philosophical genre – an argument or riddle for the sake of entertainment – or perhaps an exaggerated argument intended as satire? Or was the writer, a lifelong Catholic now facing her own mortality and more focused on the afterlife than on earthly fame, concerned about the state of her soul? After years spent navigating the often-hostile terrain faced by Renaissance women writers, maybe Lucrezia had simply wearied of the conflict and sought to save other women from the tribulations of literary fame.[8] She herself had faced charges of plagiarism when her career began to take off in the early 1600s, as would the Venetian polemicists Tarabotti and Sarra Copia Sulam. Regardless of her motivations, Lucrezia's *Exhortations* provide an ambivalent coda to a long and prolific literary career.

Over the course of more than eighty years, Lucrezia Marinella established herself as the most eminent woman writer in late Renaissance Venice and a forerunner to modern feminist methodology. She was one of the first to directly critique the motives behind misogynist literature and openly connect those motives to the exclusion of women from public life. With rigorous scholarship and acute insight, she exposed the unreliability of the philosophical "authorities" on whom centuries of patriarchal power rested and spurred her readers to view those arguments with the skepticism they deserved. Although she did not go so far as proposing concrete reforms to address gender inequality in Renaissance society, the next step in the development of modern feminism that would characterize later generations, she analyzed the situation of women in explicitly political terms, making a forceful argument for their freedom, power, and equality – even superiority – and laying the groundwork for subsequent theorists to build on. She was known and praised in her day, in Italy and beyond, including by the Dutch humanist Anna Maria van Schurman and the noted biographer of early modern women, Cristofano Bronzini, who deferred to her expertise in women's history.[9] Today, Lucrezia has returned to prominence as a major voice in early modern Italy, and her work garners attention from those interested in Renaissance philosophy, religion, and feminism as well as literature.

24 Sarra Copia Sulam (1592–1641)

Poet and Polemicist in Venice's Jewish Ghetto

With your protection, Lord, I prepare
to defend myself, since an adversary
insults and criticizes me, daring to brand as infidel
my soul which, by your grace, I arm with faith.

– Sarra Copia Sulam

In the same city as Moderata Fonte and Lucrezia Marinella, but a world away, Sarra Copia Sulam, the most famous Jewish woman writer of the Renaissance, left her mark. Her name was known far beyond the bounds of the Venetian Ghetto, the crowded neighborhood to which Jews were confined by law.

One of the oldest such quarters in Europe, the Ghetto was situated in the district of Canareggio on the site of an old foundry, or *ghèto* (from the verb *gettare*, "to throw") – likely giving rise to the modern term. A city within a city, enclosed by canals and accessible via gated footbridges, it was created in the early sixteenth century by Venetian officials to segregate and surveil the city's Jewish population (see Figure 24.1). The same republic that extolled the ideals of independence and liberty did not extend those freedoms equally to its inhabitants, neither to women nor to non-Christians. While Venice, unlike many other cities in Europe, granted Jews the freedom to worship – the Ghetto held several synagogues – Jews in Venice were restricted in many other ways, including their passage in and out of the district. Christian theologians throughout Europe perpetuated the biblical trope of Jewish enslavement, creating a racialized hierarchy that subordinated Jews – and other non-Christians – as an expression of divine will. Religious difference was thus inextricably bound up with race and racism in the Renaissance: a long and troubled history punctuated by

DOI: 10.4324/9781003081807-30

Figure 24.1 Campo del Ghetto Nuovo, Venice

Photo: Alamy

the numerous expulsions of Jews across the centuries, including from England in 1290 and Spain in 1492.[1]

Even as the Venetian Republic relied on and benefited from the economic, professional, and cultural contributions of its Jewish inhabitants – who worked as doctors and merchants, moneylenders and entrepreneurs, laborers and scholars – it created elaborate physical, legal, and symbolic barriers to limit their interactions with Christians. The original Ghetto, called the Ghetto Nuovo, housed close to a thousand Italian and Ashkenazi Jews; by the time Sarra was born, it had expanded to include the Ghetto Vecchio and would expand again into the Ghetto Nuovissimo in 1633. The area became so crowded that its residents, forbidden to spread beyond the allotted footprint, had to build upward, resulting in a kind of "vertical city" in which additional stories were added to existing buildings to create more living space.[2] The restrictions did not end there. Like prostitutes and other marginalized groups, the Ghetto's residents were required to wear identifying markers such as specially colored hats or badges and had to obtain special permission to leave the area at night. Similar discriminatory markers were required in other Italian cities, like Milan and Genoa, and reflected Christian anxieties about distinguishing the "other" through visible signs.[3]

Despite these restrictions, Venice's Ghetto was a vibrant cultural center that, by the early seventeenth century, was a major producer of Hebrew books and a hub of scholarly exchange. Christian writers and thinkers from all over Europe were also drawn to the Ghetto, creating an opportunity for the encounter of faiths even as the Counter-Reformation – the period of the Catholic Church's reaffirmation of orthodoxy spurred by the Protestant Reformation – was nearing its apex. This context shaped intellectual life for Sarra, the eldest of three daughters born to Simon Coppio (d. 1606), a merchant and moneylender from the Ionian island of Zante then part of the Venetian Republic, and his wife Ricca Grassini (d. 1645). Successful and well-educated, Simon was a patron of the prominent Jewish author Leon Modena, who dedicated works to Simon and his brother, Moisè, and later also to Sarra. Modena praised Sarra's "singular qualities and many virtues . . . and considerable knowledge," and after her death composed the epitaph for her headstone.[4] Because Jews were legally prohibited from owning property in Venice, Sarra's family rented their apartment in the Ghetto Nuovo.

At home, Sarra had an unusually extensive education, studying ancient Greek, Latin, Hebrew, and Spanish along with philosophical and religious texts, including both the Old and New Testament and rabbinic literature. She composed poetry and is reputed to have been a gifted singer, who often played the clavichord or lute as she recited verse. In his will, Simon wished his three daughters to wed "husbands to their liking, so long as they are upstanding, honest, and honourable," and he provided them with sizable dowries to do so; his will also established that each girl would have "absolute control" of her portion of inheritance, so long as she continued "to follow and abide by our Jewish law."[5] So it is likely that around 1609 when Sarra married Giacob Sulam – a well-to-do banker and leader in the religious community, originally from Mantua – she embraced the match. None of their children survived past infancy: a daughter, Rebecca, died in 1615, before turning one, and Sarra mentions a miscarriage in a letter three years later. Instead, Sarra devoted herself ever more intensively to the life of the mind, studying, writing, and engaging in conversation with other authors and scholars.

Most of our information about Sarra's life and work dates to the seven-year period from 1618 to 1624, when she was corresponding with Christian and Jewish literary and religious figures and hosting a burgeoning intellectual salon from her home. It was a high-profile period of intense activity, in which her sharp intellect and gift for philosophical debate – as well as her striking beauty – garnered attention well beyond the Ghetto Nuovo. Sarra was admired by Venetian literati, including members of the nascent Accademia degli Incogniti (Academy of the Unknowns), the literary society whose iconoclastic bent would later lead them to promote some of the most radical women in Venice, like the nun Arcangela Tarabotti. Sarra's circle included Numidio Paluzzi, a Roman author with connections to the Venetian publishing world, and his friend Alessandro Berardelli, a painter and proofreader; as well as Giovanni Francesco Coriani, a writer and jurist; and her family friend Leon da Modena.

But it was Sarra's intense epistolary relationship with the monk and Incogniti member Ansaldo Cebà, initiated by Sarra herself upon reading his 1615 epic poem, *La reina Esther* (*Queen Esther*), that sparked her turbulent journey into the public eye. The Old Testament story of Esther was a popular subject for Renaissance writers and artists, including both Lucrezia Tornabuoni and Artemisia Gentileschi, with the figure of Esther often interpreted as a model of humility for young brides. Sarra explained she was so moved by Cebà's account of the biblical heroine who saved her people from destruction that she kept the volume with her constantly, even while sleeping. Her enthusiastic letter sparked what would become a four-year exchange of letters, poems, and gifts. Significant gaps limit our understanding of their epistolary relationship, as only Cebà's side of the correspondence – published in 1623 – survives, leaving readers to fill in her missing voice. But we do know from a sonnet she composed that Sarra sent Cebà a painting of herself as a token of her admiration, calling him her "idol"; in turn, Cebà, almost thirty years her senior, fed on her flattery and infused his own letters to her with a passion that often verges on the erotic (see Figure 24.2).

Cebà's letters are filled with innuendo and wordplay: for example, he puns on Sarra's maiden name, "Coppia" (she used the feminized version of her father's surname) – meaning "couple" – to suggest that they should form a Christian couple together. After this exchange, Sarra dropped the second "p" from her surname, as if to reject the suggestion.[6] The nuances of their peculiar dynamic are further complicated by Cebà's continuous attempts to convert Sarra to Christianity. Praising Sarra for her erudition and moral uprightness "despite" her Jewish faith, he sent her religious books, hoping to sway her, and even urged his friends to join in his efforts to "make love to [Sarra's] soul,"

Figure 24.2 Possible portrait of Sarra Copia Sulam, seventeenth century, attributed to Antonio Logorio (presumed to be copied from a lost portrait by Bernardo Castello)

Photo: Alamy

describing her as his "mistress."[7] Despite these efforts, Sarra remained
unmoved in her beliefs, and even suggested that Cebà instead convert
to Judaism. As Sarra's fame grew, Cebà – frustrated by his failure to
persuade her, and unwilling to "share" her with the broader public of
her salon – became increasingly resentful and hostile, eventually going
so far as to accuse her of promiscuity. When false charges of heresy
put Sarra at risk with the Venetian Inquisition, the enforcement arm of
the Counter-Reformation, in 1621, Cebà, under scrutiny himself for
alleged religious irregularities in his *Esther*, failed to defend her.

Among those who frequented the gatherings in Sarra's home in the
Ghetto – where visitors read poetry and debated literary and religious

topics, likely during daytime given the constraints on movement after dusk – was the poet and priest Baldassare Bonifaccio. Ostensibly spurred by the "difficult and philosophical [and] theological questions" Sarra raised at one of these meetings, Bonifaccio published a treatise in 1621 titled *Dell'immortalità dell'anima* (*On the Immortality of the Soul*), which accused her of having openly denied a fundamental tenet of Christianity, one shared also by Jews. The dogma of the immortality of the soul was reasserted in Lateran Council V in 1512, but the question remained heated and even dangerous in the Renaissance. Figures like Cesare Cremonini of the University of Padua, an influential force in Sarra's Venice, echoed the views of Pietro Pomponazzi, the Aristotelian philosopher of the previous century, concluding that the soul's immortality could not be determined through reason but only as an article of faith – an implicit rejection of the doctrine. Even in the comparatively tolerant religious climate of Venice, the charge was serious enough to raise fears of repercussions from Venice's lay magistracies tasked with cases of blasphemy and Christian-Jewish relations, as well as consequences to a scapegoated Jewish community more generally – and to Sarra herself.[8] She had to answer the attack, and did so immediately, in print, with her *Manifesto of Sarra Copia Sulam, a Jewish Woman, in which she Refutes and Disavows the Opinion Denying the Immortality of the Soul, Falsely Attributed to Her by Signor Baldassare Bonifaccio* (see Figure 24.3).

As the title of Sarra's work makes clear, Bonifaccio's attack had indeed targeted her as both a Jew and a woman: anti-Semitism compounded by misogyny. The *Manifesto* – which Sarra dedicated to her "most beloved parent," Simon – is a philosophical tour de force in response, one that calls on readers and even God himself to defend her against such reckless slander. In her opening letter, Sarra acknowledges that her audience might be taken aback to find a woman venturing so publicly into theology, rather than "what might perhaps be expected from my pen."[9] Using the deflection typical of early modern women writers, she insists that the nature of Bonifaccio's claim has necessitated her forceful refutation. She publishes not out of desire for personal recognition but only to safeguard her name and faith:

[U]nder compulsion I hurriedly composed and published this short writing, not with an end or any thought to achieve glory for myself, but only to defend myself against the false accusations leveled at me by Signor Baldassare Bonifaccio. In his recently printed "Discourses on the Immortality of the Soul" he categorically says that

MANIFESTO
D I
SARRA COPIA
S VL A M H E B R E A.

Nelquale è da lei riprouata, e deteftata l'opi-
nione negante l'immortalità dell'Anima, falfamente attribuitale dal

SIG. BALDASSARE BONIFACCIO.

Con Licenza de' Superiori.

IN VENETIA, M· DCXXI·

Appreffo Giouanni Alberti.

Figure 24.3 Title page of Sarra Copia Sulam's *Manifesto* (Venice: Giovanni
Alberti, 1621)

Photo: Alamy

> I deny that infallible truth about the human soul's being immortal.
> Yet the denial is as far removed from my thinking as the capacity
> to know the inside of hearts is removed from all his knowledge.

Following two prefatory sonnets, Sarra goes on to address Bonifaccio
directly, rejecting his claim and reaffirming her belief in the doctrine –
held by both Christians and Jews – of the soul's immortality:

> The soul of man, Signor Baldassare, is incorruptible, immortal, and
> divine, created and infused by God into our body when the fetus in
> the maternal womb was made fit to receive it. This truth is as cer-
> tain, infallible, and indisputable for me as it is, I believe, for every
> Jew and Christian.

By underscoring areas of commonality between the Jewish and Christian faiths, she seeks not only to introduce her readers to the tenets of Judaism but also to protect herself – and the Jewish community – from Christian reprisal.

Freedom of inquiry, Sarra maintains, is integral to the culture of debate and learning prized by intellectuals. Such discussions only reinforce her Jewish faith and values, rather than undermine them – a critical aspect of the polemic her adversary has overlooked:

> Even if I raised some philosophical or theological difficulty in some discussion with you, it was not out of any uncertainty or indecision I have ever felt about my faith. Rather it was solely out of curiosity to hear from you some curious or uncommon teaching to provide a solution to my arguments.

The palpable weight of being perpetually forced to defend her Judaism is compounded by gender, as Sarra adds: "I reckoned that such a procedure is legitimate for any person who pursues studies, let alone a woman, in this case a Jewish woman continually drawn into these discussions by persons who do not tire of converting her, as you know, to the Christian faith."

Condemning Bonifaccio's arrogance as well as the weakness of his argument, finally, Sarra excoriates him for professing authority on matters of philosophy and theology when "it was not right for you to presume something beyond what any strength of yours allowed." Even as she employs the defensive tactic of ridiculing her antagonist for preying on a vulnerable opponent, sarcastically crediting him as a "courageous challenger of women," Sarra demonstrates her own formidable erudition by drawing on sources ranging from the Old and New Testament to Aristotle and Dante Alighieri, the magisterial medieval poet. Sarra goes further still, mocking Bonifaccio for underestimating her and venturing into linguistic arguments about Scripture without any knowledge of Hebrew, a language many Renaissance humanists aspired to learn: "In this particular, at least, when speaking with a Jewish woman, you should have been spoon-fed by someone who better understood the peculiarities of the language." Reminding him once again of the absurdity of his unfounded attack, given that "there is no reason to combat when neither in words nor in deeds is there any difference of opinion," Sarra concludes her *Manifesto* with a bold and unapologetic reassertion of her faith. "Live happily," she writes, "and hope that the same immortality you preach will be advantageous to you if you live as much to observe your Christian law as I profess to adhere to my Jewish one."

The *Manifesto* was a sensation. It was reprinted three times within a matter of weeks and inspired a new response by Bonifaccio, who accused her of having plagiarized it – a charge often leveled against women writers. But Sarra, a Jewish woman lacking the freedoms and privileges of her male Christian antagonists, was unable to hold back the turning sentiment against her. Without the protection of Cebà, who had discouraged her from "waging a war against men" by publishing her *Manifesto*, she became an easy target. Even friends who had once defended her now took advantage of her. The most blatant such treatment came at the hands of her former tutor Paluzzi, who had at first supported her against Bonifaccio's accusations. In a bizarre sequence of events, Paluzzi – who had depended on Sarra for help while recovering from a long bout of syphilis – swindled her, conspiring with her laundress and others to steal jewelry, food, wine, and other items from her. When she discovered the theft, Sarra promptly denounced Paluzzi and his conspirators to the authorities. Paluzzi's friend Berardelli (perhaps together with Paluzzi) retaliated with an obscene and libelous pamphlet about her titled *Le Sareidi* (*The Epic of Sarra*), full of "the most shameful" insults, which circulated throughout Venice. Paluzzi died from syphilis in 1625, but the attacks on Sarra did not cease. The next year, a posthumous volume of Paluzzi's poetry, edited by Berardelli, launched another volley of thinly veiled charges of plagiary against her, false charges that further threatened her reputation.[10]

Scarred by this backlash, Sarra ceased publishing around this time but did not disappear entirely from view. In a manuscript that began to circulate in 1626, to which she may have contributed, a powerful cast of characters including gods, goddesses, and famous figures from the Italian literary tradition assembles before Apollo on Mount Parnassus to defend Sarra against the accusations against her and restore her good name. Entitled *Avisi di Parnasso* (*News from Parnassus*) and signed by a certain "Giulia Solinga" ("Lonely Giulia") of whom nothing is known, the manuscript is modeled on a genre made popular in early-seventeenth-century Italy by the political writer Traiano Boccalini that commented on contemporary events. A vindication, it imagines a range of famous female poets coming to her defense, from the Greek Sappho to the sixteenth-century Italians Vittoria Colonna and Isabella Andreini, situating Sarra firmly within a genealogy of literary women.

The manuscript contains five poems attributed to Sarra herself, making it an especially important source for understanding the full range of her writing, since so few of her compositions survive.

In these poems, Sarra's hunger for knowledge vies with anger at her mistreatment and outrage at the thankless work of pursuing intellectual recognition as a woman in a male world. She struggles to reconcile the two, writing, "Let not the spite of a defaming monster/wither the green of my stalk." Though her detractors' claims are "baseless," her enemies are strangers to honor, happy to wallow "in filthy habits like a dirty pig in muck." Therefore, she concludes defiantly,

> I pay no mind
> to the poisonous breath, to the smoke of impious jaws.
> Now I sprout wings to ride the wind to greater heights.[11]

But, though Sarra longs for learning – "that desire for knowledge that in a noble heart often resides," as she puts it in another sonnet in the manuscript – the price for a public literary life is simply too steep:

> for the most part, may the truth be clear: one regrets
> ever having taken an arrow from the quiver
> or having shot a noble shaft at a foul target.

Instead, she vows to cease writing entirely, putting aside any thought of recognition and turning inward:

> Having set down the lyre which once sounded my fame
> I have been silent for some time.
> Vexing troubles clipped the wings of the noble desire
> on which poetry takes flight and seeks life.

The manuscript concludes with a victorious judgment in Sarra's favor and the elaborate punishment of her detractors as decreed by the gods: Paluzzi is pilloried and branded, and effigies of him and his coconspirators are dragged through the streets. In reality, of course, there was no such justice for Sarra, who instead simply vanishes from all records after 1626.

Sarra Copia Sulam was not the only Jewish woman writer in early modern Italy: the sixteenth-century Roman poet, Debora (Devorà) Ascarelli gained recognition for her verse and elegant translations of Hebrew hymns into Italian, but these were aimed at a devout Jewish readership. Sarra's world, despite the geographical constraints of the

Ghetto and the visible and invisible barriers she faced as a Jew and as a woman, was wider. She engaged closely with Christian and Jewish authors, clerics, and scholars, and found herself pulled into some of the most controversial philosophical and religious debates of her age. Though she did not set out to write explicitly in defense of women, she directly challenged conventional Renaissance notions of the acceptable intellectual realms and roles for women in general and for Jewish women in particular. Both the Venetian literary world and the Judaic tradition discouraged women from active public participation, yet Sarra defied these constraints to debate philosophy and religion in person and in print. Her *Manifesto* makes a forceful case for the importance of free inquiry and exchange, a cause that was increasingly threatened in the Counter-Reformation climate. Together with her sonnets, it offers the clearest picture we have of her brilliant intellect, her steadfast faith, and her important if antagonized contribution to interfaith exchange and the development of a feminist literary voice in late Renaissance Italy.

25 Arcangela Tarabotti (1604–1652)

Rebel Nun, Feminist Force

Both female and male were born free, bearing with them, like
precious gifts from God, the inestimable treasure of free will.
Therefore, woman is no less worthy than you men, though you
have deemed her such with your arrogant attacks.

– Arcangela Tarabotti

As Sarra Copia Sulam was engaging in religious and literary debate
from within the confines of the Jewish Ghetto in Venice, her contemporary Arcangela Tarabotti, dissident nun and author of some of the
most important feminist works of the early modern era, was imprisoned by walls of a different sort. By the seventeenth century, there
were nearly fifty convents active in Venice, from the wealthy San Zac-
caria, a repository for women from noble families, to more modest
houses like the Benedictine convent of Sant'Anna, near the Arsenale
shipyards (see Figure 25.1). Though Sant'Anna overlooked a canal, its
inhabitants – Arcangela among them – could not have even rested their
elbows on the windowsills to watch the boats below. The early modern
cloister was strictly regulated: after the Council of Trent – a series of
meetings held between 1545 and 1563 to define Catholic doctrine and
respond to the Protestant Reformation – female monastic houses were
required to be enclosed and their inhabitants to remain locked inside to
"protect" them from the secular world. Efforts to prohibit the interactions of nuns with outsiders included the narrowing or bricking up of
convent windows and doors and the limiting of contact with visitors,
especially men.

Despite such restrictions, however, convent walls were notoriously
permeable. Nuns conversed with friends and relatives from behind

DOI: 10.4324/9781003081807-31

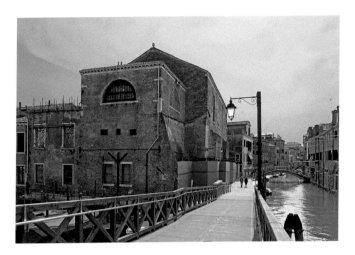

Figure 25.1 The convent of Sant'Anna in Castello (Venice) today, where Arcangela Tarabotti resided

(Open access)

the parlor grille, exchanging news, negotiating marriage prospects for female friends and relatives outside, or distributing the fine lace for which Venetian convents were famous. From within the cloister, Arcangela participated in all these activities, in addition to engaging in copious correspondence and circulating her writings condemning the misogyny of Venetian and European society and the oppression of women[1] (see Figure 25.2). Her biting prose earned her both admirers and enemies; shortly after her death, one of her works was condemned by the Church. A nun with no religious calling who yearned to be part of secular society – she bewailed the harsh, restrictive existence of the unwilling nun compared to the imagined freedoms and luxuries of the secular bride and used the aristocratic title Donna (Lady) rather than Suor (Sister) – Arcangela devoted herself instead to study. She was a self-described autodidact, who worried that others would criticize her writing, especially her imperfect use of Latin, and she read voraciously, far beyond the strictly religious diet considered appropriate for nuns. In addition to Biblical references, her works overflow with allusions to secular authors like the classical Ovid; the pillars of

Figure 25.2 Il parlatorio (The Convent Parlor), by Francesco Guardi, 1746
(Ca' Rezzonico, Venice)
[open access]

Italian poetry Dante Alighieri and Francesco Petrarca (Petrarch); and even the sixteenth-century political writer Niccolò Machiavelli, whose works the Church had placed on the Index of Forbidden Books over fifty years earlier, as she was surely aware. She also knew the feminist writings of her compatriot Lucrezia Marinella, the grande dame of Venetian letters who lived just a few minutes away, though there is no evidence that the two ever met.

Elena Cassandra Tarabotti was born in the Venetian *sestiere*, or district, of Castello, not far from the convent where she would eventually assume the religious name Arcangela. Her mother, Maria Cadena dei Tolentini, was the daughter of a jeweler; her father, Stefano Tarabotti (1574–1641), was a merchant and chemist who dabbled in alchemy, producing dyes, colors, and sublimates (the deposits left from converting solids to vapor).[2] The eldest of six daughters – with three older brothers – Elena had a condition that affected her gait and for which she termed herself "zoppa," or lame. Along with the economic pressures of so large a family, this condition likely influenced her parents' decision to place her in a convent rather than attempt to arrange a marriage for her. Marriage in early modern Italy was expensive business, requiring dowries of money, property, and other possessions. Many Venetian families, preferring not to dilute their patrimony, reserved dowries for just one or two daughters. These considerations coincided with the policies of the Venetian Republic that encouraged the cloistering of women in order to keep patrician wealth intact.

The fee to enter a convent was comparatively modest, helping to explain its prevalence: by some estimates, nearly 60 percent of all patrician women in late-sixteenth-century Venice resided in convents, many not by choice.[3] While some women voluntarily chose convent life, the ubiquity of forced cloistering – a practice against which Arcangela railed – led even Church authorities to recognize its terrible ramifications. Giovanni Tiepolo, the Patriarch of Venice – a high ecclesiastical office elected by the Senate – noted that nuns made "a gift of their own liberty (so precious even to those lacking reason) not just to God, but to their native land, to the world, and to their closest relatives," acknowledging it as a convenience to family and state more than a spiritual choice.[4] Other Church officials went further, comparing it to perpetual imprisonment and even capital punishment, a sentiment expressed by Arcangela herself, who called the convent a "hell, from which there is no hope of escape."[5] Though coercing women into taking religious vows was officially prohibited by the Church since 1563, it was difficult to enforce such a directive when daughters, under pressure from their families, did not feel free to express resistance.

Arcangela's own experience being forced to enter Sant'Anna at thirteen was the impetus for her earliest writings: the polemical and partially autobiographical *Inferno monacale* (*Convent Hell*) and *La tirannia paterna* (*Paternal Tyranny*). *Convent Hell* paints a dramatic account of the life of the forced nun, indoctrinated from birth to believe that her destiny is to serve family, city, and God by taking vows. Only too late does she come to understand that she has been tricked by her parents, often with the collusion of the older nuns who themselves had been victims of the same practice but who now falsely present convent life to young girls as a glorious Eden. Scathingly, Arcangela explains how these nuns know

> the cloister to be a damnable Inferno, yet describe it as filled with the delights of Paradise. They are so skilled at masking the truth with lies, even imitating the perfidious male sex to make it seem that beyond the cloister there is no happiness to be found.[6]

Arcangela draws liberally on Dante's fourteenth-century *Divina Commedia* (*Divine Comedy*), which opens with a journey through hell. For Arcangela, it is the convent that should bear the infamous warning inscribed above the gates to Dante's Inferno: "Abandon all hope ye who enter." Not only are the unwilling occupants of the convent consigned to it for a lifetime, but – in a terrifying paradox – their very unwillingness to embrace spiritual life ensures their eternal perdition. Only "thorns, tribulations, and unhappiness" can flourish in the cloister, and, like Dante's damned souls, the forced nuns realize too late that their sinful inability to accept their fate has damned them.

The profession ceremony, in which nuns metaphorically die to the secular world by taking their solemn vows, thus becomes a literal burial, as "with lips weakened by despair . . . [the new nun] forces herself to utter her own funeral rites." Arcangela grappled with this conundrum her entire life, repelled by the ritual cutting of long hair required of nuns and the coarse, plain habit she was made to don. In this regard she was not alone: women in wealthier Venetian convents regularly flouted religious simplicity by wearing fine fabrics or letting wisps of hair peek out from beneath their veils – much as secular Venetians, male and female, often ignored sumptuary laws that regulated ostentatious or expensive clothing.[7] Though she found convent life unbearably lonely, Arcangela took comfort in the few friends she found in Sant'Anna: a temporary boarder named Betta Polani, to whom she entrusted some of her manuscripts when Polani left to get married, and Regina Donati (Donà), whom she revered as a model of a "true" or willing nun and whose premature death in 1645 left Arcangela bereft.

In *Paternal Tyranny*, composed around the same time as *Convent Hell* but only published pseudonymously in 1654, after her death, with the milder title *La semplicità ingannata* (*Innocence Deceived*), Arcangela revisits the topic of forced cloistering, now targeting the role of fathers in the practice as well as the broader institutional mechanisms that conspire against women. Boldly, she dedicates her treatise to God himself, calling the "crime of forced enclosure" an act of "wanton defiance" of his decrees, and castigates Venice's fathers, who "defile our age with the hideous iniquity of immuring women against their will."[8] Nor did Arcangela limit her scathing critique to the convent. Her outrage targeted the oldest foundations of misogyny itself. Reinterpreting the Biblical story of Adam and Eve – a long-standing basis for misogynist arguments – she maintains that Adam, and not Eve, was responsible for humankind's expulsion from Eden and was thus "the principal cause of our woe" and the "father of pride and mendacity." Eve, "the innocent one," fell prey to the devil's deception in "a simple mistake," while Adam "knew he was offending his God" – and then blamed his wife. Arcangela imagines God's outrage at Adam's "abominable fraud," and his assurance that one day "there will come a woman who will crush the head of the serpent in revenge and for the universal glory of her whole sex": the Virgin Mary (or perhaps Arcangela herself).

Like Marinella and Fonte, Arcangela sees the exclusion of women from education as a deliberate effort to ensure their lack of access to patriarchal structures of power. "How on earth," she exclaims with striking political insight, can women reach their full potential when "they are denied entrance to political bodies such as our Venetian Senate?" "Do not scorn the quality of women's intelligence, you malignant and evil-minded men," she admonishes:

> Shut up in their rooms, denied access to books and teachers of any learning whatsoever, or any other grounding in letters, [women] cannot help being inept in making speeches and foolish in giving advice. Yours is the blame, for in your envy you deprive them of the means to acquire knowledge.

Too provocative for publication during Arcangela's lifetime, *Convent Hell* and *Paternal Tyranny* circulated in manuscript form, catching the attention of Venice's influential Accademia degli Incogniti (Academy of the Unknowns), whose members prided themselves on their libertine and anticlerical views.

Giovan Francesco Loredano, a prominent Incognito and supporter of other Venetian women such as the singer Barbara Strozzi, was especially intrigued by Arcangela's criticism of religious and political institutions and championed her first publication, the seemingly meeker and less controversial 1643 treatise, *Paradiso monacale* (*Convent Paradise*), also titled in homage to Dante's trilogy. Though ostensibly more conventional in its celebration of monastic life for willing nuns, *Convent Paradise* made a stark distinction between praise of the convent for women who choose it freely and criticism of it for those who do not. With signature feminist perspective and acerbic humor, Arcangela opens by declaring:

> God loves all creatures, but in particular Woman, and then Man, even if he doesn't deserve it. And in order to explain the nature of

his love for that most ungrateful creature, it suffices to say that the
eternal Creator loves him as only God could.[9]

Convent Paradise earned Arcangela admirers in Venice and abroad,
among them the Italian-born cardinal Jules Mazarin, chief minister to
two kings of France, and his assistant Gabriel Naudé, who sought out
Arcangela's works for the cardinal's library in Paris.

Though letter-writing was discouraged and even prohibited for
nuns, especially to contacts in the secular world, Arcangela corresponded openly with nobles, diplomats, and intellectuals throughout
Europe. Her circle ranged from the French ambassador to Venice,
Nicolas Bretel de Grémonville, to the noted mathematician and Copernican astronomer Ismäel Boulliau (Bullialdus) – a particularly surpris-
ing contact for a nun, given the heresy trial of Galileo Galilei in 1633
for promoting heliocentrism. She forged a remarkable epistolary network, which she showcased in her second published work, the carefully curated *Lettere familiari e di complimento* (*Letters Familiar and
Formal*, 1650). The collection features letters to political figures like
the doge of Venice, Francesco Erizzo; the grand duchess of Tuscany
Vittoria della Rovere, patron of many women writers and musicians;
various Incogniti members including Loredano and Arcangela's own
brother-in-law Giacomo Pighetti (d. 1647), who was probably her first
point of contact with the academy; the apostate writer Girolamo Brusoni; the librettist Giovan Francesco Busenello, whose work was set to
music by the celebrated composer Claudio Monteverdi; and numerous
others, including many women.

From the *Letters* we learn that some of Arcangela's contacts supplied her with controversial – even forbidden – reading material,
including a dangerously anticlerical work by her contemporary Ferrante Pallavicino, who was captured and executed for heresy at Avi-
gnon not long before Arcangela's *Letters* were printed; Arcangela also
claims to have read another forbidden work depicting Pallavicino as a
martyr. The *Letters* highlight Arcangela's relationships with the international community in Venice, from her friendly interactions with the
French ambassador and his family to her sometimes testy exchanges
with Renée de Clermont-Galerande, a noblewoman who commissioned an expensive lace collar from her. Notably, the volume contains
only a few, rather dispassionate, letters to just two of Arcangela's sisters and none to her parents, who moved across Venice shortly after
depositing their eldest daughter in Sant'Anna. Perhaps to soften the

remarkably public nature of this publication, Arcangela appended to her *Letters* a short work more suitable for a cloistered nun: a memorial for Regina, her beloved convent sister whose death she mourns throughout her letters and whom she praises almost as a saint.

Not everyone appreciated Arcangela's subversive voice, especially when she broadened her focus from a critique of the convent to a more general indictment of male hypocrisy. In the early 1640s, Arcangela acquired a satire of women's vanity and vice by Francesco Buoninsegni of Siena and set out to respond. Her *Antisatira* (*Antisatire*), a witty but forceful defense of women, defends women's right to fashion and luxury, from the fashionable long earrings that reach to their shoulders – the better to "open their ears" to the word of God – to their chopines, high wooden shoes that allow them to tower over men and keep their gowns from dragging in the mud. Arcangela methodically refutes Buoninsegni's allegations and turns them back upon the male sex, much like Marinella in her similar dispute with a misogynist text by Giovanni Passi in 1601. Despite its light tone, the *Antisatire* – published under the initials "D.A.T." (Donna Arcangela Tarabotti) – met a hostile reception upon its publication in 1644, due in no small part to its secular nature. Rejoinders were prepared against it, some maintaining that the author of a religious work like *Convent Paradise* could not possibly have written such an outspoken work. Leveraging her connections to the publishing world, Arcangela managed to keep at least one such response from going to press: it was a remarkable show of power by a cloistered nun, though it ignited a bitter feud with the author, the cleric Angelo Aprosio of Genoa, another one of her correspondents.

Arcangela's *Letters* mention other works that do not survive: three religious works – *La via lastricata per andare al cielo* (*The Paved Road to Heaven*), *La contemplazione dell'anima amante* (*Contemplation of a Loving Soul*), and *La luce monacale* (*Convent Light*) – as well as a *Purgatorio delle malmaritate* (*Purgatory of Unsuitably Married Women*), which apparently explored the abuse of women in the secular world and formed the middle installment of her Dantesque trilogy along with *Convent Hell* and *Convent Paradise*. But her final publication was a forceful philosophical treatise published in 1651, entitled *Che le donne siano della spetie degli uomini* (*Women Are Human, Just Like Men*). Like her *Antisatire*, it, too, was a response to a shocking misogynist provocation. An anonymous Latin treatise of 1595, attributed to the German scholar Valens Acidalius, was translated into Italian in

1647 by Arcangela's erstwhile friend Loredano. It made the satirical –
and heretical – accusation that women were not human. Despite the
risks – for to respond to the treatise was to admit to having read it –
Arcangela had no choice but to answer.

Once again, Arcangela counters the author's anti-woman arguments meticulously, refuting each one of them with examples from
religion and philosophy like a skilled theologian. With biting sarcasm,
she lambastes her opponent – whom she scornfully calls "*Signor* Philosopher" – for repeating theories about women's inferiority derived
from the ancient philosopher Aristotle and diminishing the central role
of the woman in reproduction, noting, "since both male and female
generate and are generated in the same manner, you have wandered too
far off the road." Comparing him to a litany of heedless, foolish animals – suggesting that he, not women, lacks humanity – she proceeds
to mock him for misreading his sources:

> [A]re you one of those crabs who walk backwards and always
> return on your first steps? You are a porcupine, who walks toward
> the cliff and towards evil! You are a crayfish, who is caught by the
> crazy moon, and therefore is pregnant with an infinite number of
> eggs! You have no brain, and would lie to appear a brilliant mind,
> translating the opposite of what the [original] author wrote.[10]

This highly public and polemical work was the intrepid culmination
to Arcangela's career: she was now debating men on theological and
philosophical, as well as literary, grounds. Once again, she had trespassed into dangerous territory for a woman of her religious state. It
was no accident that her treatise was published under false publishing
information, purportedly not at home in Venice, but abroad, in Germany, where the original Latin attack had been printed. She also used
a thinly veiled pseudonym, "Galerana Barcitotti." The assumed name
was a pointed play on the Italian terms for "prison" (*galera*) and "cof-
fin" (*bara*) and a commentary on her forced cloister.

Arcangela Tarabotti died on February 28, 1652, from complications
of the habitual "tightness in the chest" that had plagued her throughout
her life.[11] She was forty-eight. She had not lived to see her controversial *Paternal Tyranny* finally published, two years later, as *Innocence Deceived*, under another closely related pseudonym, "Galerana
Baratotti" and bearing the couplet: "Forced devotion/is not God's
notion."[12] Printed in the Protestant city of Leiden by a press known for

circulating clandestine books throughout Europe, *Innocence Deceived* was a dramatic coda to Arcangela's literary legacy. Though she had, astonishingly, managed to elude the attention of Church authorities in life, this posthumous publication promptly landed on the Catholic Church's Index of Forbidden Books, "prohibited in its entirety" for arguing that "all the kinds of punishment which are in Hell can be plainly found in holy convents"[13] (see Figure 25.3).

The façade of the convent where Arcangela spent her life still stands in Venice, hidden in plain sight beneath the twenty-first-century housing development that has replaced the cells of Sant'Anna. Despite her fame in the seventeenth century – which connected her to the Republic

Figure 25.3 Title page of Arcangela Tarabotti's *La semplicità ingannata* (Leiden: Sambix, 1643), published under the pseudonym Galerana Baratotti

(Rare Book Collection, Kislak Center for Special Collections, Rare Books and Manuscripts, University of Pennsylvania)

of Letters, a network of writers and pre-Enlightenment thinkers and philosophers that stretched throughout Europe – Arcangela's story fell from view over the centuries until the 1960s. Since then, scholars have dedicated increasing attention to her work. Long before what we commonly think of as the first "wave" of feminism, she articulated a clear-eyed analysis of the social, economic, and political forces that profited from the oppression of women, and the denial of education that allowed the cycle to perpetuate itself. Indeed, only in the eighteenth century did the rate of forced cloistering begin to fall, in part due to the spread of Enlightenment notions of liberty and individual freedoms.[14]

Not only a groundbreaking feminist writer, Arcangela was also an astute political theorist, adept at reinterpreting Biblical and philosophical sources and assessing the entangled and intersecting forces that fuel patriarchal power. Her spirit endures in in the continued resistance of many Roman Catholic nuns to patriarchal Church authority, like the Leadership Conference of Women Religious formed in 1956 whose rejection of a passive, submissive role for women drew the ire of the Vatican for promoting "radical" feminist ideas. Simultaneously sacred and subversive, Arcangela Tarabotti's hallmark combination of pathos, outrage, and mordant wit resonates as deeply today as it did in seventeenth-century Venice, making her writings a fundamental contribution to the development of modern feminist thought and a powerful capstone to the history of women in Renaissance Italy.

Notes and Further Reading

I have structured this work as a series of biographies, a nod to the Renaissance tradition of the biographical catalog. Where those catalogs celebrated select women as "exceptional" or "unique" among their sex, however, these biographies are meant to display the impact of Renaissance women as a collective presence, not a rare exception to the rule, drawing out their connections as well as the differences in their circumstances and trajectories. I refer to the protagonists of these biographies by their first names – as is common practice for Renaissance men ("Lorenzo," "Michelangelo," "Galileo") – not only to distinguish them from others who may have borne the same family name but also to center them as the focus of the narrative. Because this book is intended as a general introduction, I have tried to keep footnotes and academic debates to a minimum. Dates of birth and death (where known) are provided for the protagonists and their family members; dates of reign for rulers and popes mentioned are provided in an appendix.

Introduction

Epigraph: Lucrezia Marinella, *La nobiltà et l'eccellenza delle donne, co'difetti, et mancamenti de gli huomini* (Venice: Gio. Battista Ciombi, 1601); my translation.

Notes

1 Giovanni Boccaccio, *Concerning Famous Women*, trans. Guido Guarino (New Brunswick, NJ: Rutgers University Press, 1963), 127. Others followed, updating Boccaccio's catalog with contemporaneous examples, like Betussi's Italian popularization, *Il libro . . . delle donne illustri* (*Book of Famous Women*) (Florence: Torrentino, 1556).

2 On the *querelle des femmes* see the influential essay by Joan Kelly, "Early Feminist Theory and the 'Querelle des Femmes,' 1400–1789," *Signs* 8.1 (1982): 4–28; a more recent study is Steven Kolsky's *The Ghost of Boccaccio: Writings on Famous Women in Renaissance Italy* (Turnhout: Brepols, 2005).

3 Ludovico Ariosto, *Orlando Furioso: A New Verse Translation*, trans. David R. Slavitt (Cambridge, MA: The Belknap Press of Harvard University Press, 2009), Canto 20.2, 460.

4 See Chapter 22, p. 268; 23, p. 280, and 21, p. 111 in this volume.

5 For an early example, see Renate Bridenthal and Claudia Koonz, eds., *Becoming Visible: Women in European History* (Boston: Houghton Mifflin, 1977). Recent examples include Merry Weisner-Hanks, *Women and Gender in Early Modern Europe* (Cambridge: Cambridge University Press, 2019), now in its fourth edition; Virginia Cox, *Women's Writing in Italy 1400–1650* (Baltimore: Johns Hopkins University Press, 2008); and Virginia Cox, *The Prodigious Muse: Women's Writing in Counter-Reformation Italy* (Baltimore: Johns Hopkins University Press, 2011).

6 Joan Kelly, "Did Women Have a Renaissance?" in Bridenthal and Koonz, *Becoming Visible*, 137–164.

7 On the debate over the terminology, periodization, and nature of "the Renaissance," see Guido Ruggiero, "Forgetting the Italian Renaissance and Other Irreverent Suggestions," *I Tatti Studies in the Italian Renaissance* 22.2 [2019]: 355–367) and the more extensive discussion in Guido Ruggiero, *The Renaissance in Italy: A Social and Cultural History of the Rinascimento* (Cambridge: Cambridge University Press, 2015). For a concise overview of approaches to Renaissance history, see Mark Jurdjevic, "Hedgehogs and Foxes: The Present and Future of Italian Renaissance History," *Past and Present* 195 (2007): 241–268.

8 On Sofonsiba Anguissola, see Jill Burke, "Overlooking Women's Labour in Sofonisba Anguissola's Chess Game," https://jillburkerenaissance.com/2020/06/28/overlooking-womens-labour-in-sofonisba-anguissolas-chess-game/; for Annibale Carracci, see Kenna Libes at https://fashionhistory.fitnyc.edu/1583-5-carracci-african-woman-clock/. On Alessandro de' Medici, see John Brackett, "Race and Rulership: Alessandro de' Medici, First Medici Duke of Florence, 1529–1577," in T.F. Earle and Kate Lowe, eds., *Black Africans in Renaissance Europe* (Cambridge: Cambridge University Press, 2005), 303–325; Catherine Fletcher, *The Black Prince of Florence: The Specular Life and Treacherous World of Alessandro de' Medici* (Oxford: Oxford University Press, 2016); Mary Gallucci, "Mistaken Identities?: Alessandro de' Medici and the Question of 'Race'," *Journal for Early Modern Cultural Studies* 15.3 (2015): 50–81.

9 See the fundamental study by Kate Lowe, "Visible Lives: Black Gondoliers and Other Black Africans in Renaissance Venice," *Renaissance Quarterly* 66.2 (Summer 2013): 412–452.

10 Sally McKee, "Domestic Slavery in Renaissance Italy," *Slavery and Abolition* 29.3 (2008): 305–326, 312. On Isabella d'Este, see Paul H.D. Kaplan, "Isabella d'Este and Black African Women," in Earle and Lowe, *Black Africans*, 125–154.

11 See Kim Hall, *Things of Darkness: Economies of Race and Gender in Early Modern England* (Ithaca: Cornell University Press, 1996), 6.

12 For the earlier discussion, in addition to Earle and Lowe, *Black Africans in Renaissance Europe*, see Geraldine Heng, *The Invention of Race in the European Middle Ages* (Cambridge, UK: Cambridge University Press, 2018); Lindsay Kaplan, *Figuring Racism in Medieval Christianity* (Oxford:

Oxford University Press, 2018); Noemi Ndiaye, "Race and Ethnicity: Conceptual Knots in Early Modern Culture," in *The Cultural History of Race in the Reformation and Enlightenment, 1550–1760* (London: Bloomsbury Press, 2021), vol. 4, 112–126; Anna Wainwright, "Widows, Lament, and Ottoman Anxieties in Renaissance Florence," in Meredith K. Ray and Lynn Lara Westwater, eds., *Gendering the Renaissance: Text and Context in Early Modern Italy* (Newark, DE: University of Delaware Press, 2023), 23–44. See also Olivette Otele, *African Europeans* (New York: Basic Books, 2021); *Teaching Race in the European Renaissance: A Classroom Guide*, eds. Matthieu Chapman and Anna Wainwright (Tempe: ACMRS Press, 2023), https://doi.org.10.54027/GESP5156; and David Bindman and Henry Louis Gates, Jr., eds., *The Image of the Black in Western Art* (Cambridge, MA: Harvard University Press, 2010), vol. 3. Studies in the global Renaissance include Lisa Jardine and Jerry Brotton, *Global Interests: Renaissance Art Between East and West* (Ithaca: Cornell University Press, 2000); Elizabeth Horodwich and Lia Markey, eds., *The New World in Early Modern Italy, 1492–1750* (Cambridge: Cambridge University Press, 2018); Elizabeth Horodowich and Alexander Nagel, *Amerasia* (New York: Zone Books, 2023).

13 Giovan Domenico Ottonelli, *Della pericolosa conversazione con le donne* (Florence: Luca Franceschini and Alessandro Logi, 1646), 440.

14 In this volume, I apply the term "feminism" broadly (in the general sense of "supporting the equality of women") to the "prowoman" (or "protofeminist") texts of the Renaissance, as well as those that analyze more explicitly the mechanisms of oppression and possibilities for change. As Joan Kelly notes, even when remaining in the realm of argument more than action, Renaissance women understood gender to be a culturally constructed category and women to be part of a deliberately marginalized group (see Kelly, "Early Feminist Theory," 7).

15 Elena Ferrante, *In the Margins: On the Pleasures of Reading and Writing*, trans. Ann Goldstein (New York: Europa Editions, 2022), 87.

Lucrezia Tornabuoni (1427–1482): Medici Matriarch

Epigraph: My translation of Francesco da Castiglione's letter to Lorenzo de' Medici, dated 13 April 1482 (Florence, Biblioteca Laurenziana, Cod. XI). For the Italian text, see G. Levantini-Pieroni, *Studi storici e letterari* (Florence: Le Monnier, 1893), 15–16.

Notes

1 Translation amended from Christopher Hibbert, *The House of Medici: Its Rise and Fall* (New York: William Morrow, 1975), 63.

2 Leon Battista Alberti, *The Family in Renaissance Florence: Book Three (I Libri della Famiglia)*, trans. and ed. Renée Neu Watkins (Long Grove: Waveland, 1994).

3 Translated in Francis William Kent, *Princely Citizen: Lorenzo de' Medici and Renaissance Florence*, ed. Carolyn James (Turnhout: Brepols, 2013), 75.

4 Unless otherwise noted, I have translated Lucrezia's correspondence from Lucrezia Tornabuoni, *Lettere*, ed. Patrizia Salvadori (Florence: Olschki, 1993): here, 54. Later, see 55 for the 1458 letter; 62–64 for the letters from 28 March 1467; and 64–65 for the letter from 5 April 1467.

5 My translation of Poliziano, quoted in Mario Martelli, "Lucrezia Tornabuoni," in Georges Ulysse, ed., *Les femmes écrivains en Italie au Moyen Âge et à la Renaissance: actes du colloque international, Aix-en-Provence, 12, 13, 14 novembre 1992* (Aix-en-Provence: Publications de l'Université de Provence, 1994), 51–86, 65. For Lucrezia's religious poetry, see Lucrezia Tornabuoni de' Medici, *Sacred Narratives*, trans. and ed. Jane Tylus (Chicago: University of Chicago Press, 2001).

6 Lucrezia's *Storia di Giuditta* (*Life of Judith*), translated in de' Medici, *Sacred Narratives*, 118–162, 155.

7 Translated in Kent, *Princely Citizen*, 98–99.

8 Here and later, translation is adapted from de' Medici, *Sacred Narratives*, 32.

9 Translated in Kent, *Princely Citizen*, 58.

Selected Bibliography

de' Medici, Lucrezia Tornabuoni, *Sacred Narratives*, trans. and ed. Jane Tylus (Chicago: University of Chicago Press, 2001)

Kent, Francis William, *Princely Citizen: Lorenzo de' Medici and Renaissance Florence*, ed. Carolyn James (Turnhout: Brepols, 2013)

Milligan, Gerry, "Unlikely Heroines in Lucrezia Tornabuoni's *Judith* and *Esther*," *Italica* 88.4 (2011): 538–564

Tomas, Natalie, *The Medici Women: Gender and Power in Renaissance Florence* (Aldershot: Ashgate, 2003)

Caterina Sforza (c. 1463–1509): Countess, Warrior, Alchemist

Epigraph: Bartolomeo Cerretani, *Storia fiorentina*, ed. Giuliana Berti (Florence: Olschki, 266); my translation.

Notes

1 Eyewitnesses to the event stated that Caterina made an obscene gesture called "the fig," the Renaissance version of the "middle finger." On the story and its significance, see Julia Hairston, "Skirting the Issue: Machiavelli's Caterina Sforza," *Renaissance Quarterly* 53.3 (2000): 687–712; for the quotation, see 690. Versions of this story are numerous, including from Machiavelli himself.

2 On her nickname, see Elizabeth Lev, *The Tigress of Forlì: Renaissance Italy's Most Courageous and Notorious Countess, Caterina Riario Sforza de' Medici* (Boston: Mariner, 2011), 133 and 278n9.

3 On Caterina in Botticelli's paintings and others, see, among others, Maike Vogt-Lüerssen, "The Identification of Caterina Sforza in Renaissance Paintings Through Symbolism," *Kleio*, 4 March 2021, www.kleio.org/en/books/caterina_symbols/cs_en.

4 For the translation here and later, see Meredith K. Ray, *Daughters of Alchemy: Women and Scientific Culture in Early Modern Italy* (Cambridge, MA: Harvard University Press, 2015), 172n19 and 20.

5 My translation of Pier Desiderio Pasolini, *Caterina Sforza* (Rome: Loescher, 1893), 3:769, 3:617–618; later, 3:782.

6 Translated in Hairston, "Skirting the Issue," 701.

7 My translation of a letter from Francesco Tranchedini to Duke Ludovico Sforza, dated September 4, 1495, in Pasolini, *Caterina Sforza*, 3:229–230; later, my translation of 3:606, Caterina's letter from 2 November 1499.

8 The letter of Isabella d'Este, from 14 January 1500, is translated in Ray, *Daughters of Alchemy*, 20.

9 The lament is transcribed in Pasolini, *Caterina Sforza*, 3:810–823; here, my translation of 3:821.

10 Andrea Bernardi, *Cronache forlivesi dal 1476 al 1517*, ed. Giuseppe Mazzatinti (Bologna: Reale Deputazione di Storia Patria, 1895–1897), vol. 1–2:294 (my translation).

11 Translated in Ray, *Daughters*, 27.

12 See Lev, *The Tigress of Forlì*, 263; DeVries, *Caterina Sforza*, 231.

Selected Bibliography

Barker, Sheila and Sharon Strocchia, "Household Medicine for a Renaissance Court: Caterina Sforza's *Ricettario* Reconsidered," in Sara Ritchey and Sharon Strocchia, eds., *Gender, Health, and Healing, 1250–1550* (Amsterdam: Amsterdam University Press, 2020), 139–166

De Vries, Joyce, *Caterina Sforza and the Art of Appearances: Gender, Art, and Culture in Early Modern Italy* (Aldershot: Ashgate, 2010)

Lev, Elizabeth, *The Tigress of Forlì: Renaissance Italy's Most Courageous and Notorious Countess, Caterina Riario Sforza de' Medici* (Boston: Mariner, 2011)

Ray, Meredith K., *Daughters of Alchemy: Women and Scientific Culture in Early Modern Italy* (Cambridge, MA: Harvard University Press, 2015)

Isabella d'Este (1474–1539): Diplomat and Tastemaker

Epigraph: Letter of Alessandro da Baesso, 26 November 1494, quoting Niccolò da Coreggio, in Alessandro Luzio and Rodolfo Renier, "Niccolò da Coreggio," *Giornale storico della letteratura italiana* XXII (1894): 205–264, 239; my translation.

Notes

1 Stanley Chojnacki, "Getting Back the Dowry: Venice, c. 1360–1530," in Anne Jacobson Schutte, Thomas Kuehn and Silvana Seidel Menchi, eds., *Time, Space, and Women's Lives in Early Modern Europe* (Kirksville, MO: Truman State University Press, 2001), 77–96, 80.
2 Translated in Isabella d'Este, *Selected Letters*, trans. and ed. Deanna Shemek (Toronto: Centre for Reformation and Renaissance Studies, 2017), 7, 273. All citations from Isabella's letters follow this edition unless otherwise noted. Later, on Isabella's collection, see entry 7256 in Daniela Ferrari, ed., *Le collezioni Gonzaga: L'inventario dei beni del 1540–1542* (Cinisello Balsamo: Silvana, 2003), 346.
3 Translated in George R. Marek, *The Bed and the Throne: The Life of Isabella d'Este* (New York: Harper & Row, 1976), 99, ix. On Isabella and Ariosto, see Lisa Regan, "Ariosto's Threshold Patron: Isabella d'Este in the *Orlando Furioso*," *MLN* 120.1 (2005): 50–69.
4 d'Este, *Selected Letters*, 46.
5 Translated in Creighton E. Gilbert, "What Did the Renaissance Patron Buy?" *Renaissance Quarterly* 51.2 (1998): 392–450, 417.
6 Here, see d'Este, *Selected Letters*, 249–250; later, see 41–42, 46, 127–128, 73, 298–299.
7 Translated in David Alan Brown, "Leonardo and the Ladies with the Ermine and the Book," *Artibus et historiae* 11.22 (1990): 47–61, 47.
8 d'Este, *Selected Letters*, 562.
9 On this aspect of Isabella, see Paul H.D. Kaplan, "Isabella d'Este and Black African Women," in T.F. Earle and Kate J.P. Lowe, eds., *Black Africans in Renaissance Europe* (Cambridge: University of Cambridge Press, 2005), 125–154; Kate J.P. Lowe, "Isabella d'Este and the Acquisition of Black Africans at the Mantuan Court," in Philippa Jackson and Guido Rebecchini, eds., *Mantova e il Rinascimento italiano: Studi in onore di David S. Chambers* (Mantua: Sometti, 2011), 65–76.
10 See Sarah D.P. Cockram, *Isabella d'Este and Francesco Gonzaga: Power Sharing at the Italian Renaissance Court* (Farnham: Ashgate, 2013).
11 Translation adapted from d'Este, *Selected Letters*, 42.
12 d'Este, *Selected Letters*, 184; later, 132.
13 See Marek, *The Bed and the Throne*, ix.

Selected Bibliography

Cockram, Sarah, *Isabella d'Este and Francesco Gonzaga: Power Sharing at the Renaissance Court* (Farnham: Ashgate, 2013)
d'Este, Isabella, *Selected Letters*, trans. and ed. Deanna Shemek (Toronto: Centre for Reformation and Renaissance Studies, 2017)
James, Carolyn, *A Renaissance Marriage: The Political and Personal Alliance of Isabella d'Este and Francesco Gonzaga, 1490–1519* (Oxford: Oxford University Press, 2020)
Shemek, Deanna, *In Continuous Expectation: Isabella d'Este's Reign of Letters* (Toronto: Center for Reformation and Renaissance Studies, 2021)
IDEA: Isabella d'Este Archive (multidisciplinary digital project including a virtual reconstruction of Isabella's studiolo). www.isabelladestearchive.org

Lucrezia Borgia (1480–1519): Entrepreneur From Italy's Most Controversial Family

Epigraph: Ludovico Ariosto, *Orlando furioso* (Venice: Vincenzo Valgrisi, 1556), XIII.69–71, 129; my translation.

Notes

1 Translated in Niccolò Machiavelli, *The Prince*, trans. and ed. Harvey C. Mansfield (Chicago: University of Chicago Press, 1998), 2nd ed., 70.
2 For the discussion of Lucrezia's entrepreneurial activities here and later, see Diane Yvonne Ghirardo, "Lucrezia Borgia as Entrepreneur," *Renaissance Quarterly* 61.1 (2008): 53–91, 57.
3 My translation of Lucrezia Borgia, *Lettere, 1494–1519*, ed. Diane Ghirardo (Mantua: Tre Lune, 2020), 84.
4 See, for example, Borgia, *Lettere*, 91–96; my translation.
5 Translated in Hugh Shankland, trans. and ed., *The Prettiest Love Letters in the World* (New York: Vintage, 1987), 10.
6 Translated in Isabella d'Este, *Selected Letters*, trans. and ed. Deanna Shemek (Toronto: Centre for Reformation and Renaissance Studies, 2017), 178.
7 George Gordon Byron, *Letters and Journals*, ed. Leslie A. Marchand (Cambridge, MA: Belknap, 1973–1982): 5:123.
8 For the translation here, see Shankland, *Prettiest Love Letters*, letter 5; later, see the sonnet appended to letter 16.
9 Shankland, *Prettiest Love Letters*, 28.
10 Translations here and later altered from Shankland, *Prettiest Love Letters*, letter 14.
11 For the translation here, see Ghirardo, "Lucrezia Borgia," 56; later, 57n15.

Selected Bibliography

Bellonci, Maria, *The Life and Times of Lucrezia Borgia*, trans. Bernard Wall and Barbara Wall (London: Phoenix, 2003)
Bradford, Sarah, *Lucrezia Borgia: Life, Love and Death in Renaissance Italy* (New York: Viking, 2004)
Ghirardo, Diane Yvonne, "Lucrezia Borgia as Entrepreneur," *Renaissance Quarterly* 61.1 (2008): 53–91
Shankland, Hugh, trans. and ed., *The Prettiest Love Letters in the World: Letters Between Lucrezia Borgia and Pietro Bembo* (New York: Vintage, 1987)

Bona Sforza (1494–1557): The Italian Queen of Poland

Epigraph: Ludovico Domenichi, *Rime* (Venice: Giolito, 1554), Aiiiir; my translation.

Notes

1 Translated in Francesco Guicciardini, *The History of Italy*, trans. and ed. Sidney Alexander (New York: Collier, 1969), 54.
2 Ramie Targoff, *Renaissance Woman: The Life of Vittoria Colonna* (New York: Farrar, Straus and Giroux, 2018), 35–36.
3 Krysztof Zabolicki, "La regina Bona e la sua corte," in Circolo Culturale Italo-Polacco in Lombardia, ed., *Bona Sforza, "una principessa italiana sul trono di Polonia": Giornata di studio organizzata l'8 maggio 2004 al Castello Sforzesco di Milano in occasione dell'entrata della Polonia nella Unione Europea* (Milan: Mimep-Docete, 2004), 29–42, 31.
4 Colantonio Carmignano, *Viaggio de la Serenissima S[ignoria] Bona Regina in Polonia*, ed. Andrea Colelli (Rome: Lithos, 2018), 26.
5 Earlier, my translation of Giovan Battista Nenna, *Il Nennio, nel quale si ragiona di nobiltà* (Venice: Valvassore, 1542), A3r; and Domenichi, *Rime*, Aiiiir; here, of Giorgio Petrocchi, "Bona Sforza, regina di Polonia, e Pietro Aretino," in Vittore Branca and Sante Graciotti, eds., *Italia, Venezia e Polonia tra Medio Evo e età moderna* (Florence: Olschki, 1980), 325–331, 329.
6 The procession is detailed in a 1556 account by Mario Savorgnano, *La venuta della serenissima Bona Sforza et d'Aragona, reina di Polonia et duchessa di Bari nella magnifica città di Padova, á ventisette di marzo: Con l'entrata nella inclita città di Vinegia, il di 26 aprile 1556. Et la sua partita per Bari* (Venice: S.N., 1556), B1r-B1v, my translation; later, B2v.

Selected Bibliography

Bainton, Roland H., *Women of the Reformation, From Spain to Scandinavia* (Minneapolis: Augsburg, 1977), 134–155
Barycz, Henryk, "Seventeenth-Century Padua in the Intellectual Life of Poland," in Mieczysław Giergielewicz, gen. ed., *Polish Civilization: Essays and Studies* (New York: New York University Press, 1979), 135–162
Bogucka, Maria, *Women in Early Modern Polish Society, Against the European Background* (Aldershot: Ashgate, 2004)
Segel, Harold B., *Renaissance Culture in Poland: The Rise of Humanism, 1470–1543* (Ithaca, NY: Cornell University Press, 1989)

Vittoria Colonna (1490?–1547): Divine Poet, Michelangelo's Mentor

Epigraph: Vittoria Colonna, *Rime de la divina Vittoria Colonna, marchesa di Pescara* (Parma: Antonio Viotti, 1538), B3r; my translation.

Notes

1 Here and later, see Paolo Giovio, *Notable Men and Women of Our Time*, trans. and ed. Kenneth Gouwens (Cambridge, MA: Harvard University Press, 2013). Giovio wrote this celebratory work after Vittoria's request for a biography of Ferrante; see Kenneth Gouwens, "Female Virtue and the

Embodiment of Beauty: Vittoria Colonna in Paolo Giovio's *Notable Men and Women*," *Renaissance Quarterly* 68.1 (2015): 33–97.

2 Unless otherwise noted, quotations of poetry are from Vittoria Colonna, *Poems of Widowhood: A Bilingual Edition of the 1538 Rime*, trans. Ramie Targoff, eds. Ramie Targoff and Troy Tower (New York: Iter, 2021). For sonnet 22 here, see 57.

3 Translation based on Virginia Cox, trans. and ed., *Lyric Poetry by Women of the Italian Renaissance* (Baltimore: Johns Hopkins University Press, 2013), 79.

4 Here, Sonnet 18, translated in Colonna, *Poems of Widowhood*, 53; earlier, Sonnet 18, my translation.

5 Translated in Shannon McHugh, "Rethinking Vittoria Colonna: Gender and Desire in the *Rime amorose*," *Italianist* 33.3 (2013): 345–360, 348.

6 See Ramie Targoff, *Renaissance Woman: The Life of Vittoria Colonna* (New York: Farrar, Straus and Giroux, 2018), 48–51.

7 See stanzas 37.16–18 in Ludovico Ariosto, *Orlando furioso (The Frenzy of Orlando)*, trans. Barbara Reynolds (Harmondsworth: Penguin, 1975), 2:383; translation of 37.18 amended here.

8 Here and later, see sonnet 59 in Colonna, *Poems of Widowhood*, 87–89.

9 On this aspect of Vittoria Colonna's writing and thought, see Abigail Brundin, *Vittoria Colonna and the Spiritual Poetics of the Italian Reformation* (Aldershot: Ashgate, 2008); Targoff, *Renaissance Woman*, 276–287.

10 My translation of poem 235 in Michelangelo Buonarroti, *Rime*, ed. Matteo Residori (Milan: Mondadori, 1998), 363. Michelangelo's letter is translated in E. Hartley Ramsden, trans. and ed., *The Letters of Michelangelo* (Stanford: Stanford University Press, 1963), 2:120.

11 Here and later, translated in Targoff, *Renaissance Woman*, 147, 190–193.

12 Translated in Henry Wadsworth Longfellow, *The Poetical Works* (Boston: Houghton Mifflin, 1885), 393.

13 Translated in Laura Anna Stortoni, ed., *Women Poets of the Italian Renaissance: Courtly Ladies and Courtesans*, trans. Laura Anna Stortoni and Mary Prentice Lillie (New York: Italica, 1997), 29.

Selected Bibliography

Brundin, Abigail, Tatiana Crivelli and Maria Serena Sapegno, eds., *A Companion to Vittoria Colonna* (Leiden: Brill, 2016)

Colonna, Vittoria, *Poems of Widowhood: A Bilingual Edition of the 1538 Rime*, trans. Ramie Targoff, eds. Ramie Targoff and Troy Tower (New York: Iter, 2021)

Cox, Virginia and Shannon McHugh, eds., *Vittoria Colonna: Poetry, Religion, Art, Impact* (Amsterdam: Amsterdam University Press, 2021)

Targoff, Ramie, *Renaissance Woman: The Life of Vittoria Colonna* (New York: Farrar, Straus and Giroux, 2018)

Lucrezia Gonzaga (1522–1576): Epistolary Icon and Religious Dissident

Epigraph: Lucrezia Gonzaga, *Lettere della molto illustre Sig[no]ra Donna Lucretia Gonzaga da Gazuolo* (Venice: 1552), 5–6; all translations of Lucrezia's letters are my own. Subsequent page references are to the modern Italian edition by Renzo Bragantini and Primo Griguolo (Lucrezia Gonzaga, *Lettere* [Rovigo: Minelliana, 2009]).

Notes

1 Translated in Meredith K. Ray, *Writing Gender in Women's Letter Collections of the Italian Renaissance* (Toronto: University of Toronto Press, 2009), 86.
2 Gonzaga, *Lettere*, 16.
3 Biographical information on Lucrezia's daughters is scant. Both spent their early years in a convent; Isabella later married Fabio Pepoli and died in 1594.
4 Ray, *Writing Gender*, 85.
5 Translated in Meredith K. Ray, "Textual Collaboration and Spiritual Partnership in Sixteenth-Century Italy: The Case of Ortensio Lando and Lucrezia Gonzaga," *Renaissance Quarterly* 62.3 (2009): 694–747, 713n65.
6 Translated in Ray, *Writing Gender*, 83.
7 Lando's edition of the *Lettere di molte valorose donne, nelle quali chiaramente appare non esser né di eloquentia né di dottrina alli huomini inferiori* (Venice: Giolito, 1548) opens with a letter to Queen Bona Sforza, discussed here in Chapter 5.
8 Translated in Ray, "Textual Collaboration," 738.
9 Here, see Gonzaga, *Lettere*, 74; later, see 5, 108, 199, 66.
10 On such women as "learned, spiritual virtuosos," see Constance Furey, "Intellects Inflamed in Christ: Women and Spiritualized Scholarship in Renaissance Christianity," *Journal of Religion* 84 (2004): 1–22, 3–4.
11 Here, see Gonzaga, *Lettere*, 168; later, 188.
12 Translation adapted from Ray, *Writing Gender*, 85.

Selected Bibliography

Furey, Constance, "Intellects Inflamed in Christ: Women and Spiritualized Scholarship in Renaissance Christianity," *Journal of Religion* 84 (2004): 1–22

Ray, Meredith K., "Textual Collaboration and Spiritual Partnership in Sixteenth-Century Italy: The Case of Ortensio Lando and Lucrezia Gonzaga," *Renaissance Quarterly* 62 (2009): 694–747

Ray, Meredith K., *Writing Gender in Women's Letter Collections of the Italian Renaissance* (Toronto: University of Toronto Press, 2009)

Russell, Camilla, *Giulia Gonzaga and the Religious Controversies of Sixteenth-Century Italy* (Turnhout: Brepols, 2006)

Olimpia Morata (1526–1555): Humanist and Heretic

Epigraph: Olimpia Morata, *Opera omnia* (Basel: Petram Pernam, 1580), 72; my translation.

Notes

1 Quoted in Olympia Morata, *Olympia Morata: The Complete Writings of an Italian Heretic*, trans. and ed. Holt N. Parker (Chicago: University of Chicago Press, 2003), 8.
2 Only after the duke's death in 1559 was Renée able to return to France, where she offered protection to Protestant victims of the Wars of Religion that lasted from 1562 to 1572.
3 For the translation here, see letter 1 in Morata, *Olympia Morata*, 85; the translation later is adapted from Morata, *Complete Writings*, 90.
4 See Morata, *Complete Writings*, 61; for further examples, see 61–74. Later, see 22, 107.
5 Quoted in Francine Daenens, "Olimpia Morata: Storie parallele," in Claire E. Honess and Verina R. Jones, eds., *Le donne delle minoranze: le ebree e le protestanti d'Italia* (Turin: Claudiano, 1999), 101–112, 107–108 (my translation).
6 The translation here is adapted from Morata, *Complete Writings*, 108; later, from 98–99, 108, 98–99, 125, 115, 169–170, 101, 128, 140, 148, 177, 65.

Selected Bibliography

Braghi, Gianmarco, "Olimpia Fulvia Morata (1526–1555): Eloquent *Magistra*," in Kirsi I. Stjerna, ed., *Women Reformers of Early Modern Europe* (Minneapolis: Fortress, 2022), 187–191
King, Margaret L., "Book-Lined Cells: Women and Humanism in the Early Italian Renaissance," in Patricia H. Labalme, ed., *Beyond Their Sex: Learned Women of the European Past* (New York: New York University Press, 1980), 66–90
Morata, Olympia, *Olympia Morata: The Complete Writings of an Italian Heretic*, trans. and eds. Holt N. Parker (Chicago: University of Chicago Press, 2003)
Stevenson, Jane, *Women Latin Poets: Language, Gender, and Authority from Antiquity to the Eighteenth Century* (Oxford: Oxford University Press, 2005)

Laura Terracina (1519–c.1577): Bestselling Author, Defender of Women

Epigraph: My translation of canto 37.7.1–4 in Laura Terracina, *Discorso . . . sopra il principio di tutti i canti d'Orlando furioso* (Venice: Domenico Farri, 1567).

Notes

1 My translation of Laura Terracina, *Rime* (Venice: Giolito, 1548), 31r.
2 My translation of Benedetto Croce, *Storie e leggende napoletane* (Rome: Laterza, 1976), 282.
3 My translation of Luigi Tansillo, *Le lacrime di san Pietro*, ed. Barezzo Barezzi (Venice: Francesco Piacentini, 1738), 58 (of noncontinuous pagination).

4 Translated in Amelia Papworth, "Pressure to Publish: Laura Terracina and her Editors," *Early Modern Women* 12.1 (2017): 3–24, 14.

5 My translation of Terracina, *Rime*, A3r–A3v.

6 Here and later, my translation of Lodovico Domenichi, *La nobiltà delle donne* (Venice: Giolito, 1552), 238–239.

7 My translation of Laura Terracina, *Quinte rime* (Venice: Domenico Farri, 1550), 33v.

8 My translation of Terracina, *Rime*, 13 (italics added).

9 Here, my translation of the introduction to canto 5 in Terracina, *Discorso*, 11r; later, of 11v (verses 5.4.1–3), 20r-v (introduction to canto 11 and verses 11.3.1–7), and 59r-60r (introduction to canto 37 and verses 37.1.1–4, 37.2.1–3, 37.3.1–4.8, and 37.7.1–4).

10 My translation of Laura Terracina, *Settime rime sovra tutte le donne vedove di questa nostra città di Napoli* (*Seventh Book of Poetry, Concerning All the Widows of This Our City of Naples*) (Naples: Mattio Cancer, 1561), A4r.

11 My translation of Laura Terracina, *Discorsi sopra le prime stanze de' canti d'Orlando furioso*, eds. Rotraud von Kulessa and Daria Perocco (Florence: Cesati, 2017), 233.

12 My translation of Laura Terracina, *Le seste rime* (Lucca: Busdraghi, 1563), 86.

13 See Valeria Finucci, "Moderata Fonte and the Genre of Women's Chivalric Romances," in Julia Kisacky, trans., Valeria Finucci, ed., *Moderata Fonte, Floridoro: A Chivalric Romance* (Chicago: University of Chicago Press, 2006), 1–33, 20.

Selected Bibliography

Milligan, Gerry, *Moral Combat: Women, Gender, and War in Italian Renaissance Literature* (Toronto: Toronto University Press, 2018)

Papworth, Amelia, "Pressure to Publish: Laura Terracina and Her Editors," *Early Modern Women* 12.1 (2017): 3–24

Richardson, Brian, *Women and the Circulation of Texts in Renaissance Italy* (Cambridge: Cambridge University Press, 2020)

Shemek, Deanna, *Ladies Errant: Wayward Women and Social Order in Early Modern Italy* (Durham, NC: Duke University Press, 1998)

Veronica Franco (1546–1591): Celebrity Courtesan

Epigraph: Veronica Franco, *Terze rime* (Venice: No Publisher, 1575), capitolo II, 5; my translation.

Notes

1 Here and later, Thomas Coryat, *Crudities; Reprinted from the Edition of 1611* (London: Cater, 1776), 265, with modernized language and punctuation.

2 The *Catalago di tutte le principali et più honorate cortigiane di Venezia* (Catalogue of the Principal and Most Honored Courtesans of Venice) is reprinted

in Antonio Barzaghi, *Donne o cortigiane? La prostituzione a Venezia: Documenti di costume dal XVI al XVIII secolo* (Verona: Bertani, 1980), 155–167. The biographical details that follow here are based on Margaret F. Rosenthal, *The Honest Courtesan: Veronica Franco, Citizen and Writer in Sixteenth-Century Venice* (Chicago: University of Chicago Press, 1992); the letter to Tintoretto later is translated in Veronica Franco, *Poems and Selected Letters*, trans. and eds. Ann Rosalind Jones and Margaret F. Rosenthal (Chicago: University of Chicago Press, 1998), 37.

3 Translations of Veronica Franco's poetry are based, with some adjustments, on Franco, *Poems and Selected Letters*; here, 25–28; later, capitolo 2 (63).

4 Capitolo 12 in Franco, *Poems*, 127; later, capitolo 2 (63–65) and capitolo 13 (133–137); see the discussion in Rosenthal, *Honest Courtesan*.

5 My translation of Maffio Venier, *Poesie diverse*, ed. Attilio Carminati (Venice: Corbo e Fiore, 2001), 102. On misogynist dynamics in Venetian literary culture, see Courtney Quaintance, *Textual Masculinity and the Exchange of Women in Renaissance Venice* (Toronto: University of Toronto Press, 2015).

6 Capitolo 16 in Franco, *Poems*, 161–171; later, see 29 (letter 4) and 39 (letter 22).

7 The trial records are transcribed (but not translated) in Rosenthal, *Honest Courtesan*, 197–203.

8 My translation of Michel de Montaigne, *Journal de voyage*, ed. François Rigolot (Paris: Presses Universitaires de France, 1992), 68.

Selected Bibliography

Franco, Veronica, *Poems and Selected Letters*, trans. and eds. Ann Rosalind Jones and Margaret F. Rosenthal (Chicago: University of Chicago Press, 1998)

Miguel, Marilyn, *Veronica Franco in Dialogue* (Toronto: University of Toronto Press, 2022)

Ray, Meredith K., *Writing Gender in Women's Letter Collections of the Italian Renaissance* (Toronto: University of Toronto Press, 2009)

Rosenthal, Margaret F., *The Honest Courtesan: Veronica Franco, Citizen and Writer in Sixteenth-Century Venice* (Chicago: University of Chicago Press, 1992)

Gaspara Stampa (1523–1554): Renaissance Sappho

Epigraph: Gaspara Stampa, *Rime* (Venice: Plinio Pietrasanta, 1554), 309; my translation.

Notes

1 See Jane Tylus, "Volume Editor's Introduction," in Jane Tylus, trans., Jane Tylus and Troy Tower, eds., *Gaspara Stampa, the Complete Poems: The 1554 Edition of the Rime, a Bilingual Edition* (Chicago: University of Chicago Press, 2010), 1–45, 2–3.

2 Both are translated in Martha Feldman, "The Courtesan's Voice: Petrarchan Lovers, Pop Philosophy, and Oral Traditions," in Martha Feldman and Bonnie Gordon, eds., *The Courtesan's Arts: Cross-Cultural Perspectives* (Oxford: Oxford University Press, 2006), 105–123, 105, 108. For an exploration of this dynamic in music, see, for example, Bonnie Gordon, *Monteverdi's Unruly Women: The Power of Song in Early Modern Italy* (Cambridge: Cambridge University Press, 2004).

3 Translated in Tylus, "Volume Editor's Introduction," 7.

4 Translated in Martha Feldman, *City Culture and the Madrigal at Venice* (Berkeley: University of California Press, 1995), 373.

5 My translation of Francesco Sansovino, "Ragionamento," in Giuseppe Zonta, ed., *Trattati d'amore del Cinquecento* (Bari: Laterza, 1912), 150–184, 184.

6 Unless otherwise noted, all references to Gaspara Stampa's poems follow the numbering and translation in Gaspara Stampa, *Complete Poems*; here, sonnet 16, 73.

7 My translation of Lucrezia Gonzaga, *Lettere* (Venice: Scotto, 1552), 325.

8 Tylus, "Volume Editor's Introduction," 3.

9 See sonnet 2 in Stampa, *Complete Poems*, 61.

10 Translation amended from poems 68 and 41 in Stampa, *Complete Poems*, 116–121, 93; and later, 65 (poem 7).

11 Sonnet 1 in Francesco Petrarca, *Lyric Poems: The Rime Sparse and Other Lyrics*, trans. and ed. Robert Durling (Cambridge, MA: Harvard University Press, 1976), 36.

12 Sonnet 1 in Stampa, *Complete Poems*, 59; later, 139 (sonnet 91).

13 Translation amended from Stampa, *Complete Poems*, 241 (sonnet 206).

14 Tylus, "Volume Editor's Introduction," 12; later, 1.

15 Courtney Quaintance, *Textual Masculinity and the Exchange of Women in Renaissance Venice* (Toronto: University of Toronto Press, 2015), 215n61.

16 Abdelkader Salza, ed., *Gaspara Stampa-Veronica Franco: Rime* (Bari: Laterza, 1913).

17 See Antonio Rambaldo di Collalto and Luisa Bergalli, eds., *Rime, con alcune altre di Collaltino, di Vinciguerra, conti di Collalto, e di Baldassar Stampa* (Venice: Francesco Piacentini, 1738); Luisa Bergalli, ed., *Componimenti poetici delle più illustri rimatrici d'ogni secolo* (Venice: Antonio Mora, 1726). The count's volume included verse by Collaltino (an amateur poet himself), as well as by Gaspara's brother Baldassare.

18 On possible sources for this likeness, see Tylus, "Volume Editor's Introduction," 37–41.

19 Fiora Bassanese, *Gaspara Stampa* (Boston: Twayne, 1982).

Selected Bibliography

Bassanese, Fiora, *Gaspara Stampa* (Boston: Twayne, 1982)

Falkeid, Unn and Aileen A. Feng, eds., *Rethinking Gaspara Stampa in the Canon of Renaissance Poetry* (New York: Routledge, 2016)

Smarr, Janet, "Gaspara Stampa's Poetry for Performance," *Journal of the Rocky Mountain Medieval and Renaissance Association* 12 (1991): 61–83

Stampa, Gaspara, *The Complete Poems: The 1554 Rime, a Bilingual Edition*, trans. Jane Tylus, eds. Jane Tylus and Troy Tower (Chicago: University of Chicago Press, 2010)

Tarquinia Molza (1542–1617): *Virtuosa* and Philosopher

Epigraph: My translation of Tarquinia Molza, *Opusculi inediti . . . con alcune poesie*, ed. Domenico Vandelli (Bergamo: Lancellotti, 1750), 20–21.

Notes

1 This account is attributed to Sigonio in Francesco Patrizi, *L'amorosa filosofia*, ed. John Charles Nelson (Florence: Le Monnier, 1963), 19; my translation; see also Francesco Patrizi, *The Philosophy of Love*, trans. Daniela Pastina and John W. Crayton, notes and intro. John W. Crayton (Philadelphia: Xlibris, 2013), 47. Tarquinia's eighteenth-century biographer, Domenico Vandelli, based much of his account on the information offered by Patrizi. Little is known of Tarquinia's mother, except that her marriage took place in 1539.

2 The letter is quoted in Progetto Donne e Futuro, "Tarquinia Molza: donna letterata tra le pi[ù] erudite alla corte del duca Alfonso II," *Progetto Donne e Futuro*, July 20, 2020, www.progettodonneefuturo.org/2020/07/20/tarquinia-molza-una-donna-e-letterata-tra-le-piu-erudite-presso-la-corte-del-duca-alfonso-ii; my translation.

3 See Muzio Manfredi, ed., *Per donne romane: Rime di diversi raccolte e dedicate al Signor Giacomo Buoncompagni* (Bologna: Alessandro Benaco, 1575).

4 My translation of Torquato Tasso, *Prose*, ed. Ettore Mazzali (Milan: Ricciardi, 1959), 205.

5 My translation of Molza, *Opusculi*, 81.

6 See the madrigal "Eran le vostre lagrime" with music by Giovanni Pierluigi da Palestrina in Giacomo Vincenzi, ed., *Canto de floridi virtuosi d'Italia: il secondo libro de madrigali à cinque voci* (Venice: Vincenzi & Amadino, 1585), 4; translation altered from Mick Swithinbank's translation in *Choral Public Domain Library*, 27 December 2022, www.cpdl.org/wiki/index.php/Eran_le_vostre_lagrime_(Giovanni_Pierluigi_da_Palestrina). See also Tarquinia's madrigal for Angela Beccaria in Stefano Guazzo's 1595 *La ghirlanda della contessa Angela Beccaria*, discussed in Virginia Cox, *Women's Writing in Italy, 1400–1650* (Baltimore: Johns Hopkins University Press, 2008), 139–142.

7 Translation amended from Laurie Stras, "Recording Tarquinia: Imitation, Parody and Reportage in Ingegneri's 'Hor che'l ciel e la terra e'l vento tace'," *Early Music* 27.3 (1999): 358–377.

8 My translation of Camillo Camilli, *Imprese illustri di diversi* (Venice: Francesco Ziletti, 1586), 51.

9 Translated in Jacomien Prins, "Early Modern Angelic Song in Francesco Patrizi's *L'Amorosa Filosofia*," in Alicia C. Montoya, Sophie van Romburgh and Wim van Anrooij, eds., *Early Modern Medievalisms: The Interplay Between Scholarly Reflection and Artistic Production* (Leiden: Brill, 2010), 111–135, 117.

10 My translation of Francesco Patrizi, *Lettere ed opuscoli inediti*, ed. Danilo Aguzzi Bargagli (Florence: Istituto Palazzo Strozzi, 1975), 17.

11 See Prins, "Early Modern Angelic Song," 119.

12 Translation amended from Francesco Patrizi, *Philosophy of Love*, trans. Daniela Pastina and John W. Crayton (Philadelphia: Xlibris, 2003), 34; later, 69, 165.

13 My translation of Tasso, *Prose*, 205. Tarquinia is also featured in a 1585 dialogue on love by Annibale Romei titled *Discorsi* (*Discourses*). On the lectures attributed to her, see Jane Stevenson, *Women Latin Poets: Language, Gender, and Authority from Antiquity to the Eighteenth Century* (Oxford: Oxford University Press, 2005), 290.

14 Translated in Patrizi, *Philosophy*, 69.

15 See Anthony Newcomb, *The Madrigal at Ferrara (1579–97)* (Princeton: Princeton University Press, 1980), 7.

16 See Paola Di Pietro, "La biblioteca di una letterata del Cinquecento modenese Tarquinia Molza," *Atti e memorie della Deputazione di Storia Patria per le Antiche Provincie Modenesi* 10.8 (1973): 55–64.

17 My translation of Molza, *Opuscoli*, 27.

Selected Bibliography

Plastina, Sandra, "Is Francesco Patrizi's *L'Amorosa Filosofia* a Heterodox Reading of the *Symposium*?" *Intellectual History Review* 29.4 (2019): 631–648

Ray, Meredith K., "Tarquinia Molza and 'Le cose del cielo': Gender, Natural Philosophy, and Celebrity in Early Modern Italy," in Mary Lindemann and Deanna Shemek, eds., *Redreaming the Renaissance: Essays in Honor of Guido Ruggiero* (Newark: University of Delaware Press, 2024)

Riley, Joanne, "Tarquinia Molza (1542–1617): A Case Study of Women, Music, and Society in the Renaissance," in Judith Lang Zaimont, gen. ed., *The Musical Woman: An International Perspective; Volume II, 1984–1985* (New York: Greenwood, 1988), 470–493

Stras, Laurie, "Recording Tarquinia: Imitation, Parody and Reportage in Ingegneri's 'Hor che 'l ciel e la terra e 'l vento tace'," *Early Music* 27.3 (1999): 358–377

Isabella Andreini (1562–1604): Diva of Stage and Page

Epigraph: Isabella Andreini, *Rime* (Milan: Girolamo Bordone, 1601), 1; my translation.

Notes

1 Translated in Rosalind Kerr, *The Rise of the Diva on the Sixteenth-Century Commedia dell'Arte Stage* (Toronto: University of Toronto Press, 2015), 127.

2 Translated in Margaret Rose, "The First Italian Actresses, Isabella Andreini and the *Commedia dell'Arte*," in Jan Sewell and Clare Smout, eds., *The Palgrave Handbook of the History of Women on Stage* (Cham: Palgrave Macmillan, 2019), 107–126, 108–109. Though women performed on stages everywhere in Italy but Rome, and though many – like Vincenza Armani, Barbara Flaminia, Diana Ponti, and Virginia Ramponi – earned praise and occasionally led their own companies, in England they would not take the stage until nearly a century later, leaving women's roles to be performed by men.

3 For an analysis of this portrait, see Maria Ines Aliverti, "An Icon for a New Woman: A Previously Unidentified Portrait of Isabella Andreini by Paolo Veronese," *Early Theatre* 11.2 (2008): 159–180.

4 Anne MacNeil, *Music and Women of the Commedia dell'Arte in the Late Sixteenth Century* (Oxford: Oxford University Press, 2005), 50–51; Sarah Gwyneth Ross, "Performing Humanism: The Andreini Family and the Republic of Letters in Counter-Reformation Italy," in Ann Blair and Anja-Silvia Goeing, eds., *For the Sake of Learning: Essays in Honor of Anthony Grafton* (Leiden: Brill, 2016), 140–156; see also Sarah Gwyneth Ross, *The Birth of Feminism: Woman as Intellect in Renaissance Italy and England* (Cambridge: Harvard University Press, 2009), 212–234.

5 Translation amended from Isabella Andreini, *Mirtilla, a Pastoral: A Bilingual Edition*, trans. Julia Kisacky, ed. Valeria Finucci (Toronto: Iter, 2018), 147.

6 See the dedicatory letter in Isabella Andreini, *Lettere* (Venice: Zaltieri, 1607), A3r.

7 See Chiara Cedrati, "Isabella Andreini: La vicenda editoriale delle 'Rime'," *ACME* 40.2 (2007): 115–142.

8 My translation of Isabella Andreini, *Rime* (Milan: Girolamo Bordone e Pietromartire Locarni, 1601), 3v.

9 Here and later, translation adapted from Isabella Andreini, *Selected Poems*, trans. James Wyatt Cook, ed. Anne MacNeil (Lanham: Scarecrow, 2005), 31.

10 Here, my translation of Andreini, *Lettere*, A3r–A3v; later, A2v, E2v, E3v.

11 A shorter, "intermediate" edition of Isabella's *Rime* was printed in France in 1603; see Isabella Andreini, *Rime* (Paris: Claude de Monstr'oeil, 1603).

Selected Bibliography

Andreini, Isabella, *Mirtilla, a Pastoral: A Bilingual Edition*, trans. Julia Kisacky, ed. Valeria Finucci (Toronto/Tempe: Iter Academic Press/Arizona Center for Medieval and Renaissance Studies, 2018)

Andrews, Richard, "Isabella Andreini and Others: Women on Stage in the Late Cinquecento," in Letizia Panizza, ed., *Women in Renaissance Culture and Society* (London: Legenda, 2005), 316–333

Kerr, Rosalind, *The Rise of the Diva on the Commedia dell'Arte Stage* (Toronto: University of Toronto Press, 2015)

MacNeil, Anne, *Music and Women of the Commedia dell'Arte in the Late Sixteenth Century* (New York: Oxford University Press, 2005)

Francesca Caccini (1587–post-1641): Opera's Star at the Medici Court

Epigraph: Cristofano Bronzini, *Della dignità e nobiltà delle donne* (Biblioteca Nazionale, Florence, Magl. VIII, 1525/1), 54–77; my translation. The original text is transcribed in Suzanne G. Cusick, *Francesca Caccini at the Medici Court: Music and the Circulation of Power* (Chicago: University of Chicago Press, 2009), 331–338.

Notes

1 Though his family came from Tuscany, Giulio studied music in Rome and is often referred to as "Romano" to distinguish him from the wealthy Florentine family of the same name; see Cusick, *Francesca Caccini*, 2. Cusick's is the most complete study of Francesca to date; biographical details throughout are based on it. For the translation here, see Cusick, *Francesca Caccini*, 9; later, 3.

2 See Anthony Newcomb, "Courtesans, Muses, or Musicians? Professional Women Musicians in Sixteenth-Century Italy," in Jane Bowers and Judith Tick, eds., *Women Making Music: The Western Art Tradition, 1150–1950* (Chicago: University of Illinois Press, 1987), 90–115.

3 Translated in Carolyn Raney, "Francesca Caccini (1587-c. 1630)," in James R. Briscoe, ed., *Historical Anthology of Music by Women* (Bloomington: Indiana University Press, 1987), 22–38, 22.

4 For the translation here, see Cusick, *Francesca Caccini*, 19; later, 62.

5 See Suzanne Cusick, "'La stiava dolente in suono di canto': War, Slavery, and Difference in a Medici Court Entertainment," in Emily Wilbourne and Suzanne Cusick, eds., *Acoustemologies in Contact: Sounding Subjects and Modes of Listening in Early Modernity* (Cambridge: Cambridge University Press, 2021), 201–237.

6 See Cusick, *Francesca Caccini*, 66.

7 On early modern equestrian ballet and opera, see Jessica Goethals, "The Patronage Politics of Equestrian Ballet: Allegory, Allusion, and Satire in the Courts of Seventeenth-Century Italy and France," *Renaissance Quarterly* 70.4 (2017): 1397–1448. Caccini was the first woman to compose music for a horse ballet, while the first female-authored libretto for one was written by the prolific Baroque author Margherita Costa in 1647.

8 Translated in Carolyn Raney, "Francesca Caccini, Musician to the Medici, and Her *Primo libro* (1618)" (dissertation, New York University, 1971), 51; see also Francesca Caccini, Il primo libro delle musiche *of 1618: A Modern*

Critical Edition of the Secular Monodies, eds. Ronald James Alexander and Richard Savino (Bloomington: Indiana University Press, 2004), 4.

9 See Cusick, *Franecsa Caccini*, 247–363.

10 On theater as an important facet of early modern convent life, see Elissa B. Weaver, *Convent Theatre in Early Modern Italy: Spiritual Fun and Learning for Women* (Cambridge: Cambridge University Press, 2002).

11 Translated in Cusick, *Francesca Caccini*, 276; italics added.

Selected Bibliography

Cusick, Suzanne G., *Francesca Caccini at the Medici Court: Music and the Circulation of Power* (Chicago: University of Chicago Press, 2009)

Harness, Kelly, *Echoes of Women's Voices: Music, Art, and Female Patronage in Early Modern Florence* (Chicago: University of Chicago Press, 2006)

Newcomb, Anthony, "Courtesans, Muses, or Musicians? Professional Women Musicians in Sixteenth-Century Italy," in Jane Bowers and Judith Tick, eds., *Women Making Music: The Western Art Tradition, 1150–1950* (Chicago: University of Illinois Press, 1987), 90–115

Raney, Carolyn, "Francesca Caccini (1587-c.1630)," in James R. Briscoe, ed., *Historical Anthology of Music by Women* (Bloomington: Indiana University Press, 1987), 22–38

Barbara Strozzi (1619–1677): Trailblazing Composer

Epigraph: Giovanni Francesco Loredano, *Lettere* (Geneva: Widerhold, 1669), vol. II, 249; my translation.

Notes

1 See Ellen Rosand, "Barbara Strozzi, *Virtuosissima cantatrice*: The Composer's Voice," *Journal of the American Musicological Society* 31.2 (1978): 241–281, 242. My thanks to Beth Glixon for sharing new biographical information about Strozzi's family included in the forthcoming volume, *Barbara Strozzi in Context*, edited by Wendy Heller and Beth Glixon (Cambridge University Press).

2 See Robert L. Kendrick, "Intent and Intertextuality in Barbara Strozzi's Sacred Music," *Recercare* 14 (2002): 65–98, 66–68, 95–97.

3 For the translation here, see Rosand, "Barbara Strozzi," 251; later, 251n34, 253.

4 Cited in the epigraph to this chapter.

5 Rosand, "Barbara Strozzi," 256n64. Tarabotti's *Antisatira (Antisatire)* was a sharp and witty defense of women against charges of vanity and luxury, published by the Valvasense press in Venice in 1644.

6 My translation of Barbara Strozzi, *Il primo libro de' madrigali* (Venice: Vincenti, 1644), A2r. Vittoria della Rovere was the focus of several dedications by women writers and composers, including in addition to Strozzi and Tarabotti, Barbara Tigliamochi's 1640 epic, *Ascanio errante*.

7 My translation of Barbara Strozzi, *Sacri musicali affetti* (Venice: Gardano, 1655), 1.

8 See Francesco Tonalli, ed., *Arie a voce sola di diversi auttori* (Venice: Vincenti, 1656); Bartolomeo Marcesso, ed., *Sacra corona* (Venice: Francesco Magni, 1656).

9 Letter dated 24 September 1678; translated in Beth L. Glixon, "More on the Life and Death of Barbara Strozzi," *Musical Quarterly* 83 (1999): 134–141, 136. The information that follows about Barbara's relationship with Vidman and about their children is based on Glixon; see also Beth Glixon, "New Light on the Life and Career of Barbara Strozzi," *Musical Quarterly* 81.2 (1997): 311–335.

10 My translation of Glixon, "More on the Life," 138.

Selected Bibliography

Glixon, Beth L., "New Light on the Life and Career of Barbara Strozzi," *Musical Quarterly* 81.2 (1997): 311–335

Glixon, Beth L., "More on the Life and Death of Barbara Strozzi," *Musical Quarterly* 83.1 (1999): 134–141

Heller, Wendy, "Barbara Strozzi and the Taming of the Male Poetic Voice," in Dinko Fabris and Margaret Murata, eds., *Passaggio in Italia: Music on the Grand Tour in the Seventeenth Century* (Turnhout: Brepols, 2016), 131–169

Rosand, Ellen, "Barbara Strozzi, *Virtuosissima cantatrice*: The Composer's Voice," *Journal of the American Musicological Society* 31.2 (1978): 241–281

Sofonisba Anguissola (c. 1532–1625): Portraitist to Kings

Epigraph: Giorgio Vasari, *Delle vite de' più eccellenti pittori, scultori, e architettori*, III.1 (Florence: Giunti, 1568), 74; my translation.

Notes

1 Baldassare Castiglione, *The Book of the Courtier*, trans. Charles Singleton, ed. Daniel Javitch (New York: Norton, 2002), 155.

2 Michael Cole, *Sofonisba's Lesson: A Renaissance Artist and Her Work* (Princeton: Princeton University Press, 2019), 4.

3 In 1554, the painter Francesco Salviati described Sofonisba to Campi as "the beautiful painter from Cremona, your creation"; for this translation and the analysis later, see the classic study by Mary D. Garrard, "Here's

ist," *Renaissance Quarterly* 47.3 (1994): 556–622, 560.

4 See Germaine Greer, *The Obstacle Race: The Fortunes of Women Painters and Their Work* (New York: Farrar, Straus and Giroux, 1979), 181. Michael Cole suggests that Campi himself may have painted this double portrait, but the attribution to Sofonisba is accepted by most experts; see Cole, *Sofonisba's Lesson*, 54–67.

5 Translated in Charles De Tolnay, "Sofonisba Anguissola and Her Relations with Michelangelo," *Journal of the Walters Art Gallery* 4 (1941): 114–119, 117. The anecdote was recounted by Tommaso Cavalieri to Cosimo I and is also alluded to by Vasari; see Garrard, "Here's Looking at Me," 611n97.

6 For the translations here and later, see De Tolnay, "Sofonisba Anguissola," 116–117.

7 For this analysis, see Garrard, "Here's Looking at Me," 603; on her letter to Campi later, see 617n104.

8 For the translation here, see Cecilia Gamberini, "Sofonisba Anguissola at the Court of Philip II," in Sheila Barker, ed., *Women Artists in Early Modern Italy: Careers, Fame, and Collectors* (London: Harvey Miller, 2016), 28–38, 32; later, see 34.

9 Translated in Cole, *Sofonisba's Lesson*, 147 and later, 150.

10 Translated in Christopher Brown, *Van Dyck* (Ithaca, NY: Cornell University Press, 1982), 84.

11 Translated in Maria H. Loh, " 'Cross My Heart, Hope to Die, Stick a Needle in My Eye': Friendship, Survival, and the Pathos of Portraiture," *Res: Anthropology and Aesthetics* 65–66 (2014): 375–385.

12 Translated in Frederika H. Jacobs, "Woman's Capacity to Create: The Unusual Case of Sofonisba Anguissola," *Renaissance Quarterly* 47.1 (1994): 74–101, 76.

Selected Bibliography

Barker, Sheila, ed., *Women Artists in Early Modern Italy: Careers, Fame, and Collectors* (London: Harvey Miller, 2016)

Cole, Michael, *Sofonisba's Lessons: A Renaissance Artist and Her Work* (Princeton: Princeton University Press, 2020)

Garrard, Mary D., "Here's Looking at Me: Sofonisba Anguissola and the Problem of the Woman Artist," *Renaissance Quarterly* 47.3 (1994): 556–622

Gómez, Leticia Ruiz, ed., *A Tale of Two Women Painters: Sofonisba Anguissola and Lavinia Fontana* (Madrid: Museo Nacional del Prado, 2019)

Lavinia Fontana (1552–1614): Pioneering Professional Artist

Epigraph: Giulio Cesare Croce, *La gloria delle donne* (Bologna: Alessandro Benacci, 1590), 19; my translation.

Notes

1 See Germain Greer, *The Obstacle Race: The Fortunes of Women Painters and Their Work* (New York: Farrar, Straus and Giroux, 1979),
208–226; Babette Bohn, *Women Artists, Their Patrons, and Their Publics in Early Modern Bologna* (College Park: Pennsylvania State University Press, 2021). See also Babette Bohn, "Celebrating Bologna's
Women Artists," *Art Herstory*, 23 March 2021, https://artherstory.net/
celebrating-bolognas-women-artists.
2 On this painting, see Katherine R. McIver, "Lavinia Fontana's Self-Portrait
Making Music," *Woman's Art Journal* 19.1 (1998): 3–7.
3 Carolyn Murphy, *Lavinia Fontana: A Painter and Her Patrons in Sixteenth-
Century Bologna* (New Haven: Yale University Press, 2003), 91, 105–106.
Murphy's examination of Lavinia Fontana and her work remains the most
substantial study devoted to the artist and informs the analysis here.
4 On this portrait, see Merry Weisner-Hanks, *The Marvelous Hairy Girls:
The Gonzales Sisters and Their World* (New Haven: Yale University Press,
2009).
5 See Liana De Girolami Cheney, "Lavinia Fontana's Nude Minervas,"
Woman's Art Journal 36.2 (2015): 30–40.

Selected Bibliography

Bohn, Babette, *Women Artists, Their Patrons, and Their Publics in Early Mod-
ern Bologna* (State College: Pennsylvania State University Press, 2021)
Gómez, Leticia Ruiz, ed., *A Tale of Two Women Painters: Sofonisba Anguissola
and Lavinia Fontana* (Madrid: Museo Nacional del Prado, 2019)
Murphy, Caroline, "Lavinia Fontana and *Le dame della città*: Understanding
Female Artistic Patronage in Late Sixteenth-Century Bologna," *Renaissance
Studies* 10.2 (1996): 190–208
Murphy, Caroline, *Lavinia Fontana: A Painter and Her Patrons in Sixteenth-
Century Bologna* (New Haven: Yale University Press, 2003)

Artemisia Gentileschi (1593–1656?): Fearless Painter, Feminist Icon

Epigraph: Letter of Artemisia Gentileschi to her patron Antonio Ruffo,
13 November 1649. The Italian text is in Vincenzo Ruffo, "Galleria Ruffo
nel secolo XVII in Messina," *Bollettino d'Arte* 10, 51, https://archive.
org/stream/bollettinodarte10italuoft/bollettinodarte10italuoft_djvu.txt;
my translation.

Notes

1 Mary D. Garrard, *Artemisia Gentileschi and Feminism in Early Modern Europe* (London: Reaktion, 2020), 140.
2 References to the trial and translations of the transcript are taken from Mary D. Garrard's foundational study, *Artemisia Gentileschi: The Image of the Female Hero in Italian Baroque Art* (Princeton: Princeton University Press, 1989), 407–487.
3 See Jesse Locker, "Artemisia Gentileschi: The Literary Formation of an Unlearned Artist," in Sheila Barker, ed., *Artemisia Gentileschi in a Changing Light* (London: Harvey Miller, 2017), 89–101.
4 See the discussion in Garrard, *Artemisia Gentileschi*, 183–209.
5 On Artemisia's Florentine years and her business strategies, see Sheila Barker, "Artemisia's Money: The Entrepreneurship of a Woman Artist in Seventeenth-Century Florence," in Sheila Barker, ed., *Artemisia Gentileschi in a Changing Light* (London: Harvey Miller, 2017), 59–88.
6 Probably at Artemisia's direction, Bronzino's account omits any mention of the trial in Rome; see Sheila Barker, "The First Biography of Artemisia Gentileschi: Self-Fashioning and Proto-Feminist Art History in Cristofano Bronzini's Notes on Women Artists," *Mitteilungen des Kunsthistorischen Institutes* 60.3 (2018): 405–435.
7 Barker, "Artemisia's Money," 61n29.
8 See Francesco Solinas, ed., *Lettere di Artemisia* (Rome: De Luca, 2011), 74; translation from the National Gallery booklet accompanying the exhibition, Artemisia, from 2020–2021, www.nationalgallery.org.uk/media/35472/letters-transcription-booklet_final_online-version-1.pdf.
9 These letters are translated in Barker, "Artemisia's Money," 66.
10 Translated in Garrard, *Artemisia Gentileschi*, 386.
11 Translations of Artemisia's letters – dated 12 June, 23 October and 13 November 1649 – are from Garrard, *Artemisia Gentileschi*, 393–397, with some adjustments.
12 Linda Nochlin, "Why Have There Been No Great Women Artists?" *Art News* 69.9 (1971): 22–39.
13 Artemisia's letter to Ruffo, dated 7 August 1649, is translated in Garrard, *Artemisia Gentileschi*, 394.

Selected Bibliography

Barker, Sheila, ed., *Artemisia Gentileschi in a Changing Light* (London: Harvey Miller, 2017)
Bissell, R. Ward, *Artemisia Gentileschi and the Authority of Art* (University Park: Pennsylvania State University Press, 1999)

330 Notes and Further Reading

Christiansen, Keith and Judith W. Mann, eds., *Orazio and Artemisia Gentile-schi: Father and Daughter Painters in Baroque Italy* (New Haven: Yale University Press, 2001)

Garrard, Mary D., *Artemisia Gentileschi: The Image of the Female Hero in Italian Baroque Art* (Princeton: Princeton University Press, 1989)

Camilla Erculiani (d. post-1584): Pharmacist-Philosopher

Epigraph: Camilla Erculiani, *Lettere di philosophia naturale* (Krakow: Lazaro, 1584), aii–v; my translation.

Notes

1 See Paula Findlen, "Aristotle in the Pharmacy: The Ambitions of Camilla Erculiani in Sixteenth-Century Padua," in Hannah Marcus, trans., Eleonora Carinci, ed., *Camilla Erculiani, Letters on Natural Philosophy* (Toronto: Iter, 2021), 1–49, 6; Sharon Strocchia, *Nuns and Nunneries in Renaissance Florence* (Baltimore: Johns Hopkins University Press, 2009); Sharon Strocchia, *Forgotten Healers: Women and the Pursuit of Health in Late Renaissance Italy* (Cambridge, MA: Harvard University Press, 2019).
2 Biographical information throughout is based primarily on Erculiani, *Letters*, 67–75.
3 See Findlen, "Aristotle in the Pharmacy," 10.
4 Unless otherwise noted, translations from Camilla's letters are based, with some adjustments, on Erculiani, *Letters* (here, 125; later, 125, 111).
5 My translation, amended from Erculiani, *Letters*, 110. On Camilla's *Letters* in the context of the Renaissance debate over women, see Meredith K. Ray, *Daughters of Alchemy: Women and Scientific Culture in Early Modern Italy* (Cambridge, MA: Harvard University Press, 2015), 111–154.
6 Translated in Johanna Kostyło, "Commonwealth of All Faiths: Republican Myth and the Italian Diaspora in Sixteenth-Century Poland-Lithuania," in Karen Friedrich and Barbara M. Pendzich, eds., *Citizenship and Identity in a Multinational Commonwealth: Poland-Lithuania in Context, 1550–1772* (Leiden: Brill, 2008), 171–205, 185.
7 Findlen, "Aristotle in the Pharmacy," 39. The discussion of Camilla's philosophical concepts later is based on Findlen, "Aristotle in the Pharmacy," 34–44; Carinci, *Letters*, 85–106.
8 Here, see Erculiani, *Letters*, 114; later, 139 and 156.
9 Menochio's defense of Camilla is reproduced in Erculiani, *Letters*, 155–168; later, see 96–106, 114.

Selected Bibliography

Erculiani, Camilla, *Letters on Natural Philosophy*, trans. Hannah Marcus, ed. Eleonora Carinci (Toronto: Iter, 2021)

Findlen, Paula, "Aristotle in the Pharmacy: The Ambitions of Camilla Erculiani
in Sixteenth-Century Padua," in Hannah Marcus, trans., Eleonora Carinci, ed.,
Camilla Erculiani, Letters on Natural Philosophy (Toronto: Iter, 2021), 1–49

Ray, Meredith K., *Daughters of Alchemy: Women and Scientific Culture in
Early Modern Italy* (Cambridge, MA: Harvard University Press, 2015)

Shaw, James and Evelyn Welch, *Making and Marketing Medicine in Renaissance Florence* (Amsterdam: Rodopi, 2011)

Margherita Sarrocchi (c. 1560–1617): Reader of the Stars, Galileo's Correspondent

Epigraph: Dedicatory letter to the third edition of Margherita Sarrocchi, *Scanderbeide* (Naples: Bulifon, 1701), 2: a3r–a3v; my translation.

Notes

1 Cristofano Bronzini, *Della dignità e nobiltà delle donne. Dialogo . . .
diviso in quattro settimane, e ciascheduna in esse in sei giornate* (Florence: Pignoni/Ciotti, 1622–1628), 2:130; translation amended from Meredith K. Ray, *Daughters of Alchemy: Women and Scientific Culture in
Early Modern Italy* (Cambridge, MA: Harvard University Press, 2015),
133–134.

2 Giulio Cesare Capaccio, *Il forastiero* (Naples: Rongagliolo, 1634), 823.

3 Translated adapted from Margherita Sarrocchi, *Scanderbeide*, trans. and
ed. Rinaldina Russell (Chicago: University of Chicago Press, 2006), 9n15.

4 Francesco Agostino Della Chiesa, *Theatro delle donne letterate* (Mondovì:
Giflaudi and Rossi, 1620), 253–254.

5 Here and later, see Bronzini, *Della dignità*, 130, 135; translated in Ray,
Daughters of Alchemy, 134–135.

6 Translated in Mario Bucciantini, Michele Camerota and Franco Giudice,
Galileo's Telescope: A European Story, trans. Catherine Bolton (Cambridge, MA: Harvard University Press, 2015), 182–183.

7 My translation of the dedication in Meredith K. Ray, "Statecraft and the
Politics of Knowledge in Margherita Sarrocchi's *Scanderbeide*," *Bruniana & campanelliana* 25.2 (2019): 475–491, 477.

8 Here and later, my translation of Margherita Sarrocchi, *Scanderbeide*
(Rome: Lepido Facio, 1606), 3:38.

9 Bronzini, *Della dignità*, 134.

10 Here and later, translation adapted from Meredith K. Ray, ed., *Margherita Sarrocchi's Letters to Galileo: Astronomy, Astrology, and Poetics in Seventeenth-Century Italy* (New York: Palgrave, 2016), 55n87,
70 and 74.

11 Valerio's letter to Galileo is in Galileo Galilei, *Opere: Edizione nazionale*,
ed. Antonio Favaro (Florence: Barbèra, 1890–1909), 10:362–363; translated in Ray, *Daughters of Alchemy*, 146.

12 Here and later, translation adapted from Ray, *Margherita Sarrocchi's Letters*, 71, 77.

13 See Dava Sobel, *Galileo's Daughter: A Historical Memoir of Science, Faith, and Love* (New York: Walker & Company, 1999); Dava Sobel, *Letters to Father: Suor Maria Celeste to Galileo, 1623–1633* (New York: Walker & Company, 2001).
14 See Ray, *Margherita Sarrocchi's Letters*, 40.

Selected Bibliography

Cox, Virginia, *The Prodigious Muse: Women's Writing in Counter-Reformation Italy* (Baltimore: Johns Hopkins University Press, 2011)

Ray, Meredith K., *Daughters of Alchemy: Women and Scientific Culture in Early Modern Italy* (Cambridge, MA: Harvard University Press, 2015)

Ray, Meredith K., ed., *Margherita Sarrocchi's Letters to Galileo: Astronomy, Astrology, and Poetics in Seventeenth-Century Italy* (New York: Palgrave, 2016)

Sarrocchi, Margherita, *Scanderbeide*, trans. and ed. Rinaldina Russell (Chicago: University of Chicago Press, 2006)

Laudomia Forteguerri (1515–1555?): Queer Poet, Civic Hero

Epigraph: Giovanni Betussi, *Le imagini del tempio della signora Giovanna d'Aragona* (Florence: Torrentino, 1556), 31r; my translation.

Notes

1 So wrote Girolamo Gigli; see *Parlour Games and the Public Life of Women in Renaissance Italy*, trans. George McClure (Toronto: University of Toronto Press, 2013), 161.
2 Betussi, *Le Imagini*, 31r.
3 See Virginia Cox, "Members, Mascots, and Muses: Women and the Italian Academies," in Jane E. Everson, Denis V. Reidy and Lisa Sampson, eds., *The Italian Academies 1525–1700: Networks of Culture, Innovation, and Dissent* (New York: Legenda 2016), 132–169, 134.
4 My translation of the unpaginated dedication in Alessandro Piccolomini, *De la sfera del mondo* (Venice: Al Segno del Pozzo, 1540). Piccolomini also dedicated to Laudomia, upon the birth of her son, his 1539 *De la institutione di tutta la vita de l'homo nato nobile e in città libera* (*About the Upbringing of the Entire Life of a Noble Man, Born in a Free City*).
5 Though there is still debate over the identity of Alessandro's mother, a number of recent studies focus on Alessandro and the interplay of race, power, and politics in Renaissance Italy: see, for example, Catherine Fletcher, *The Black Prince of Florence: The Spectacular Life and Treacherous World of Alessandro de' Medici* (Oxford: Oxford University Press, 2016); Olivette Otele, *African Europeans: An Untold History* (New York: Basic, 2021), 39–46; and, more broadly, T.F. Earle and K.J.P. Lowe, *Black*

Africans in Renaissance Europe (Cambridge: Cambridge University Press, 2005).

6 On the episode, see Stefano dall'Aglio, *The Duke's Assassin: Exile and Death of Lorenzino de' Medici* (New Haven: Yale University Press, 2015), 176–186.

7 Charlie R. Steen, *Margaret of Parma: A Life* (Leiden: Brill, 2013), 35.

8 Konrad Eisenbichler, *The Sword and the Pen: Women, Politics, and Poetry in Sixteenth-Century Siena* (Notre Dame: Notre Dame University Press, 2012), 124; later, see 123.

9 For Laudomia's verse as a bid for patronage, see Diana Robin, *Publishing Women: Salons, the Presses, and the Counter-Reformation in Sixteenth-Century Italy* (Chicago: University of Chicago Press, 2013), 149–159; for Piccolomini's description later, see 150.

10 For the translation here, see Eisenbichler, *The Sword and the Pen*, 121; later, 126.

11 All translations of Laudomia's poetry are in Robin, *Publishing Women*, 153–155.

12 Eisenbichler, *The Sword and the Pen*, 130–131.

13 For the translation here, see Robin, *Publishing Women*, 124; later, 127.

14 Translated in McClure, *Parlour Games*, 50.

Selected Bibliography

Eisenbichler, Konrad, "Laudomia Forteguerri Loves Margaret of Austria," in Francesca Canadé Suatman and Pamela Sheingorn, eds., *Same Sex Love and Desire Among Women in the Middle Ages* (New York: Palgrave, 2001), 277–304

Eisenbichler, Konrad, *The Sword and the Pen: Women, Politics, and Poetry in Sixteenth-Century Siena* (Notre Dame: Notre Dame University Press, 2013)

McClure, George, *Parlour Games and the Public Life of Women in Renaissance Italy* (Toronto: University of Toronto Press, 2013)

Robin, Diana, *Publishing Women: Salons, the Presses, and the Counter-Reformation in Sixteenth-Century Italy* (Chicago: University of Chicago Press, 2013)

Moderata Fonte (1555–1592): Visionary of Women's Equality

Epigraph: Moderata Fonte, *Il merito delle donne* (Venice: Domenico Imberti, 1600), 20; my translation.

Notes

1 Other early influential pro-woman models include Giovanni Boccaccio's *Concerning Famous Women*, trans. Guido Guarino (New Brunswick, NJ: Rutgers University Press, 1963) from 1361–1362, a source for Christine

de Pizan; Galeazzo Flavio Capra's 1525 *Della eccellenza e dignità delle donne* (*On the Excellence and Dignity of Women*); Cornelius Agrippa's *On the Nobility and Preeminence of the Female Sex* from around 1529.

2 Virginia Cox, "On Moderata Fonte's Feminist Reimagining of 16th-Century Venice: Female Friendships and Single Women in the Merits of Women," *Literary Hub*, 27 March 2018, https://lithub.com/on-moderata-fontes-feminist-reimagining-of-16th-century-venice.

3 Doglioni's biography of Fonte is translated in *The Worth of Women: Wherein Is Clearly Revealed Their Nobility and Their Superiority to Men*, trans. and ed. Virginia Cox (Chicago: University of Chicago Press, 1997), 31–40; for the translations later, see 35–36, 133.

4 Moderata Fonte, *Floridoro: A Chivalric Romance*, trans. Julia Kisacky, ed. Valeria Finucci (Chicago: University of Chicago Press, 2006), 49; for the translation of stanza 4.3 later, see 262.

5 See Ippolito Zucconello, ed., *Viridiarium poetarum tum latino, tum graeco, tum vulgari eloquio scribentium in laudes serenissimi atque potentissimi D.D. Stephani regis Poloniae, magni ducis Lituaniae, Russiae, Prussiae, Semofitiae, Kioviae, Liboniae[que], domini ac principis Transilvaniae* (Venice: Hyppogryph/Guerra, 1583), 2:14, 48–57.

6 For the translation here, see Fonte, *Worth of Women*, 113–114; later, 36.

7 Translated in Laura Cereta, *Collected Letters of a Renaissance Feminist*, trans. and ed. Diana Robin (Chicago: University of Chicago Press, 1997), 31–32.

8 For the translation here, see Fonte, *Worth of Women*, 65; later, 59, 61, 76, 157, 171.

9 My translation of Cristofano Bronzini, *Della dignità & nobiltà delle donne: dialogo . . . diviso in quattro settimane; e ciascheduna di esse in sei giornate* (Florence: Zanobi Pignoni, 1625), 116.

Selected Bibliography

Castiglione, Caroline, "Why Political Theory Is Women's Work: How Moderata Fonte Reclaimed Liberty for Women Inside and Outside Marriage," in Merry Wiesner-Hanks, ed., *Challenging Women's Agency and Activism in Early Modernity* (Amsterdam: Amsterdam University Press, 2021), 141–161

Fonte, Moderata, *The Worth of Women*, trans. and ed. Virginia Cox (Chicago: University of Chicago Press, 1997)

Ray, Meredith K., *Daughters of Alchemy: Women and Scientific Culture in Early Modern Italy* (Cambridge, MA: Harvard University Press, 2015)

Ross, Sarah Gwyneth, *The Birth of Feminism: Woman as Intellect in Renaissance Italy and England* (Cambridge, MA: Harvard University Press, 2009)

Lucrezia Marinella (1571?–1653): Champion of Women's History

Epigraph: Lucrezia Marinella, *La nobiltà et l'eccellenza delle donne, co' difetti et mancamenti de gli huomini* (Venice: Ciotti, 1601), 2; my translation.

Notes

1 For this translation, see Letizia Panizza, "Introduction to the Translation," in *The Nobility and Excellence of Women and the Defects and Vices of Men*, trans. and eds. Anne Dunhill and Lucrezia Marinella (Chicago: University of Chicago Press, 1999), 1–34, 1; later, 17. Virginia Cox suggests a revised birthdate of c. 1579 for Lucrezia Marinella (see *The Prodigious Muse: Women's Writing in Counter-Reformation Italy* (Baltimore: Johns Hopkins University Press, 2011, 271n5).

2 This discussion of Lucrezia's devotional writing draws from the analysis in Meredith K. Ray and Lynn Lara Westwater, "Polemics That Might Seem Spiteful in Heaven: Female Spiritual Authority in Arcangela Tarabotti's *Paradiso Monacale*," in Meredith K. Ray and Lynn Lara Westwater, eds., *Gendering the Renaissance: Text and Context in Early Modern Italy* (Newark, DE: University of Delaware Press, 2023), 231–262.

3 For the translation here, see Lucrezia Marinella, *The Nobility and Excellence of Women and the Defects and Vices of Men* (Chicago: University of Chicago Press, 1999), 41; later, 45, 51, 83.

4 Translated in Marinella, *Nobility*, 79. The reference is to Moderata Fonte's unfinished chivalric romance, *Tredici canti di Floridoro [Thirteen Cantos on Floridoro]*, published in Venice in 1581. Though Marinella does not cite Fonte's more overtly feminist work, *Il merito delle donne (The Worth of Women)*, she must have known it by at least by 1601, when an expanded edition of her *Nobility and Excellence of Women* was printed.

5 Marinella, *La nobiltà et l'eccellenza delle donne*, 2; my translation.

6 Translated in Marinella, *Nobility*, 119. Lucrezia's treatise was published in an expanded second edition almost immediately; see Lynn Lara Westwater, "'Le false obiezioni de' nostri calunniatori': Lucrezia Marinella Responds to the Misogynist Tradition," *Bruniana & campanelliana* 12.1 (2006): 95–109.

7 Here and previously, translated in Marinella, *Nobility*, 167.

8 See Lynn Lara Westwater, "The Disquieting Voice: Women's Writing and Antifeminism in Seventeenth-Century Venice" (dissertation, University of Chicago, 2003), 111–162.

9 See Sarah Gwyneth Ross, *The Birth of Feminism: Woman as Intellect in Renaissance Italy and England* (Cambridge: Harvard University Press, 2009), 293–295.

Selected Bibliography

Malpezzi Price, Paola and Christine M. Ristaino, *Lucrezia Marinella and the "Querelle des Femmes" in Seventeenth-Century Italy* (Teaneck: Fairleigh Dickinson Press, 2008)

Marinella, Lucrezia, *The Nobility and Excellence of Women*, trans. Anne Dunhill, ed. Letizia Panizza (Chicago: University of Chicago Press, 1996)

Ross, Sarah Gwyneth, *The Birth of Feminism: Woman as Intellect in Renaissance Italy and England* (Cambridge: Harvard University Press, 2009)

Westwater, Lynn Lara, "Lucrezia Marinella [1571–1653]," in Diana Maury Robin, Anne Larson and Carol Levin, eds., *Encyclopedia of Women in the Renaissance: Italy, France, and England* (Santa Barbara: ABC-CLIO, 2007), 234–237

Sarra Copia Sulam (1592–1641): Poet and Polemicist in Venice's Jewish Ghetto

Epigraph: Sarra Copia Sulam, *Manifesto* (Venice: appresso Antonio Pinelli, 1621), sonnet 2, no page number; my translation. Sarra's name is spelled with many variations; the spelling with which she published, adopted by most scholars, is used here.

Notes

1 See Lindsay Kaplan, *Figuring Racism in Medieval Christianity* (Oxford: Oxford University Press, 2018), 2.

2 See Dana Katz, *The Jewish Ghetto and the Visual Imagination of Early Modern Venice* (Cambridge: Cambridge University Press, 2017).

3 See Flora Cassen, *Marking the Jews in Renaissance Italy: Politics, Religion, and the Power of Symbols* (Cambridge: Cambridge University Press, 2017).

4 In 1619, Modena dedicated an Italian translation of Salomon Usque's *Esther* to Sarra, calling her his "most admired mistress" and praising her exceptional "virtue and learning"; for the translation, see Don Harrán, *Sarra Copia Sulam: Jewish Poet and Intellectual in Seventeenth-Century Venice* (Chicago: University of Chicago Press, 2009), 511.

5 Lynn Lara Westwater, *Sarra Copia Sulam: A Jewish Salonnière and the Press in Counter-Reformation Venice* (Toronto: University of Toronto Press, 2020), 193. Much of the biographical information here and later is based on Westwater's comprehensive study of Sarra and her world; see especially 187–198.

6 See Howard Tzvi Adelman, "Sarra Copia Sullam," in Jennifer Sartori, ed., *Shalvi/Hyman Encyclopedia of Jewish Women*, *Jewish Women's Archive*, 23 June 2021, https://jwa.org/encyclopedia/article/sullam-sara-coppia.

7 See Harrán, *Sarra Copia Sulam*, 44–45.

8 See Westwater, *Sarra Copia Sulam*, 81.

9 All following translations from the *Manifesto* follow Harrán, *Sarra Copia Sulam*, 317–348.

10 On this episode, see Westwater, *Sarra Copia Sullam*, 126–148.

11 Translations from the *Avvisi* are taken from Westwater, *Sarra Copia Sulam*: here, 155; later, 167–168.

Selected Bibliography

Adelman, Howard Tzvi, "Sarra Copia Sullam," in Jennifer Sartori, ed., *Shalvi/Hyman Encyclopedia of Jewish Women*, *Jewish Women's Archive*, 23 June 2021. https://jwa.org/encyclopedia/article/sullam-sara-coppia

Bonfils, Roberto, *Jewish Life in Renaissance Italy*, trans. Anthony Oldcorn (Berkeley: University of California Press, 1994)

Harrán, Don, *Sarra Copia Sulam: Jewish Poet and Intellectual in Seventeenth-Century Venice* (Chicago: University of Chicago Press, 2009)

Westwater, Lynn Lara, *Sarra Copia Sulam: A Jewish Salonnière and the Press in Counter-Reformation Venice* (Toronto: University of Toronto Press, 2020)

Arcangela Tarabotti (1604–1652): Rebel Nun, Feminist Force

Epigraph: Galerana Baratotti [Arcangela Tarabotti], *La semplicità ingannata* (Leiden: Sambix, 1654), 23; my translation.

Notes

1 Meredith K. Ray, "Letters and Lace: Arcangela Tarabotti and Convent Culture in Seicento Venice," in Julie D. Campbell and Anne R. Larsen, eds., *Early Modern Women and Transnational Communities of Letters* (Aldershot: Ashgate, 2009), 45–73.

2 For the intriguing but inconclusive hypothesis that the Tarabotti family had Jewish origins, see Francesca Medioli, "Tarabotti fra omissioni e femminismo: Il mistero della sua formazione," in Anna Bellavitis, Nadia Maria Filippini and Tiziana Plebani, eds., *Spazi, poteri, diritti delle donne a Venezia in età moderna* (Verona: Qui Edit, 2012), 221–239.

3 See Meredith K. Ray and Lynn Lara Westwater, "Introduction," in *Convent Paradise*, trans. and eds. Arcangela Tarabotti, Meredith K. Ray and Lynn Lara Westwater (Toronto: Centre for Reformation and Renaissance Studies, 2020), 1–61, 3. A religious career was frequently chosen for unmarried or younger sons, often also under pressure from their families, but men were not subject to the same strict cloister as women nor did they pay a "spiritual dowry"; see Anne Jacobson Schutte, *By Force and Fear: Taking and Breaking Monastic Vows in Early Modern Europe* (Ithaca: Cornell University Press, 2011), 56.

4 Translated in Letizia Panizza, "Introduction," in *Paternal Tyranny*, trans. and eds. Arcangela Tarabotti and Letizia Panizza (Chicago: University of Chicago Press, 2004), 1–31, 4n6.

5 Translation adapted from Arcangela Tarabotti, *Letters Familiar and Formal*, trans. and ed. Meredith K. Ray and Lynn Lara Westwater (Toronto: Centre for Reformation and Renaissance Studies, 2012), 210.

6 Here and later, my translation of Arcangela Tarabotti, *L'Inferno monacale*, ed. Francesca Medioli (Turin: Rosenberg & Sellier, 1990), 32, 70.

7 See Isabella Campagnol, *Forbidden Fashions: Invisible Luxuries in Early Venetian Convents* (Lubbock: Texas Tech University Press, 2020).

8 Here, see Arcangela Tarabotti, *Paternal Tyranny* (Chicago: University of Chicago Press, 2004), 119; later, 51–53, 99.

9 Translated in Arcangela Tarabotti, *Convent Paradise*, trans. and eds. Meredith K. Ray and Lynn Lara Westwater (Toronto: Centre for Reformation and Renaissance Studies, 2020), 115.

10 Translation adapted from Prudence Allen, *The Concept of Woman* (Grand Rapids: Eerdmans, 2017), 3:169.

11 Translation adapted from Tarabotti, *Letters*, 123.

12 My translation of Arcangela Tarabotti, *La semplicità ingannata*, ed. Simona Bortot (Padua: Il Poligrafo, 2007), 178.
13 Tarabotti, *Paternal Tyranny*, 27.
14 Schutte, *By Force and Fear*, 262–263.

Selected Bibliography

Laven, Mary, *Virgins of Venice: Broken Vows and Cloistered Lives in the Renaissance Convent* (New York: Viking, 2003)

Tarabotti, Arcangela, *Paternal Tyranny*, trans. and ed. Letizia Panizza (Chicago: University of Chicago Press, 2004)

Tarabotti, Arcangela, *Letters Familiar and Formal*, trans. and eds. Meredith K. Ray and Lynn Lara Westwater (Toronto: Centre for Reformation and Renaissance Studies, 2012)

Weaver, Elissa B., ed., *Arcangela Tarabotti: A Literary Nun in Baroque Venice* (Ravenna: Longo Editore, 2006)

Dates of Reign

Alessandro de' Medici, Duke of Florence (1532–1537)

Alfonso II, Duke of Calabria, afterward King of Naples (1494–1495)

Alfonso II d'Este, Duke of Ferrara (1559–1597)

Anna Jagiellon, Queen of Poland and Grand Duchess of Lithuania (1575–1587)

Bianca Cappello, Grand Duchess consort of Tuscany (1579–1587)

Caterina de' Medici, Queen consort of France (1547–1559), Queen regent of France (1560–1563)

Charles I, King of England (1625–1649)

Charles V, Holy Roman Emperor (1519–1556)

Charles VIII, King of France (1483–1498)

Christine de Lorraine, Grand Duchess consort of Tuscany (1589–1609), co-regent (1621–1628)

Cosimo I de' Medici, Grand Duke of Tuscany (1537–1569)

Cosimo II de' Medici, Grand Duke of Tuscany (1609–1621)

Elizabeth I, Queen of England (1558–1603)

Ercole II d'Este, Duke of Ferrara (1534–1559)

Ferdinando I de' Medici, Grand Duke of Tuscany (1587–1609)

Ferdinand II, King of Naples (1495–1496)

Holy Roman Emperor Ferdinand II (1619–1637)

Francesco I de' Medici, Grand Duke of Tuscany (1574–1587)

Francesco Erizzo, Doge of Venice (1631–1646)

Henrietta Maria, Queen consort of England (1625–1649)

Henri II, King of France (1547–1559)

Henri IV, King of France (1589–1610)

Henry VIII, King of England (1509–1547)

Livia Feltria della Rovere, Duchess of Urbino (1599–1631)

Louis XII, King of France (1498–1515)

Maria de' Medici, Queen consort of France (1600–1610), Queen regent of France (1610–1614)

Maria Magdalena of Austria, Grand Duchess consort of Tuscany (1609–1621), co-regent (1621–1628)

Marguerite de Navarre, Queen consort of Navarre (1527–1549)

Maximilian I, Holy Roman Emperor (1508–1519)

Ottavio Farnese, Duke of Parma (1547–1586)

Philip II, King of Spain (1556–1598)

Sigismund I, King of Poland and Grand Duke of Lithuania (1506–1548)

Stefan Batory, King of Poland and Grand Duke of Lithuania (1576–1586)

Renée de France, Duchess consort of Ferrara (1534–1559)

Suleiman I, Sultan of the Ottoman Empire (1520–1566)

Vittoria della Rovere, Grand Duchess consort of Florence (1637–1670)

Popes (by date, 1455–1655)

Callixtus III (Alfonso de Borja), 1455–1458

Pius II (Enea Silvio Piccolomini), 1458–1464

Paul II (Pietro Barbo), 1464–1471

Sixtus IV (Francesco della Rovere), 1471–1484

Innocent VIII (Giovanni Battista Cybo), 1484–1492

Alexander VI (Rodrigo de Borja [Borgia]), 1492–1503

Pius III (Francesco Todeschini Piccolomini), 1503

Julius II (Guiliano della Rovere), 1503–1513

Leo X (Giovanni di Lorenzo de' Medici), 1513–1521

Adrian VI (Aryaen Floriszoon Boeyens), 1522–1523

Clement VII (Giulio di Giuliano de' Medici), 1523–1534

Paul III (Alessandro Farnese), 1534–1549

Julius III (Giovanni Maria Ciocchi del Monte), 1550–1555

Marcellus II (Marcello Cervini degli Spannochi), 1555

Paul IV (Giovanni Pietro Carafa), 1555–1559

Pius IV (Giovanni Angelo Medici), 1559–1565

St. Pius V (Antonio Ghislieri), 1566–1572

Gregory XIII (Ugo Boncompagni), 1572–1585

Sixtus V (Felice Peretti di Montalto), 1585–1590

Urban VII (Giovanni Battista Castagna), 1590

Gregory XIV (Niccolò Sfondrati), 1590–1591

Innocent IX (Gregory Antonio Facchinetti), 1591

Clement VIII (Ippolito Aldobrandini), 1592–1605

Leo XI (Alessandro Ottaviano de' Medici), 1605
Paul V (Camillo Borghese), 1605–1621
Gregory XV (Alessandro Ludovisi), 1621–1623
Urban VIII (Maffeo Barberini), 1623–1644
Innocent X (Giovanni Battista Pamphilj), 1644–1655

Acknowledgments

This book is the product of a life-long fascination with the women of the Italian Renaissance. I set myself a challenge in telling the stories of twenty-five women active in so many different areas, and I am grateful to all those who generously shared their knowledge with me, including Suzanne Cusick, Beth Glixon, Liz Horodowich, Mark Jurdjevic, Dana Katz, Cindy Klestinec, Lia Markey, Tim McCall, Jill Pederson, Courtney Quaintance, and Elissa Weaver. Conversations with Lynn Westwater about Arcangela Tarabotti and all topics early modern are always inspirational; many thanks, too, to Alison Parker and Eva del Soldato.

My heartfelt appreciation to the Rockefeller Foundation for a once-in-a-lifetime writing residency that allowed me to complete this book, and to my fellow residents at the Bellagio Center in Fall 2022. I also thank the University of Delaware College of Arts and Sciences and the University of Pennsylvania FIGS program for their support. At Routledge, Laura Pilsworth and Tiffany Cameron shepherded this volume to print with enthusiasm and care. My gratitude to Troy Tower for providing valuable editorial assistance, and to Luciana Vernola for helping to assemble bibliographic information.

I am so fortunate for the love and encouragement of my family over the course of this long project (begun in the middle of a pandemic), and always: my wonderfully curious and insightful son, Owen; Sam, my partner in life and research adventures; and my parents – especially my brilliant mother Crennan, who is my inspiration and ideal reader. This book is for them, and for all the amazing women in my life.

Index

Note: Page numbers in *italics* indicate a figure on the corresponding page.

Academies: 112, 141, 181, 183, 254; Arti del Disegno 222; Dubbiosi 143; Incogniti (Naples) 112; Incogniti (Venice) 183, 224, 277, 288, 301; Infiammati 256; Innominati 154; Informi 278; Intenti 163, 278; Intronati 254–255; Lincei 240; Ordinati 183; Oscuri 176; San Luca 213; Umoristi 242; Unisoni 184
Adam and Eve, interpreting Biblical story of 300–301
Adoration of the Magi 21, *21*
Aeneid 116, 151, 240
Alberti, Leon Battista 23
Albertini, Ludovico 40
alchemical experimentation, interest in 34–35, 40, 298
Alcibiades, Albrecht II 108
Aldrovandi, Ulisse 212
Alexander VI, Pope 38, 53, 56–57, 60–61; *see also* Borgia, Cesare
Alfonso II, King 57, 58, 67, 150
Alighieri, Dante 11, 28, 84, 126, 129, 254, 256, 260, 292, 298, 300, 301, 303
Allegory of Inclination 222, *223*
altar painting 27, 206, 212, 213, 226
Amore innamorato, et impazzato (Love Enamoured and Driven Mad) 281
Andreini, Francesco 158, 162, 166–167

Andreini, Giovan Battista 162, 166
Andreini, Isabella 13, 158–167, 222; commemorative medal depicting 166, *166*; death of 166; education of 161; family background of 161; letters 164–166; literary works of 162–167; marriage 162; portrait of 160–161, *161*; stage performances of 158–160, 162
Anguissola, Amilcare 194–195, 198, 200–202
Anguissola, Sofonisba 193–204; accomplishments of 202; apprenticeship of 194–195; aristocratic marriage of 202; artistic successors of 204; as court painter 200–204; devotional paintings by 203; education of 194; familial support to 194–195; family background of 194; featured in exhibitions 204; genre painting by 198–199; official state portraiture by 200–201; portrait of 203; portrait paintings by 195–198, *196*, *197*; reputation of 201–202, 204; second marriage of 202–203; self-portraits by 6, 198, *199*, 203; works of 6, *7*, 13, 206;
apothecaries 229–232, *230*

Arcadia felice (*Happy Arcadia*) 281
Aretino, Pietro 71
Ariosto, Ludovico 3, 9, 11, 42,
　　44, 53, 60, 84, 114–119,
　　174–175, 218, 243, 246,
　　267, 269, 281
Aristotelian philosophy 245, 279
Aristotle 97, 104, 148, 153, 156,
　　231–232, 292
Ascarelli, Debora (Devorà) 294
Assumption of San Petronio
　　212–213
astrology 14, 236–237, 240–241, 245
astronomy 14, 147, 241, 245, 254, 256
Augustus, Sigismund 69
Austria 14, 150, 171, 174, 222, 254,
　　256, 260, 261, 263
autonomy, women's 2, 29, 83, 127,
　　130, 135, 253, 262, 273
Avisi di Parnasso (*News from
　　Parnassus*) 293–295

Bandello, Matteo 45, 66, 91
Bardi, Contessina de' 22
Baschi, Gentile 27
Batory, Stefan 75, 232
Battle of Marciano 262–263
Battle of Pavia 82
Belcari, Feo 27
Bellincioni, Bernardo 27
Bellini, Giovanni 46
Bembo, Pietro 46, 60–61, 84, 135
Bentivoglio, Camilla 90
Berecci, Bartolommeo 69
Bergalli, Luisa 131, 139, 144, 145
Bertari, Giovanni 147
Bettoli, Guido 248
Bianca degli Utili Maselli, depiction
　　of 210, *210*
Biandrata, Giorgio 71
Bible: divine events in 236; natural
　　phenomena described
　　in 234; in vernacular
　　languages 101, 104
Boccaccio, Giovanni 2, 28, 84, 137,
　　233–234
Bologna 7, 13, 168, 205–206,
　　208, 211, 213–215, 223,
　　240, 259; "Bolognese
　　phenomenon" 205

Bonardis, Antonia de 205
Bonifaccio, Baldassare 290,
　　291–293
Borgia, Cesare 38, 39, 53, 55, 58, 59,
　　60, 61
Borgia, Lucrezia 5, 6, 11, 24–25,
　　50, 53–64; annulment
　　of marriage of 57–58;
　　betrothed to Spanish
　　noblemen 55–56; children
　　of 60; diplomatic skills
　　56–57, 61; early life of
　　54–55; education of 55;
　　friendship with Bembo
　　60–61; historical legacy
　　of 53; leadership abilities
　　58–59; letter to father 56,
　　57; marriage to Alfonso
　　d'Aragona 58–59; marriage
　　to Alfonso I d'Este 59–60;
　　persona of 53–54; political
　　activities of 54, 60; in
　　popular culture 64; portraits
　　of *54*, 62–64, *63*; proxy
　　marriage to Giovanni Sforza
　　56; reclamation projects 62;
　　religious commitment 62
Borgia, Rodrigo 11, 38, 53
Borgias, rumours about 58, 59
botanical gardens 33
Botticelli, Sandro 21, 32, 257
Bronzini, Cristofano 168, 170, 222,
　　240, 243, 245, 274, 284
Brucioli, Antonio 231
Brusoni, Girolamo 302
Buonarroti, Michelangelo 1, 79,
　　98, 116; *Crucifixion*
　　88–89, *89*; friendship with
　　Vittoria Colonna 87–88;
　　and Sofonisba Anguissola
　　197–198, 204
Buonarroti, Michelangelo, the
　　Younger 172–173, 174,
　　176, 222
Busenello, Giovan Francesco 302

Caccini, Francesca 13, 168–179;
　　connections to Medici
　　women 171–173, 177–178;
　　economic security of

176–177; family background
of 168–169; marriage of
173; music and composition
career of 169–170,
174–176; performed for
Henri IV 170; portrait of
170, *171*; and publication
175; second marriage of 176;
success of 175

Caccini, Giulio 13, 168, 173, 176;
aspirations for daughters
169; concerto featuring
family members 169–170

Calcagnini, Celio 103

Callixtus III, Pope 55

Cambio, Perissone 137

Campi, Benardino 194–196

*Bernardino Campi Painting
Sofonisba Anguissola*
195–196

Canale, Carlo 55

Caraglio, Gian Giacomo 69

Carnesecchi, Pietro 85, 86, 87

Carracci, Annibale 7–8

Casa delle Zitelle (Venice) 131

Castiglione, Baldassare 44, 70, 84,
93, 193

Catholic Church 14, 29, 87, 104,
131, 152, 212–213, 236,
287; cosmology 282–283,
286;

doctrine 12, 99, 104, 105, 245, 237;
and prohibited books 101,
152, 231, 297, 298

Cattanei, Vanozza dei 55

Cebà, Ansaldo 288–289

Cenci, Beatrice 242

Centelles, Cherubino Joan de 56

Cereta, Laura 6, 103, 165, 270

Cesi, Federico 241

chamber music 13, 168–169, 180,
186, 188–189

Chapel, Sigismund 69–70

charitable institutions 136; women's
support of 29, 157

charitable works 29, 38, 87

Charles VII, King 56

*Che le donne siano della spetie degli
uomini (Women Are Human,
Just Like Men)* 303–304

The Chess Game 6, *7*, 199–200

chivalric literature 3, 11, 115,
128–130, 174, 267

Christian faith 245, 278, 292

Christianity 4, 269, 277, 288,
290

Cibo, Caterina 86

Clement VII, Pope (Giulio de'
Medici) 8, 29, 51, 83

cloistering of women 15, 296, 297,
299–301, 306; *see also*
convents

Collalto, Collaltino di 138, *139*,
139–142, 144

Colonna, Fabrizio 80

Colonna, Giovanni 80

Colonna, Isabella 113

Colonna, Marcantonio II 242

Colonna, Vittoria 1, 12, 68, 72,
79–89, 148, 158, 242,
259, 280, 293; conjugal
love 82–85; education of
80–81; friendship with
Michelangelo 87–88, 98;
literary works of 81–88;
marriage of 81; persona
of 79, 84; Petrarchan style
82, 84, 88, 89; presumed
portrait of 79, *80*; religious
devotion of 82–83, 85–87,
255; widowhood 83

commedia dell'arte, women in 13,
159–160, *160*, 164, 167

Compagnoni, Marsilio 39

concerto delle donne 13, 100, 136,
154–156, 169

convents: education in 241, 265,
301; fee to enter 299;
Florence 178–179, 248;
forced cloistering 299–301;
as perpetual imprisonment
299; pharmacies 229;
prevalence of 299;
restrictions 296–297;
Sant'Anna 296, *297*;
Venice 188–189, 296; and
women artists 205; *see also*
Tarabotti, Arcangela

Copernicus, Nicolaus 70, 110, 152,
230, 243

Copia Sulam, Sarra 15, 243,
285–295, 296; admired
by Incogniti 288; backlash
against 293; charges of
plagiary against 293;
defense of Judaism
292; education of 287;
epistolary exchange with
Ansaldo Cebà 288–289;
false charges of heresy
against 289–290; family
background of 287; libelous
pamphlet about 293;
marriage of 287; music 287;
poetry 294; portrait of *289*;
salon 287–288; targeted by
Baldassarre Bonifaccio 290;
work on soul's immortality
290–292
Coppio, Simon 287
Correggio, Niccolò da 42, 51
Coryat, Thomas 122–123
cosmology: Galileo and 245–248,
282; planetary revolution
151–153; tensions with
Catholic doctrine 280;
women's study of 24, 153,
157, 230, 241, 245, 256,
272; *see also* astronomy
cosmos, ancient and medieval
notions 151; influence on
human temperament 236
Costa, Lorenzo 45
Costa, Margherita 6
Council of Trent 10, 12, 245,
275, 296
Counter-Reformation 14, 86, 98, 99,
120, 212, 215, 222, 234,
237, 246, 255, 275, 277,
278, 287, 288, 295
courtesans 6, 10, 11, 59, 62, 77,
122–126, 128–131,
144–145, 180, 182, 267;
and courtiers 126–129;
images of 123, *124*;
meaning of 123; musical
proficiency of 136; numbers
of 122; *see also* Franco,
Veronica

Credi, Lorenzo di 35, *37*
Curione, Celio Secondo 104, 106,
108, 109, 110

da Collevecchio, Simonetta 7–8, 258
d'Allegre, Yves 39
Dangerous Beauty (film) 132
D'Annunzio, Gabriele 146
Dantiscus, Johannes 69
d'Aragona, Alfonso 58–59
d'Aragona, Federico 67
d'Aragona, Giovanna 113
d'Aragona, Tullia 6, 126
d'Ávalos, Costanza 81
d'Ávalos, Ferdinando (Ferrante)
Francesco I 81–83
Decameron 103
Decjusz, Justus Ludwik *66*
De claris mulieribus (*Concerning
Famous Women*) 2
d'Este, Alfonso I 44, 59
d'Este, Anna 102, 104, 106
d'Este, Cardinal Ippolito 45
d'Este, Ercole II 47, 91, 100
d'Este, Isabella 9, 11, 39, 42–52,
90; correspondence of
42, 51–52; early life of
42; education of 42–43;
fascination with antiquity
44; interest in collecting
46–48; leadership skills of
48–50; love of music 45;
as marchioness of Mantu
48–49; marriage of 43–44,
48; overseeing Mantua's
affairs 48–51; partnership
with Francesco 48; political
and diplomatic decisions
48–51; portrait of 42, *43*,
46, *47*; studiolo of 45–46;
tensions in marriage of 50
d'Este, Luigi 130
*Dialogue between Theophila and
Philotima* 106
Diporti di Euterpe (*Euterpe's
Amusements*) 187
Discorso (*Commentary* on *Orlando
furioso*)115–116, 118,
121, 122

Discussiones peripateticae 152
Divina Commedia (*Divine Comedy*),
    11–12, 256, 300
Doglioni, Giovanni Niccolò 265, 269
Domenichi, Lodovico 71, 112–114,
    121, 137, 256
Donati, Regina 300
Doré, Gustave 115
Dossi, Dosso 63

Edict of Châteaubriant 106
education and access to knowledge
    by women 2, 14, 273–274,
    301; inequities in 256, 272,
    281; translation of scientific
    works 256
Elizabeth I 11, 75, 110
enslaved women 6–7, 48
epic poetry 14, 131, 148, 181,
    213, 240–241, 242,
    245–246, 249, 275, 278,
    281–282, 288
epistolary networks 60, 232,
    288–289, 302
epistolary writing 95–97, 130–131,
    288–289; *see also* letters
Erasmus, Desiderius 69, 98, 104, 110
Erculiani, Camilla Greghetta 14,
    229–239; and Anna
    Jagiellon 232–234;
    first marriage of 231;
    heresy trial 237–238;
    intellectual network of
    230–232; *Letters on
    Natural Philosophy*
    230, 233–238; natural
    philosophical arguments
    236–238; practical
    experience in medicine
    230; second marriage of
    231; theologically sensitive
    debate 232, 234–237; work
    at Tre Stelle 229–232
Essortationi alle donne et a gli altri
    (*Exhortations to Women and
    Others*) 282–284
Esther, Queen (Old Testament figure)
    28, 288
Experimenti (*Experiments*) 35, *36*, *40*

Fanino, Fanio 104
Farnese, Giulia 55
Fedele, Cassandra 6, 73, 103, 165,
    232, 280
female honor 10, 28, 64, 120–121,
    123, 135, 173, 179, 188,
    198, 220
feminism, women's role in: access
    to education and knowledge
    256, 274; and chivalric
    poetry 269; civic and
    political activism 261–263;
    cosmology 256; feminist
    thought 264, 268, 306;
    gender equality 270–275,
    280, 284; historiography
    272; methodology 15; moral
    and intellectual superiority
    279–281; natural
    philosophy 256; philosophy
    and theology 255, 278;
    social critique 273
Feo, Giacomo 37
Ferdinand of Aragon 10–11
Ferrara 11, 12, 13, 42, 44, 46, 47, 54,
    59–63, *63*, 71, 84, 86–87,
    91–92, 98, 100–106, 130,
    136, 150, 154–157, 169,
    243, 267
Forlì 31, 33–35, 38–39, 53
Ficino, Marsilio 21, 151
Fiorentino, Francesco 69
Flaminio, Marcantonio 86
Florence 4, 6, 8, 13–14, 19, 21–29,
    32–34, 38–40, 50, 62, 69,
    84, 101, 114, 120, 151,
    156, 158, 168–172, 174,
    176–178, 180–181, 205,
    217, 220–224, 249, 254,
    256–258, 262, 265, 267
Florentine Camerata 168
Fontana, Lavinia 1–2, 6, 14, 204,
    205–215; artistic training
    of 206; and Bolognese
    noblewomen 208, 210,
    209, 215; education of 206;
    female nude 213–214;
    heroic poetry influencing
    213; honors and recognition

of 213–214; impact on women artists 215; marital agreement 207; *Minerva Dressing* versions 214, *214*; monumental ruins influencing 213; portraits of children 211–212; religious paintings by 212–213; self-portraits by 206–208, *207*; works attributed to 215; young mother with children 210, *210*

Fontana, Prospero 205, 207–208, 212

Fonte, Moderata 3, 15, 120, 126, 131, 200, 244, 264–275, 278, 280, 281, 287, 301; dedicatory letters 267; education of 265; family background of 265; feminist dialogue 268–269; on gender equality 264, 270–274; literary works 265–269; marriage of 269; and natural philosophy 232; portrait of 265, *266*; pseudonym 266, 267; regard for Doglioni 265; religious poems 270; secluded life 266–267; sonnets 265; success of literary works 269, 275

Forteguerri, Alessandro di Niccodemo di 254

Forteguerri, Laudomia 6, 14–15, 232, 253–263; civic and political activism of 261–263; devotion to Margaret of Austria 150, 256–257; education of 254; family background of 254; featured in literary dialogue 255; intellectual curiosity 256; love poetry by 256–257, 259–262; marriages of 254; natural philosophy studies 256; poetic relationship with Margaret 259–261

Fourth Crusade 282

Fracassa, Paola 123

France 2, 11–12, 36, 38, 47, 49, 56, 66, 70–72, 74, 80, 86–87, 95, 100, 104, 106, 111, 121, 130–131, 159, 162, 166–167, 170, 194, 200, 254, 262, 278, 302

Franco, Veronica 11, 122–132; assessment of courtesan's life of 130–131; chivalric literature 128–130; courtesan's life 123–124, 126, 132; education of 125; encounter with Henri III of Valois 126; fame of 131; female sexuality and authority 123, 126–129, 132; feminist sensibility of 131; Inquisition trial of 131; letters of 126–127, 130–131; marriage of 125; poetry of 126–130; in popular culture 132; portrait of 125, *125*

French invasion of Italy 49, 66

French Wars of Religion 106

Galateo 138

Galen 230–232

Galenism 230, 238

Galilei, Galileo 99, 172, 181, 222, 230, 236, 240, 246, 249, 282, 302; and astrology 236, 245; discovery of Jupiter's satellites 247–248; "Galileo affair" 14; heresy trial 237, 241, 282; and Margherita Sarrocchi 241, 243, 245, 245–250; objections to discoveries of 245; portrait of *247*; scientific community support needed by 241, 246–248

Galilei, Vincenzo 168

Gallerani, Cecilia 49

Gambara, Veronica 6, 89, 113, 118

Garzone, Giovanna 6

Garzoni, Lucia Bonasoni 215

Gatti, Bernardino 195

Gelosi troupe 158, 162, 166, 167; *see also* Andreini, Isabella

gender equality 2, 3, 15; efforts to promote 238; and knowledge 273; and liberty 274; in Renaissance Venice 265–274; and superiority 275, 284; *see also* women's equality

gender inequality 15, 264, 272, 272, 284

Gentileschi, Artemisia 14, 28, 204, 213, 216–228; *Allegory of Inclination* 222, *223*; celebration of female strength 222; culture of credit exploited by 221–222; death of 227; depiction of Judith killing Holofernes 216–218, *217*; dowry dispute with Orazio 224; early life of 218; in England 226–227; exhibits of works of 228; involvement with Maringhi 224; *Judith and her Maidservant* 225–227, *225*; marriage of 220–221; mythological figures 227; in Naples 226–227; patronage networks navigated by 221; rape and sexual exploitation of 188, 216–217, 219–220; reputation of 226; return to Rome 224–225; *Susanna and the Elders* 218–219, *219*; training in art 218

Gentileschi, Orazio 218–220, 224, 226, 228

Germany 12, 35, 65, 98, 105–107, 110, 304

Gerusalemme liberata (*Jerusalem Delivered*) 148, 213, 242, 282

Ghetto Nuovo (Venice) 285–288; as cultural center 287; *see also* Copia Sulam, Sarra

Ghirlandaio, Domenico 19

Giovio, Paolo 81

Gli asolani (*The People of Asolo*) 60

Gonzaga, Aloisio 90

Gonzaga, Elisabetta 44

Gonzaga, Emilia Cauzzi 97

Gonzaga, Ercole 50

Gonzaga, Ferrante 51

Gonzaga, Francesco II 42–44, 48–50, 60

Gonzaga, Giulia 86, 98

Gonzaga, Lucrezia 6, 12, 90–99, 101, 106, 138, 243, 255; abusive marriage of 91–92; as cultural arbiter 97; early life of 90–91; education of 91; epistolary writing of 95–99; Inquisition trial of 99; in literary works 93, 99; persona of 95; portrait of *94*; reformist religious views of 97–99; reputation of 93

Gonzaga, Pirro 90

Gonzaga, Vespasiano 92

Gonzales, Antonietta (Tognina) 211–212, *211*

Gozi, Lucrezia 102

Gozzadini, Bettisia 206

Gozzadini, Laudomia, Lavinia Fontana's painting of 208–209

Gozzadini, Ulisse 209

Gozzoli, Benozzo 23

Gramsci, Antonio 40–41

Greghetti, Andrea 231

Gregory XIII 213

Guarini, Antonio 147

Guarnier, Georges 232

Guicciardini, Francesco 58, 67

Henri III of Valois 126

Henry VIII 51, 280

heresy 87; Camilla Greghetta Erculiani 237–238; Copia Sulam, Sarra 289; heresy trial 237–238, 241; *see also* orthodoxy

Heroides 81

heterodoxy 12, 71–72, 98; *see also* orthodoxy

History of Monsters 212
history, women's role in 3–4,
    280–281, 285, 306; *see also*
    Marinella, Lucrezia
humanism 23, 70, 106–107
humanist education 28, 55, 67
Hungary 72, 244

Iasolino, Giulio 242
*I donneschi difetti (The Defects of
    Women)* 270, 278
*Il Libro del Cortegiano (The Book of
    the Courtier)* 13, 44, 70, 84,
    93, 193
*Il merito delle donne (The Worth
    of Women)* 264, 266–267,
    270–274, 271
Il Padovano *see* Mosca,
    Giovanni Maria
Il parlatorio (The Convent Parlor)
    297, 298
*Il primo libro de' madrigali (First
    Book of Madrigals) see*
    Opus 1
Inferno monacale (Convent Hell)
    299–300, 303
Inquisition 99, 105, 132, 238, 246;
    Paduan 14, 231, 237;
    Roman 104, 181; Spanish
    11; Venetian 131, 289
intellect of women 93, 103, 109,
    119, 121, 123, 126, 137,
    147, 159, 200, 234, 238,
    239, 255–256, 264, 269,
    280, 294
Isabela I of Castile 10
Isabella of Aragon 67–68
Ischia 67, 80–81, 83, 242
Italian evangelism 12, 72,
    106–107, 255
Italian Wars 56, 66, 80, 100

Jagiellon, Anna 69, 75, 231–234,
    233
Jewish and Christian faiths, areas
    of commonality between
    291–292; *see also* Copia
    Sulam, Sarra; Ghetto Nuovo

Jews 9–10, 285–287, 290, 291,
    295; attempts to convert
    288–293; denigrating
    treatment of 285–287;
    discriminatory markers
    for 286; and gender 290;
    and race 9, 285; *see also*
    Ghetto Nuovo
John III of Sweden, King 72
John of Hungary, King 72
Judaism 15, 289, 292
judicial astrology 236–237
Judith Slaying Holofernes 23;
    depiction of 216–218,
    217; versions of 223, 225,
    225, 227
Julius II, Pope 61

Kelly, Joan 4
knowledge, women's access to
    35, 153, 193–194, 229,
    231–233, 240, 245,
    256, 263, 272–273,
    292–293, 301
Kraków 66, 68–70, 74, 230,
    233–235
Krzycki, Andrzej 69

La Crocetta 178; *see also* convents
*L'Enrico, ovvero Bizanzio acquistato
    (Enrico, or Byzantium
    Conquered)* 281–282
*La filosofia amorosa (The Philosophy
    of Love)* 153
*La Liberazione di Ruggiero
    dall'isola di Alcina (The
    Liberation of Ruggiero from
    Alcina's Island)* 174–175
La Molza 153
*La semplicità ingannata (Innocence
    Deceived)* 304–305
Lando, Ortensio 72, 91, 93, 97–99,
    107, 138
Landriani, Lucrezia 32
*La nobiltà et l'eccellenza delle
    donne, co' difetti et
    mancamenti de gli
    uomini (The Nobility and*

Excellence of Women and the Defects and Vices of Men) 15, 278, *279*, 281–282

La passione di Christo (*The Passion of Christ*) 269

La reina Esther (*Queen Esther*) 288–289

La stiava (*The Slave*) 172–173

La tirannia paterna (*Paternal Tyranny*) 299–301, 304

Leadership Conference of Women Religious 306

Le feste (*The Celebrations*) 269

Le Livre de la Cité des Dames (*The Book of the City of Ladies*) 2, 119, 264, 278

Le vite de' più eccellenti pittori, scultori, e architetti (*Lives of the Most Excellent Painters, Sculptors, and Architects*) 198–199, 205

Leo X, Pope 29

Lettere amorose (*Love Letters*) 137

Lettere di philosophia naturale (*Letters on Natural Philosophy*) 230–239

Lettere familiari e di complimento (*Letters Familiar and Formal*) 302–303

letters 6, 13, 14, 19, 24, 25, 30, 42, 43, 48, 50, 59, 60, 62, 67, 72, 87, 90, 92–99, 104–110, 126, 130–132, 137, 151, 164–166, 178, 206, 218, 224, 227, 230–239, 247, 249, 259, 288, 302–303

letter-writing 94–95, 164–166; *see also* epistolary writing; letters

Liombeni, Giovanni Luca 46

Lippi, Filippo 22

Lismanini, Francesco 71

literature: Latin 103, 106–107, 148, 165; misogynist 2, 129, 184, 264, 270, 277, 278, 284; religious devotion 84–85,

107, 270; religious subjects 277–278, 301–302; spiritual contemplation 82–83, 85, 87; tropes of female fidelity 82, 84–85, 93, 95, 97; vernacular literature 28, 60, 84, 98, 103, 138, 246, 256, 277, 169; women's study of 11–12, 24, 32, 44, 194, 206, 240–241, 277, 287; *see also* Andreini, Isabella; Colonna, Vittoria; Copia Sulam, Sarra; Erculiani, Camilla; Fonte, Moderata; Forteguerri, Laudomia; Franco, Veronica; Gonzaga, Lucrezia; Marinella, Lucrezia; Molza, Tarquinia; Morata, Olimpia; poetry; Sarrocchi, Margherita; Stampa, Gaspara; Tarabotti, Arcangela; Terracina, Laura; Tornabuoni, Lucrezia

Lomellino, Orazio 202–203

Loredano, Giovan Francesco 184, 224, 301, 302, 304

Lorraine, Christine de 158, 170–174, *172*, 177–179, 222

Louis XII, King 38, 49, 59, 100

Luciani, Sebastiano 79, *80*

Luther, Martin 65, 100–101, *101*, 104, 106–107

Machiavelli, Niccolò 1, 25, 31, 33, 35, 38, 53, 59, 80, 273, 298

Madonna of the Assumption of Ponte Santo 212

Manfredi, Muzio 131

Manfrone, Giampaolo 91–97

Manifesto of Sarra Copia Sulam 290–293, 295

Mantegna, Andrea 45

Mantua 5, 9, 11, 39, 42–45, 48–51, 59–60, 69, 90–91, 98, 156, 287

Margaret of Parma: Laudomia's devotion to 256–257;

352 *Index*

Laudomia's poetic relationship with 259–261; portrait of *257*; sexual orientation of 259; solitary life of 259; wedding with Alessandro 257; wedding with Ottavio 259
Margherita Sarrocchi (drama) 250
Margraves' War *108*
Maria, Galeazzo 33, 67
Maria Magdalena of Austria 171, 174, 222
Marinella, Lucrezia 3, 15, 120, 131, 181, 186, 222, 225, 244, 267–270, 275–284, 298, 301; defense of women 278–281; depiction of *276*; dialectic 277; education of 276–277; epic 282–283; family background of 275–276; feminist methodology 275, 284; literary career of 275, 277, 284; literary persona 275; pastoral romance 281; *querelle des femmes* 278–281, 303; religious subjects 277–278; women's history 3, 280, 284
Maringhi, Francesco Maria 224
Marino, Giambattista 163, 184, 187, 242, 246
Marot, Clément 100
Matraini, Chiara 6
matronage 222
Maximilian I 35, 68
medical-alchemical recipes 35, 36, 40
Medici, Alessandro de' 8, 257–258
Medici, Anna Maria Luisa de' 40
Medici, Catherine de' 11
Medici, Cosimo de' 19–22
Medici, Cosimo I de' 33, 39–40, 197, 263
Medici, Cosimo II de' 171, 223
Medici court 13, 168–179, 222
Medici, Ferdinando de' 158, 170
Medici, Francesco I de' 40, 171

Medici, Giovanni de' ("Il Popolano") 38
Medici, Giuliano de' 25–27; Pazzi Conspiracy and 27
Medici, Lorenzino de' 258–259
Medici, Lorenzo de' 1, 19, 21, 25, 29, 30, 33, 40; marriage with Clarice 25–26; Pazzi Conspiracy and 27, 33; poetry of 28
Medici, Ludovico di Giovani de' (Giovanni dalle Bande Nere) 38
Medici, Piero di Cosimo de' 19–21, 24–26, 39; death of 26; marriage with Lucrezia 20–22; transfer of power by 26
medicine 34–35, 70, 73, 90, 97, 105, 109, 229–231, 270, 272–273, 276; botanical 33; early modern alchemy 34–36, 40; medical-alchemical manuscript 35, 36; medicine and herbs, women's role in study of 273; and natural philosophy 230, 273, 276; preventive and therapeutic medicine 72
Medici Palace, Florence *22*, 22–23, 27–28
Mediterranean slave trade 9
Menochio, Giacomo 237–238
Michelozzo (architect) 22
Mila, Adriana de 55
Minerva, Amilcare, and Asdrubale Anguissola 200, *201*
Minerva Dressing, versions of 214, *214*
Minerva Expelling the Vices From the Garden of Virtue 45
Mirtilla (*The Blueberry Bush*) 162–163
misogyny 118, 228, 238, 264, 290, 297, 300–301
Modena 98, 136, 147–148, 150, 153, 154, 156–157, 168, 169

Modena, Leon 287–288
Molza, Francesco Maria 147
Molza, Tarquinia 13, 100, 136, 145,
    147–157, 158, 164, 169,
    202, 206, 242, 244; accused
    of affair with Wert 156; birth
    of 147; commonplace book
    of 147–148; and concerto
    delle donne 154–156; death
    and will of 157; education
    of 147; legal dispute with
    in-laws 154; marriage of
    148; metaphysical and
    theological concepts 151;
    music 150, 151, 153;
    persona of 153; on planetary
    revolution 151–153; Plato's
    Symposium and 153; poetry
    works 148–150; portrait
    of *149*; recognition of
    achievements of 156–157;
    reputation of 154, 156;
    salon 148, 244; singing
    practices of 154–155; on
    theorics of cosmos 153;
    widowed state of 151
Moncada, Fabrizio 202
monodic music 168
Montaigne, Michel de 131
Montoni, Prudenzia di Ottaviano 218
Morata, Olimpia Fulvia 12, 98,
    100–110; with burning
    Schweinfurt in background
    108; commentaries on
    ancient texts 103; early
    life 102; education of
    102–104; as humanist 103,
    106–107; intellect of 103,
    106, 109–110; literary
    works 106–109; marriage
    of 105; passion for learning
    103; poetry of 103; portrait
    of *102*; Protestant beliefs
    104–107; recognition of
    109–110; religious conflict
    and political instability
    107–109; religious
    exile 105

Morato, Fulvio Pellegrino 102, 104
Mosca, Giovanni Maria 69
motherhood 10, 40, 254, 270
music and performance: book for
    pedagogical use 175–176;
    chamber music 186,
    188–189; compositions
    187–188; concerts 45;
    concerto delle donne 136,
    154–156; courtesans 125,
    136, 267, 182; at court of
    Ferrara 100, 136, 154–156;
    instruments 46, 135, 154,
    169, 173, 182, 206, 277;
    love lyric 138–142, 144,
    150; at Medici court 169,
    171–175; "musica segreta"
    155; natural philosophy 151;
    opera 13, 136, 169–170,
    174, 180–182, 189, 222;
    patronage 10, 45, 51, 60;
    performed for Henri IV 170;
    Petrarchism 139–140, 144,
    150; professionalization
    155–156; as professional
    musicians 170; professional
    singers 45; sacred and
    religious music 136, 181,
    188; secular music 13,
    137, 169, 181, 187–188; at
    Unisoni meetings 184; in
    Venice 135–136, 180–181;
    vocal ornamentation 176;
    women's contributions to
    6, 13, 137, 169, 180, 277;
    see also Andreini, Isabella;
    Caccini, Francesca; Molza,
    Tarquinia; Stampa, Gaspara;
    Strozzi, Barbara
music of the spheres, concept of 151
Muzio, Girolamo 97

Naples 1, 6, 11, 42, 56–58,
    66–68, 74, 79, 81, 84,
    111–112, 120, 226–227,
    241–242, 249
natural phenomena, women's study
    of 14, 147, 230, 240;

Camilla Erculiani's *Letters* 230–239; causes of natural phenomena 273; influence of cosmos 236–237; origin of flood 234–236; rainbows 236; theologically sensitive debate 232, 234

natural philosophy, women's contributions to 151, 230, 232, 241–242, 256, 265, 276; metaphysical and theological concepts 151; philosophical arguments 237; planetary revolution 151–153; theologically sensitive debate 232, 234–237; theories of cosmos 153; women's equality 239, 273

Nelli, Plautilla 205
Nenna, Giovan Battista 71
Neoplatonism 165, 279
Newton, Isaac 35
Nogarola, Isotta 6, 103, 165, 280
nuns 2, 15, 51, 60, 62, 83, 95, 135–136, 173, 178, 205, 229, 241, 265, 288, 296–297, 298–306; solemn vows of 200; *see also* convents; Arcangela Tarabotti

Ochino, Bernardino 72, 85, 87, 98, 101, 104, 255
On the Revolutions of the Heavenly Spheres 152
opera 13, 136, 168, 169–170, 173–174, 179–182, 189, 222
oppression of women 2, 270, 271, 273, 297, 306
Opus *see* Strozzi, Barbara
Orlando furioso (The Frenzy of Orlando) 42, 60, 84, *115*, 115–116, *117*, 120, 174, *175*, 246, 267
Orsini, Clarice 25–27
orthodoxy 87, 104, 237, 241, 282, 287; *see also* heterodoxy

Ottonelli, Jesuit Giovanni Domenico 12

painting, women's contributions to *see* Anguissola, Sofonisba; Fontana, Lavinia; Gentileschi, Artemisia
Palazzo Medici *see* Medici Palace
Paleotti, Gabriele 212–212
Pappacoda, Arturo 73, 74
Pappacoda, Gian Lorenzo 73
Parabosco, Girolamo 137
Paradiso monacale (Convent Paradise) 256, 301–303
Parthenopeus, Suavius 68–69
Passero, Marc'Antonio 112
Passi, Giuseppe 270, 278, 280, 303
pastoral play 162–163
pastoral romance 281–282
Pastori Frattegiani (Shepherds of Fratta) 93
Patrizi da Cherso, Francesco 151–154, *152*
Pazzi conspiracy of 1478 27, 33, 35
periodization 4
Perugino, Pietro 45
Petrarca, Francesco (Petrarch) 1, 9, 12, 28, 80, 82, 95, 111, 114, 116, 136, 139–141, 145, 150, 164, 218, 242, 260, 298
Petrarchism 12, 82, 84, 88, 89, 112, 121, 138–140, 144, 150, 260; spiritual 89
Petrucci, Petruccio 254
Phillip II of Spain, King 74, 75
philosophy and theology, women's role in study of: Copia Sulam, Sarra 290, 292; Erculiani, Camilla 232–234, 236–238; Forteguerri, Laudomia 255; Marinella, Lucrezia 278; Tarabotti, Arcangela 304
Piccolomini, Alessandro 231–232, 256, 259
Piccolomini, Marcantonio 255
Piola, Pietro Francesco 203

Pizan, Christine de 2, 119, 264,
    273, 278
Platonic love 153–154, 214
Poetics 97
poetry: commentary on *Orlando
    Furioso* 117, 120, 121;
    criticisms of Renaissance
    society 116–118; debates
    among literary circles
    245–246; dedicated to
    widows of Naples 120;
    encomiastic 120; epic
    poetry 243–246; erotic
    language 149–150;
    femininity as novel
    selling point 113; feminist
    116–119; Greek and Latin
    103, 106, 148, 151, 169;
    love 80, 136, 144, 162, 164,
    256–257, 259–262, 263;
    masculine rhetorical stance
    150; patronage-seeking
    113, 114; Petrarchism 112,
    114, 121, 150; political
    subjects 121; religious
    devotion 84–85, 107, 270;
    religious themes 112–113,
    120; spiritual contemplation
    82–83, 85, 87; tropes of
    female fidelity 82, 84–85;
    see also Andreini, Isabella;
    Colonna, Vittoria; Copia
    Sulam, Sarra; Franco
    Veronica; literature;
    Marinella, Lucrezia; Molza,
    Tarquinia; Morata, Olimpia;
    Sarrocchi, Margherita;
    Stampa, Gaspara; Terracina,
    Laura; Tornabuoni, Lucrezia
Poland 7, 11, 14, 65–66, 68–71,
    73, *74*, 75, 103, 174, 213,
    230–233, 237, 255
politics, women's role in: alchemical
    experimentation 34–35,
    40; civic unrest following
    Sixtus's death 33–34;
    formation of Polish state
    72; Mantua's affairs 48–49;

Medici Florence 24, 29–30;
    patronage and charitable
    works 29; persuasive
    diplomacy 49; private
    dealings and investments
    24–25; queens 10–11; *see
    also* d'Este, Isabella; Sforza,
    Bona; Sforza, Caterina;
    Tornabuoni, Lucrezia
Poliziano *see* Bertari, Giovanni
Poliziano, Angelo 24
*Portrait of a Young Woman with
    Jasmine* 35, *37*
Portrait of a Woman 7–8
Portrait of Lady 125
Pozzo, Modesta *see* Fonte, Moderata
Primavera (Spring) 32, *32*
*Primo libro delle musiche (First
    Volume of Musical
    Compositions)* 175–176,
    177
The Procession of the Magi 23
Procida, Gasparo 56
Protestantism 245, 255
Protestant Reformation 1, 12, 65,
    275, 287, 296; upheaval of
    100, 234; *see also* Morata,
    Olimpia
Pulci, Luigi 24, 27, 29

querelle des femmes 2, 255, 264,
    186, 278–279
Question de amor (On Love) 68

race 7–9, 258; and religious
    difference 9, 285
racism and discrimination 9–10, 285
Radziwill, Barbara 72
Raffaelli, Maria Francesca 179
Raffaelli, Tommaso 176
Ravaldino, Rocca di 34
reform, religious, and women
    77, 85–87, 97–99,
    103–104, 255
religion 1, 3, 5, 9, 14–15, 105–106,
    109, 258, 284, 295, 304
religious and philosophical debates,
    women's role in 2, 14, 87,

232, 234, 238; religious
devotion 82–83, 85–87;
religious reformist views
97–99
religious conflict 107; and political
instability 107–109;
between Protestants and
Catholics 66; Wars of
Religion 5, 106
religious difference 285
religious freedom 109
"Renaissance" 4–10; meaning of 4;
periodization 4–5
Renaissance feminism 14, 251, 268
Renée of France 12, 47, 71, 86, 87,
100, 104, 106
Riario, Girolamo 31, 33–34
Rime (Poems) 71, 84–86, *86*, 94,
112, 127, *127*, 139, 142,
145, 163
*Rime de la signora Laura Terracina
(Poems of Lady Laura
Terracina)* 112
*Rime di Madonna Gaspara Stampa
139, 142*
*Rime seconde (Second Book of
Poems)* 114
Robortello, Francesco 97
Roches, Catherine des 110
Rome 2, 4, 8–9, 14, 26, 33, 39, 54–56,
59–60, 62, 80, 84, 88, 104,
116, 120, 147, 156, 159, 168,
197, 205, 211, 213–215, 216,
218, 220–221, 224–225,
241–242, 247, 249,
258–259, 262; Sack of 51,
83, 254
Rovere, Vittoria della 178, 179, 184,
186, *186*, 302
Rucellai, Bernardo 25
Ruffo, Don Antonio 227
Ruskin, John 180

Salza, Abdelkader 144
Sannazaro, Jacopo 58, 81
Sansovino, Francesco 137–138
Sarrocchi, Margherita 9, 148,
183, 240–250, 269, 282;

active in academies 242;
Bronzini's praise of 240;
and Colonna family 242;
debates among literary
circles 245–246; early
life of 242; education of
241; and Galileo 241,
243; interest in cosmology
245–249; on Jupiter's
satellites 248; literary
works 243–246; marriage
of 242–243; multitalented
241–243; relation with Valerio 243,
249; *Scanderbeide* 240,
243–246, *244*; salon 243;
support to Galileo 248–249;
in works by others 249–250
Savonarola, Girolamo 38
Savorgnani, Ippolita 212
Scanderbeide 14, 240, 243–244,
246, 282
Schurman, Anna Maria van 110, 284
Scientific Revolution 5, 14, 241, 250
scientific works, translations and
summaries of 231, 256
Senf, Chilian 104
Senf, Johannes 104
Serenissima Repubblica *see* Venetian
Republic
Sforza, Ascanio 56
Sforza, Bona 11, 65–75, 103, 126,
232, 269; artistic interests
69; birth of 66; children
of 69; death of 75; early
life of 67–68; education
of 67; interest in medicine
73; marriage to Sigismund
I 65–66, 68; poisoning
of 74–75; Polish court
of 69–70; political and
economic power 70–71;
political instincts of 72–74;
popularity in Italy 71–73;
regiment of 73; religious
views 71–72; return to Bari
72–74; voyage to Kraków
68–69; woodcut of *66*

Sforza, Caterina 6, 11, 31–41, 53; captured by Cesare Borgia 38–39; charitable works 38; children of 33; civic unrest following Sixtus's death 33–34; death of 40; diplomacy 36–37; education of 32–33; first marriage of 33; interest in alchemical experimentation and medicine 33, 34–35, 40; inventories of possessions of 34; Machiavelli on 31; medical-alchemical manuscript 35, 36; political life of 35–40; political qualities of 32; portrait of 35, *37*; public persona of 31–32, 40; public works by 34; as ruler of Imola and Forlì 34–36; secret wedding with Feo 37; as symbol of independence and resistance 40–41; third marriage of 38

Sforza, Galeazzo Maria 32, 33, 67
Sforza, Gian Galeazzo 67
Sforza, Giovanni 56–57
Sforza, Isabella 98
Sforza, Ludovico 38, 43, 49, 67
Sforza, Ottaviano 33, 36–38
siege of Siena 262–263
siege of Zara 282, *283*
Sigismund II, King 72, 73, 75
Sigismund I, King 65–66, 68
Signorini, Giovanni Battista 173
Signorini, Margherita 173, 178–179
Sigonio, Carlo 147, 206
Sinapius, Johannes 104, 105; *see also* Senf, Johannes
Sirleto, Guglielmo 241
Sixtus IV, Pope 27, 33, 67
social norms and criticism of women: as authors 29, 185, 234, 246, 267; as performers 12, 135, 162, 173, 182
Sojaro, Il *see* Gatti, Bernardino

sola fide, doctrine of 86, 88, 98–99, 255
soul's immortality 290–292; *see also* Copia Sulam, Sarra
spas, and health 25, 38, 73; and leisure culture 25
Spain 10, 34, 37, 55–56, 66, 74, 80, 121, 194, 200, 204–205, 212, 226, 234, 254, 259, 262, 286
Spirituali (Spirituals) 87, 98, 255
Stampa, Bartolomeo 136–137
Stampa, Cassandra 136–137, 144
Stampa, Gaspara 13, 129, 135–146, 164, 188, 267; affair with Collaltino 138–142, 144; as cultural mediator 138; death of 143; death of brother of 137; debate over legacy of 144–145; education of 136–137; family background of 136; love lyric 138–142, 144; modern legacy of 144–146; and music 137; performances of 138; and Petrarchism 139–140, 144; poetry 138–143; portrait of *145*; publication of *Rime* 144–144; recognition of 143; relationship with Zen 142–143; source of inspiration for 138; works dedicated to 137–138
Starry Messenger 241, 246–247
Stella, Alvise (Alovisio) 231
Stiattesi, Giovan Battista 220–221
Stiattesi, Pierantonio 220–221, 224, 226
Stoic Paradoxes 103
Stones of Venice 180
Strozzi, Alessandra Macinghi 6, 24
Strozzi, Barbara 3, 13, 72, 136, 156, 180–189, 224, 301; children 188–189; dedication to Vittoria della Rovere 185–186; death of 189; fame as singer 186; family

background of 181–182;
music education of 182;
Opus 1 184–186, *185*; Opus
2 187; Opus 3 188; Opus 4
187; Opus 5 185; Opus 7
187; Opus 8 187
portrait of 182, *183*; relationship with
Giovanni Paolo Vidman
188–189; sexual innuendo
against 182, 183
Strozzi, Barbara, musical career of
180; chamber music 186,
188–189; compositions
187–188; legacy 189;
paradoxes of 189;
publication 184–187;
sacred music 188; secular
music 188; sensual music
187–188; at Unisoni
meetings 184
Strozzi, Filippo 24
Strozzi, Giulio 180; founder of
Unisoni 184; musical
undertakings of 181–182;
will of 181
Susanna and the Elders 218–219,
219
Symposium 153

Tansillo, Luigi 81, 112
Tarabotti, Arcangela (Elena
Cassandra) 2, 15, 120,
184, 225, 274–275,
288, 296–306; Biblical
story of Adam and Eve
300–301; coda to literary
legacy of 305; convent life
experience of 296–297,
299–300; criticism of
institutions 301; death of
304; defense of women
303; earliest writings
of 299–300; epistolary
network of 302; exclusion
of women from education
301; family background of
298; feminism 306; against
forced cloistering 299–300;

forceful philosophical
treatise of 303–304; and
Incogniti 301, 303–304;
letter-writing by 302–303;
polemical writing 299–302,
303–304; pseudonym of
304; religious works of
301, 303
Tassi, Agostino 219–221
Tasso, Bernardo 81
Tasso, Torquato 9, 100, 148–149,
154, 163, 242–243,
246, 282
Terracina, Laura Bacio 3, 11, 93,
97, 111–121, 122, 181,
243, 277, 280; family
background of 111;
marriage 120; portrait of
113, *114*; reputation and
influence of 120–121
Terracina, Laura Bacio, poetry works
of: commentary on *Orlando
Furioso* 117, 120, 121;
criticisms of Renaissance
society 116–118; dedicated
to widows of Naples
120; encomiastic 120;
femininity as novel selling
point 113; feminist work
116–119; patronage 113,
114; Petrarchan style 112,
114, 121; political subjects
121; recognition of 112;
religious themes 112–113,
120; sources of inspiration
for 115
Terracina, Polidoro 120
theology 14, 67, 87, 151, 231, 236,
238, 240, 255, 290, 292
Tiepolo, Giovanni 300
Tornabuoni, Lucrezia 1, 11, 19–30,
40, 239; achievements of
29–30; children of 25; death
of 29; education of 23–24;
literary compositions
28–29; literary interests
of 24, 27–29; marital
negotiations for Lorenzo

25–26; marriage with Piero 20–22; meeting with Clarice Orisini 26; patronage and charitable works 29; persona of 19–20; political activity of 24, 26–27; portrait of *20*; private dealings and investments 24–25; widowhood of 27–28

Tredici canti di Floridoro (*Thirteen Cantos of Floridoro*) 267–269, *268*

Tre Stelle apothecary 229–332; *see also* Erculiani, Camilla Greghetta

Tromboncino, Bartolomeo 51

Uccello, Paolo 22

Valdés, Juan de 85, 87, 98, 109, 234
Valerio, Luca 241, 243, 246–247, 249
Van Dyck, Anthony 203
Vannitelli, Ridolfo 131
Vasari, Giorgio 198–200, 204–206, 263
Vega, Lope de 121
Venetia edificata (*Venice Edified*) 181
Venice 61, 72–74, 112, 129, 131–132, 135–138, 143–144, 148, 156, 180–189, 205, 222, 224–225, 233–234, 244, 265, 269, 275, 277, 278, 282, 284, 288–290, 293, 300, 302, 305–306; ghetto 285–287, 296; Venetian Republic 9, 15, 48, 91–92, 122–123, 125, 130, 229, 265, 282, 285–287, 299; Venetian Senate 73, 299, 301; Venetian women 265–267, 270, 273, 276, 299, 301
Veneto, Bartolomeo *54*, 62
Venier, Domenico 126, 131,138

Venier, Maffio 129
Venier, Marco 127–129, 132
Veronese, Paolo 160, *161*
Vesalius, Andreas 230
Vidman, Paolo, Giovanni 188–189
Vinci, Leonardo da 1, 21, 27, 43, 46–47, 49, 67

Wawel Castle 69, *70*
Weiglowa, Katarzyna 72
Wert, Giaches de 156
women: African 7–8; artists 194, 193–204, 205–214, 215–228; capabilities, debate about 2–3; coerced into taking religious vows 299, 300; of color, Renaissance 6–7; countering arguments against inferiority of 278–281, 304; defense of 238, 264, 278–284, 293, 295, 303; education and gender equality 2–3, 10, 273–275, 280, 301; enslaved 6–7, 48; excellence of 15, 278, 281, 282; excluded from education and training 3, 193, 280, 301; health of 24, 50, 72–73, 87, 270, 273; intellect of 103, 109–110, 121, 126, 238, 269, 288; lack of freedom and access to education 281, 301; lives, circumstances of 10; as moral and erudite 281; musicians and composers 135–146, 147–157, 168–179, 189–190; nobility and excellence of 15, 278, 281, 282; nobility of 15, 21, 72–73, 136, 156, 169, 278–281, 282; origins of Italian and Latin words for 280; patrician 10, 123, 299; political life 1, 10–11, 15–16, 19–30, 31–41,

42–52, 53–64, 65–75,
262–263, 265, 275, 301;
potential of 234, 239, 255,
269, 301; renowned for
their intellect 280–281;
right to enhance their
beauty 281; servants 6–7,
9, 40, 131; and scientific
culture 5, 14, 35, 153, 231,
238–239, 240, 28–250,
254, 280; superiority of
275, 278, 280–281, 284;
writers 11–12, 28–29,
79–89, 95,100, 103–107,
109–110, 111–121,
126–131,139–144,
147–151, 162–167,
223–239, 241–246, 256,
259–261, 166–274,
277–284, 290–294,
299–306; *see also* querelle
des femmes
women's equality 2, 3, 238, 165,
268, 270–274, 275, 284;
and freedom 274; and
liberty 274

Zappi, Gian Paolo 208
Zappi, Severo 207, 208
Zieglerin, Anna 35
Zuccanello, Ippolito 232
Zwingli, Huldrych 104